Women, Writing, and Revolution
1790–1827

Women, Writing, and Revolution
1790–1827

GARY KELLY

CLARENDON PRESS · OXFORD

Oxford University Press, Great Clarendon Street, Oxford OX2 6DP

Oxford New York
Athens Auckland Bangkok Bogota Bombay Buenos Aires
Calcutta Cape Town Dar es Salaam Delhi Florence Hong Kong
Istanbul Karachi Kuala Lumpur Madras Madrid Melbourne
Mexico City Nairobi Paris Singapore Taipei Tokyo Toronto Warsaw

and associated companies in
Berlin Ibadan

Oxford is a trade mark of Oxford University Press

Published in the United States
by Oxford University Press Inc., New York

First published 1993
Reprinted 1997

British Library Cataloguing in Publication Data
Data available

Library of Congress Cataloging in Publication Data
Kelly, Gary.
Women, writing, and revolution, 1790–1827/Gary Kelly
Includes bibliographical references and index.
1. Revolutionary literature, English—History and criticism.
2. France—History—Revolution, 1789–1799—Foreign public opinion,
British. 3. Williams, Helen Maria, 1762–1827—Political and social
views. 4. Hamilton, Elizabeth, 1758–1816—Political and social
views. 5. Hays, Mary, 1759 or 60–1843—Political and social views.
6. English literature—Women authors—History and criticism.
7. France—History—Revolution, 1789–1799—Influence. 8. Women and
literature—Great Britain—History. 9. English literature—French
influences. 10. France in literature. I. Title.
PR129.F8K44 1993
820.9'9287'09034–dc20   92–47261
ISBN 0–19–812272–1

Printed in Great Britain
on acid-free paper by
Bookcraft Ltd
Midsomer Norton, North Somerset

Preface

THE following chapters investigate women's writing as a major factor in the relationship of class and gender during a crucial stage in the cultural revolution that founded the modern state in Britain. This relationship was central to that revolution, and I use particular terms to investigate it.

'Feminism' was not in English usage then, but 'advocacy of women's rights on grounds of equality of the sexes' (*Concise Oxford Dictionary*, seventh edition, 1982) did exist, even though its precise terms might now be considered more femininist than feminist. Opposition to feminism I call 'counter-feminism', since 'anti-feminism' has long meant 'criticism of women in general'. I use 'feminine' and 'masculine' for particular social and cultural constructions of what is taken to be 'natural' or appropriate to the 'male' or 'female'. Similarly, I use 'masculinization' (or 'remasculinization') to mean 'making something seem proper to or the property of males' (however 'maleness' might be constructed at the time), and 'feminization' to describe initiatives, mostly by women writers, to reverse the subordination of women by the discursive, social, and political order and transform that order according to attributes conventionally assigned to women then, especially under the ideology of 'domestic woman'. I use 'gender' in a sense now widely received—differences of 'masculine' and 'feminine' that are socially and culturally constructed rather than biologically determined.

I use 'class' in the sense of historically specific social identities based on perceived differences of interest, verging on conflict. In most cases I use 'professional' for a subdivision of the middle class rather than a certain way of working, although the nature of professional work— certain practices of critical thought—grounded professional middle-class ideology and culture. Whether women share in such a class identity or constitute a class of their own has been debated, but it seems that particular social identities are learned and articulated for particular situations and purposes, within the framework of a historically and socially specific 'language' of such identities. As I argue here, in a revolutionary situation this language, like others, becomes both more open to change and more hotly contested.

'Revolution' itself has been transformed historically. It came from science and was applied to politics and society in the eighteenth century first as a complete cycle and then as a 'complete change, turning upside down, great reversal of conditions', often sudden and dramatic. The cultural revolution was not sudden or dramatic but it was a complete change. Partly for this reason and partly because it is not yet recognized as one of the major transformations of the late eighteenth and early nineteenth century, I do not capitalize it. I use 'Britain' for Great Britain, after union with Ireland in 1801 known as the United Kingdom. I use 'writing' for the field of manuscript and printed documents and the cultural practices and socio-economic institutions that enable the creation and understanding of those documents. I use 'literature' to mean 'written verbal art'—artistic according to particular historical, social, and cultural criteria held by particular social groups. During the period under investigation here, literature became the cultural property and ideological weapon of the middle classes, and, as I try to show, women took a major if contradictory role in fashioning this weapon.

I focus on women writers here because they initiated the feminization of culture and civil society in the cultural revolution and the Revolution debate, because authorship was thoroughly gendered at the time and the same utterance was read differently when from a man or woman author, and because the women writers have not been much studied as yet, though the different role of men writers in feminizing literature and culture during this period also needs study. In order to reconcile the particular and the general, contingency and explanation, I discuss the conditions of women's writing in the cultural revolution and the Revolution debate and aftermath in Chapters 1 and 5, and then concentrate on three women writers in Chapters 2–4 and 6–8. I choose Helen Maria Williams, Mary Hays, and Elizabeth Hamilton because they were prominent in their time and they challenged discursive, generic, and stylistic orders that subordinated women and their writing, yet they differed in responding to the revolutionary conditions of their time and in negotiating contradictory identities of gender, class, and nation and demands of commerce, career, and political commitment.

I have carried out the research for this book over a decade and a half and during that time much has happened in women's literary studies, but historical enquiry still has much to offer these studies and literary and cultural studies in general. As Rita Felski argues, 'the political

value of literary texts from the standpoint of feminism can be determined only by an investigation of their social functions and effects in
relation to the interests of women in a particular historical context, and
not by attempting to deduce an abstract literary theory of "masculine"
and "feminine", "subversive" and "reactionary" forms in isolation
from the social conditions of their production and reception' (*Beyond
Feminist Aesthetics: Feminist Literature and Social Change*, p. 2). And as
Laurie A. Finke writes, 'Uncovering the full range of social meanings
attached to gender within any particular cultural formation . . . requires
a method sensitive to the historical particularities of time and place, as
well as to the heterogeneity of socioeconomic formations, the intersect-
ing and competing interests of different groups, and the hegemonic
practices that work to smooth over or to suppress these conflicts'
(*Feminist Theory, Women's Writing*, p. 9).

   I could not have attempted such a study without the support of the
Social Sciences and Humanities Research Council of Canada, the
Killam Foundation of the Canada Council, the University of Alberta,
and the staffs of the University of Alberta Library, the Bodleian
Library, the British Library, Dr Williams's Library, the Pforzheimer
Library, and the Cambridge University Library. I am particularly
grateful to Lord Abinger for permission to use the Godwin circle
correspondence now on deposit in the Bodleian Library, and to the
Pforzheimer Collection of the New York Public Library and Dr
Williams's Library, London, for the use of Hays correspondence in
their possession. I want to thank Gina Luria, Mitzi Myers, and William
St Clair for encouragement and help of several kinds. I dedicate this
book to my sister and friend, Gemey Kelly.

                                                              G.K.

Contents

PART I

*Women and Writing in the
Revolutionary Decade*

I

Introduction

THE late eighteenth and early nineteenth century saw a striking increase in the participation of women in print culture, as both writers and readers. Such participation was facilitated and conditioned by a cultural revolution interacting with the political, economic, and commercial revolutions of the time.[1] This cultural revolution was carried out by and for the professional middle class and had two linked objectives.[2] The first was to consolidate the middle classes under the leadership of the professionals, detach them from ideological and cultural dependence on the dominant classes of court, aristocracy, and gentry, and secure them from cultural and ideological contamination by the lower classes.[3] Secondly, and somewhat later, the cultural revolution aimed to professionalize the dominant classes and form a coalition with them while detaching the lower classes from their historic subordination to the upper classes and conferring on them a diminutive version of middle-class culture and consciousness.[4] In this way the cultural revolutionaries would secure hegemony for themselves without using court government's resource of main force or the lower classes' resource of riot, and without the kind of revolutionary violence that haunted Britain from the seventeenth century and that took place across the Channel in the 1790s. The cultural revolution would not only achieve these objectives by transforming the apparatus of the state, but would guarantee this transformation by internalizing the new

[1] On definitions and theories of revolution see Michael S. Kimmel, *Revolution: A Sociological Interpretation* (Cambridge, 1990).

[2] On the rise of the professionals see Geoffrey Holmes, *Augustan England: Professions, State and Society, 1680–1730* (London, 1982). For a survey of the professions among the other middle classes in a European context see Pamela M. Pilbeam, *The Middle Classes in Europe 1789–1914: France, Germany, Italy and Russia* (Basingstoke, 1990); Pilbeam points out that the history of the professions has only recently begun to be written and so research is patchy (p. 78).

[3] On gentry hegemony see G. E. Mingay, *The Gentry: The Rise and Fall of a Ruling Class* (London, 1976).

[4] For a recent survey of 'pre-industrial' society and 'modernization' see Patricia Crone, *Pre-Industrial Societies* (Oxford, 1989).

WRITING IN THE REVOLUTIONARY DECADE

state in individual consciousness, embedding it in the practice of everyday life, and thus naturalizing it and masking its revolutionary character.[5]

In order to do so, the cultural revolution relied on an array of rhetorical topics, especially subjectivity and domesticity in relation to ideas of community, region, and nation, developed in intellectual and cultural discourses of Enlightenment and Sensibility.[6] In this revolutionary rhetoric a certain figure of 'woman' was constructed to represent a professional middle-class discourse of subjectivity as opposed to communal or courtly sociability, 'nature' rather than decadent 'civilization', domesticity as opposed to the public and political spheres, and the 'national' culture, identity, and destiny rather than local, temporary, narrow interests of rank or region.[7]

In the decades leading up to the 1790s, subjectivity was a leading theme in the cultural revolution, formalized in the literature of Sensibility and rationalized by the materialist epistemology of the Enlightenment.[8] If the individual mind was constructed by reflection on sensory

[5] On cultural revolution see Philip Corrigan and Derek Sayer, *The Great Arch: English State Formation as Cultural Revolution* (Oxford, 1985). On reform movements see Eckhart Hellmuth (ed.), *The Transformation of Political Culture: England and Germany in the Late Eighteenth Century* (London, 1990). On the rise of bourgeois critique of court government, though in the Continental absolutist states rather than Britain, see Reinhart Koselleck, *Critique and Crisis: Enlightenment and the Pathogenesis of Modern Society* (1959), trans. (Oxford, 1988). On the transformation of the state apparatus and its operation as a consequence of cultural revolution see Eugene Kamenka, *Bureaucracy* (Oxford, 1989), ch. 4.

[6] There is much recent work in these areas. On subjectivity see Huck Gutman, 'Rousseau's *Confessions*: A Technology of the Self', and Michel Foucault, 'The Political Technology of Individuals', in Luther H. Martin *et al.* (eds.), *Technologies of the Self: A Seminar with Michel Foucault* (Amherst, Mass., 1988), 99–120, 145–62; Regenia Gagnier, *Subjectivities: A History of Self-Representation in Britain, 1832–1920* (New York, 1991). For a recent survey of changes in family structure see James Casey, *The History of the Family* (Oxford, 1989). On some aspects of moral and social reform see Joanna Innes, 'Politics and Morals: The Reformation of Manners Movement in Later Eighteenth-Century England', in Hellmuth (ed.), *Transformation of Political Culture*, 57–118. On national identity see Gerald Newman, *The Rise of English Nationalism: A Cultural History 1740–1830* (London, 1987); Eric J. Hobsbawm, *Nations and Nationalism since 1780: Programme, Myth, Reality* (Cambridge, 1990); Benedict Anderson, *Imagined Communities: Reflections on the Origin and Spread of Nationalism*, rev. edn. (London, 1991). On Sensibility see John Dwyer, *Virtuous Discourse: Sensibility and Community in Late Eighteenth-Century Scotland* (Edinburgh, 1987).

[7] For cross-cultural and anthropological investigations of these issues see the essays in Michelle Zimbalist Rosaldo and Louise Lamphere (eds.), *Woman, Culture and Society* (Stanford, Calif., 1974).

[8] See John Mullan, *Sentiment and Sociability: The Language of Feeling in the Eighteenth Century* (Oxford, 1988); R. F. Brissenden, *Virtue in Distress: Studies in the Novel of Sentiment from Richardson to Sade* (London, 1974), pt. 1, ch. 2.

impressions from the surrounding natural and social worlds, as a certain line of empirical philosophers argued, then subjectivity was implicitly democratized and posited as uniquely individual and authentic, justifying a wide range of political, social, economic, and cultural programmes, including reform of Parliament, expansion of the 'political nation', professionalization of institutions and society as a whole, reward for merit and abolition of 'privilege', encouragement of competition and an investment economy, and modernized and extended education for participation in such an economy. This professionalized subject was constituted by certain technologies of the self, denominated 'virtue' and 'reason'.[9] 'Virtue' stood for professionalized affectivity, or 'sensibility' disciplined into a moral self capable of deferring immediate gratification for future benefits, declining material gratification for moral and intellectual benefits, and thus acting ethically according to 'truth' and 'justice'—code words for professional middle-class ways of creating knowledge and evaluating individuals and their actions free from 'custom', 'tradition', or codes of value controlled by the upper classes or controlling the common people. For the cultural revolution's 'reason' and 'virtue' were developed from professional ways of working, or modes of production in intellectual service industries. 'Reason' stood for the method and order necessary in 'learned' professions, those with the highest status, such as lawyers, the clergy, medical practitioners, and those in professions based on theoretical or speculative discourse.[10] Professionalized 'virtue' was developed from but also against earlier, aristocratic and courtly usage, as subjective rather than courtly manliness, civil rather than martial courage, in the transformation of 'chivalry' by Enlightenment historians and sociologists during the mid-eighteenth century.

Women had at best a problematic relation to this professional middle-class culture of subjectivity. Since women in both upper and middle classes continued to serve the economic function of transferring property from one man to another, the 'virtue' assigned to them was predominantly private, restraint of the erotic 'passions' ensuring the stability and integrity of the family as a property trust continuing through the generations.[11] Female 'virtue' meant sexual chastity guard-

---

[9] On the linking of reason and virtue see Koselleck, *Critique and Crisis*, 57 n. 15.

[10] For a survey of reason as socially and historically specific see Ernest Gellner, *Reason and Culture: The Historic Role of Rationality and Rationalism* (Oxford, 1992).

[11] See Susan Moller Okin, 'Patriarchy and Married Women's Property in England: Questions on Some Current Views', *Eighteenth-Century Studies*, 17 (Winter 1983/4), 121–

ing those subordinated within their own class against seduction by a social superior or contamination by an inferior. Female 'virtue' was moral propriety concealing and defending the material property, social interests, and cultural power of 'their' class. Since women continued to be excluded from public and professional life they were denied the kind of 'reason' required by men in their professional work. The gendering of 'reason' also had a long history, associated with the culture, identity, and power of professional men since classical antiquity, equated with the divine in human 'nature', distinguishing 'man' from lesser animals, and associated with spirit, divinity, and transcendence of the 'merely' material, physical, natural, and bodily.[12] Because of a parallel social subordination of women and the labouring classes, both were associated with these inferior spheres and modes of being, and seen as more limited to the body by the nature of the 'work'— reproductive or productive—performed by their bodies, correspondingly less intellectually reflective, accordingly more responsive to appeals to the passions, thereby associated with disorder of various kinds from the bodily to the political, and therefore to be excluded from the public, political life shared by men.[13] In Gerda Lerner's account, women became a class within each class.[14]

Moreover, in Renaissance and Enlightenment humanism, 'reason' became a slogan to legitimize professional middle-class critiques of court government's mystification, artifice, decadence, 'effeminacy', injustice, and despotism, and of plebeian ignorance, 'superstition', unreason, improvidence, impulsiveness, violence, and criminality. Since women were excluded by education and profession from participating

38; Susan Staves, *Married Women's Separate Property in England, 1660–1833* (Cambridge, Mass., 1990).

[12] See Genevieve Lloyd, *The Man of Reason: 'Male' and 'Female' in Western Philosophy* (London, 1984).

[13] Mullan, *Sentiment and Sociability*, 217–24; Londa Schiebinger, 'Skeletons in the Closet: The First Illustrations of the Female Skeleton in Eighteenth-Century Anatomy', in Catherine Gallagher and Thomas Laqueur (eds.), *The Making of the Modern Body: Sexuality and Society in the Nineteenth Century* (Berkeley, Calif., 1987), 42; Thomas Laqueur, *Making Sex: Body and Gender from the Greeks to Freud* (Cambridge, Mass., 1990), 201; Michelle Zimbalist Rosaldo, 'Woman, Culture, and Society: A Theoretical Overview', in Rosaldo and Lamphere (eds.), *Woman, Society and Culture*, 17–42 (31–2); Sherry B. Ortner, 'Is Female to Male as Nature is to Culture?', in Rosaldo and Lamphere (eds.), *Woman, Society and Culture*, 67–87; Natalie Zemon Davis, 'Women on Top: Symbolic Sexual Inversion and Political Disorder in Early Modern Europe', in Barbara A. Babcock (ed.), *The Reversible World: Symbolic Inversion in Art and Society* (Ithaca, NY, 1978), 147–90.

[14] Gerda Lerner, *The Creation of Patriarchy* (New York, 1986), 214–16.

in these Enlightenment rationalist critiques, they tended to be associated with what 'reason' criticized.[15] This association reinforced the view that women were liable to seduction from above or contamination from below because they had more to gain by class treason. Furthermore, women's political practices, or 'female politics', were seen as part of the court system of intrigue and patronage, in which women used their sexual desirability and erotic skills to achieve power not available to them by 'legitimate' means. This image of courtly woman was widely diffused through society and led to a middle-class construction of 'domestic woman' naturally restricted to the domestic sphere for her own good, the good of her family, and the good of society and the nation. The ways in which women—in all classes—were forced to practise politics in a court-dominated society and culture were read as illegitimate if not criminal.[16] In order to fix their 'domestic' character, women were assigned 'reason' as rote-learning rather than independent critical thought, as domestic order and policing rather than public discourse, while being allowed freer rein in domains of 'fancy' and 'imagination', in 'light', 'ornamental', 'entertaining', and domestically useful discourses of 'taste' that could add an inflection of gentility to middle-class private life. This figure of 'domestic woman' was of most use to the professional middle-class cultural revolution, but it had use in other classes as well, a fact which may explain the rapid dissemination of the figure as part of the new culture of 'respectability' during the nineteenth century. Restricting though it was in reality, this figure was used by many women writers to gain access to the public, political, and professional domains otherwise considered unsuitable or too difficult for them—in a word, unfeminine. Among the leaders in that venture were Helen Maria Williams, Mary Hays, and Elizabeth Hamilton.

They and others were quick to exploit the revolutionary and feminist potential of 'sensibility' in the construction of woman and subjectivity. While 'reason' and 'virtue' guaranteed professional middle-class subjectivity, even when inflected for gender, 'sensibility' as 'sympathy' guaranteed social relations, co-operation, and cohesion against excesses

[15] On 18th-century philosophy's treatment of 'woman', see Susan Moller Okin, *Women in Western Political Thought* (Princeton, NJ, 1979), pt. 3; Jane Rendall, *The Origins of Modern Feminism: Women in Britain, France and the United States 1780–1860* (Basingstoke, 1985), ch. 1; Ruth Salvaggio, *Enlightened Absence: Neoclassical Configurations of the Feminine* (Urbana, Ill., 1988), ch. 1.

[16] See Jane Fishburne Collier, 'Women in Politics', in Rosaldo and Lamphere (eds.), *Woman, Society and Culture*, 89–112.

of individualism. Women were to preside over the first arena of socialization by nurturing sympathy in the family members, thus preparing them to withstand the competitive pressures of the public sphere. Women were also assigned sympathetic roles beyond the domestic sphere, repairing individuals or groups unsuccessful in social competition, such as the poor, the 'fallen', the oppressed—in part as recognition of women's own subordinate social position. This extended domestic role was exploited, for example, in mid-century by the 'Bluestocking' culture's feminization of gentry capitalism and later in religious reform movements such as Evangelicalism.[17] But 'sensibility' was also a contradictory practice. On the one hand it was associated with excessive or sublime selfhood of the imagination and 'genius', it validated the authenticity of the subjective self against competing models of identity, such as inherited rank and ascribed status, and it was often treated as aristocracy of soul, equal or superior to aristocracy of birth and designed to subvert it. On the other hand 'sensibility' could lead to social transgression, crime, or 'madness', as social categories designed for the wilfully or unwillingly extra-social. Yet such transgression had considerable glamour, enabling the middle-class individual's social dependence or failure to be heroized. The 'man of feeling', too good for a bad world, subsumed the aristocratic hero of classical epic or chivalric romance. Women were of course excluded from these dangerous heroics by being harboured in the domestic sphere.

Nevertheless, a particular figure of 'woman' became central to the professional middle-class cultural revolution partly because women were associated historically with key elements in the cultural revolution—the subjective self, the private and domestic sphere, and the class's social and cultural reproduction over time.[18] Yet women remained subordinate in the revolutionary class because 'woman' could be a figure for both the 'virtues' and 'vices' of their class. Thus professional men subordinate to upper-class patrons could also identify with the figure of 'woman'. This figure addressed men and women of the same class differently, yet both could read themselves there and thus seem united through a cultural revolution that was in fact class-

---

[17] For the 'Bluestocking' programme, see Sarah Scott's *Millenium Hall* (1762).

[18] See Nancy F. Cott, *The Bonds of Womanhood: 'Woman's Sphere' in New England 1780–1835* (New Haven, Conn., 1977), ch. 3; Nancy Armstrong and Leonard Tennenhouse (eds.), *The Ideology of Conduct: Essays on Literature and the History of Sexuality* (New York, 1987); Sandra Burman (ed.), *Fit Work for Women* (London, 1979).

based and thereby gender-biased. For this reason 'woman' continued to be a field of struggle within a cultural revolution that was itself a field of struggle.

The figure of 'domestic woman' conditioned not only the experience of women in the cultural revolution but also their participation in one of the revolution's main weapons—writing. The cultural revolution was facilitated by a revolution in cultural consumption, including print of all kinds, from newspapers to novels, but cultural revolutionaries were ambivalent about both the revolution in consumption and the so-called 'rise of the reading public'.[19] Print and especially fashionable 'literature of the day' were forms of commercialized consumption that the upper classes could still influence through their social prestige and cultural leadership, if no longer directly through literary patronage. Print was not only a widely disseminated form of cultural consumption among the revolutionary class, it was also a cultural practice that professionals had already mastered through their work as specially trained and paid readers, interpreters, and writers. Furthermore, print was particularly suitable for a revolution that aimed to operate within individual consciousness rather than by external forces and constraints. As T. J. Mathias wrote in the middle of the Revolutionary decade, 'Literature'—by which he meant any kind of writing—'well, or ill conducted, is the great engine by which ... all *civilized* states must ultimately be supported or overthrown'.[20]

Print enabled women to participate in the cultural revolution, and thus in public political life, without relinquishing the feminine character of 'domestic woman'. Commercialized print offered new opportunities to women lacking professional education, authorship did not require leaving the actual or notional confines of domestic life, and the prominence of 'domestic woman' in the cultural revolution encouraged a feminization of culture on which women could claim to have some authority. Print was thoroughly and hierarchically gendered, but through it many women could extend their accepted domestic domains of expertise into public and political activities of various kinds,

[19] See Neil McKendrick, John Brewer, and J. H. Plumb, *The Birth of a Consumer Society: The Commercialization of Eighteenth-Century England* (London, 1982); Colin Campbell, *The Romantic Ethic and the Spirit of Modern Consumerism* (Oxford, 1987).

[20] [Thomas J. Mathias,] *The Pursuits of Literature: A Satirical Poem; in Four Dialogues*, 7th edn., rev. (London, 1798), 161–2 n. The remark was published in the Third Dialogue (1796).

particularly education and popularization of men's learned discourses. Hence the cultural revolution and the 'rise of the reading public' were accompanied by a great increase in the number and variety of published women writers.[21]

Yet by publishing, a woman put herself in a 'double bind'.[22] As a woman she was supposed to be domestic; once published she became public, risking loss of femininity. Moreover, women were assumed to lack the rhetorical training, intellectual range, and even technical competence (correct grammar, spelling, and punctuation) necessary to the professional writer. Restriction of women to the face-to-face culture of domesticity implied an orientation to speech rather than writing, and a long cultural tradition associated women with gossip, orality, narrativity, and fictionality.[23] Such writing as women did was supposed to support their domestic lives and relations, in personal, familial, epistolary forms not meant for publication. But because this writing was private did not mean it lacked rhetorical and formal conventions. It was informal, desultory, candid, personal, and occasional, incorporating discussion of literature, culture, and public affairs into the subjective, domestic text. In the late eighteenth-century culture of Sensibility, these characteristics were associated with the 'authentic' subjective and domestic spheres against the artfully rhetorical, learned, and stylized discourses dominated by men and used in the political and professional spheres still subject to upper-class hegemony, and so characteristics of unpublished writing came to be carried over into published work by both men and women opposing that hegemony.

Yet publication continued to be considered 'unfeminine' and many women published anonymously, especially if they wrote on themes or in forms considered more appropriate for men. Most women who published kept to topics and genres seen as expressions or extensions of 'woman's' subjective, domestic domain. Many women authors kept

---

[21] Judith Phillips Stanton, 'Statistical Profile of Women Writing in English from 1660 to 1800', in Frederick M. Keener and Susan E. Lorsch (eds.), *Eighteenth-Century Women and the Arts* (New York, 1988), 247–54.

[22] See Rhoda K. Unger, 'Psychological, Feminist, and Personal Epistemology: Transcending Contradiction', in Mary McCanney Gergen (ed.), *Feminist Thought and the Structure of Knowledge* (New York, 1988), 132–3; Mary Poovey, *The Proper Lady and the Woman Writer: Ideology as Style in the Works of Mary Wollstonecraft, Mary Shelley, and Jane Austen* (Chicago, 1984), ch. 1.

[23] See Patricia Meyer Spacks, *Gossip* (Chicago, 1986); on the relegation of narrativity and fictionality to women, children, and primitive peoples, see Jean-François Lyotard, *The Postmodern Condition: A Report on Knowledge*, trans. Geoff Bennington and Brian Massumi (Minneapolis, 1984), 27, 30.

(or even enhanced) their femininity by publishing as amateur belletrists, especially in the miscellany magazines accommodating such work.[24] Women who wrote for pay often concealed or extenuated the fact. Most women writers faced practical difficulties likely to deter them from learned, controversial, or noble literary genres. Most had less formal education than men and were unwilling to attempt scholarly or sublime genres. Women also needed the literary patronage and protection of men. Women were hindered from entering contracts on their own and securing the profits of their intellectual and literary labour. Furthermore, men were gatekeepers of the literary institution as publishers, agents, critics, and editors, and in order to publish women needed them or men relations and friends who could deal with them.

The biggest obstacle faced by women writers, however, was the gendering of written discourse, and indeed all aspects of culture and the arts.[25] The Revd James Fordyce's often-reprinted conduct book, *Sermons to Young Women*, expressed a commonplace in basing this division on women's 'nature'. Their 'faculties', he writes, are formed 'for the most part with less vigour' than men's, according to the 'more delicate frame' of the female body.[26] Women's 'natural' role is 'to be the mothers and formers of a rational and immortal offspring; to be a kind of softer companions, who, by nameless delightful sympathies and endearments, might improve our pleasures and soothe our pains; to lighten the load of domestic cares, and thereby leave us more at leisure for rougher labours, or severer studies; and finally, to spread a certain grace and embellishment over human life' (i. 208). Women's writing should be determined by these 'natural' spheres of activity and interest. Thus 'war, commerce, politics', 'abstract philosophy, and all the abstruser sciences, are most properly the province of men', and 'those masculine women, that would plead for your sharing any part of this province equally with us, do not understand your true interests'. This does not mean women 'are not capable of the judicious and the solid'; nevertheless, 'it is not the argumentative but the sentimental talents, which give you that insight and those openings into the human heart, that lead to your principal ends as Women' (i. 272–3). The

---

[24] See Robert D. Mayo, *The English Novel in the Magazines 1740–1815* (Evanston, Ill., 1962).

[25] Ellen Messer-Davidow, ' "For Softness She": Gender Ideology and Aesthetics in Eighteenth-Century England', in Keener and Lorsch (eds.), *Eighteenth-Century Women and the Arts*, 45–55.

[26] James Fordyce, *Sermons to Young Women*, 3rd edn., corr., 2 vols. (London, 1766), i. 271–2.

'female mind' is particularly inclined to 'works of imagination' or fiction 'blended with instruction', 'where Fancy sports under the controul of Reason' and 'a strict regard is paid to decorum' by 'a chaste, yet elevated imagination'. Women may read history, biography, and memoirs; voyages and travels; geography and astronomy; natural history and natural and moral philosophy; and the Scriptures and some devotional writing. These narrative and descriptive genres illustrate God's Providence and are both 'solid' and 'useful'. Fordyce warns against theology, especially 'Religious Controversy', because it requires advanced learning and leads to public dispute—both considered unfeminine and distracting women from their domestic duties. He recommends periodicals such as the *Spectator* and disapproves of novels disseminating court culture and encouraging social emulation (i. 278, 274–6, 279).

Fordyce clearly assigns women a subaltern place in professional culture:

For my part, I could heartily wish to see the female world more accomplished than it is; but I do not wish to see it abound with metaphysicians, historians, speculative philosophers, or Learned Ladies of any kind. I should be afraid, lest the sex should lose in softness what they gained in force; and lest the pursuit of such elevation should interfere a little with the plain duties and humble virtues of life. (i. 201–2)

Women writers were usually careful to acknowledge this gendering of discourse in the prefaces, dedications, and other preliminaries to their books. When they did stray into men's literary and cultural territory they usually pretended to be extending acceptably feminine subjects in acceptably feminine genres, including narrative fiction in verse and prose, comic and sentimental drama, 'light' verse, and essays of personal and quotidian life, though men practised these kinds too, for 'feminine' genres and subjects disregarded by official canons and culture were the most widely and avidly read by both men and women. Nevertheless, the sex of the author played a fundamental role in determining the import of a particular text for readers: women venturing into topics and genres gendered masculine were uniformly condemned; men venturing into topics and genres gendered feminine were usually seen as conferring new dignity and seriousness on them.

The novel, for example, was the genre most closely identified with women as readers and writers.[27] Hannah More expressed a widespread

[27] Joyce M. S. Tompkins, *The Popular Novel in England 1770–1800* (1932; Lincoln,

view when she wrote, 'women cannot be excelled' in the romance and novel 'because here, "Invention labours more, and judgment less" '.[28] But because of this predominance of imagination over reason, novels were a source of cultural and social anxiety. Prose fiction carried the main burden of disseminating the cultural revolution throughout the 'reading public', yet it had low moral, literary, and intellectual status because it was both a vehicle for and an article of commercialized cultural consumption, or the 'fashion system'. Most novels were not even purchased by their readers, but rented from circulating libraries. With the rise of 'print capitalism' the distinction between 'serious' and commercialized literature reinforced the historic distinction between 'solid' and 'useful' reading, usually for professional training, and 'mere' entertainment, which was justified only as necessary recreation from the other kind of reading. There was also a historic association between the novel and decadent court culture: in the late 1770s Vicesimus Knox argued that 'modern novels' were descended from court romances and novellas imported during the Restoration and thanks to them 'the effects of the coarse taste introduced in the reign of Charles the Second, have scarcely yet decreased'. Classic novels by Richardson, Fielding, and Smollett contained 'the beauties of true genius', 'but the multitude of memoirs, private histories, and curious anecdotes, imported from our neighbouring land of libertinism [France], have seldom any thing to recommend them to perusal but their profligacy'.[29] The ideological work of novels was figured as courtly seduction directed at women, supposed to be the weak link in class consciousness and solidarity. Accordingly, the association of women and novels was paradigmatic for the 'problem' of the woman writer in the late eighteenth-century cultural revolution.

This 'problem' was greatly complicated during the last decade of the century, for the French Revolution had a catalysing and divisive effect on every aspect of the cultural revolution in Britain, including the social and cultural importance of 'domestic woman' and the gendering

---

Nebr., 1961); Jane Spencer, *The Rise of the Woman Novelist: From Aphra Behn to Jane Austen* (Oxford, 1986); Dale Spender, *Mothers of the Novel: 100 Good Women Writers before Jane Austen* (London, 1986); Terry Lovell, *Consuming Fiction* (London, 1987), ch. 3.

[28] Hannah More, *Essays on Various Subjects, Principally Designed for Young Ladies* (London, 1777), 11.

[29] Vicesimus Knox, *Essays Moral and Literary*, 2 vols. (London, 1778–9), ii. 189.

of writing.[30] At first many British cultural revolutionaries thought that the French had achieved what they themselves wanted—the overthrow of court politics, patronage, paternalism, social hierarchy based on inherited rank and wealth, and the established Church.[31] Among the first to welcome the Revolution were the Dissenters, leaders among the professional and commercial bourgeoisie and campaigning in the late 1780s to end restrictions on their civic rights.[32] As early as the autumn of 1788 Richard Price, a leading Dissenting philanthropist, philosopher, and political writer, told James Wodrow, Presbyterian minister at Stevenston in Ayrshire, Scotland, that he had 'great hopes of the extension of Liberty from the present struggles in France'.[33]

The outbreak of the Revolution in France seemed to confirm these hopes and in November 1789 Price delivered a *Discourse on the Love of Our Country*, reminding his audience of the 'principles' of the English Revolution of 1688: 'First; The right to liberty of conscience in religious matters. Secondly; The right to resist power when abused. And, Thirdly; The right to chuse our own governors; to cashier them for misconduct; and to frame a government for ourselves.' The 'inequality of our representation' enabled the government to deny these 'rights', but 'a diffusion of knowledge, which has undermined superstition and error', had already produced the French Revolution, in turn spreading 'the ardour for liberty'. Price concluded, 'Tremble all ye oppressors of the world! . . . Restore to mankind their rights; and consent to the correction of abuses, before they and you are destroyed together.'[34] As an appendix to his discourse Price printed a copy of the

[30] See Albert Goodwin, *The Friends of Liberty: The English Democratic Movement in the Age of the French Revolution* (London, 1979); J. Ann Hone, *For the Cause of Truth: Radicalism in London 1796–1821* (Oxford, 1982); James T. Boulton, *The Language of Politics in the Age of Wilkes and Burke* (London, 1963).

[31] S. Maccoby, *English Radicalism 1786–1832: From Paine to Cobbett* (London, 1955), chs. 1–7; Ronald Paulson, *Representations of Revolution (1789–1820)* (New Haven, Conn., 1983); Carl B. Cone, *The English Jacobins: Reformers in Late 18th Century England* (New York, 1968); Harry T. Dickinson, *Liberty and Property: Political Ideology in Eighteenth-Century Britain*, repr. (London, 1979), chs. 6–7. See also Norbert Elias, *The Court Society*, trans. Edmund Jephcott (Oxford, 1983), ch. 9, 'On the Sociogenesis of the French Revolution'.

[32] Ursula Henriques, *Religious Toleration in England 1787–1833* (London, 1961), ch. 3; Martin Fitzpatrick, 'Heretical Religion and Radical Politics in Late Eighteenth-Century England', in Hellmuth (ed.), *Transformation of Political Culture*, 339–72.

[33] Letter from Richard Price to James Wodrow, Dr Williams's Library, London.

[34] Richard Price, *A Discourse on the Love of Our Country, Delivered on Nov. 4, 1789, at the Meeting-House in the Old Jewry, to the Society for Commemorating the Revolution in Great Britain*, 2nd edn. (London, 1789), 34, 39, 49, 50–1.

French National Assembly's Declaration of the Rights of Men. Writing to James Wodrow again in January 1790 Price rejoiced, 'Never perhaps did an event happen more favourable to civil and religious liberty than the late Revolution in *France*. . . . A spirit is gone forth which is likely to shake to the foundations the long establish'd fabricks of Superstition and tyranny.'[35]

Many echoed these sentiments through 1789 and 1790, but others were alarmed by acts of Revolutionary violence as early as the summer of 1789. On 5 August James Wodrow wrote to his old friend Samuel Kenrick, Dissenter and banker at Bewdley in Worcestershire:

What think you of the state of France[?] I had flat[t]ered myself that a grand & glorious revolution in favour of Liberty woud have been effected without bloodshed & that it woud have made the Tyrants of Europe tremble on their Thrones; but now I see the purchase must be made by blood[.] The Tiers Etats seem to have lost their influence & France from one end of the kingdom to the other to be under the power of an enraged Mob the most dreadful of tyrants.

Edmund Burke's *Reflections on the Revolution in France*, published in November 1790, confirmed such a view and warned of dire consequences for Britain. In January 1791 Wodrow wrote again to Kenrick: 'The French Revolution! I have read Burks attack upon it a much stronger one than I expected . . . It glows with warm eloquence contains some argument that really deserves the attention of the French Patriots & their friends here . . .'[36] Burke had been seen as an advocate of political reform, religious toleration, and other 'liberal' causes. Now he argued that the French Revolution was led by people with no right to membership in the 'political nation'—the lower-class 'mob', women, disaffected professionals and 'men of letters', and a few ambitious aristocrats. He accused the Revolution's British sympathizers of the same political illegitimacy.

Significantly, Burke uses figures of gender difference inscribed in the professional middle-class cultural revolution to condemn the Revolution and rehabilitate the *ancien régime*. He claims that the characteristic Revolutionary event was the march of a Parisian mob 'in the abused shape of the vilest of women' (i.e. prostitutes) on Versailles in October

---

[35] Letter from Richard Price to James Wodrow, 20 Jan. 1790, Dr Williams's Library.

[36] Letter from James Wodrow to Samuel Kenrick; Wodrow–Kenrick Correspondence, Dr Williams's Library. Subsequent quotations from letters by Wodrow and Kenrick are from this collection. On Kenrick and Wodrow see John Creasey, 'The Birmingham Riots of 1791: A Contemporary Account', *Transactions of the Unitarian Historical Society*, 13 (1963–6), 111–17.

1789—an unfeminine and therefore unnatural eruption into the public, political domain. This mob then transgressed into the domestic sphere of the royal family, 'insulting' the queen and threatening the royal family in their domestic quarters. Burke imagines the queen fleeing 'almost naked' from her own room and concealing in her bosom a means of committing suicide lest she be subjected to 'the last disgrace'—rape. He casts the Revolution as a desecrator of femininity, domesticity, and the domestic affections:

I thought ten thousand swords must have leaped from their scabbards to avenge even a look that threatened her [the queen] with insult.—But the age of chivalry is gone.—That of sophisters, oeconomists, and calculators, has succeeded; and the glory of Europe is extinguished for ever. Never, never more, shall we behold that generous loyalty to rank and sex, that proud submission, that dignified obedience, that subordination of the heart, which kept alive, even in servitude itself, the spirit of an exalted freedom.

A series of oxymorons represents 'antient chivalry' as a coalescence of masculine and feminine virtues validating historic upper-class culture as that of the political nation.[37]

At the centre of this culture are particular figures of 'woman', domesticity, and the 'domestic affections', the foundation of community, state, and nation:

We begin our public affections in our families. No cold relation is a zealous citizen. We pass on to our neigbourhoods, and our habitual provincial connections. . . . Such divisions of our country as have been formed by habit . . . were so many little images of the great country in which the heart found something which it could fill. The love to the whole is not extinguished by this subordinate partiality. Perhaps it is a sort of elemental training to those higher and more large regards, by which alone men come to be affected, as with their own concern, in the prosperity of a kingdom so extensive as that of France. (p. 315)

Burke's model of the family is an *embourgeoisement* of the economic and cultural institution of the landed estate, the unit of local and national political power. He uses figures of 'woman', domesticity, and the 'domestic affections' not to undermine court government and aristocratic culture but to defend them as already imbued with the values of the professional middle-class cultural revolution.

This comprehensive rhetorical strategy divided cultural revolutionaries in Britain, initiating a 'paper war' that lasted through most of the

---

[37] Edmund Burke, *Reflections on the Revolution in France*, ed. Conor Cruise O'Brien (Harmondsworth, 1968), 170–1.

decade.[38] In view of Burke's strategy it is not surprising that one of the first replies to him was by a woman—Mary Wollstonecraft's *A Vindication of the Rights of Men* (November 1790). Wollstonecraft was familiar with intellectual circles of liberal Dissent, knew and admired Richard Price, and had been influenced by his social and political thinking. Price argues that individual salvation is gained by choosing good over evil, but doing so requires a cultivated 'mind', a proper balance of passions and reason, and personal liberty. In her earlier writings Wollstonecraft had applied this philosophy to the education of girls and young women; here she applies it in a broad critique of the system Burke defends. She accuses Burke of being seduced by the 'effeminate' glamour of court culture, represented by Marie Antoinette. She argues that Burke's own effeminacy is seen in his personal tone, ostentatious 'sensibility', susceptibility to passion rather than reason, and rhetorical and stylistic excess. By contrast, Wollstonecraft attempts to display a style and method of argument that is both feeling and 'philosophical', both 'feminine' and 'masculine'. A year later she used this rhetorical strategy to exemplify a feminist argument in *A Vindication of the Rights of Woman*.[39] Though some reviewers ridiculed Wollstonecraft's venture into the 'masculine' domain of politics, it was well received among Revolutionary sympathizers. Samuel Kenrick called it a 'handsome drubbg of Mister Burke' and had it bound with replies by Catharine Macaulay Graham, Joseph Priestley, and James Mackintosh.

But most replies to Burke by women were ignored, and the reply that was most popular—in both senses—was Tom Paine's *Rights of Man* (1791–2). Events soon made middle-class observers wary of 'popular' politics in both Britain and France, however. In Birmingham on 14 July 1791 a 'Church and King' mob was incited to attack Revolutionary sympathizers celebrating the anniversary of the fall of the Bastille. Samuel Kenrick lamented, 'What must foreign nations think & say of us, particularly the enlightened French.' In the spring of 1792 Kenrick noted increasing social conflict: 'so many competitions for superiority, so many little clashing imaginary interests, in politics & religion,—not to mention deep rooted prejudices with the authority of Burke to love & hug them the closer because they are prejudices.' Yet the popularity of books such as Paine's and the appearance of *A Vindication of the Rights of Woman* gave Kenrick renewed hope:

---

[38] See Marilyn Butler (ed.), *Burke, Paine, Godwin, and the Revolution Controversy* (Cambridge, 1984).
[39] See Gary Kelly, *Revolutionary Feminism: The Mind and Career of Mary Wollstonecraft* (London, 1992), chs. 4–5.

Add to all this Mrs. Woolstonecraft's Rights of Woman—wch will delight you & still more perhaps your daughters. She possesses the same original genius [as Paine], undaunted intrepidity, & benevolent intention—added to the most liberal notions of God, Providence & the christian religion—with the most sov[er]eign contempt of every frivolous aristocratical folly wch have so long enslaved the world.

The lot of women was linked to that of other oppressed groups, and the Revolution was seen as promising emancipation for all.

In the autumn of 1792, events in France again altered the course of the Revolution debate in Britain, confirming the warning of the Birmingham Riots. Wodrow told Kenrick that the September Massacres at Paris had 'hurt the reputation of the cause of Liberty more than any thing which has yet happened, & silenced many of it's friends in this Country'. Kenrick took the common liberal view that Revolutionary excesses were the 'natural' result of court tyranny. The struggle between Girondins and Jacobins in late 1792, the trial and execution of Louis XVI early in 1793, and the outbreak of war between France and Britain in February 1793 further damped Revolutionary sympathy in Britain.[40] Wodrow wrote to Kenrick in March:

the Jacobin faction in France have done more by their rash violence & madness to hurt the sacred cause of Liberty than all its open enemies. They seem resolved to destroy & have in part accomplished their purpose, all sense of order & subordination in the minds of men[,] the only sure basis on which the fabric of civil & political Liberty can stand.

In Britain, many were turning against reform of any kind, labelled 'innovation' or 'French principles'.[41]

Others thought these changes were orchestrated by the 'privileged orders' and government in their own interest, and political repression increased. Leaders of a 'British Convention' held in Edinburgh were convicted of treason after a perfunctory trial in 1793. Movements such as feminism and opposition to slavery were accused of subverting 'order and good government'. The possibility of a coalition between middle-class reformers and politicized artisans receded. The professional

[40] Clive Emsley, British Society and the French Wars 1793–1815 (London, 1979), ch. 2.

[41] Harry T. Dickinson, 'Popular Loyalism in Britain in the 1790s', in Hellmuth (ed.), Transformation of Political Culture, 503–33; David Eastwood, 'Patriotism and the English State in the 1790s', in Mark Philp (ed.), The French Revolution and British Popular Politics (Cambridge, 1991), 146–68.

middle-class cultural revolution was dividing into opposed factions, and by early 1794 Kenrick and Wodrow, like many others of their class, were quarrelling over the Revolution. Kenrick was depressed by the tide of social, religious, and political reaction in Britain and disgusted at the way the terms 'presbyterians, republicans, levellers & lastly jacobins' were being used 'as op[p]robrious names of the same import'. Yet he thought France still 'exhibits an awful spectacle to rash hot-headed tyrants—& Liberty, however disfigured by rage & violence & bismeared wth the mingled blood of slaves & patriots, still rears her triumphant head, & proclaims aloud to the astonished world, that her Cause is invincible'. But his vehemence suggests desperation rather than conviction. Wodrow saw France differently: 'Their present Govt is a most ferocious Despotism marked with more outrages of injustice & cruelty than any other at present in Europe, and as the professed friends of Liberty they have dishonoured & hurt its sacred—it's glorious cause more than it's worst enemies.'

Kenrick condemned government repression and intimidation in Britain, 'when infamous spies & informers are encouraged & protected, & when the very sounds, knowledge liberty, & improvement, are treated as synonymous wth faction, discontent, sedition & rebellion'. Wodrow agreed, but feared that 'the meer Mob have certainly imbibed levelling principles to a higher degree than I ever knew before & by any thing I can learn, their attachment to the French still continues'. Kenrick saw little difference between the Jacobin government and its regime of Terror in France and the 'anti-Jacobin' government in Britain, which he called 'terrorism—alias Toryism': 'The same head-strong violence in the ruling party to extinguish their opponents—the same impatience of controul & disregard of justice, humanity & ancient usage', producing 'that most degrading of human passions, fear—& its inseparable concomitant implacable revenge'. Wodrow again agreed, but felt that the 'British Convention', mass demonstrations in various cities, and the discovery of stockpiled arms in Sheffield justified the government in acting to avoid civil war. By the summer of 1794 a political crisis seemed imminent and Kenrick almost believed a violent revolution might be necessary; Wodrow cautioned, 'Submission to order & Govt is certainly a natural as well as a Scriptural duty, as much founded on the eternal principle of morality, as resistance to tyranny.' But acquittals in the Treason Trials of autumn 1794 relieved political and social tensions. By early 1795 Kenrick and Wodrow were writing more amicably and agreed in condemning the war, but they feared signs of an imminent famine, Government legislation such as the 'Two Bills' suppressing reform clubs, and the rise of local military volunteers, ostensibly to resist French invasion but in fact to intimidate reformers.

Both Kenrick and Wodrow now blamed radical reformers for the excesses of political reaction. In December 1795 Wodrow wrote:

The Errours & abuses of [established] Religion & Govt are certainly very great, and the prejudices men have in their favour very strong. These Reformers (who are unworthy of the honourable name) take the most effectual means to rivet them by tearing them up by the roots and along with them all religion and subordination & instead of dealing tenderly with them, or at least with what is pardonable & sometimes amiable in them by so doing they make men cling the closer to their old faulty religions & govts.

Like many others, they came to see Revolutionary feminism and especially the career of Mary Wollstonecraft as unfortunate examples of such counter-productive vanguardism. Wodrow confessed that the publication of William Godwin's *Memoirs* of his late wife, Mary Wollstonecraft, had 'lowered her not a little in my Esteem; yet not so much as in that of many'. Kenrick, as usual, took a more liberal view, and remembered reading Wollstonecraft's *Vindication of the Rights of Woman*, an 'able defence of her own sex against the degrading theory' of conduct writers such as James Fordyce.

Kenrick and Wodrow became increasingly concerned with conditions in Britain itself. The famine of 1795 and dislocations of a wartime economy caused widespread distress among the common people, increasing the poor rates for parish relief and leading to business failures, political unrest in Ireland and elsewhere, and the banking crisis of 1797. Like most people of their class, Kenrick and Wodrow avidly followed events at home and abroad by reading the publications of the day. For Kenrick and Wodrow these included the reformist *Cambridge Intelligencer*, Godwin's attack on political extremism in his *Considerations* (1795), Coleridge's *Watchman* (1796), and the reformist *Monthly Magazine* (begun 1796), where Mary Hays was defending Revolutionary feminism. Kenrick was shocked by the French invasion of Switzerland, but confessed that Helen Maria Williams's *A Tour in Switzerland* (1798) 'has opened my eyes, wth regard to this celebrated people, & demonstrated, that they were as ripe for a revolution as ever France was'. Both Kenrick and Wodrow were sceptical of attempts, such as John Robison's *Proofs of a Conspiracy*, to blame the Revolution on secret societies of Freemasons and

'Illuminati'.[42] Nor did they blame the spread of literacy and cheap print; as Kenrick wrote to Wodrow in October 1798, 'The printers first & next the restorers of polite literature [Renaissance humanists], wth our religious Reformers, were our illuminati, to whom we are indebted for all the improvements wch are now spreading abroad wth an accelerated rapidity in every direction: wch boundless effects, I think, could never be produced, by isolated secret clubs of sedentary enthusiasts.' But like many other former Revolutionary sympathizers they were now inclined to trust Providence and gradual intellectual improvement. Kenrick confessed in October 1798, 'As to politics & the present posture of affairs, I am as averse as you to meddle wth them: & with you, our chief comfort is a reliance on that mysterious energy of an over-ruling Divine Providence, wch turns what appears to us to be evil into the greatest good.' Wodrow concurred: 'Every impartial man detached from the strife of party may now see, that the noble spirit of benevolence & liberty which animated some of the first french reformers, is now extinguished, I fear never to kindle again in our days.'

The letters of Kenrick and Wodrow show how 'woman' and women writers became important concerns in the British Revolution debate.[43] The turn against feminism accelerated in both Britain and France after the avant-garde political amorousness of the early Revolutionary salons seemed to degenerate into courtly decadence during the Directory of the mid-1790s.[44] In Britain, conservative conduct-books for women, such as Fordyce's *Sermons to Young Women*, were published in new editions.[45] In the later 1790s women writers such as Elizabeth Hamilton and Hannah More, though similar in background to feminists such as Mary Wollstonecraft and Mary Hays, rejected Revolutionary feminist civic 'woman' for a renewed model of 'domestic woman' as professionalized custodian of the 'national' conscience, culture, and destiny. Yet even this model could have feminist and revolutionary potential, as Hamilton and other counter-Revolutionary writers showed.

The French Revolution and the British Revolution debate simply recontextualized major elements of the professional middle-class cultural revolution, including the nature of 'domestic woman' and the

[42] John M. Roberts, *The Mythology of the Secret Societies*, repr. (London, 1974), chs. 6–7.
[43] See Joan B. Landes, *Women and the Public Sphere in the Age of the French Revolution* (Ithaca, NY, 1988).
[44] Annette Rosa, *Citoyennes: Les Femmes et la Révolution Française* (Paris, 1988), 184.
[45] William St Clair, *The Godwins and the Shelleys: The Biography of a Family* (London, 1989), app. 2.

role of women writers. As Janet Todd argues, one sign of 'the greatly improved status of authorship for women' was the lively political debate in women's writing 'over whether or not women should *write* overtly about political matters'.[46] In fact, this debate extended far beyond women's writing. At first the Revolution seemed to affirm the cultural revolution's social critique, encouraging women writers, among others, to turn that critique to Revolutionary events and issues. In the early 1790s many women writers, especially religious Dissenters, brought acceptably 'feminine' pre-Revolutionary topics of social sympathy and humanitarianism into the Revolution debate. Helen Maria Williams moved easily from a Sentimental critique of imperialism in her poem *Peru* to enthusiasm for the Revolution in her series of *Letters from France* (1790 on). Women such as Wollstonecraft, A. L. Barbauld, Catharine Macaulay Graham, and Ann Jebb moved from acceptably feminine subjects such as education and devotional religion to participation, though usually anonymously, in the French Revolution debate.

Many women writers had participated in the cultural revolution's critique of court culture before 1789, focusing on the corruption and degradation of women by courtly gallantry and the 'mistress system'. This work was carried over into the early 1790s; courtly decadence was blamed for producing the Revolution in France and internal crisis and external weakness in other European countries, including Britain. In 1794, for example, Lady Sophia Burrell published an epyllion entitled *The Thymbriad*, written some years before. Based on Xenophon's *Cyropædia*, the classical Greek quasi-novel of a prince's education, her poem describes the triumph of the virtuous and austere Persians, led by the youthful prince Cyrus, over the luxurious and decadent Medes, and was probably written around the American Revolution, when British cultural revolutionaries accused the King and court of using patronage and corruption to override the will of the people and suppress the independence of a youthful, energetic American meritocracy. Central to Burrell's social critique is the contrast between the morally inspiring, virtuous, and properly domestic woman and the effeminizing, disruptive, and coquettish courtly intriguer.

The working-class poet Ann Yearsley had made her mark before the Revolutionary decade, like most women poets, celebrating the local, quotidian, domestic, and familial and engaging in social criticism as an

---

[46] Janet Todd, *The Sign of Angellica: Women, Writing, and Fiction 1660–1800* (London, 1989), 225.

extending borders...

extension of acceptably feminine social sympathy and nurture of the domestic affections. But she too was moved by the Revolution to attempt the theme of social oppression under 'antient chivalry', in the more ambitious form of a blank-verse tragicomedy, *Earl Goodwin: An Historical Play* (1791). It is influenced by the earlier moral dramas of Yearsley's erstwhile literary patron, Hannah More, offers the kind of pastiche Shakespeare fairly common at the time, and attacks court government and priestcraft for using women as instruments of ambition and power. The priest Lodowicke boasts how he persuaded the king that women had to be ideologically subjugated, through the church, in order to ensure the stability of state and society: 'Thro' ev'ry age it had been *our* chief care | To rule the thought of *Woman*', for 'kingly leagues, | Order of government, and social ties, | Depend on woman's faith' (p. 14). Yearsley glorifies virtuous, domestic, and heroic woman as the antithesis of these courtly evils and therefore destined to be their victim. The play stays within acceptably feminine discourse by this focus on domestic woman, but her victimization is linked to numerous other social evils resulting from court politics—a linking that might have seemed an unfeminine intrusion into the public, political sphere. *Yamba*

Like many others, Yearsley took a different view of the Revolution after the events of 1793. In her *Reflections on the Death of Louis XVI* (1793) she feminizes Revolutionary violence as a courtly coquette, and deplores the way 'fancied Liberty, with rude Excess, | Courts Man from sober Joy, and lures him on | To frantic War, struck by her gaudy Dress'. Pessimistically, she concludes that true liberty exists not in France, or even Britain, but only in the 'fancy', a mental faculty usually gendered female:

> Ask ye! where joyous Liberty resorts,
>   In France, in Spain, or in Britannia's Vale?
> O no!—She only with poor Fancy sports
>   Her richest Dwelling is the passing Gale.   (p. 5)

Charlotte Smith takes a similar line in her blank verse poem, *The Emigrants*, written in the spring of 1793 and set in November 1792. Though the poem sympathizes with the French *émigré* clergy and condemns the excesses of the Revolution, it affirms that the *émigrés* themselves are bigots and that Britain is the scene of 'proud oppression' and 'legal crimes' (p. 3). Indeed, the poem's narrator claims a privileged viewpoint for sympathizing with the emigrants' sorrows, 'for I too have known | Involuntary exile' and suffered from systemic oppression.

Unlike the *émigrés*, however, she has come to a rational understanding and critique of the causes for her oppressed condition.

Women writers also assumed a 'feminine' role in allaying plebeian revolt by extending their domestic activities and expertise into local society and thus into national life.[47] Before the Revolution, Sarah Trimmer's *Œconomy of Charity* (1787) called middle-class women to a variety of tasks in reform, management, and policing of the lower classes. In the 1780s Hannah More and her sisters promoted Sunday schools for the poor by promising local gentry that if the poor were 'better principled' they 'would be more industrious' and less inclined to crime, thus lowering the poor rates.[48] In the 1790s these schemes were directed to pre-empting subversion of the lower classes by 'Jacobinism'.[49] The popularity of Paine's *Rights of Man* among the 'lower orders' was attributed to their previous reading of chapbooks and street ballads, seen by More as a 'sans-culotte library'.[50] More was called on to merge her Sunday-school literacy campaign with a programme of pseudo-popular literature. Thousands of copies of her pamphlet *Village Politics*, first published anonymously in 1792, were bought and given away to labouring people—testimony to professional middle-class faith in the power of print. In 1795 More followed with a massive programme of similar works called the 'Cheap Repository'. Many thought it staved off lower-class revolution but some thought it was designed to separate the lower classes from their historic masters, the landed gentry.[51] The fictitious 'Rev. Sir Archibald MacSarcasm' attacked 'Cheap Repository' for 'puritanizing' the lower classes: 'To puritanize is to revolutionize the people, and to revolutionize is to confound all order, subordination, religion, and regular government.'[52]

While the Revolution debate offered new opportunities for women writers to extend 'feminine' discourse into politics, it also drew increas-

[47] Frank K. Prochaska, 'Women in English Philanthropy, 1790–1830', *International Review of Social History*, 19 (1974), 426–45.

[48] Letter from Hannah More to William Wilberforce, 1789, in William Roberts, *Memoirs of the Life and Correspondence of Mrs. Hannah More*, 3rd rev. edn., 2 vols. (London, 1835), ii. 206–8.

[49] Ibid. 340.

[50] Susan Pedersen, 'Hannah More Meets Simple Simon: Tracts, Chapbooks, and Popular Culture in Late Eighteenth-Century England', *Journal of British Studies*, 25 (Jan. 1986), 84–113.

[51] Roberts, *Memoirs of More*, ii. 383.

[52] 'Rev. Sir Archibald MacSarcasm, Bart.' (possibly Abraham Elton), *The Life of Hannah More, with a Critical Review of Her Writings* (London, 1802), 206.

ing condemnation to such work and the pre-Revolutionary social critique that lay behind it. Women who attempted 'men's' discourses such as learning, criticism, and satire had long been ridiculed and to many the terms 'bluestocking' and 'learned lady' were synonymous with 'unfeminine', as seen in Fordyce's *Sermons to Young Women*. Such terms now acquired a sharper edge, suggesting not only pro-Revolutionary sympathies but moral, social, and literary transgression ultimately threatening 'order and good government'. Satires such as William Gifford's *Baviad* (1791) and *Mæviad* (1794) attacked the pre-Revolutionary feminization of culture for contributing to Revolution in France and national crisis in Britain. By 1797 T. J. Mathias associated plebeian readers and female writers together as signs of decadence and disorder and as dangers to the state: 'Our peasantry now read the *Rights of Man* on mountains, and moors, and by the way side . . . Our *unsexed* female writers now instruct, or confuse, us and themselves in the labyrinth of politicks, or turn us wild with Gallick frenzy'—references to Mary Wollstonecraft and Helen Maria Williams.[53] Women's greater 'sensibility' and 'imagination' were also supposed to incline them to Revolutionary sympathy. A reviewer of Helen Maria Williams's *Letters from France* (1790) suggested that 'the susceptibility of the feminine mind receives more ardent impressions even than that of the most honest patriots; and when the *imagination* is considered as *patriotism*, every literary female becomes a patriot'.[54] Women who professed Revolutionary 'reason' and 'philosophy' were seen as only more completely the dupes of their passions.

Those most obviously caught in this double bind were the Revolutionary feminists. Their work was conditioned by the cultural revolution, the Revolution in France, and the Revolution debate in Britain but rooted in the female conduct-book tradition, liberal Dissenting theology, and the literature and culture of Sensibility.[55] In the late 1790s British 'anti-Jacobins' welcomed revelation of Mary Wollstonecraft's sexual transgressions as proof that Revolutionary feminism was inimical to bourgeois domesticity and femininity. But Wollstonecraft was only the most prominent woman to develop a feminism for the 1790s, and her early entry into the Revolution debate against

---

[53] Mathias, *Pursuits of Literature*, 238.
[54] *English Review*, 20 (July 1792), 57.
[55] See Joyce Hemlow, 'Fanny Burney and the Courtesy Books', *Publications of the Modern Language Association of America*, 65 (1950), 732–61; Kelly, *Revolutionary Feminism*, ch. 1.

Burke precipitated the feminism latent in her work before 1790. *A Vindication of the Rights of Woman*, published early in the critical Revolutionary year of 1792, attacks the cultural revolution's figure of 'domestic woman' as merely a re-formation of dependent, eroticized, trivialized, and subjugated courtly 'woman'. Wollstonecraft warns that both the cultural revolution and the Revolution in France would be vitiated from within unless they purged their residue of courtly gender culture by granting women intellectual, professional, and some civic rights. Only then would women be able effectively to discharge their 'natural' domestic roles and thereby serve the state and the nation.

In *A Vindication* Wollstonecraft plays down the sexual passions because she here blames them for the exploitation of women in courtly amorous culture. She also gives a feminist turn to the familiar conduct-book warning that sexual passion inevitably decayed in marriage, and therefore women should be prepared emotionally and intellectually to replace passion with the 'higher' and more lasting 'domestic affections'. In stressing women's need to 'exercise' reason by suppressing the passions, Wollstonecraft responds to the Western philosophical tradition's relegation of 'woman' to the sphere of matter, body, and the passions. In other texts Wollstonecraft argues for women's erotic equality with men and right to sexual pleasure, at a time when philosophy and science were increasingly asserting the incompatibility of femininity and sexual desire or pleasure.[56]

Wollstonecraft's views were strengthened by her involvement with avant-garde cultural revolutionaries in London and Paris who rejected marriage and sexual chastity as oppressive property institutions and cultivated an apparently egalitarian sexuality informed by an eroticized culture of Sensibility.[57] In France Wollstonecraft fell in love with the American entrepreneur Gilbert Imlay, had a child by him, and under the shadow of Jacobin rule wrote *An Historical and Moral View of the Origin and Progress of the French Revolution* (1794). But she was abandoned by Imlay and, having invested her identity as a female cultural revolutionary in her relationship with him, she came close to personal disintegration. She travelled to Scandinavia on business for Imlay in the summer of 1795 and published *Letters Written During a Short Residence in Norway, Sweden, and Denmark*. Here the personal experience and 'sensibility' used to validate her political views in the *Vindications*

---

[56] See Thomas Laqueur, 'Orgasm, Generation, and the Politics of Reproductive Biology', in Gallagher and Laqueur (eds.), *The Making of the Modern Body*, 1–41.

[57] Claire Tomalin, *The Life and Death of Mary Wollstonecraft* (London, 1974), ch. 11.

are deployed again to imply an authoritative Revolutionary subjectivity heralding the elimination of inequalities of class and gender and thus the success of a cultural revolution led by those like herself. *Letters* subsumes her earlier feminism and Revolutionary sympathy in ways similar to those being explored by many women writers around the same time, including Helen Maria Williams and Mary Hays, and like their work, *Letters* is another essay in formulating a woman's political discourse for the Revolutionary decade.

Back in London Wollstonecraft formed a new relationship with the leading 'English Jacobin' philosopher and novelist William Godwin, who was just then advising Mary Hays on her autobiographical feminist novel, *Memoirs of Emma Courtney*. Wollstonecraft again became pregnant, and married Godwin to secure herself from public criticism that would vitiate her revolutionary usefulness. She too was working on a novelization of Revolutionary feminism, entitled *The Wrongs of Woman; or, Maria*, when she died from complications of childbirth in September 1797. In 1798 Godwin published her unfinished novel and other papers with a biography of her, setting forth her Revolutionary feminist views of gender, sexuality, and domesticity and her attempts to live out those views. But this attempt to disseminate her feminism beyond her death only gave counter-revolutionaries and counter-feminists ammunition in their struggle for control and leadership of the cultural revolution. Even a sympathetic reader of Wollstonecraft such as James Wodrow felt that Godwin's revelations showed 'a wish to trample on the general sense of mankind expressed by the Apostle . . . yet against his will he serves the cause of religion, by exhibiting a striking view of a Woman of fine Talents & amiable dispositions, meanly deserting her station & sinking a Victim to the strength of her Passions & feelings because destitute of the support of Religious principles'.

By the late 1790s there was growing insistence by many cultural revolutionaries in Britain that professional middle-class culture alone could save the country from the incompetence of its aristocratic rulers, the disaffection of the 'lower orders', and the military threat from Revolutionary France. Hannah More, for example, turned her attention from the *embourgeoisement* of the lower ranks through 'Cheap Repository' to *embourgeoisement* of the ruling classes and the entire nation through 'domestic woman'. More had rejected Revolutionary feminism, refusing even to read Wollstonecraft's *Vindication of the Rights of Woman*. Yet in *Strictures on the Modern System of Female*

Education (1799) she asserts, like Wollstonecraft, that 'the general state of civilized society depends . . . on the prevailing sentiments and habits of women, and on the nature and degree of the estimation in which they are held' by men.[58] Like Wollstonecraft she denounces court society in which women can 'use their boasted power over mankind to no higher purpose than the gratification of vanity or the indulgence of pleasure' (i. 3). Like Wollstonecraft she calls on her countrywomen not to 'content themselves . . . with captivating for a day, when they may bring into action powers of which the effects may be commensurate with eternity', and to extend their feminine domestic character into social reform and cultural revolution (i. 4). But she also calls on women to chasten public 'manners', deter ridicule of religion, discourage men of 'gallantry', and abjure 'that sober and unsuspected mass of mischief' going under the name 'of science, of philosophy, of arts, of belles lettres', especially 'German dramas' and novels such as those of Rousseau and Wollstonecraft that undermine marriage and thus public morality. Above all women should supervise their children's domestic education—the ideological and cultural reproduction that is the basis of the state.

This programme for 'domestic woman' to become a social and cultural, and thereby a political revolutionary merges Wollstonecraft's Revolutionary feminism with the earlier conduct book tradition.[59] Fordyce's *Sermons to Young Women* also argued that the domestic character and thus the public influence of women must affect the national destiny. More wrote as Britain faced a renewed nationalist and imperialist Revolution under Napoleon. In 'this moment of alarm and peril' she calls on women 'to come forward, and contribute their full and fair proportion towards the saving of their country', 'without departing from the refinement of their character, without departing from the dignity of their rank, without blemishing the delicacy of their sex', but rather by using 'that power delegated to them by the courtesy of custom, by the honest gallantry of the heart, by the

---

[58] Hannah More, *Strictures on the Modern System of Female Education, with a View of the Principles and Conduct Prevalent among Women of Rank and Fortune*, 2 vols. (London, 1799), i. 2.

[59] On the parallels between More and Wollstonecraft, see Mitzi Myers, 'Reform or Ruin: "A Revolution in Female Manners"', in Harry C. Payne (ed.), *Studies in Eighteenth-Century Culture*, 11 (Madison, Wis., 1982), 199–216; cf. Donna Landry, *The Muses of Resistance: Labouring-Class Women's Poetry in Britain, 1739–1796* (Cambridge, 1990), 57–60, and Elizabeth Kowaleski-Wallace, *Their Father's Daughters: Hannah More, Maria Edgeworth, and Patriarchal Complicity* (New York, 1991), 41–4.

imperious control of virtuous affections, by the habits of civilized states, by the usages of polished society' (i. 5). The passage echoes Burke's paean to 'antient chivalry', as Burke in turn echoes Fordyce's paean to women's social influence.

To distance herself from Revolutionary feminism More assures her readers that 'I am not sounding an alarm to female warriors, or exciting female politicians: I hardly know which is the most disgusting and unnatural character' (i. 6). But she also rejects crypto-courtly Burkean feminism, declaring, 'I do not wish to bring back the frantic reign of chivalry, nor to reinstate women in that fantastic empire in which they then sat enthroned in the hearts, or rather in the imaginations of men' (i. 19). Nevertheless, she insists that women's influence will determine, 'in no low degree, the well-being' of civilized states:

At this period, when our country can only hope to stand by opposing a bold and noble *unanimity* to the most tremendous confederacies against religion and order, and governments, which the world ever saw; what an accession would it bring to the public strength, could we prevail on beauty, and rank, and talents, and virtue, confederating their several powers, to come forward with a patriotism at once firm and feminine for the general good! (i. 5–6)

More does not reject Revolutionary feminism so much as modify its version of 'domestic woman' for the Revolutionary aftermath and Romantic nationalism.[60] The call would be repeated many times in various forms over the next decade and a half, opening new opportunities for women writers to participate in the public, political sphere as cultural revolutionaries, while attempting to reshape civil society according to repeatedly revised and at times contradictory versions of the professional middle-class cultural revolution.

[60] Gary Kelly, 'Revolutionary and Romantic Feminism: Women, Writing and Cultural Revolution', in Keith Hanley and Raman Selden (eds.), *Revolution and English Romanticism: Politics and Rhetoric* (Hemel Hempstead, 1990), 107–30.

2

Feminizing Revolution:
Helen Maria Williams

HELEN MARIA WILLIAMS provided readers in Britain with a sustained eyewitness account and analysis of the French Revolution, yet her position as a writer was trebly marginal.[1] She was from the geographical and cultural borders of Britain, born in 1761 of Welsh and Scottish parents and raised in Berwick after the early death of her father, an army officer. Her intellectual culture came from religious Dissent and its provincial Enlightenment. But she was marginalized even within these cultures by being a woman. Like other women Dissenters such as Anna Lætitia Barbauld and Mary Hays she was well educated and found liberal Dissent receptive to women intellectuals, but she could no more attend a Dissenting Academy than Oxford or Cambridge University, and no more preach in a Dissenting chapel than an Anglican church. She did not have to, for, like many women of her time in Britain and France, she achieved literary and political influence through coteries and salons. These created a social space at once public and domestic to develop Enlightenment culture, disseminate a discourse of merit, harmonize differences of class and gender through intellectual, political, professional, and personal relations and correspondence, and provide the encouragement and contacts necessary to support publication of books and periodicals, thus rivalling court society and culture.[2] It was a space that nourished women intellectuals and Williams had the personality to make full use of it. The banker and poet Samuel Rogers met her around 1787 and spoke of her 'as a very fascinating person, though not handsome', with 'much conversa-

---

[1] Biographical information in this chapter is heavily indebted to Lionel D. Woodward, *Une anglaise amie de la Révolution française: Hélène-Maria Williams et ses amis*, repr. (Geneva, 1977).

[2] See Sylvia Harcstark Myers, *The Bluestocking Circle: Women, Friendship, and the Life of the Mind in Eighteenth-Century England* (Oxford, 1990); Dena Goodman, 'Enlightenment Salons: The Convergence of Female and Philosophic Ambitions', *Eighteenth-Century Studies*, 22 (Spring 1989), 329–50.

tional power', 'the charm of sympathy', and 'the art of bringing people together'.[3] The remark indicates that Williams's ability to be 'fascinating', with its suggestions of erotic seductiveness, depended on subjective qualities—her 'sensibility'—rather than the physical attributes conventionally supposed to give a woman such power, especially in courtly society. Salon and coterie culture was well suited to the exercise of her power, and Williams went on to make a public and literary career of it by finding formal means to 'express' what would be taken to be 'her' subjectivity in writing.

Williams was one of many women writers helped in her career by male mentors, often men who themselves participated in the feminization of culture as a way to reform civil society in the image and interests of the professional middle class. Williams's first mentor was Andrew Kippis, a scholar, advocate of social and political reform, and leader of the English Dissenting Enlightenment who belonged to several different coteries, from that of the Tory Samuel Johnson to those of eighteenth-century 'commonwealthmen' and classical republicans.[4] Kippis helped her to publish her first work, *Edwin and Eltruda: A Legendary Tale* (1782), and its success then enabled her to settle with her family in London, where Kippis introduced her to an international literary and political circle, including the Burneys, the Wartons, Benjamin Franklin, the Corsican leader General Paoli, the painter Romney, the Italian writer Alfieri, the leading 'Bluestocking' Elizabeth Montagu, the English provincial Enlightenment poet, Anna Seward, and the connoisseur and patron William Hayley. Through Dr John Moore she corresponded with Robert Burns and promoted his work in England. She probably met the Scottish master of Sensibility, Henry Mackenzie, and knew Hester Piozzi and her circle, the avant-garde literary and political circle of William Godwin, the 'Della Cruscan' literary coterie around Robert Merry, and figures such as Joshua Reynolds, Sarah Siddons, Arthur Murphy, and Edmund Burke. After the outbreak of the Revolution debate in Britain it would be difficult for one person to circulate in such varied companies. Williams's early work reflects the interests of the more Sentimental and reformist of these associates and, like much writing of the 1780s, especially by women, suggests the Revolutionary potential of Sensibility.

Edwin and Eltruda: A Legendary Tale is an anti-war poem, foregrounding

---

[3] P. W. Clayden, *The Early Life of Samuel Rogers* (London, 1887), 77.

[4] Isaac Kramnick, *Republicanism and Bourgeois Radicalism: Political Ideology in Late Eighteenth-Century England and America* (Ithaca, NY, 1990).

the sorrows of a young woman deprived of her father and lover by an
armed conflict that seems to have no legitimate cause and no positive
outcome—an implied critique of the conflicted public and political
sphere dominated by men. It is one of several similar poems by
women that purport to be taken from popular oral and 'traditionary'
culture, supposedly within the purview of women writers because they
did not require learning and were narrative in character. *An Ode on the
Peace* (1783) also resembles other poems by women on the same
subject; it celebrates the end of the American war as an end to
domestic grief and goes on to anticipate Britain's assumption of
American freedom and prosperity, opening a new era of peace and
progress in the arts. Again, the subject of war and politics would
conventionally be gendered masculine but the treatment would be seen
as acceptably feminine. *Peru: A Poem; in Six Cantos* (1784) is an
epyllion, an acceptably feminine form because it is briefer and less
formal than the epic, which was conventionally reserved for men. *Peru*
is again 'feminine' in treatment because it portrays the evils of war and
imperialism through their effect on the individual sensibilities and
domestic relations of the victims—a central theme of Williams's later
Revolutionary writing. Williams's *Poems* (1786) is dedicated to the
Queen, known as a patron of intellectual and genteel women writers,
and it was published by subscription, a major way for women writers
to make the most of their social connections. The subscribers included
artists, writers, intellectuals, Dissenting ministers and Anglican church-
men, noblemen, the Prince of Wales, Scots, and women writers who
promoted the cultural revolution. *Poems* collects Williams's earlier
poems and contains a variety of minor kinds often practised by women,
including songs, hymns, paraphrases from Scripture, a verse epistle, a
Gothic piece, an elegy to a woman friend, a sonnet ('To Expression'),
and the love complaint of a woman, in this case the common Sentimental figure of Mary Queen of Scots. In 1788 Williams published a poem
On the Bill . . . for Regulating the Slave-Trade, another favourite subject
of women poets and one that enabled them to capitalize on their
'sensibility' to discourse on public, political issues. Williams does
sentimentalize slavery, but she is more interested in exploiting the issue
to feminize civil society as a whole, anticipating her major work of the
1790s Revolution debate. Here she does so by setting conventionally
'feminine' virtues such as mercy and interests such as home and the
domestic affections against the conventionally 'masculine' pursuits of
martial glory on one hand and commerce on the other.

In the spring of 1790 Williams attempted to transfer her version of the Sentimental feminization of literature and culture into the more widely read form of prose fiction. *Julia: A Novel; Interspersed with Some Poetical Pieces* takes up the early novel of passion developed by Frances Sheridan in *Memoirs of Miss Sidney Biddulph* (1761), Frances Burney in *Evelina* (1778) and *Cecilia* (1782), Sophia Lee in *The Recess* (1783–5), and Charlotte Smith in *Emmeline* (1788). It also develops the work of the more 'liberal' writers among Williams's friends and anticipates her imminent transformation of pre-Revolutionary Sensibility into Revolutionary sympathy. The novel's 'Advertisement' designates the subject as excessive passion, implies that the story is factual—Sentimental validation of fiction as an expression of subjective if not material reality—and advances the Sentimental aesthetics of expressivity by insisting that 'the perfection' of the 'picture' depends not on the matter but the manner of telling. Williams had already established this as her forte in her poems. The plot is purposely thin and most characters are merely social in order to foreground the heroine's subjectivity as she struggles against an illicit love. The heroine has a feeling yet cultivated and disciplined mind, representing a professionalized subjectivity, and her silent suffering represents unrecognized merit oppressed by a seductive, corrupt, and oppressive world. *Julia* also reworks Mackenzie's *Julia de Roubigné* and their common ancestor, Rousseau's *Julie; ou, la nouvelle Héloïse*—the heroine's name invites the reader to read one Julia against the other—by dampening their extravagance of plot, character, setting, and language. Williams uses third-person narration to contain, relativize, or even criticize her novel's central subject consciousness, partly by narratorial irony and partly through free indirect discourse, or the filtering of characters' inward speech and sensations through the narrator's 'voice'. The narrator is moralizing—one reviewer extracted six columns of moral aphorisms from the novel[5]—yet 'poetic', implying a model consciousness like Julia's, a resemblance reinforced by 'her' poems, with themes ranging from the pleasures of nature to 'philanthropy' and pre-Revolutionary libertarianism. This feminization of culture and politics was anticipated by the 'Della Cruscan' poets, who had already transformed these themes into Revolutionary enthusiasm by the time *Julia* was published.[6] In fact, *Julia* could be described as a 'Della Cruscan' novel with the thematic and stylistic extravagance of those writers toned down.

---

[5] *European Magazine*, 17 (June 1790), 435–8.

[6] See W. N. Hargreaves-Mawdsley, *The English Della Cruscans and Their Time, 1783–1828* (The Hague, 1967).

Reviewers recognized this by praising Williams for showing the same 'properly' feminine sensibility and taste exhibited in her poems, along with a cultivation of mind, artistic discipline, and moral correctness thought unusual for a woman. Even Mary Wollstonecraft, who condemned most Sentimental novels by women for merely arousing their readers' sensibility and thereby contributing to their oppression, approved of *Julia*.[7] But the *General Magazine* thought this very achievement set a dangerous example and Williams's efforts should have been directed to 'cultivating and discharging the tender and heart-felt duties of domestic life'. 'Ladies' of rank and fortune, above 'the cares of a family', might indulge in literature, but 'many young creatures . . . early smitten by a generous love of letters, have found their favourite passions' used against them by courtly seducers. Even if they escape this fate, 'Their taste is not deemed most friendly to domestic œconomy, to personal quiet, or to social accommodation', and a 'man of modesty, or sound discretion' would seldom 'select a wife' from among them.[8] Literature is associated with seductive court culture leading to sexual 'ruin' and contrasted with domesticity as a figure for professional middle-class ideology and culture.

The *General Magazine*'s fears would be confirmed by the course Williams's career was about to take. Around 1786 she had met Augustin du Fossé and his wife Monique (Coquerel). Du Fossé's father was a member of the French *noblesse de robe*, disapproved of the marriage, and like other aristocratic parents used a *lettre de cachet* to prevent 'contamination' of his noble blood by his son's 'romantic' action. When the Baron died in 1787 the *lettre de cachet* was revoked, and young du Fossé claimed his patrimony after the fall of the Bastille, symbol of the regime that supported such patriarchal tyranny. Williams found here a political cause more inspiring than any that had interested her earlier. In June 1790 she wrote to a friend that she was going to 'renounce' the literary and social pleasures of England 'for the sublimer delights of the French Revolution'. The Williamses were invited to visit the du Fossés and while in Paris witnessed the Revolutionary 'Festival of the Federation' on 14 July, when National Guards from all over France met to renew their oaths, led by the king. It was 'an occasion of genuine enthusiasm, marking perhaps the high-point of

---

[7] *Analytical Review*, 7 (May 1790), 98. The review is unsigned but followed by one signed 'M.', almost certainly one of Wollstonecraft's signatures at this time.

[8] *General Magazine*, 4 (Apr. 1790), 162–3.

national consensus about what the Revolution had achieved, and was achieving'.[9] As Williams wrote years later, 'The impressions of this unforgettable day determined my political opinions forever' ('Les impressions de cette journée mémorable ont fixé pour toujours mes opinions politiques').[10] As with the 'Della Cruscans' and many other writers, especially women, pre-Revolutionary Sensibility easily became Revolutionary sympathy, a transformation that counter-revolutionaries would later turn against Sensibility and any movement that resembled it, including certain forms of Romanticism.

Williams's account of her political tourism appeared at the end of 1790 as *Letters Written in France, in the Summer of 1790, to a Friend in England; Containing, Various Anecdotes Relative to the French Revolution; and Memoirs of Mons. and Madame du F——*. The story of the du Fossés is the climax of the book, intended as an illustration of the Revolutionary Declaration of the Rights of Man, passed in August 1789. Williams later wrote, 'I recounted what I myself felt, and my stirring account created quite a sensation in my native country, where perhaps more than anywhere else we find injustice repugnant' ('je racontai ce que je sentais moi-même; et ce récit, d'un effet frappant, fit quelque sensation dans mon pays natal, où plus qu'autre part peut-être on abhorre l'injustice'), for her rhetorical strategy was to write as both a Briton and a woman.[11] She uses the acceptably feminine form of personal letters to describe her arrival in Paris, the Festival of the Federation, leading Revolutionary figures, her visit to the National Assembly, the emancipation of Protestants from restrictions still suffered by Dissenters in England, the misrepresentations of various British commentators, her visit to Rouen and the progress of the Revolution there, the history of the du Fossés as the first cause of her sympathy for the Revolution, and her return to England.

Thus she insists that her support for the Revolution arises from her feminine, domestic character and affections. She tells her (unnamed) correspondent:

I am glad you think that a friend's having been persecuted, imprisoned, maimed, and almost murdered under the antient government of France, is a

[9] William Doyle, *The Oxford History of the French Revolution* (Oxford, 1989), 129.

[10] Helen Maria Williams, *Souvenirs de la Révolution française*, trans. Charles Coquerel (Paris, 1827), 7. The English original was never published and the translations here and elsewhere are my own, corrected by Marianne Krajicek. For a discussion of *Souvenirs* see Ch. 6.

[11] Ibid. 10.

good excuse for loving the revolution. What, indeed, but friendship, could have led my attention from the annals of imagination to the records of politics; from the poetry to the prose of human life? In vain might Aristocrates have explained to me the rights of kings, and Democrates have descanted on the rights of the people. How many fine-spun threads of reasoning would my wandering thoughts have broken; and how difficult should I have found it to arrange arguments and inferences in the cells of my brain! But however dull the faculties of my head, I can assure you, that when a proposition is addressed to my heart, I have some quickness of perception. I can then decide, in one moment, points upon which philosophers and legislators have differed in all ages: nor could I be more convinced of the truth of any demonstration in Euclid, than I am, that, that system of politics must be best, by which those I love are made happy. (pp. 195–6)

Williams accepts the conventional gendering of intellectual, professional, and public discourse, with 'reasoning', the 'head', 'prose', philosophy, legislation, geometry, and politics on one side and 'imagination', 'poetry', the heart, and 'those I love' on the other. But she suggests that women's domestic experience confers greater quickness of perception and accuracy of judgement than the public, political experience of men does, and that feminized politics transcend conflict between parties and factions such as 'Aristocrates' and 'Democrates'. She characterizes the Revolution as the embodiment of feminine sympathy and the domestic affections, freeing them from the patriarchy of the 'antient government', yet she also represents the Revolution as 'sublime'—a category conventionally gendered masculine—but comprehensible to her confessedly 'feminine' mind and sensibility.

Later she claims that this response is validated by Frenchwomen, who have been inspired by the Revolution to overcome their exclusion from politics, class differences, and their 'natural' femininity, eagerly sacrificing 'titles, fortune, and even the personal ornaments, so dear to female vanity, for the common cause' (p. 37). In fact the Revolution originated in feminine sympathy and humanity: 'The women have certainly had a considerable share in the French Revolution: for, whatever the imperious lords of the creation may fancy, the most important events which take place in this world depend a little on our influence; and we often act in human affairs like those secret springs in mechanism, by which, though invisible, great movements are regulated' (pp. 37–8). This is a dangerous suggestion. Court government was criticized for giving women illegitimate influence through the 'mistress system' of sexual and political intrigue, and Williams does retain vestiges of courtly 'gallantry' in her feminization of the Revolution, for example describing a procession of young women at a Revolutionary festival: 'Thus have the leaders of the revolution engaged beauty as one of their auxiliaries, justly concluding, that, to the gallantry and sensibility of Frenchmen, no argument would be found more efficacious than that of a pretty face' (pp. 62–3).

Otherwise she contrasts the condition of women under the 'antient government' and the Revolution. For example the only portrait that interests her in Paris is of the virtuous and unfortunate mistress of Henry IV, Louise de la Vallières, in the nun's habit she assumed on withdrawing from the delusive glory of court life. This is obvious criticism of the 'mistress system' but also suggests that the Revolution has ended such evils. Similarly, while in Normandy she visits Rouen and its monuments to Joan of Arc, the national liberator of France in an earlier age. Williams feels momentarily ashamed of being English but reflects that the French now depend on themselves rather than a monarch for their freedom. By contrast, she refuses to visit the nearby tomb of William the Conqueror, confessing that the Revolutionary festivals of July are too fresh in her mind to permit travelling 'twelve leagues in order to see the tomb of a tyrant'. The male conqueror and founder of feudalism in England contrasts with the female liberator of France from English rule, echoing the lament of British 'commonwealthmen' for the loss of 'Anglo-Saxon liberty' and implying that Britain in the 1790s needs liberation from the 'Norman yoke' just as France did centuries earlier. Williams folds Enlightenment political writing and historiography—men's discourses—into her feminization of the Revolution.

Her description of Revolutionary debates, institutions, and acts aims for the same effect, as in her account of the National Assembly:

The leaders of the French revolution, are men well acquainted with the human heart. They have not trusted merely to the force of reason, but have studied to interest in their cause the most powerful passions of human nature, by the appointment of solemnities perfectly calculated to awaken that general sympathy which is caught from heart to heart with irresistible energy, fills every eye with tears, and throbs in every bosom. (pp. 61–2)

Williams even treats victims of Revolutionary violence in terms of the 'domestic affections', for the first time lamenting the Revolution and painting in her 'imagination the agonies of their families and friends'. But she characterizes such violence in terms of negative masculine traits, an aberration from the 'true' character of the Revolution (pp. 81–2).

Her celebration of the Festival of the Federation also foregrounds values conventionally treated as feminine but here at the centre of an organized yet spontaneous spectacle of national unanimity evoking those sentiments of sympathy that Williams represents as the key to the Revolution. The Festival was similarly celebrated by others present, and later seemed to mark both the end of the old order and the beginning of the new, a turning-point of world history recognized in its power to address a host of individuals as one.[12] In Williams's account, the Festival transformed individual sentiment and domestic affections into a public and political revolutionary force, not only remaking the state but refounding it within each person, regardless of class or sex.

The climax of Williams's feminization of the Revolution is the du Fossés' story, which is assimilated to the chief discourse of women's literary culture as Williams asks, 'Has it not the air of a romance? and are you not glad that the denouement is happy?—Does not the old Baron die exactly in the right place; at the very page one would choose?' (p. 193). Underlying this novelization of the Revolution is the plot of romantic comedy, figuring social conflict as a conflict of generations resolved through love and marriage in the younger genera-tion. By drawing attention to the novelistic as well as political character of the du Fossés' story, Williams suggests the revolutionary potential of women's novelistic discourse, its ability to prefigure social and political revolution. This 'charming little nouvelle', as one reviewer called it,[13] was even republished as a chapbook entitled *The Unfortunate Young Nobleman; A Tale of Sympathy, Founded on Fact, in Which Are Depicted the Unprecedented Sufferings of an Affectionate Husband, and the Forlorn State of an Amiable Mother, and Her Infant Child.*[14] Such narratives were a staple of pre-Revolutionary political propaganda and were used by all sides in the Revolution debate.

Williams feminizes the Revolution formally and rhetorically as well as thematically, mainly through use of the familiar letter, well estab-lished as a predominantly feminine discourse, conventionally seen as

---

[12] See Mona Ozouf, *La Fête révolutionnaire 1789–1799* (Paris, 1976), ch. 2; also Jean Ehrard and Paul Viallaneix (eds.) *Les Fêtes de la Révolution: Colloque de Clermont-Ferrand* (Paris, 1977).

[13] *Critical Review*, NS 1 (Jan. 1791), 117.

[14] Woodward, *Williams et ses amis*, 32 n. 72.

informal, immediate, personal, private, and domestic, and thus suited to the supposedly more emotional character, limited education, domestic interests, and quotidian experience of women, and long associated with the novel of domestic and sentimental realism.[15] The *Critical Review* later commented that it was immaterial whether Williams's 'letters really passed' or 'the author merely made choice of the epistolary form to convey her sentiments, as most congenial with her own disposition', 'passing freely from the gay to the grave, from the colloquial to the argumentative, the pathetic, and the sublime'. For 'no other form can so suitably express the countless varieties and gradations of the soul, when actuated by a lively sensibility and a brilliant imagination'.[16] Any letter may combine description, anecdote, self-reflection, apostrophe, and journalistic narrative, united by the narrator's 'voice' as a stylistic representation of the 'author' in the text. Each successive letter may continue, amplify, echo, or contrast with points made previously, producing both open texture and progressive movement and favouring the appearance of immediacy, spontaneity, and responsiveness to the varied phenomena to be expected in a revolutionary situation of rapid and complex change.

Other elements reinforce the impression of structured openness and purposeful spontaneity. The overall form is a romance journey from the narrator's 'proper' sphere of home, family, and friends to the apparently unfamiliar and public-political domain, concluding with her imminent return home, more aware of the difference between 'home' and 'not home', between Revolutionary France and unrevolutionized Britain. Thus there are explicit or implied contrasts between Britain and France throughout—between the French National Assembly and British Parliament, French Revolutionary enthusiasm and British criticism of the Revolution, and so on until the last letter's contrast between false impressions of the Revolution circulated by British travellers and French *émigrés* and the account just given by Williams. These contrasts are reinforced by the narrator's reminders that she is a foreigner and outsider but also a woman who therefore can overcome national difference and sympathize with the Revolution, affirming its trans-national character. France has learned from Britain, but now Britain may have something to learn from France, helped by precisely the kind of person conventionally accepted as mediator of differences.

[15] See Bruce Redford, *The Converse of the Pen: Acts of Intimacy in the Eighteenth-Century Familiar Letter* (Chicago, 1986), Introduction.

[16] *Critical Review*, NS 31 (Feb. 1801), 183.

The loose romance form is dominated by the illustrative anecdote—such as the story of the du Fossés—apparently improvised yet constructing a cumulative and distinctive representation of the Revolution experienced at the individual, domestic, local level. This structure was well established in the literature of Sensibility, invoking a rhetoric of authenticity that privileges the personal, spontaneous, improvised, and 'natural' over the impersonal, learned, stylized, and 'polished' and implicitly associating the latter with a courtly, aristocratic, authoritative, and even autocratic culture and the former with a dialogical, egalitarian, 'liberal', and feminized culture created by the professional middle class. According to theories such as Edward Young's *Conjectures on Original Composition* (1759), authority in the rhetoric of Sensibility depends on 'genius', which arises from plenitude of self rather than acquired knowledge or social status, manifested not in learning, rhetorical training, and forensic skill but in style and manner, the lyrical expressiveness produced by 'surplus' of self in the immediacy of subjective response before the local and particular. Although such theories assume that the 'genius' is a man, the discourse of 'genius' was open to women writers because it relied on subjectivity and the local and particular, accepted domains of women's experience and expertise.

Williams invoked this association in her pre-Revolutionary writing and does so again here. The *Critical Review* later argued that 'the patriots of France have adopted new and powerful measures, for adding to the number of converts in this kingdom' because most readers were better able to resist the 'eloquence', 'arguments', or 'energy' of men writers than 'the seductive insinuations of miss Williams'.[17] The Della Cruscan poet Edward Jerningham addressed a poem to Williams in the *European Magazine* portraying her as simple 'Maid' in contrast to the 'literary Knight' Edmund Burke:

> She tries no formal refutation
> Of his elab'rate speculation,
> Nor raves of Government and Laws,
> For she to Nature trusts her cause;
> Makes to the heart her strong appeal,
> Which all who have a heart must feel[18]

Other readers found Williams's feminization of politics more menacing. Six months after *Letters* was published Horace Walpole associated

[17] *Critical Review*, NS 6 (Sept. 1792), 65–6.
[18] *European Magazine*, 18 (Dec. 1790), 472.

Williams with a wide range of subversives including the Della Cruscan poets, English Dissenters, politicized British artisans, and the plebeian Parisiennes denounced by Burke in *Reflections on the Revolution in France*.[19]

The success of *Letters* made Williams eager to return to France, but first she published *A Farewell, for Two Years, to England* (1791), a poem obliquely responding to recent British criticisms of the Revolution. The poet—another textual figure devised for the occasion—eulogizes Britain as both her native land and the land of liberty, made dear to her by nature, memory, 'ties' of the domestic affections, and constitutional freedom. But Freedom, personified as feminine, now 'treads the banks of Seine, | Hope in her eye, and Virtue in her train!' (p. 5), though Britons will surely not deny to others what they themselves enjoy, and what France first learned from them. The poet admits the Revolution's excesses—an allusion to the 'Massacre of the Champ de Mars' of 17 July 1791 and the suppression of the Parisian popular movement—but insists that 'that purifying tempest now has past'. The poet then compares the Revolution to the divine Creation (pp. 9–10) and hopes that passions causing discord and war will now be banished: 'may the ardent mind, that seeks renown, | Claim, not the martial, but the civic crown!' (p. 10). The poet laments that while the example of Britain has freed France, Britain has failed to free the slaves—an allusion to Parliamentary defeat in April 1791 of a bill to abolish the slave trade. She refers obliquely to the National Assembly's extension of rights to people of mixed race in May 1791 and hopes that France, in its Revolutionary enthusiasm, may go further, taking 'home' to Britain her own lessons in liberty. The poet closes with the hope that on returning from 'exile' all her ties of domestic affections will remain intact.

The poem feminizes and domesticates the Revolution as a ploy in the Revolution debate. Against Burke's representation of the Revolution and its British sympathizers as alien, it familiarizes and assimilates the Revolution to 'British' culture and politics. It links opposition to the slave trade and sympathy for the Revolution, implying that the latter is a natural extension of the former. There were grounds for this suggestion, since Williams had published an anti-slavery poem in 1788

---

[19] *Horace Walpole's Correspondence with Mary and Agnes Berry and Barbara Cecilia Seton*, ed. W. S. Lewis and A. Dayle Wallace, vol. i (London, 1944), 320 (26 July 1791).

and many of the liberal Dissenters and intellectuals she knew were supporters of the Revolution and opponents of slavery in the early 1790s, to the consternation of anti-slavery campaigners such as Wilberforce and to the later detriment of the cause.[20] The poem's circular form, from Britain to France and back 'home', not only suggests the path of Williams's journey, as in *Letters*, but also implies the circulation of political sensibility that the poet herself (as a character in the poem) exemplifies. Nevertheless, the poem only alludes indirectly to particular events, thereby keeping its argument on a general, apparently non-partisan plane. Furthermore, the heroic couplets, occasional Miltonic echoes, and ode-like apostrophes give a sublime and epic tone to what might otherwise seem a 'merely' feminine, sentimental view of the Revolution.

Williams followed up *A Farewell* with a poetical epistle *To Dr. Moore*, written from France and even more forthright in defence of the Revolution against Burke. The poet compares the landscape of France at harvest time with that of her native Wales, which Moore has just described in a letter to her, and goes on to argue that the scene before her is as inspiring because the French now pursue those liberties they learned from Britain. She treats the now 'happy peasant' as sympathetically as she had treated the natives of Peru and the African slaves in her poems of the 1780s, argues that he is now able to enjoy the domestic affections thanks to 'those equal rights impartial heav'n bestows' through the Revolution, and represents the Revolution as the erection of a home—'a mansion worthy of the human race'—on the site of the demolished 'Gothic pile', or Bastille, symbol of the 'feudal governments' defended by Burke. Dr John Moore was a well-known pre-Revolutionary social critic, his 'philosophical' novel *Zeluco* was referred to in Williams's *Julia*, and he would later publish his own eyewitness account of the Revolution. Williams uses their friendship here to suggest that though they are separated by distance they are united in sympathy with 'the great, the glorious triumph of mankind' against growing British criticism of the Revolution.

Meanwhile, the Williamses were moving closer to the centre of Revolutionary power. Williams's mother and sister had participated during the summer in men's Revolutionary politics in Rouen, where

---

[20] Roger Anstey, *The Atlantic Slave Trade and British Abolition 1760–1810* (London, 1975), 276.

they gave a copy of *Letters* to the Société des Amis de la Constitution, who praised its author's 'pure and feeling heart' and 'energetic mind' for giving 'suitable expression to the noble enthusiasm of a great people at the moment when they became free', and who confessed that the account of the du Fossés 'made us shed tears of wonder'. Williams herself attended the Société in September and assured them that 'to feel the general happiness it is not necessary to have the wisdom of a philosopher; it is enough to have the sensibility of a woman'. The Société called on Frenchwomen to follow Williams's example and exercise a properly feminine influence in politics and the state by using their natural amorous power to instil in men 'a love for Peace, Concord, Fraternity, but above all for our country' and later, 'as mothers of families', to 'inspire your children with love of liberty and the deepest respect for the law': 'Thus our courage has brought about the Revolution and your virtues will consolidate it.'[21] But Williams joined this company of French Revolutionaries only temporarily and as a guest, in contrast to men such as Joseph Priestley and Tom Paine, who were elected to the National Convention.

Williams arrived in Paris in summer 1791, stayed in Rouen and Orléans until December, and settled in Paris, where her involvement with John Hurford Stone caused scandal back in England. She had returned home by mid-June 1792.[22] During this period the Revolutionaries consolidated the gains of 1789 and 1790, but there was continuing political factionalism, the threat from Parisian *sansculottes* and Jacobins, regional resistance to expropriation of the Church and centralization of government, plotting by royalist *émigrés*, a slave rebellion in Saint-Domingue, and increasing hostility from other European powers. In this situation Williams published *Letters from France: Containing Many New Anecdotes Relative to the French Revolution, and the Present State of French Manners* in mid-1792.

At the end of *Letters* (1790) Williams hoped that the National Assembly would 'answer the objections of its adversaries' in France and Britain 'by forming such a constitution as will render the French nation virtuous, flourishing, and happy'. *Letters* (1792) picks up this hopeful note, starting again with the emancipation of the du Fossés: 'we are so framed that, while we contemplate the deliverance of millions with a sublime emotion of wonder and exultation, the tears of

---

[21] Quoted in Woodward, *Williams et ses amis*, 46.
[22] *Thraliana: The Diary of Mrs. Hester Lynch Thrale (Later Mrs. Piozzi) 1776–1809*, ed. Katharine C. Balderstone, 2nd edn., 2 vols. (Oxford, 1951), ii. 849.

tenderness, throbbings of sympathy, are reserved for the moment when we select one happy family from the great national groupe, and when, amidst the loud acclamations of an innumerable multitude, we can distinguish the soothing sounds of domestic felicity.'[23] She now uses this line, however, to reply indirectly to Burke's *Reflections on the Revolution in France*. Burke claimed that the Revolution exalted general philanthropy at the expense of the individual and the domestic affections, so Williams insists that the Revolution restores domestic relations persecuted under the *ancien régime* and can be 'loved' and 'admired' only in so far as it promotes such relations. Burke derided the French Revolutionaries and their British supporters as impractical speculators, abstract 'philosophers', and 'romantic' visionaries. Williams replies that 'living in France at present, appears to me somewhat like living in a region of romance' because 'events the most astonishing and marvellous are here the occurrences of the day'. She appropriates 'antient chivalry', which Burke portrays as the spirit of the old order, to the Revolution that has swept away that order, observing that 'the age of chivalry, instead of being past for ever, is just returned', not in 'erroneous notions of loyalty, honour, and gallantry' but in the Revolution's 'noble contempt of sordid cares, its spirit of unsullied generosity, and its heroic zeal for the happiness of others' (pp. 4–5). In the remaining twenty-three letters Williams continues to refute criticism of the Revolution while addressing the major issues of 1791–2—the new constitution, slavery, deteriorating foreign relations, the *émigrés* and war with Austria, legal toleration for Protestants and secularization of the Church, social transformation, provincial resistance to the Revolution, economic crisis, and cultural and educational policy.

As in *Letters* (1790), these issues are presented in terms of the Revolution's feminization of culture and society in contrast to the 'antient government of France'. Again Williams uses telling allusions and comparisons to incorporate history into her account of a sublime present, again made immediate through epistolary form and devices such as apostrophe, typographical representation of strong emotion (dashes and exclamation marks), and lyrical verse. But there is a stronger sense of chronological development in *Letters* (1792). *Letters*

---

[23] Helen Maria Williams, *Letters from France: Containing Many New Anecdotes Relative to the French Revolution, and the Present State of French Manners*, 2nd edn. (London, 1792), 1–2. Between *Letters* (1790) and *Letters* (1792) Williams had evidently changed publishers from Thomas Cadell to the more liberal firm of Robinsons, leading publisher of the English and Scottish Enlightenments.

(1790) portrayed the Revolution as a sublime moment, transcending history while giving it a new meaning and point of departure. *Letters* (1792) admits that the Revolution is a social, material process and may be as subject to temporal vicissitudes and relativities as earlier, superseded eras and orders. Hence Williams insists more strongly because more anxiously that sublimity inspires Revolutionary social transformation from within each subject. For example, after visiting Orléans she believes the Austrian armies will fail to overturn the Revolution:

> wherever we journeyed, liberty seemed to have run like electric fire along the country, and pervaded every object in its passage. Do you think all the Austrians of the earth will subdue this people? Oh no: nothing is more true than, that a people are free whenever with one unanimous sublime sentiment they determine to be so. (pp. 7–8)

This sublimity addresses all classes, unlike the insulting condescension of the old aristocracy, and underlies the new egalitarianism and dignity of the common people. The same subjective principle motivates Revolutionary transformation in culture and education. Invoking Enlightenment 'philosophical history', Williams argues that despotism and 'the progress of literature' are incompatible, as shown by the Revolution, which 'has surely been the work of literature, of philosophy, of the enlarging views of mankind' (p. 70).

Significantly, the new educational projects and cultural institutions of the Revolution, such as the public Lycée, have no parallel in England (pp. 132–3), implying that Britain remains too close to the oppressive despotism from which France is escaping. For to meet growing British criticism of the Revolution Williams now gives a more decided advantage to France in comparison with Britain, especially in politics and public institutions. She denies that the debates in the National Assembly are too tumultuous and counters that in Britain government control of Parliamentary votes through bribery and corruption renders any argument, however eloquent, useless. She contrasts the intellectual vitality of the Paris Lycée with dull evenings of cards and 'fashionable conversation' in London. If Britain has social and intellectual advantages despite its unrevolutionized government and institutions, these are due to greater feminization and domestication of culture. Protestantism, with its emphasis on spiritual inwardness, also makes Britain more domestic than France, which still retains elements of the too social, unreflecting culture of the *ancien régime* and its support, Catholicism. Such comparisons exemplify Williams's central defence of the Revolution—France pursues a path of political, social, and cultural revolution first taken by Britain, but will soon surpass its teacher.

This thesis is again exemplified in the individual case by a story of domestic affections that is novelistic yet based on 'fact', removing the Revolution from the vicissitudes and relativities of history. A year before the Revolution Auguste and Madelaine fell in love, but his father would forbid the match as unequal in rank and fortune. Then the Revolution occurred:

Madelaine was a firm friend to the revolution, which she was told had made every Frenchman free. 'And if every Frenchman is free,' thought Madelaine, 'surely every Frenchman may marry the woman he loves.' It appeared to Madelaine, that, putting all political considerations, points upon which she had not much meditated, out of the question, obtaining liberty of choice in marriage was alone well worth the trouble of a revolution; and she was as warm a patriot from this single idea, as if she had studied the declaration of rights made by the Constituent Assembly, in all its extent and consequences. (pp. 174–5)

Nuns urge Madelaine to avoid family conflict by taking the veil, but at that moment (13 February 1790) the National Assembly forbids any more women to enter monastic life. Providentially, Auguste's uncle leaves him a fortune in his will, provided that Auguste's father agrees to the match with Madelaine, and the couple are married.

This tale, though based on 'fact', has all the characteristics of a late eighteenth-century Sentimental tale, and like the du Fossés' story, it was also issued as a chapbook. Like the du Fossés' sentimental comedy, it resolves in the younger generation social conflicts characteristic of the older generation and their outmoded social order, but Williams politicizes the form by making the young couple's helpers not sympathetic servants or other social outsiders but a political revolution and the will (both legal document and desire) of an 'enlightened' member of the older generation. Specific Revolutionary legislation enables the subjective absolute of romantic love to triumph over social 'prejudice' produced by a false political and social structure. Again the tale is positioned in the text as a climactic illustration of the Revolution's benefits, for *Letters* (1792) also closes with Williams's return to England, facing criticisms of the Revolution and doubts about its future, but expecting fulfilment of its promise.

Soon after she published *Letters* (1792) Williams was back in France and frequenting the Paris salons of the Girondins, where politics, culture, and the domestic affections were mingled in self-conscious vanguardism. But after the last events discussed in *Letters* (1792) the Revolutionary consensus had begun to crumble. In June and July 1792 Brissot's ministry was dismissed, Prussia declared war on France, the Paris sections went into permanent session, and the Duke of Brunswick's manifesto threatened restoration of the pre-Revolutionary monarchy. Tension, fear, and suspicion were intensified in August when *sansculottes* attacked the Tuileries and overthrew the monarchy. Williams arrived in Paris in time to witness this event. Constitutional monarchists such as Lafayette defected, Prussian armies invaded France, and in early September Revolutionary crowds lynched many held in the Paris prisons. But then the French 'citizen armies' defeated the Prussians at Valmy, the new National Convention met, and a republic was declared, inspiring a new wave of Revolutionary sympathy in Britain and elsewhere. Williams shared these feelings, even defending Revolutionary violence.[24]

By now she had a literary reputation in France as a friend of the Revolution. But she entered Girondin circles thanks to John Hurford Stone, who had subscribed to her *Poems* in 1786. He too was a product of both the English Nonconformist and the provincial Enlightenment and his friends were leaders of liberal Dissent. He knew the Whig politicians Fox and Sheridan, belonged to the English Revolution Society, and welcomed the French Revolution, perhaps witnessing the fall of the Bastille. He was married but his wife had taken lovers. When Hester Piozzi was in Paris in September 1792 she was shocked to find Williams and Stone together, but such relationships were part of avant-garde Revolutionary culture, a rejection of both the court 'mistress system' and petty bourgeois respectability. By autumn 1792 Stone was a leader of the British and American Revolutionary sympathizers who met at White's Hotel in Paris. In November 1792 they celebrated French military victories with a dinner where a toast was drunk to English women distinguished for their writings on the Revolution. In the worsening Revolutionary situation of early 1793 many expatriates left the country and the White's group dissolved. But Stone and other British entrepreneurs such as Thomas Christie were

---

[24] Baron Dieudonné Thiébault, *Mémoires du Baron Thiébault*, 5 vols. (Paris, 1893–7), i. 313.

establishing commercial and industrial concerns, including stocking manufacture, a printing house, and a wallpaper factory. Stone knew the president of the Committee for Commerce as well as politicians, administrators, and generals, had agents in Germany, Switzerland, and Italy, and corresponded with leading liberals in Britain.

As a woman, Williams could participate in Revolutionary salons, and here important personal, social, political, and literary contacts were made and women were important mediators and leaders. By late 1792 Williams frequented the most important of these salons, that of Marie Roland and her husband. He became the Girondin government's Minister of the Interior in March 1792, and she was the most politically powerful woman in Paris, her husband's political adviser, and author of his important political letters. They lived an ostentatiously simple life in an elegant aristocrat's mansion assigned to them as official residence, where they held salons two evenings a week.[25] Here Williams met leading Revolutionaries, including a previous acquaintance, Bancal des Issarts, who fell in love with her. She did not return his feeling, but persuaded him to vote against the death sentence for Louis XVI in January 1793.[26] By the autumn of 1792, however, the Rolands and the Girondins were under attack by the Jacobins. When discovery of the king's secret papers revealed his betrayal of the Revolution, Roland, as minister responsible for the investigation, was accused of hiding evidence incriminating himself and others. His wife was attacked for intruding into politics and compared to courtly intriguers such as Lucrezia Borgia and Marie Antoinette, supposedly rewarding her supporters with sexual favours.[27] When she fell in love with the Girondin Buzot her husband lost his will to resist the Jacobins and resigned his ministry in January 1793.

Through this deepening crisis Williams was close to the Rolands and other Girondins, many of whom frequented her salon, with foreign political tourists such as Thomas Christie, Joel Barlow, J. G. Forster, Count Gustav von Schlabrendorf, and Mary Wollstonecraft, who visited Williams in late December 1792, just after arriving in Paris, and commented:

[25] Gita May, *Madame Roland and the Age of Revolution* (New York, 1970), 205.

[26] Williams, *Souvenirs*, 39. Claire Tomalin believes, however, that Bancal was in love with Mary Wollstonecraft, who had just arrived in Paris in December 1792, and not Williams; *The Life and Death of Mary Wollstonecraft* (London, 1974), 140–1.

[27] Dorinda Outram, *The Body and the French Revolution: Sex, Class and Political Culture* (New Haven, Conn., 1989), 127.

Miss Williams has behaved very civilly to me and I shall visit her frequently, because I *rather* like her, and I meet french company at her house. Her manners are affected, yet the *simple* goodness of her hearts [*sic*] continually breaks through the varnish, so that one would be more inclined, at least I should, to love than admire her.—Authorship is a heavy weight for female shoulders especially in the sunshine of prosperity.[28]

Williams's advice was sought by writers and intellectuals and she used her influence for other expatriates, helping the South American Francisco Miranda get a commission in the French army.

Through the early months of 1793 the situation of Williams's Girondin friends worsened with the execution of the king, war between France and Britain, counter-revolutionary revolt in the Vendée, growing economic crisis, creation of the Committee of Public Safety, deterioration of the military situation on the frontiers, and the defection of General Dumouriez, hero of the victories of autumn 1792. On 31 May there was a rising in Paris and on 2 June leading Girondins were purged from the National Convention. Hester Piozzi heard—incorrectly—that Stone had been guillotined and expected that Williams would share his fate. But in August Piozzi had a letter from her: 'Poor soul! she adverts to our felicity at Streatham Park, and says how happy we all are here . . . while she listens only to the sound of the Tocsin', or Revolutionary alarm-signal.[29] For Williams the 'good', feminized Revolution was over.

Williams describes this personal and public disaster in *Letters from France: Containing a Great Variety of Interesting and Original Information Concerning the Most Important Events that Have Lately Occurred in that Country, and Particularly Respecting the Campaign of 1792*. It was published in autumn 1793 with an 'Advertisement' stating that 'for particular reasons, the author's name could not be prefixed to these Letters', though 'the reader will . . . be at no loss to determine from what quarter they proceed'. Five of the seven letters (II to VI) in the first volume deal with 'the campaign of 1792' and according to the *Analytical Review* were written by Stone, while the fifth and last letter in the second volume, dealing with British critiques of the Revolution, was

---

[28] To Everina Wollstonecraft, 24 Dec. 1792, in *Collected Letters of Mary Wollstonecraft*, ed. Ralph M. Wardle (Ithaca, NY, 1979), 226.

[29] *The Intimate Letters of Hester Piozzi and Penelope Pennington 1788–1821*, ed. Oswald G. Knapp (London, 1914), 96.

by Christie.[30] This division of labour in itself represents the disintegration of the unified and feminized Revolution of the earlier *Letters* into 'feminine' and 'masculine' discourses, affirmed by Williams's representation of the Revolution as having a new, apocalyptic character.

The first letter declares that the conflict of 1789–92 between executive and legislature, court and people, has been 'succeeded by a conflict far more terrible: a conflict between freedom and anarchy, knowledge and ignorance, virtue and vice' (iii. 3).[31] The tyranny of the *ancien régime* has been replaced by a tyranny of demagogues, dictatorship of court and aristocracy by mob dictatorship. These social and political extremes have met by crushing the 'good', implicitly middle-class and feminized Revolution. Recalling the Festival of Federations celebrated in *Letters* (1790) Williams laments:

Ah! . . . What is become of the transport which beat high in every bosom, when an assembled million of the human race vowed on the altar of their country, in the name of the represented nation, inviolable fraternity and union—an eternal federation! This was indeed the golden age of the revolution.— But it is past!—the enchanting spell is broken, and the fair scenes of beauty and of order, through which imagination wandered, are transformed into the desolation of the wilderness, and clouded by the darkness of the tempest. (iii. 6)

'The golden age' mythologizes the early Revolution and 'beauty and order' feminize and domesticate it. 'But it is past!' pointedly echoes the most notorious passage in Burke's *Reflections on the Revolution in France*, lamenting the death of 'antient chivalry' in the Revolution. With 'the enchanting spell is broken' Williams insists, as in *Letters* (1790), that the spirit of chivalry and romance is embodied in neither the feudal past nor modern-day court aristocracy, but in the Revolution. That 'spell' has been broken by a renewed despotic alliance of aristocrats and mob, led by the demagogues Robespierre, Danton, and Marat, who, she claims, are suspected of selling out to foreign monarchies anxious to restore court government in France.

Stone's letters then describe the campaigns of the Republic's 'citizen armies' against the 'leagued despots' of Europe. By resigning such matters to a male correspondent Williams distances herself and her woman's political vision from the predominantly male activity of

---

[30] *Analytical Review*, 17 (Oct. 1793), 127.

[31] The two volumes of *Letters* (1793) are numbered on their title-pages 'Vol. III' and 'Vol. IV', indicating that they are to be taken as continuations of *Letters* (1790) and *Letters* (1792). *Letters* (1792), 2nd edn., was designated 'Vol. 2' on its title-page.

armed defence of the republic. Her correspondent could see places and things inaccessible to a woman, especially of Williams's nationality and class, and he can describe them with an authority ill-suited to her authorial character as woman of feeling and domestic sympathies. This ploy lets Williams suggest that the foreign military threat had altered the 'natural', feminized course of the Revolution; at the same time, the account of heroic and admirable French resistance to invasion diverts attention from negative aspects of the Revolution. This diversion is reinforced by an appendix portraying General Dumouriez as a Revolutionary hero and his conduct of the war as intelligent, philosophical, and practical in contrast to the conduct of French aristocrats serving the armies of the 'leagued despots'.

Williams unites the two different aspects of the Revolution by again using the pattern of a journey and evoking a Revolutionary 'space'. She appropriates Stone's account of civic martial heroism on the frontiers by framing it between her opening and closing letters on events in Paris, the Revolution's 'centre'. This structuring device is reinforced by differences in the letters' contents and places and dates of writing. Williams's opening letter is dated from Paris four days after the king's execution on 21 January 1793. The following letters on the military campaign are dated from various places on the north-east frontier in October and November 1792. Letter VII by Williams is dated from Lille, 12 December 1792, as she and her correspondent are about to meet and her account of Revolutionary politics and his of Revolutionary heroism are about to converge.[32] Two parallel accounts are linked not only by the relation between external military threat and internal political upheaval, but also by an implicit parallel and political relationship between barbarous Prussians invading France from without and barbarous Jacobins undermining the Revolution from within.

Finally, Williams suggests that the parallel accounts of the Revolution's external and internal crises are linked by their common origin in the old order. Under the *ancien régime* 'political servitude' produced a nation of fops, in which 'follies, and even crimes' were 'naturalized into manners from the continued contemplation of those manners in a corrupted court'. But since the Revolution, 'a wonderful reverse has been effected'. The 'effeminacy' with which the British hitherto

---

[32] Letter VII is misnumbered VI; this letter and the actual sixth letter are both misdated '1793'.

reproached the French 'has been changed alternately into Roman firmness and Tartarean ferocity', for 'effeminacy and cruelty are oftentimes not remote from each other' (iii. 150). Because of their former oppression the people commit Revolutionary excesses but also defend their Revolution heroically, making their own history, or 'destiny', rather than relying mistakenly on rulers, providence, or luck, as they formerly had to do.

Williams's closing letter invokes history and nature to excuse Revolutionary excess and violence. First she uses a commonplace of Enlightenment 'philosophical history' to reinforce the relation of both Revolutionary martial heroism and political violence to the vices of the *ancien régime* and to each other: 'the history of former times instructs us, how superior is that state of society in which civil broils for political rights continually disturb the state, and which, nevertheless, is flourishing in arts, enriched by philosophy, and great in population, to that of despotism.' Ancient Greece, 'even when the assassination of tyrants was the Marseillois song of the people', was superior to 'Greece of the present hour, the tranquil province of an ignorant barbarian [the Turks], and the peaceful habitation of slaves'. Rome, 'even when agitated by the contentions of the heated multitude, torn by factions, diminished by civil wars, and horrid proscriptions', was superior to present-day Rome, 'the seat of priestly government' (the Papacy) and proverbial for 'poverty and superstition'. These examples show that revolutionary excess is preferable to decadent despotism and imply that the Revolution operates by historical law. Secondly, Williams argues that France was infested 'by traitors within', 'menaced by a host of foes from without', and 'depended on the entire infraction of the laws' for its safety. Thus it is not surprising 'that the genius of liberty, in rushing forward to strike at the formidable hosts of its external foes, should crush . . . the pigmies of aristocracy or despotism which stood in its way' (iii. 238–40). The image suggests that the Revolution is a natural force operating by some physical law. Both history and nature absolve the Revolution of responsibility for its excesses.

The second volume of *Letters* (1793) gives this argument new direction. The first letter is dated two weeks after the first letter of the previous volume and is written after the execution of Louis XVI, the event that decisively alienated moderate opinion in France and Britain from the Revolution. Williams now distances herself from the Revolution—or rather from the new, unfeminine, undomestic, and unsocial Revolution led by the Jacobins, called the 'Mountain' from their occupying the upper tiers in the National Convention:

The faction of the anarchists desired that the French king should be put to death without the tedious forms of a trial. This opinion, however, was confined to the summit of the Mountain, that elevated region, where, aloof from all the ordinary feelings of our nature, no one is diverted from his purpose by the weakness of humanity, or the compunction of remorse; where urbanity is considered as an aristocratical infringement of les grandes principes, and mercy as a crime de leze-nation. (iv. 1–2)

Sarcasm distances Williams from the 'Mountain' while her punning implies superiority to them. Natural mountains were a familiar example of the sublime—elevated, lofty, grand, non-human, and non-social, but also conventionally gendered masculine, whereas the human, social, and familiar were conventionally gendered feminine, as in Edmund Burke's well-known treatise on the sublime and beautiful. These commonplaces of eighteenth-century aesthetics reinforce Williams's characterization of the Jacobin Revolution as remote from the human, domestic, and social ('elevated region', 'aloof from . . . ordinary feelings of our nature'). And whereas the earlier *Letters* show Revolutionary sublimity nurturing 'the ordinary feelings of our nature', now this union of the sublime and the social disintegrates as the Revolution breaks into contending factions, contrasting Revolutions.

The king, formerly symbol of the anti-domestic *ancien régime*, now symbolizes the feminized Revolution:

It was enough to consider this unfortunate person as a man, a husband, a father! Ah, surely, amidst the agonies of final separation from those to whom we are bound by the strongest ties of nature and affection! surely when we cling to those we love, in the unutterable pang of a last embrace—in such moments the monarch must forget his crown, and the regrets of disappointed ambition must be unfelt amidst the anguish which overwhelms the broken heart. (iv. 29)

This passage echoes Burke's lament for the 'former elevation' of the royal family and his characterization of them in domestic rather than political terms. But Burke claimed that all Revolutionaries lack humane, domestic, and social feelings; Williams indicts only certain 'philosophers' (mainly atheists) and the Jacobins and maintains that the original Revolution and the French people remain virtuously feminized. For example, the Jacobins prevented the king from addressing the crowd from the scaffold lest he should touch their feelings, but Williams imagines the moved populace, led by the women, rescuing him (iv. 35–6). The feminized Revolution still lives in the 'natural' sensibility of the people, to be reawakened one day.

For Williams represents the events of early 1793 as a necessary and even desirable test of the Revolution, proving 'that the passage from despotism to liberty is long and terrible—like the passage of Milton's Satan from hell to earth' (iv. 72). This simile represents the Revolution as a passage from darkness and bondage to light and freedom. The Jacobin Revolution is a test, perhaps divinely ordained, of the Revolutionary will to paradise, a repetition in history of the archetypal rebellion of angels and humans that precipitated history by subjecting humanity to time, toil, and mortality. The implication, as in the *Letters* of 1790 and 1792, is that the early Revolution was potentially paradise regained, now lost again through demonic wilfulness and rebellion. The Revolution seemed to end human history initiated by the Fall, and thus to represent humanized divinity or Christ in everyone, human freedom and capacity for self-redemption through divinely implanted desire and reason. But Williams now portrays the Revolution as another Fall, representing human inability to achieve redemption without divine intervention. Such a theologico-political vision was intrinsic to the liberal Dissenting culture shared by Williams and many other Revolutionary sympathizers in Britain, such as Samuel Kenrick and James Wodrow, and it continued to guide their response to the Revolution. Critical refiguring of the Revolution from history to myth, like the use of historical and natural laws, implicitly removes the Revolution from the domain of human will. Like Williams's contrast of 'feminine' and 'masculine' Revolutions, this schema would also inform Romantic representations of revolution.

The Jacobin Revolution as second Fall is illustrated in a friend's account in Letter III of the exemplary defection from the Revolution of its former hero and saviour, Dumouriez. But Williams returns in Letter IV to the military situation, Burke's apocalyptic vision of the Revolution's outcome, and the issue of religion and the state; she concludes with a biblical vision of Revolutionary paradise regained: 'where equal laws, wise instruction, rational faith, and virtuous conduct, constitute order and happiness, all mankind will become worshippers in the Temple of Liberty; whose corners will extend to the farthest ends of the earth, and whose arch will be the vault of Heaven' (iv. 154). This is not the only image in Williams's Revolutionary epic that anticipates the poeticized political images of Shelley's poems such as *Laon and Cythna* and *Prometheus Unbound*, for the Shelleys certainly knew Williams's work. As in Shelley's poems, Williams's Revolutionary paradise has been postponed by 'tumult and anarchy', but it will embody professional middle-class culture ('equal laws, wise instruction, rational faith, and virtuous conduct') and extend to global dominion. This is Williams's conclusion, for the volume's fifth and last letter is a friend's long review of British opinions of the Revolution, ranging from Burke to Wollstonecraft. By this point such discussion would be unavoidable, but by assigning the task to someone else Williams implies that she herself has a detached, impartial view of the extensive 'paper war' over the Revolution. By avoiding treatment of this subject herself Williams also avoids entanglement in polemical controversy that would vitiate her assumed role of direct and immediate respondent to the Revolution.

Williams's latest instalment of her prose epic was read eagerly in Britain.[33] It even drew a book-length attack by another woman, Lætitia Matilda Hawkins. Hawkins did not put her name on the title-page of *Letters on the Female Mind, Its Powers and Pursuits; Addressed to Miss H. M. Williams, with Particular Reference to her Letters from France* (1793). By her own argument to do so would be unfeminine: 'I consider the regulation of a kingdom's interests as far too complex a subject for me to comprehend. I would dissuade my countrywomen from the study, and I shun it myself' (i. 142). Yet she attacks the Revolution and defends Britain in a way characteristic of the Revolution debate as conducted by men. Hawkins deplores Williams's Revolutionary sympathy as all too feminine—too emotional, 'romantic', impractical, irrational—and expresses a growing hostility to women's political writing, both in France and Britain.[34]

Meanwhile Williams was arrested in October along with other British subjects and sent to the Luxembourg prison with her mother and sister. Friends in Britain feared the worst. Williams was known as 'a warm adherent of the Girondist party' and according to Samuel Rogers only an 'oversight' prevented her from being 'carried with their leaders to the guillotine'.[35] But through the intervention of her sister's brother-in-law, M. Coquerel, and Jean Debry, a member of the National Convention, Williams and her family were transferred to an English convent and then house arrest in November. Thanks to a sympathetic police inspector she was even able to destroy personal papers that might have incriminated her.[36]

[33] *Letters of Piozzi and Pennington*, ed. Knapp, 100.
[34] Joan B. Landes, *Women and the Public Sphere in the Age of the French Revolution* (Ithaca, NY, 1988), 142–3.
[35] Clayden, *Early Life of Rogers*, 77.   [36] Williams, *Souvenirs*, 80–1.

Stone remained free and did what he could for his friends. He tried to buy several Girondins out of prison, including the husband of Mme de Genlis.[37] Though Stone now considered himself a Frenchman he remained under surveillance and was arrested in October 1793 and again in April 1794. He corresponded with United Irishmen who hoped for a French invasion to help them throw off the British yoke, but the conspirators, including his brother, were arrested in Britain in 1794. His wife divorced him around the same time. By July 1794 Hester Piozzi heard that Williams's proven 'partiality' to the Revolution 'repays her *at present* with a splendid situation'. But Stone was warned that he was about to be rearrested, and in early July he and the Williamses fled to Switzerland, to return after the fall of Robespierre and the Jacobins in the reaction of Thermidor (July and August) 1794. There were reports that while in Switzerland Stone spied for the French government. Certainly on their return he and Williams were well treated by the new government. Years later Williams recorded that 'a friend in power' had offered them 'an easy and honourable means of obtaining a fortune', enabling them to have a mansion in Paris and 'a delicious Country House in the English Taste'. In December 1795 Hester Piozzi stated confidently that Williams's 'friends are uppermost in Paris now'.[38]

During her imprisonment Williams translated her friend Bernardin de Saint-Pierre's Sentimental novella, *Paul et Virginie* (1795). This would become Williams's most often reprinted work, so widely-read for a century that it was used as an instantly recognizable reference by writers from Maria Edgeworth to Charles Dickens and Thomas Hardy.[39] Translation, especially from the modern languages, was a major form of cultural appropriation by the late eighteenth century, though conventionally represented as a subordinate and secondary literary practice and thus well-established women's literary work.[40] But Williams turns her translation into an act of political defiance, another expression of her feminization of Revolution.

The Preface is dated June 1795 and declares that the translation 'was

---

[37] Williams, *Souvenirs*, 66.

[38] *Letters of Piozzi and Pennington*, ed. Knapp, 113, 133.

[39] John Donovan, Introduction, Jacques-Henri Bernardin de Saint-Pierre, *Paul and Virginia*, trans. John Donovan (London, 1982), 10.

[40] Lori Chamberlain, 'Gender and the Metaphorics of Translation', *Signs*, 13 (Spring 1988), 454–72.

written at Paris, amidst the horrors of Robespierre's tyranny', when
'society', or natural human relations, 'had vanished' and 'Jacobinical
despotism', which 'murdered in *mass*' but 'persecuted in detail', made
'the resources of writing, and even reading', dangerous. Police surveillance had driven her to destroy 'a manuscript volume, where I had
traced the political scenes of which I had been a witness, with the
colouring of their first impressions on my mind'. Because her pen was
'accustomed to follow the impulse of [her] feelings' she could only
write the truth, which would have condemned her if discovered. But
'even reading had its perils; for books had sometimes aristocratical
insignia, and sometimes counter revolutionary allusions: and when the
administrators of police happened to think the writer a conspirator,
they punished the reader as his accomplice'. Mere private acts of
writing and reading, uniting individuals in an invisible relationship, are
subversive in the eyes of a regime hostile to autonomous subjectivity
and domestic affections of any kind, even those subsisting between
reader and writer.

Accordingly, she translated her feelings into a different discourse,
finding 'the most soothing relief' in Saint-Pierre's 'enchanting scenes'
of nature and sentiment and being inspired to write a few sonnets,
interspersed in her translation. But this work too was suspect, 'as
English papers', and was confiscated by the police, 'where they still
remain, mingled with revolutionary placards, motions, and harangues'.
The Jacobin Terror levelled everything, including varieties of discourse.
In her translation, as in her Revolutionary writing, she aimed for the
feminine role of transparent mediation, deserving 'the humble merit of
not having deformed the beauty of the original', though she had to
respect national difference by omitting some philosophical reflections:
unlike the French reader, the English reader requires, 'in novel-writing,
as well as on the theatre, a rapid succession of incidents, much bustle,
and stage-effect, without suffering the author to appear himself, and
stop the progress of the story'. Her sonnets render more lyrical an
already lyrical text, and omission of 'several pages of general observations' so as not to 'interrupt the pathetic narrative' further feminizes
Saint-Pierre's already powerful representation of the feminized culture
of Sensibility.

The translation appropriates this representation to Williams's Revolutionary project. Saint-Pierre's novella was published in 1788 as an
illustrative supplement to his popular *Études de la nature*, a series of
Rousseauist meditations on the harmony of the scientific laws of

nature, the 'moral laws' of nature in relation to individual subjectivity, and 'the application' of these laws 'to the evils of society'. Saint-Pierre's Sentimental economy of nature, self, and society under a divine plan spoke directly to Williams's experience in the English Nonconformist Enlightenment and anticipated her use of similar narratives to illustrate her view of the Revolution in the *Letters*. Like Rousseau, Saint-Pierre uses nature to attack both the courtly society and imperialistic commercialism of Europe. In a framed narrative a sentimental traveller to the Île-de-France (Mauritius) hears an old man's tale of two women from different classes, victims of women's oppression in European society. The peasant Margaret was seduced and abandoned by a 'gentleman' and forced to flee society; the aristocratic Mme de la Tour married 'beneath' her, was rejected by her haughty relatives, and then widowed. But the two women co-operated to raise their children, Paul and Virginia, in a remote valley on the island, living off the land and according to nature, assisted by two faithful slaves. When Paul and Virginia approached sexual maturity their domestic relationship promised to evolve into paradisal conjugality, but European society and the state, in the form of Mme de la Tour's rich aunt seconded by the governor of the island and the local priest, had Virginia returned to France for a 'proper' education and marriage. Eventually she rejected this attempt to appropriate her to the courtly system of wealth, power, and gender relations, but her great-aunt maliciously allowed her to return to the island only during the dangerous hurricane season and she died when the ship was wrecked on the coast.

Paul et Virginie exemplifies pre-Revolutionary social criticism, but by translating and publishing it in the 1790s Williams recontextualizes it and appropriates it for her own view of the Revolution. Readers familiar with Williams's *Letters* would see another version of the du Fossés' story but lacking the happy ending created by the Revolution, thus showing that the Revolution had to occur to end the social division and injustice that exiled Margaret and Mme de la Tour and prevented the union of Paul and Virginia. Williams's translation of Saint-Pierre's pre-Revolutionary novel into the Revolutionary situation is another act of justifying 'her' Revolution. *Paul et Virginie* portrays the Edenic world as thoroughly feminized, not only lacking a central adult male presence but validating 'feminine' values of domesticity and philanthropy as the product of 'nature' marginalized, despised, and oppressed by pre-Revolutionary European society. This was the feminized culture of Sensibility in which Williams had first made her literary reputation as a cultural revolutionary. By recurring to Sensibility while herself imprisoned Williams returns to the origins of 'her' Revolution, no longer oppressed by court government and society but by the Jacobin Terror, and only publishable after that Revolution has been overthrown. This appropriation succeeded. Reviewers were generally sympathetic, the *Critical Review* finding Williams 'eminently qualified'—by her earlier work and her literary character—'not only to transfuse every beauty of the original, but to embellish it with new and peculiar graces' such as the sonnets.[41] Later editions also retained the 1795 Preface, indicating that publishers thought sales would be stimulated by the translator's piquant situation under the Terror.[42]

Williams's direct account of the Jacobin Revolution began appearing late in 1795. *Letters Containing a Sketch of the Politics of France from the Thirty-first of May 1793, till the Twenty-eighth of July 1794, and of the Scenes which Have Passed in the Prisons of Paris* was published in two volumes, followed by a third entitled *Letters Containing a Sketch of the Scenes which Passed in Various Departments of France During the Tyranny of Robespierre, and of the Events which Took Place in Paris on the 28th of July 1794*. A fourth volume appeared in 1796 entitled *Letters Containing a Sketch of the Politics of France, from the Twenty-eighth of July 1794, to the Establishment of the Constitution in 1795, and of the Scenes which Have Passed in the Prisons of Paris*.[43] *Letters* (1795–6) takes the Revolution from the fall of the Girondins to the approval of the Constitution of the Year III in August and September 1795. Inevitably, the new work repeats central figures, patterns, and arguments found in the earlier *Letters*, but the outline is now clearer and the tone sharper.

More clearly than before, Revolutionary history is mythologized as a passage from the hell of Jacobin Terror to another Revolutionary paradise regained. Williams again compares the Jacobin Revolution to Milton's Hell, where Hébert, Clootz, Danton, and their followers outdo one another in schemes for tormenting humanity, like so many demons led and finally betrayed by a satanic Robespierre. Such

---

[41] *Critical Review*, NS 18 (Oct. 1796), 183.

[42] For example the elegant edition printed by C. Whittingham in 1819 and sold by John Sharpe; Longman, Hurst, Rees, Orme, & Brown; Baldwin, Cradock, & Joy; & George Cowie.

[43] The title-pages of successive issues and editions of these four volumes have variations on this wording.

allusions are reinforced by quotations from a well-known poetic representation of the horrors of civil discord, Nicholas Rowe's translation of Lucan's *Pharsalia*, set in the late Roman republic. The allusions to Milton and Lucan place the Jacobin Revolution in relation to both cosmic and historic rebellions. The Revolution is also more obviously split between feminine and masculine, positive and negative aspects, with 'vulgar' lower-class characteristics added to the latter. For example, the first volume opens with a letter from the refuge of Switzerland, dated September 1794, after the fall of the Jacobins and deploring the Jacobin coup d'état 'which seated a vulgar and sanguinary despot' (Robespierre) on the ruins of Liberty's throne. Thus the correspondence frames the Jacobin Terror which the letters recount within a conventionally feminine discourse and a feminized Revolutionary consciousness that the Jacobins tried and failed to suppress, as the mere existence of the new letters testifies.

Working from this mythologizing and feminizing initial impetus, Williams shows the Jacobin Revolution in contrast to and resisted by various feminized values celebrated in her earlier *Letters* and *Paul and Virginia*—feminized domesticity, Enlightenment and Dissenting historical optimism, and the beauty of nature. She also continues personal and immediate representation of Revolution with discursive elements that would have been seen as feminine at the time, thereby suggesting that the Jacobin interlude has not radically disrupted the feminized Revolution. For example, she frequently adduces personal observation, claiming, 'I have seen those infectious cells' of the Conciergerie, and 'I have seen the chamber, where the persons condemned by the revolutionary tribunal' were prepared to face the guillotine (ii. 100). She again uses anecdotal narrative much more than general description or analysis and insists that many of her anecdotes come from friends and personal contacts, quoting some information directly. This is not merely factual validation, however: 'Those scenes, connected in my mind with all the detail of domestic sorrow, with the feelings of private sympathy, with the tears of mourning friendship, are impressed upon my memory in characters that are indelible' (i. 2–3). The intensity of immediate experience guarantees the authenticity of memory—hence the authority of her retrospective narrative. Furthermore, the Revolution is viewed anecdotally and mainly from the level of daily domesticity, both because the Revolution's character is shown by its treatment of individuals and their domestic relations and because only such a portrayal can give Revolutionary history meaning for the individual.

This is history taking place not at the public, political level but at the personal, domestic level, where experience is most immediate and intense.

Meshing with this quotidian, immediate reality, however, is the cycle whereby the Revolution, true to its name, overturns those who previously overturned others. This Revolutionary irony relativizes the cycles of Revolutionary violence in contrast both to the constancy of the domestic affections and to the permanence of nature. Williams gives numerous examples of the domestic affections resisting Terror— son sacrificing himself for father, father for son, devotion unto death of the wives, daughters, and mothers of the Terror's victims, whole families dying together rather than face separation by Revolutionary death. She translates the poem of a condemned young man to his beloved (ii. 40–1). She notes that 'many young women who had lost their parents or lovers on the scaffold' simply shouted 'Vive le roi!', a passport to death (ii. 65). In such examples the feminized Revolution resists the masculine Revolution of the Jacobin Terror to constitute a heaven in the heart of hell.

This point is again reinforced by foregrounding women as Revolutionary heroes and martyrs. In the first volume Charlotte Corday is the heroine, inspired not by Revolutionary faction but by the 'feminine' virtues of sympathy and compassion informing Williams's earlier response to the Revolution. Aimée Cecile Renaud, would-be assassin of Robespierre, is the heroine in the second volume. Other female victims of all classes are presented through anecdotes illustrating their domestic devotion, while male victims of the Terror are described in terms of their domestic, feminine qualities. Dominating this catalogue is Marie Roland, whose patriotic death symbolizes the feminized Revolution temporarily obscured by the brutally masculine, individualistic, anti-domestic Jacobin Revolution. Roland's self-defence and account of the Revolutionary leaders, with other documents protesting the Jacobin coup, are printed as appendices to volumes one and two, again grounding Williams's personalized account in 'objective', documentary fact.

Williams justifies Mme Roland's prominence as a tribute to the domestic affections:

Merciful Heaven! and among those who have thus suffered were persons to whom my heart was bound by the ties of friendship and affection.—But though I have survived such scenes, they have left upon my heart that settled melancholy which never can be dissipated. . . . death, the idea most familiar to my imagination, appears to my wearied spirit the only point of rest. (ii. 100)

This is more than self-pity. The same domestic affections that once validated the Revolution for her now affect her for the worse. The movement of the passage, from addressing a 'merciful heaven' remote from the unmerciful Revolution to wishing for death as the only 'point of rest' from Revolutionary violence, suggests a profound alteration in Revolutionary subjectivity. The relation between heaven and earth, formerly represented as divine validation of Revolutionary paradise regained, has now become an abyss to be bridged, following the example of the Revolution's victims, only by death.

Revolutionary death is a major theme in these *Letters*, levelling Revolutionary leaders Williams knew, monarchs, and a host of ordinary individuals and families, ironically uniting the nation under Jacobin Terror. Death even mediates contrasting figures of Revolution—on one hand 'ferocious crimes' and on the other 'the sublime enthusiasm of the virtuous affections' that bid 'us cease to despair of humanity', that convert 'the throb of indignant horror into the glow of sympathetic admiration', and that bid us 'turn from the tribunal of blood, from Robespierre and his jury of assassins' to parents and children dying with or for their loved ones, individuals such as Mme Bousquet, the sister-in-law of the Girondin Guadet, 'scorning the impious laws which punished humanity with death, affording shelter to her proscribed friends, and dying with them on the scaffold for having done so' (ii. 102–4).

This passage comes shortly after Williams's confession of Revolutionary despair and longing for death, and announces her rediscovery of Revolutionary sublimity in the Revolution's victims and their assumption in death of the same domestic virtues and civic heroism celebrated in her earlier *Letters*. The sublimity of Revolutionary death transcends present evils and prefigures the restoration of Revolutionary virtue. But chastened by Terror she cannot confidently greet the post-Jacobin cycle as the return of feminized Revolution. She can only hope 'that this stormy revolution will at least produce some portion of felicity to succeeding generations, who have not, like us, felt the tumultuous horrors of this convulsion of the passions, who will owe their happiness to the struggles of a race that is passed away, and whom they have never known' (ii. 117).

A further solace is nature, like sublime death outside the political and social domains and thus beyond their relativities and conflicts. Even in Luxembourg prison, symbol of Revolutionary division and failure, Williams escapes to nature. By standing on a table in her cell she can see into the Luxembourg gardens and soothe her 'afflicted spirit', for 'it is scarcely possible to contemplate the beauties of nature without that enthusiastic pleasure which swells into devotion; and when such dispositions are excited in the mind, resignation to sufferings, which in the sacred words of scripture "are but for a moment," becomes a less difficult duty' (i. 16–17). Prison and garden, adjacent and bearing the same name, symbolize the alternatives for sensibility—afflictions or pleasures—leading to religious devotion and resignation, validated by the biblical quotation.

A striking contrast opens volume two: 'While far along the moral horizon of France the tempest became every hour more black and turbulent, the spring, earlier and more profuse of graces than in the climate of England, arose in its unsullied freshness, and formed a contrast at which humanity sickened.' After their release from prison Williams and her family vainly sought nature in the woods and gardens of estates around Paris, 'once the residence of fallen royalty' but 'now haunted by vulgar despots, revolutionary commissaries', 'spies of the police', and sometimes 'the sanguinary decemvirs themselves'. They held their 'festive orgies' in these 'scenes of beauty', 'cast their polluting glance on nature', and trod 'with profane step her hallowed recesses'. The imagery suggests a scene of rape that parodies the scenes of courtly seduction and sexual intrigue that the Jacobins boast of having ended. Even 'the revolutionary jury' sometimes suspended 'their work of death, to go to Marly or Versailles' where, 'without being haunted by the mangled spectres of those whom they had murdered the preceding day, they saw nature in her most benign aspect, pleading the cause of humanity and mercy, and returned to feast upon the groans of those whom they were to murder on the morrow' (ii. 2–3). Williams sees nature in feminine and domestic terms, but the Jacobins see 'her' as a victim of their lust or their cannibalistic politics. Nature is no longer a refuge from a too-masculine Revolution, but a feminine force for social good that this Revolution must violate and subdue. This opposition is reinforced by Williams's suggestions that Jacobin leaders, like court despots, used their illicit powers for illicit pleasure and sexual victimization of women.

Such figural representation of internecine Revolutionary struggle gives a powerful yet acceptably feminine character to Williams's political analysis. Though she again uses the conventionally feminine and apparently desultory form of letters, once again the structure is more artful than she intends to appear. The first two volumes present the oppositions just described, illustrating the persistence of feminized Revolutionary values even under Jacobin 'tyranny' and death. Volume three deals directly with the operations of the Jacobin Revolution in the regions of France, showing the dissemination of Terror, Revolutionary discord, and resulting royalist reaction, but also illustrating the existence of feminized Revolution there, resisting both Jacobin Terror and royalist counter-revolution. For example, Williams describes resistance to the Vendéan rebels at Grandville by local 'republicans', not Jacobins:

I have been told by one of my acquaintance who fought on the republican side, that the spectacle was truly sublime. Not only every man, but every woman and every child, was that day a warrior: the artillery was served by the children, who, forming chains from the arsenal to the ramparts, conveyed the ammunition, while the women were employed in assisting their husbands, brothers, and fathers. (iii. 30–1)

The resistance of Grandville typifies feminized Revolution rather than Jacobin Terror and anticipates Williams's account of the French republican armies at the end of volume four. In fact, Williams even refers to the Terror as 'this revolutionary, or rather counter-revolutionary, impulse', thus implying what many in Britain such as Samuel Kenrick and James Wodrow believed, that Jacobinism was not advancing but undermining the Revolution, even more than internal opponents such as the Vendéan rebels or the external 'leagued despots' of Europe. Williams even compares the Jacobin leaders to notoriously licentious, bloodthirsty, and despotic rulers of antiquity such as Nero, Caligula, and Heliogabalus, thus equating Jacobinism and monarchic absolutism.

Accordingly, volume three not only shows the dissemination of Jacobinism and resistance to it, from Paris to the whole of France, but also intensifies the contrast of the Terror and the feminized Revolution in episodes of increasing horror, especially affecting women and the domestic affections. Under the Jacobin agent in the Vendée, mothers are butchered and their infants tossed on bayonets. Female modesty is outraged when young women and men are stripped and tied together before being executed. A peasant woman and nursing mother who dropped a remark of horror at Jacobin cruelties was herself executed: 'When she received the fatal stroke, the streams of maternal nourishment issued rapidly from her bosom, and, mingled with her blood, bathed her executioner' (iii. 122). The Revolution has become the maternal body of an ordinary citizeness, in the moment of death shedding two life-streams in a final act of female Revolutionary redemption. Other outrages are described, such as the massacre of an entire village, in the immediacy of the present tense. Eventually Williams confesses that imagination fails before such horrors, fearing to lose its creative sensibility and thus its revolutionizing potential by dwelling on the ghastly details.

Having reached this ineffable sublime of the Terror, the Revolution, by an internal mechanism of recoil that was intrinsic to the nature of the Jacobin regime, swings back to the imaginable, the social, and the feminized, in the reaction of Thermidor (July 1794). Robespierre's elimination of Danton, Hébert, and the leaders of the Paris commune roused his rivals and the otherwise docile 'plain', or moderates in the National Convention, into destroying him. In the last letter of the volume Williams's racy journalistic description of the coup is followed by a rapid sketch of sudden release of joy, with 'affecting scenes' of family reunion and the disclosure of domestic affection's hidden triumphs even under the Terror. The volume closes anticipating a new constitution to settle the Revolution on these values.

The fourth and last volume continues, supplements, and contrasts with the previous ones, tracing events from the aftermath of Thermidor to the new constitution of August 1795. Williams opens by reaffirming that the very sensibility that authenticates her account hinders it when the Terror is her subject: 'in describing those scenes of desolation, how often have I experienced that my pen was unfaithful to my purpose! how faint is the impression which I have conveyed to you at a distance, of those local emotions which are felt on the spot!' (iv. 1). She goes on both to track the punishment of Jacobins whose 'crimes' were recounted in the previous volume and to illustrate the gradual restoration of the feminized and domestic Revolution in the aftermath of Thermidor, including the liberation of prisoners, the remission of death sentences, the return of exiles, the reunion of families, and the revival of arts and sciences, culminating in the new constitution. This volume too has its inset tale, of an aged priest who had secretly married during the *ancien régime*, was arrested by the Jacobins, saved from the guillotine by Robespierre's fall, and reunited with his loyal wife—a private life that parallels the history of the Revolution. Thus volume four balances its predecessor, offering a structural counterpart to description of the Terror, reinforcing the compensatory alternatives to the Terror outlined in volumes one and two, and implying a finality and permanence to the restoration of feminized Revolution.

Yet this restoration is haunted by the horrors of the Jacobin past, revealed in the trials of Jacobin leaders. Williams had insisted since *Letters* (1790) that the basis of the 'true' Revolution is Revolutionary sensibility such as hers and those she celebrates in her pages. She had validated this claim by demonstrating such a sensibility in her own immediacy of response to the Revolution in all its phases, good and bad, rendered in the style and structure of her texts. But now that immediacy has become self-obstructing, occluded by memory of hopes disappointed and joys turned to horrors, for memory revives the immediacies of the past, making them present. If, as Williams claims, the Revolution was produced by and lives in the sensibility of the people, that Revolution has begun to consume itself as individual and collective memory of the Revolutionary past begins to supersede the immediacy of the Revolutionary present.[44] Restoration of the 'good' Revolution is qualified by the regret of those now liberated from prison for time lost with friends and family and their grief for others (including the author's friends) now lost forever. Revolutionary death may have validated the feminized Revolution even under the Terror, but such death has transformed the living. Even the Revolutionary present seems insecure, with renewed food shortages, the revival of counter-revolutionary revolt in the Vendée and elsewhere, the Jacobin insurrection of Prairial (20–3 May) 1795, and the tragic British-assisted invasion by *émigrés* at Quiberon in July. 'But', Williams insists, the 'barbarous triumphs' of the Jacobins 'are past, and anarchy and vandalism can return no more'. The new constitution, like the spear of Romulus, Rome's founder, 'will fix itself in the earth, so that no human force can root it up, and will become, like the budding wood, the object of a people's veneration' (iv. 179). The magically vivified weapon, symbolizing the turn from conflict to peace and resembling the Revolutionary liberty tree, is evoked to prefigure a new and equally significant historical era. Yet the image seems strangely far-fetched, pertaining to myth rather than history, to carry new burdens of Revolutionary optimism.

But Williams still has to explain the Revolutionary war, for the

---

[44] For a survey of individual and social memory see James Fentress and Chris Wickham, *Social Memory* (Oxford, 1992); see also the discussion of Williams's *Souvenirs de la Révolution française* in Ch. 6 below.

Revolutionary citizen armies saved the Revolution from exiled French royalists, defeated the major military powers of Europe, and took the Revolution beyond France's historic borders. Jacobins claimed that this success was only possible because of their government's strong central powers and policy of Terror. France's enemies claimed that these military successes exported Jacobinism to Europe and the world, that revolutions inevitably become militarist and expansionist, and that Revolution was merely a cover for French imperialism. Williams counters by showing the relationship between war and feminized Revolution, exemplified in her new ability, as a woman writer, to represent the domain of war and military affairs with authority. If war still eludes her understanding and literary competence, the authority of her general representation of the Revolution may be vitiated. She now claims authority on military affairs not because she has changed her 'feminine' outlook and character, but because the martial character of the French has been feminized.

She had assigned the topic to other correspondents in *Letters* (1793), and in *Letters* (1795–6) the two letters on Revolutionary war are relegated to the end of the last volume. She also insists that 'I am not, like some of the females of this country, skilled in the art of war', and declares that her materials have mostly been supplied 'by the actors in the scenes they record', which she has 'only the task to relate' (iv. 180–1), thus seeming to accept a modest and mediating role again. But her account of the war in *Letters* (1795–6), unlike that in *Letters* (1793), is related to her argument that the 'true' Revolution survived despite the Terror. She claims that her description of the military campaigns will present 'the brighter side' of the Revolution during the Jacobin regime, denies that measures of the Jacobin government necessarily saved the military situation, and insists that such measures could have been instituted legally rather than by the Terror. She notes that even the Jacobins dared not push the armies too far, for example by ordering them to execute English prisoners. Furthermore, the Jacobins broke the armies as soon as they safely could. Thus the Jacobin Terror not only had little to do with the armies' success but was actually inimical to the spirit that motivated the armies—the spirit of 'her' Revolution.

She argues that the republican armies defeated the 'leagued despots' because they were morally and politically superior, inspired by inward rather than outward forces. This has 'changed the national military character' (iv. 188). The republican soldier fights for his country's liberty rather than mere pay, vain martial pomp, or fear of brutal discipline that alone motivates monarchic armies. He is inspired by his 'honour', formerly an aristocratic value, 'his personal courage, his dexterity and vivacity, the cultivation of his mind, his liberty of thinking, the general knowledge that he possesses of the public affairs of his country; while his enthusiasm is animated by patriotic songs and martial music analogous to his feelings' (iv. 191)—elsewhere Williams announces her friendship with Rouget de Lisle, author of 'La Marseillaise'. In fact these sentiments extend to the entire people, as seen at the siege of Grandville, and the fact that foreign invasion was resisted not only by the republican armies but by local 'citizens', as well as women and children (iv. 198), and the fact that the French victory at Fleurus (26 June 1794) has been compared to the victory of the Swiss over the Austrians in 1386, founding Swiss independence and national identity.

Williams insists that this Revolutionary military character had no connection with the Jacobin government and Terror:

The horrors which desolated the interior part of France had too long formed a melancholy contrast with the resplendent glories that hung around its frontiers; and the honour of the French name, sinking beneath the obloquy with which it was loaded by the crimes of its domestic tyrants, was only sustained by the astonishing achievements of the French armies. They alone remained pure and unsullied by the contagious guilt which overspread their country. They alone appear to have been the true representatives of the French nation, and every family in France could boast of having a deputy upon the frontier. (iv. 206)

Williams feminizes the Revolutionary armies by attributing their achievements not to masculine aggressiveness and bellicosity but to the combined inspiration of the domestic affections and patriotism. But this character could only be kept 'pure and unsullied'—the phrase would suggest female chastity—by remaining isolated from internal Revolutionary politics: 'It was the duty of the French soldiers not to deliberate upon the internal commotions, but to repulse the hostile invader: and Europe, which has been the theatre of their exploits, has been awed by their overwhelming greatness' (iv. 206–7). In fact, Williams claims, the Jacobins concealed their crimes from the armies. But even this was unnecessary, for the armies could be inspired only by 'that holy flame which liberty kindles in every heart but that of the base and degenerate', and 'that unconquerable love of their country, which animates a people, when, after a long night of oppression, they have at length a country to hail' (iv. 217). The two letters on military affairs now seem the crowning piece in Williams's insistence that the feminized Revolution survived and even triumphed over both Jacobin Terror and royalist counter-revolution, appropriating even the conventionally masculine domain of war to her feminization of the Revolution.

Letters (1795–6) ends with the implication that the now firmly established feminized Revolution will continue to spread beyond the borders of France. Williams developes this theme in *A Tour in Switzerland; or, A View of the Present State of the Government and Manners of those Cantons: with Comparative Sketches of the Present State of Paris* (1798). As the title suggests, it combines travels with politics, but Williams lost nothing in giving up the epistolary form, for travel narrative conventionally allowed for a degree of apparent immediacy, desultoriness, and spontaneity, especially with women travel-writers such as Elizabeth Craven, Hester Piozzi, and Mary Wollstonecraft. By contrast, men travel-writers, especially political travellers such as Arthur Young, Dr John Moore, and William Coxe, employed a more matter-of-fact, factual, and detached discourse. Williams would certainly have known Piozzi's, Moore's, and Coxe's books, and probably Wollstonecraft's as well. Williams avoids both the experimental play of Piozzi's *Travels* and the narrative manner of Moore, but equals Wollstonecraft's *Letters* from Scandinavia in exhibiting a vanguard female Revolutionary consciousness while displacing Coxe's well-established but conservative account of Switzerland. *A Tour* incorporates travel-writing, the most important and widely read form of non-fiction prose at the time, into Williams's project of feminizing politics and the Revolution.

Williams establishes at the outset that she is a political refugee and writer, seeking solace in Switzerland's sublime nature and the society it has formed. Switzerland becomes another figure for the ideal revolution. But it also becomes an example of why such revolution is desirable and necessary. Rousseau and other Sentimental writers represented Switzerland as a professional middle-class arcadia—a society shaped by its sublime and beautiful environment into an economic and social ideal of patriarchal, domestic, democratic pastoralism—contrasting with societies shaped by court government and their fictional arcadias. Britons revered Switzerland as a cradle of Protestantism, and British 'commonwealthmen' admired the exploits of William Tell and the fifteenth-century Swiss as exemplary triumphs of 'the people' over aristocracy and despotism. The relationship of Swiss landscape and

Swiss democracy was celebrated by James Thomson, Oliver Goldsmith, and other writers. William Coxe saw a close resemblance between the Swiss and the English. Williams reshapes these cultural figures of Switzerland to show that, like the French and British, the Swiss have deviated from 'nature' and so were ripe for revolution. For while Switzerland's sublime nature and rural domestic society are as she expected, the social and political structure of Swiss towns imitates the old European order. Switzerland shows the relevance of the feminized French Revolution to the rest of Europe—perhaps even to Britain, with which Switzerland was commonly compared.

It is this internationalized Revolution, embodied for her in the figure of Bonaparte, that Williams promotes in *A Tour*. Pro-revolutionary Swiss had been in France since the early 1790s, urging establishment of democratic regimes in oligarchic cantons such as Basle and liberation of fiefs of the more powerful cantons. After Williams's return to France in 1795, Bonaparte's Italian victories of 1796 transformed Switzerland from a byway of Europe to a highroad of Revolutionary expansion. By the time Williams's *Tour* was published Bonaparte had sparked revolutions in Switzerland and Italy, had become the military saviour of France, and appointed himself disseminator of the Revolution. Thus he too becomes a figure for Williams's Revolutionary sublime.

A Tour opens with Williams announcing her intention to flee the conflicts and relativities of the Revolution for the sublimities of Switzerland. As she explained to a friend:

I am going to gaze upon images of nature ... I am going to repose my wearied spirit on those sublime objects—to soothe my desponding heart with the hope that the moral disorder I have witnessed shall be rectified, while I gaze on nature in all her admirable perfections; and how delightful a transition shall I find in the picture of social happiness which Switzerland presents! (i. 4)

But in Basle she finds a mirror of the Revolution's degeneration from sublime origins to the ambition, self-interest, commercialism, social emulation, and surrogate courtliness of the Directory: 'industry flourishes on the ruins of vanity; and, as the impetuous French are ever in extremes, their ancient disdain of mercantile occupations is succeeded by a sort of rage for commerce.' Memory of Revolutionary Terror has made people live for the moment: 'They seek amusement with new eagerness, and the dangers which they find attendant on a revolution, only serve to attach them more to the present moment, on the Epicurean principle of uncertainty respecting the future' (i. 18–19).

It is true that 'the Epicurean principle' has transformed parasites into producers: 'Gothic abbies are transformed into manufactories, cloisters become work-shops, chapels are converted into warehouses, the recesses of solitary superstition are invaded, and the hollow echoes of the long-resounding aisles, which were once only responsive to the solemn, slow-breathed chant, now repeat the rude dissonance of the workman's tools' (i. 21–2). Through Stone Williams could appreciate the ideas of the French 'économistes', or 'physiocrats', who opposed the interventionist and regulatory policies of the *ancien régime* and favoured a free market economy, here represented by the contrasting figures of monastery and workshop.[45] Yet the passage has a note of regret for what has passed. Like Wollstonecraft, Williams was critical of the commercial bourgeoisie and shared the growing resistance of professional middle-class intellectuals to commerce and industry in the Revolutionary aftermath. This resistance would have a long history, and though some post-Revolutionary women writers such as Maria Edgeworth saw the industrial spirit as an extension of Enlightenment political economy, others such as Williams saw that spirit as incompatible with feminized civil society.

Williams sees the commercial spirit as a return of court politics, with women participating in a bourgeois version of the 'mistress system' of mingled sexual and political intrigue: 'A few of the most beautiful, and the most intriguing of the fair Parisians, became the agents and emissaries of their friends, lovers, or husbands, in the public offices', and 'republican committees made no better defence than polished courts, against the formidable artillery of bright eyes, gay smiles, lively sallies, and animated graces'. Thus 'the women of France, to whom, by the Constitutional Act, all rights have been denied, find that they still have a tolerably despotic empire over their lords and masters, the sovereign people' (i. 25–6). Like the court system of the *ancien régime*, the Revolutionary Constitution bars women from legitimate political activity and forces them to use the only power they have. Mary Wollstonecraft makes a similar argument in *A Vindication of the Rights of Woman* (1792).[46]

Williams turns from this falsely feminized society to the natural and

[45] Doyle, *French Revolution*, 57–8.
[46] See Gary Kelly, *Revolutionary Feminism: The Mind and Career of Mary Wollstonecraft* (London, 1992), ch. 5.

social beauty of rural Switzerland. Here she finds sublime and 'romantic' nature, the democratic structures and patriotism it inspires, and the
social and economic life it imposes (i. 53). She finds traditional popular
culture, or folklore, embodying this social structure and passing it on
through 'the oral tale', for 'many a traditionary tale gives a moral
interest to the picturesque scenes of this enchanting country' (i. 53, 54).
Such sublimity can even construct authentic subjectivity through
imagination alone: 'so long, so eagerly, had I desired to contemplate
that scene of wonders, that I was unable to trace when first the wish
was awakened in my bosom—it seemed from childhood to have made
a part of my existence' (i. 57). Thus Williams and rural Swiss society
have both been constructed by the same transcendent force, and its
revolutionary potential is now affirmed by presence, as Williams
describes the Rhine falls:

That stupendous cataract, rushing with wild impetuosity over those broken,
unequal rocks, which, lifting up their sharp points amidst its sea of foam,
disturb its headlong course, multiply its falls, and make the afflicted waters
roar—that cadence of tumultuous sound, which had never till now struck
upon my ear—those long feathery surges, giving the element a new aspect—
that spray rising into clouds of vapour, and reflecting the prismatic colours,
while it disperses itself over the hills—never, never can I forget the sensations
of that moment! when with a sort of annihilation of self, with every past
impression erased from my memory, I felt as if my heart were bursting with
emotions too strong to be sustained.—Oh, majestic torrent! which hast conveyed a new image of nature to my soul, the moments I have passed in
contemplating thy sublimity will form an epocha in my short span!—thy
course is coeval with time, and thou wilt rush down thy rocky walls when this
bosom, which throbs with admiration of thy greatness, shall beat no longer! (i.
60–1)

Subjective revolution ('a sort of annihilation of self, with every past
impression erased') is made immediate by familiar devices of Sentimental writing such as the incomplete first sentence, the dashes, exclamations, and direct address. Like the Revolution as represented in her
Letters, it is a moment in time transcending time, thereby remaking the
individual and history, both of which had become burdensome since the
Jacobin Terror, and anticipating a similar function of sublime nature in
Wordsworth and Shelley, both of whom knew Williams's work.
    Though Williams claims that the sublime moment remakes and
transcendentalizes her, she shows her capacity both to respond to it and
to represent it in writing and thereby master it. By contrast, those who

merely make their living near the cataract are oblivious to it: 'accustomed to the neighbourhood of the torrent, the boatman unloads his merchandize, and the artisan pursues his toil, regardless of the falling river . . . while the imagination of the spectator is struck with the comparative littleness of fleeting man, busy with his trivial occupations, contrasted with the view of nature in all her vast, eternal, uncontrolable grandeur' (i. 63). The sublime not only reveals the difference between temporal and transcendent, historical and permanent, relative and absolute, it also reveals human difference—based not on class or gender but on 'imagination' or subjective capacity. This is a commonplace of contemporary political and cultural theory: only those with the necessary leisure can participate in politics and culture. Unlike working men and those 'very wise men, who admit no scope to that faculty of the mind called imagination, and are for ever bringing every theory to the square and the compass' (i. 66–7), Williams has a manifest capacity for the sublime, showing that she and readers who feel with her are qualified subjectively to constitute the cultural and political nation. This would exclude both the plebeians and the merely rationalist *philosophes* ('very wise men') who together perpetrated the Jacobin Revolution.

Williams also grounds the politics of the Revolutionary sublime in the revolutions of the past. On seeing the Lake of the Four Cantons she understands how sublime landscape can inspire revolutionary heroism such as William Tell's: 'No place could surely be found more correspondent to a great and generous purpose, more worthy of an heroical and sublime action, than the august and solemn scenery around us' (i. 141). Unlike the Revolution, this sublimity endures, for the landscape that inspired Swiss revolutionaries of the twelfth century still speaks to the revolutionary subject: 'There must surely be some defect in the heart, which feels no enthusiastic glow, while we tread over the spots where those heroes have trod, who have struggled for the liberties of mankind, or bled for their rights' (i. 146). History is again grasped for the present by being feminized—in this case by being personalized and made affectively immediate. The past is also feminized by being embodied in the conventionally feminine discourse of narrative, especially oral narrative, the 'sublime traditions' or folk-tales that transform Swiss popular memory into a 'national' heritage and destiny. Such 'traditions' also unite Swiss and Britons in a common democratic mythology: 'Tell is in England, as well as Switzerland, the hero of our infancy; the marvellous tale of the apple is one of our earliest lessons'

(i. 147). Williams uses Tell to recall the revolutionary, libertarian, democratic origin of Swiss independence because the sublime landscape that once inspired such a revolution may do so again, and not only for the Swiss.

Williams shows how this may happen with another extended narrative based on 'fact' and positioned climactically near the end of her first volume. An upper-class French couple, Mme C—— and her husband, had differing views on the Revolution. He detested it but his wife 'had often wept over the miseries of the oppressed people, and was more disposed to rejoice in the amelioration of solid substantial wretchedness, than to lament the ideal deprivations of greatness' (i. 288). They fled France separately but before they could meet in Switzerland he took up with Mme de ——, an impecunious Parisian aristocrat and accomplished coquette who turned to supporting herself by sexual intrigues with wealthy *émigrés*. Meanwhile, Mme C—— gladly supported herself and child by needlework and drawing: 'the precious purpose of sustaining her child, filled her mind with the sweetest sensations of maternal tenderness . . . it was an effort of virtue, which, while it shielded the object of her fond solicitude from suffering, was interwoven with an immediate recompense in the soothing effect it produced on her own mind' (i. 313–14). Soon after, her husband was abandoned by his mistress for a German count, fell ill, and returned to his forgiving wife. A friend secured enough of their property to support them in a 'neat' cottage in Switzerland, where Monsieur C——hoped to recover his physical and mental health amidst the nurturing beauties of nature (i. 321).

Like similar stories in the *Letters*, this tale transforms the plot of the Revolution on to the domestic plane that Williams represents as authentic political reality, where women operate best as political agents. The tale also novelizes and feminizes the Revolution up to the re-establishment of bourgeois leadership and control in 1794–5. The loyal wife and the faithless mistress represent different elements of the French upper class before and during the Revolution. The seduction of Monsieur C—— by Mme de —— illustrates the corruption of the aristocracy by courtly decadence. Mme de ——'s alliances with *émigrés* and a foreign nobleman parallel the royalists' self-interested betrayal of the Revolution and collusion with foreign powers. Mme C——'s conversion of her merely ornamental upper-class 'accomplishments' into means of livelihood illustrates how the Revolution has abolished luxury and will replace it with selfless rather than merely commercial industry. The reunion of Monsieur and Mme C—— in bourgeois cottage life illustrates the social psychology of Revolutionary transformation of individual and family, even when the Revolution imposes persecution, exile, and hardship, and suggests that Revolutionary conflict and counter-revolutionary threat will be resolved by 'natural' values, which turn out to be those of the leisured middle class.

The tale also links the first volume of *A Tour*, which contrasts the French Revolution with the sublimity of Switzerland, to the second volume, which relates Swiss sublimity to revolution in Switzerland. Monsieur and Mme C—— settle down in the Grisons, and early in volume two Williams describes the political revolution there. According to Williams, 'Swiss democracy', like pre-Revolutionary French despotism, has come to depend on 'ignorance' arising 'from a state of social degradation' (ii. 41). But, she claims, the restoration of original Swiss democracy has already begun in the Valtelline, formerly subject to the Grisons but inspired by Bonaparte's northern Italian Cisalpine Republic to establish itself on 'the imprescriptible rights of mankind' (ii. 49). In fact, the Valtelline 'revolution' was part of Bonaparte's scheme to establish a dependent 'Helvetic Republic', but Williams sees Bonaparte as he portrayed himself—the embodiment of the French Revolution and consequently the liberator of Europe (ii. 54–7). In the remaining chapters Williams describes various revolts in undemocratic Swiss cantons, foreshadowing the grand Revolution of 1798 which would bring Swiss history full circle. Earlier she suggested that Switzerland's heroic, democratic, revolutionary past was inspired by the same sublime landscape that consoled her for the French Revolution's loss of its original sublime yet feminine character. Now she insists that Switzerland's heroic, democratic, revolutionary future will be inspired by a French Revolution as sublimely inspiring as the Swiss Alps (ii. 270–1). Naturalizing the Revolution in this way gives it transcendent, trans-historical, and international significance. This significance is reinforced by a scientific appendix on the Alpine glaciers as a figure for the entire temporal, climatic, and environmental system of nature, later developed by writers such as Percy and Mary Shelley.

Williams returns from these sublime heights, however, and concludes with reflections on the unsublime character of pre-revolutionary Swiss society, culture, and government, and her own return to unsublime Paris under the Directory. Nevertheless, she is consoled by the pleasures of the domestic affections and the realization that, just as the French Revolution has 'awakened new ideas' in Switzerland, presaging imminent revolution there, so 'Switzerland has opened to me a new world of ideas' (ii. 277), offering solace from Revolutionary evil and presaging a return of sublime Revolution in France.

Just after she had published *A Tour* Williams reclaimed another cause she had supported in the 1780s and now associated with the triumph of the Revolution—opposition to slavery. In a memoir of the Swedish anti-slavery campaigner Charles Berns Wadstrom, published in French in the *Décade philosophique* and in English in the liberal *Monthly Magazine*, she claimed that Wadstrom must have approved of the Revolution: 'Yes, our philanthropic enthusiast must have discerned with transport, that liberty, irresistible in its progress as the majestic waters of the Nile, when they overflow their banks and rush over the land, and, benevolent in its effects, as that fructifying stream which spreads only blessings in its course; liberty would soon diffuse over the African continent the benign influence of civilization . . . '[47] In a nice example of articulate energy, this sentence also overflows its banks, as Williams again represents the Revolution as an overpowering but benign force of nature, a feminized power. Yet such a reference was perilous, considering the contemporary struggle between Britain and France for control of the land of the Nile, a connection that Williams seems to encourage by asserting that at the end of his life Wadstrom rejoiced in the victories of the French armies as a step in the ending of slavery everywhere. The memoir goes further than Williams had done so far in expressing approval for a Revolution that she continued to insist was essentially feminized and positive, despite its militarism and expansionism.

Certainly Williams was now seen by many in Britain as an advocate of the Revolution in any aspect. In early 1798 letters from Stone and Williams to Joseph Priestley were intercepted and published as part of a campaign orchestrated by the British government to discredit its critics at home and abroad.[48] A few months later the anti-Jacobin *British Critic* reviewed both *A Tour* and its author's career, linking her literary, political, and moral transgressions: 'She caught the infection of Gallic liberty' and her publications 'were more remarkable for the gaudy glare of declamation, than for sound reason or sober argument', for 'female modesty, the lovely ornament of our countrywomen,

---

[47] *Monthly Magazine*, 7 (July 1799), 463–4.
[48] *Copies of Original Letters Recently Written By Persons in Paris to Dr. Priestley in America, Taken on Board of a Neutral Vessel* (London, 1798).

opposes in France but a feeble barrier to Jacobinical principles, which laugh at morality, and despise religion'.[49] The same link was seen in the career of the late Mary Wollstonecraft, whose biography had recently been published by her husband William Godwin. The Revd Richard Polwhele, in a note to his counter-feminist poem *The Unsex'd Females* (1798), asked of Williams, 'is it not extraordinary, that such a genius, a female and so young, should have become a politician' and 'stand forward, an intemperate advocate for Gallic licentiousness'.[50] Hester Piozzi, who once thought Williams 'a very fine genius', now saw her as not only 'a wicked little Democrate' but more dangerous than Wollstonecraft because she 'infuses *her* venom in such sweetness of style, and in such moderate quantities; I think no corruption has a better chance to spread'.[51] Nevertheless, by the late 1790s Williams's Revolutionary prose epic had made her an international figure. Her books were quarried for illustrations in the Revolution debate. Perceptions of the Revolution were influenced by her contrast between 'feminine' and 'masculine' Revolutions. Her work was translated by leading French writers, and a French critic claimed that her works 'n'ont pas peu contribué à multiplier en Angleterre les partisans des principes français, et doivent placer Miss Williams au rang des auteurs à qui l'on devra l'affermissement de notre République'.[52] Her representation of feminized Revolutionary culture was taken up by Romantic writers seeking alternatives to Revolutionary conflict.

Yet response to her view of the Revolution, her rhetorical strategies, and even her participation in such a subject remained divided. Most critics saw in her work intellectual deficiencies commonly attributed to women writers, especially those venturing beyond 'feminine' subjects. The *English Review* thought her work 'not so much addressed to the sagacious politicians of the day, as to the more amiable, though perhaps less sagacious ones'—'the politicians in petticoats', for 'it seems to have been the intention of Miss Williams to collect the small talk of the French patriots; and this task she has executed with all the ability peculiar to her sex'. The *Critical Review* asked condescendingly, 'Sweet enthusiasm, why should we check thy ardour, why tinge thy glowing colours with the sombre tint of philosophical investigation?' The

[49] *British Critic*, 12 (July 1798), 24.
[50] [Richard Polwhele,] *The Unsex'd Females: A Poem* (London, 1798), 19 n.
[51] *Thraliana*, ii. 895; *Letters of Piozzi and Pennington*, ed. Knapp, 159.
[52] *La Décade philosophique, littéraire et politique*, no. 22 (10 Floréal An VI [29 Apr. 1798]), 221.

Monthly Review thought both Burke and Williams showed the limitations of 'poetical politicians', for 'all sound moral and practical reasoning, to which the science of politics eminently belongs, is totally incompatible with the giddy flights of an unrestrained and impassioned fancy'.[53] Though her accounts of the Revolution were widely read, influential, and even plagiarized by others, they seldom received the detailed consideration given to similar accounts by men.

Her form and style were also seen to have characteristically 'feminine' defects. The *British Critic* complained that she had a 'prompt, we had almost said pert, and decisive way of speaking, on matters far too perplexed for her sagacity, and far too abstruse for her acquirements'. The *English Review* found her style exhibited 'exaggeration, accumulation, and floridity and turgidity of expression. This vitiated taste, by which so many female writers, even of lively parts, are corrupted, has the unhappy effect of throwing an air of novelism or romance on tales of real woe.' The *Monthly Review* thought her work had 'no regular form of composition; seeming chiefly to consist of detached memorandums, occasional reflections, and descriptive strokes of a luxuriant pen'. The *English Review* recognized that her aim was not to write Enlightenment 'philosophical history' but rather to give immediacy to the history of the present. Yet 'even this humble plan' is 'not well executed', and 'the sketches are not well arranged, clear, and satisfactory, but desultory, confused, and uninteresting'.[54] Like most women writers, Williams also endured repeated criticism of her 'inaccuracies' in syntax, spelling, scholarship, and understanding of foreign languages.

But some critics recognized the originality and importance of her work, it received increasing respect through the 1790s, and by 1796 it was, according to the *Critical Review*, acknowledged to be both distinctive and important:

If [her *Letters*] want the profound investigation of the statesman or legislator,—if they are destitute of those political discussions, in which historians of the higher order are fond of indulging,—they will be found to contain what is more valuable,—a picture of the times. What they lose in stateliness they gain in interest; if they plunge not deeply into the intrigues of cabinets or the views of politicians, they delineate correctly the fluctuations of popular sentiment;

---

[53] *English Review*, 20 (July 1792), 57; *Critical Review*, NS 6 (Sept. 1792), 68; *Monthly Review*, NS 27 (Oct. 1798), 140.
[54] *British Critic*, 6 (Nov. 1795), 493; *English Review*, 26 (Nov. 1795), 363; *Monthly Review*, NS 19 (Mar. 1796), 336; *English Review*, 26 (Oct. 1795), 247–8.

and if they enter but little on the disgusting and generally tiresome details of senatorial debates or military exploits, they paint the manners, and, by a variety of engaging anecdotes, expose the human heart.

In the same year the *Monthly Review* wrote:

Her ideas of government, and of its various effects on human affairs, take a flight far above the common female range. Her language, too, if not always strictly correct, frequently aims at higher excellence; it soars to the regions of eloquence and of pathos; and if it will not, in every instance, secure the frigid plaudits of the philologist, it will seldom fail to interest the feelings of humanity, and (*party prejudice* aside) it will command the approbation of the heart.

The *Critical Review* praised her work as 'our most characteristic accounts' of 'the tumults of the French revolution' and 'a pleasing, succinct, and . . . dramatic history of the French revolution'.[55] Despite reservations and criticism, by the end of the Revolutionary decade Williams was recognized as a leading interpreter of it.

---

[55] *Critical Review*, NS 16 (Jan. 1796), 1; *Monthly Review*, NS 21 (Nov. 1796), 325–6; *Critical Review*, NS 23 (May 1798), 10; 17 (June 1796), 177.

3

Mary Hays and Revolutionary Sensibility

MARY HAYS read Wollstonecraft's *A Vindication of the Rights of Woman* soon after it was published in 1792 and felt it to be a personally revolutionary text. By that time she was in her early thirties and already transforming the limitations of gender into a feminist identity and politics within the professional middle-class cultural revolution. Like Helen Maria Williams, she had a double intellectual inheritance from liberal Dissent and the culture of Sensibility. Born in 1760, she was raised in a large middle-class Dissenting family in Southwark. When she was 16 or 17 she fell in love with John Eccles, a young man of similar background. She assigned him the role of mentor-lover and they carried on an intense epistolary courtship, informed by Rousseau and British Sentimental writers. Like many others of her class, Hays used Sentimental subjectivity as an alternative to social categories and hierarchies of identity that marginalized her.[1] Since their marriage was for a time forbidden by Eccles's father, they rehearsed Sentimental self-validation as a sense of being victimized by the merely social values of 'the world'. In their letters they practised the Sentimental aesthetics of expressivity, writing as self-authentication, and to create an imaginative space distinct at once from the false values of courtly gallantry and coquetry and the narrow self-interest of the petty bourgeoisie to which they both belonged. Through this correspondence Hays also reconciled the secular culture of Sensibility with her liberal Dissenting background, merging Sentimental subjectivity and independence from the social world with Dissenting spiritual self-examination and unmediated address to the deity, the Sentimental ethics of social sympathy with Dissent's ethics of humanitarianism, Sensibility's cult of simplicity and the sublime with Dissenting 'unworldliness', and Sensibility's emphasis on the local, particular, and quotidian with Dissenters' cultivation of the humble life.

More important, Sensibility's foregrounding of the 'feminine' in

[1] Gina Luria, 'Mary Hays: A Critical Biography', Ph.D. thesis (New York University, 1972), 39.

social practice, culture, and discourse converged with the spiritual egalitarianism implicit in liberal Dissent's argument that intellectual cultivation and ethical freedom were necessary to gain salvation. Like many others, Hays treated Sensibility and liberal Dissent as variants of the professional middle-class cultural revolution. But like Wollstonecraft, Hays also found a contradiction in the cultural revolution's ideal of 'domestic woman'. Writing to Eccles, she made the commonplace observation that education constructed gender difference, preparing men for professional life, material independence, and struggle with the 'world', and preparing women for domesticity and a debilitating 'sensibility'. As she told Eccles, 'in general I have but an indifferent opinion of the natural capacities of your sex; had the women half your advantages, depend upon it they would make more shining figures in the world of literature'.[2] Aware of this contradiction in the ideal of 'domestic woman', Hays fluctuated between a Rousseauist sense of liberation and a confining despondency, though this only further confirmed for her the plenitude of self she was constructing in order to transcend the limitations of her class and gender.

Just before Hays and Eccles were to be married he fell ill and died, in August 1780. Hays considered the role of 'domestic woman' in marriage now barred to her and sought an alternative identity, reading widely in both Sentimental literature and philosophy. In the spring of 1786 she published 'The Hermit: An Oriental Tale' in the *Universal Magazine*—one of many amateur miscellany magazines for those who wished to participate publicly in genteel literary culture. The tale is an allegory of the evils resulting from excessive passion. A sonnet of about the same time asks, 'Ah! say can reason's feebler power controul, | The finer movements of the feeling soul?'[3] But Hays maintained her religious commitment and tried to connect herself to liberal Dissenting coteries by writing to prominent Dissenters with her theological and personal problems. In 1782 she used this approach with Robert Robinson, a popular writer, opponent of the slave trade, political liberal, and founder of the Cambridge Constitutional Society.[4] She outlined her difficulties and confessed to being tempted by deism. He replied:

[2] *The Love-Letters of Mary Hays (1779–1780)*, ed. A. F. Wedd (London, 1925), 173.
[3] Mary [and Elizabeth] Hays, *Letters and Essays, Moral, and Miscellaneous* (London: T. Knott, 1793), 257.
[4] Graham W. Hughes, *With Freedom Fired: The Story of Robert Robinson, Cambridge Nonconformist* (London, 1955).

Short as the narration you give of yourself is, it is a miniature portrait of a lady in danger and distress, the work of an exquisite artist calculated to touch the heart. . . . The power of deism lies in its dress, that of christianity in itself. Who would not prefer innocence and beauty in rags before deformity and prostitution in fashionable finery?

Deism was seen as a consequence of rationalism and associated with upper-class religious scepticism and 'worldliness', and Robinson grasps Hays's religious difficulties in terms of gender difference and class conflict, even attributing feminine seductiveness to Hays's epistolary style.[5] Hays adopted the role she had taken with Eccles, transforming gender difference into a 'philosophical' and dialogical relationship that gave her a kind of equality and power, in spite of educational and material limitations conventionally attributed to women. When Robinson died in 1790 Hays was establishing similar relations with his associates William Frend and George Dyer.

Since Hays did not have the means to entertain guests, these relations remained almost entirely epistolary, but they gave her the confidence and connections necessary to enter a field of writing rarely attempted by women—controversial theology. In 1791 Gilbert Wakefield, a leading Nonconformist scholar and 'commonwealthman', published *An Enquiry into the Expediency and Propriety of Public or Social Worship*. Using his formidable learning, he argued that worship should preferably be a private and personal rather than public act. A number of writers replied to him, including Hays. She concealed her name but not her sex by identifying herself as 'Eusebia' on the title-page of *Cursory Remarks on an Enquiry into the Expediency and Propriety of Public or Social Worship: Inscribed to Gilbert Wakefield*. She begins with a conventionally 'feminine' apology for herself as 'a woman, young, unlearned, unacquainted with any language but her own; possessing no other merit than a love of truth and virtue, an ardent desire of knowledge, and a heart susceptible to the affecting and elevated emotions afforded by pure and rational devotion'. Though 'under great disadvantages' she has nevertheless 'made some little progress in this most important of all pursuits, and by rectifying, in a measure, my judgment, opened a source of exquisite intellectual entertainment and moral improvement'.[6] This resembles Helen Maria Williams's profession of incapacity

---

[5] Robert Robinson to Mary Hays, 11 Jan. 1783, in the Pforzheimer Library.
[6] *Cursory Remarks*, 2nd edn. (London: T. Knott, 1793), 3–4. Knott was a friend of John Disney.

for the abstruse and abstract arguments of philosophers and politicians, and makes a virtue of necessity in suggesting that a woman may have intellectual attributes unavailable to the learned but validated in the culture of Sensibility—simplicity, directness, modesty, intuitiveness, sympathy, and benevolence.

In fact, Hays plays gendered conventions of discourse against Wakefield, avoiding both his display of learning and occasional sarcasm, concentrating on central points rather than abstruse ones, and taking the practical and tolerant approach conventionally expected of a woman. She relies on knowledge a woman might be expected to have, arguing that most people need the support of communal activity and respond to the immediacy of the senses in public worship. She keeps to a 'woman's' range of reading, citing not scholarly sources but Rousseau's well-known description of the Savoyard vicar. She uses dextrous deference in admitting that Wakefield would be right if all Christians were as 'refined, elevated, and philosophic' as he. She closes by suggesting that the conventions of discourse, including those based on gender, have been altered by 'the spirit of freedom and enquiry universally disseminated' by the French Revolution. Masculine rationalism, scholasticism, and professional rivalry have been exaggerated, obscuring major human concerns, which turn out to be those conventionally pursued by women: 'in general the disputes which have disturbed the peace of mankind, have not been about justice, mercy, and love; but concerning curious, and perplexing points of speculation . . . containing no very material practical consequences'. 'Evil tempers have mixed themselves with the love of truth', making 'the mildest and most benevolent religion in the world . . . a scourge to the nations,' but in the life hereafter all will become 'true philosophers'— that is, feminized ones (pp. 20–1).

The response to Hays's bold venture into men's discourse was positive. The *English Review* thought the author had no reason to conceal her name: 'Eusebia needs only claim the merit of a performance which, in the compass of a few pages, contains all the most striking authorities, as well as the most cogent arguments, for public worship, expressed in a very lively and pleasing manner.' The *Critical Review* also thought the book successfully combined 'masculine' and 'feminine' discourses, though its appeal was ultimately in its feminine character: 'Rational religion appears with peculiar beauty in a female mind, for it is generally animated with warmth of devotion, and rendered interesting by the feminine weakness, which requires support.'[7] Wakefield himself praised her and her friend John Disney: 'If all the professors of the gospel had imbibed at those *living waters* the amiable dispositions of these most respectable individuals, *mere differences of opinion* would excite no animosities in the heart, no disagreements of affection.'[8] The reformer William Frend, then embroiled in controversy, confessed that 'no higher gratification could be offered' to him 'than that of hearing sentiments unsophisticated by scholastick learning and drawn without prejudice from the source of truth', and he thought Hays made a specifically feminine contribution to public debate: 'So much candour and sound reasoning cloathed in insinuating language excite in us the hopes that the aid of the fair sex may in future be often called in to soften the animosity and fervour of disputation.'[9]

She became more determined to fashion a woman's way of participating in 'men's' discourse after reading Wollstonecraft's *A Vindication of the Rights of Woman*. Her friend George Dyer sent her a copy which she read, marked up, and passed on to her sister.[10] Like many women of their class, the Hays sisters had few outside intellectual resources and developed their own domestic method of study and enquiry. Stimulated by *A Vindication*, they were soon completing a collaborative work and Hays sought Wollstonecraft's advice.[11] Wollstonecraft was a seasoned professional, with no patience for the 'lady' writer. She scolded Hays for adopting a humble pose and disapproved of the conventional feminine apology in Hays's preface: 'Disadvantages of

---

[7] *English Review*, 19 (June 1792), 476; *Critical Review*, NS 4 (Feb. 1792), 231.

[8] *An Enquiry into the Expediency and Propriety of Public or Social Worship*, new edn. (London, 1792), 60.

[9] William Frend to Mary Hays, Apr. 1792, Dr Williams's Library, London.

[10] The copy is in the Pforzheimer Library, New York. It seems that Mary made her many marks and few written comments in the right margin of each page, and Elizabeth added a few marks in the left margin, and occasionally commented on her sister's remarks. Mary particularly marked out passages in which Wollstonecraft attacked the subordination of women, the way they were trivialized by denial of education and physical or mental exercise, and then blamed for their physical and mental weaknesses. Elizabeth seems to have been more interested in passages that depict women's life as a struggle to attain moral discipline and intellectual cultivation, thus fulfilling the divine plan for all humans. In general, Mary marked passages calling for radical, revolutionary change; Elizabeth marked passages emphasizing the degraded, almost hopeless condition of most women's lives. Occasionally the lines in the left margin extend before or after the passage of text marked off by the right-hand lines. At one point the right margin has the question, 'Do you [agree]?' At another point, where the text states that many women are intellectually superior to their husbands, the right margin has the inscription, 'A very common case', but another hand has written immediately below, 'Not at all'.

[11] *Love-Letters of Hays*, ed. Wedd, 5.

education &c ought, in my opinion, never to be pleaded (with the public) in excuse for defects of any importance, because if the writer has not sufficient strength of mind to overcome the common difficulties which lie in his way, nature seems to command him, with a very audible voice, to leave the task of instructing others to those who can.'[12] She condemned Hays's parade of approval by prominent men: 'Rest, on yourself—if your essays have merit they will stand alone, if not the shouldering up of Dr this or that will not long keep them from falling to the ground.'[13] After revisions Wollstonecraft found 'fewer of the super-latives exquisite, fascinating, &c, all of the feminine gender', than she expected, though some ideas were 'obscurely expressed', the result of the untrained woman writer's tendency to 'confusion of thought'.

The Hays sisters' *Letters and Essays, Moral, and Miscellaneous* was published early in 1793, though Mary Hays wrote most of it and her name alone appeared on the title-page. The Preface restates *A Vindica-tion*'s central argument that society subjugates women intellectually and then uses their resulting intellectual deficiencies to justify continued subjection. Hays does apologize for her intellectual weaknesses and disadvantages, but relates these to the general oppression of women that is being overcome in the larger revolution now taking place, to which her book aims to contribute. Like Hays's first book, *Letters and Essays* does so by merging conventionally 'feminine' and 'masculine' discourses. Its title associates it with the *belles-lettres* and it is epistolary and personal, miscellaneous and desultory—genres and modes long associated with women writers. Yet many of the pieces treat convention-ally masculine discourses.

For example, the letter 'To Mr. ——' continues Hays's debate with Wakefield and discusses a 'masculine' topic, the place of eloquence in the pulpit. Some argue that eloquence has no place in the pulpit because it is a kind of feigning, a form of personal display, and addresses the passions rather than reason. Hays argues that true elo-quence is sincere belief shaped to a particular situation and audience, it is legitimate personal display as the expression of a unique individual, and it properly addresses the passions in order to guide them. Her argument derives from the classical rhetoric of ethos, found in Aristotle, Cicero, and Quintilian, popularized in the late eighteenth century by

---

[12] Like most writers of her time, Wollstonecraft used the masculine pronouns as general ones where the antecedent could be either male or female.
[13] Mary Wollstonecraft to Mary Hays, 12 Nov. 1792, in *Collected Letters of Mary Wollstonecraft*, ed. Ralph M. Wardle (Ithaca, NY, 1979), 219.

Hugh Blair and other Enlightenment rhetoricians, and adapted by writers of Sensibility. She follows A. L. Barbauld's feminization of theology in 'Thoughts on the Devotional Taste' (1775) and argues that liberal Dissenters were too concerned over their reputation for 'enthusiasm' and 'unreason' and should now accept passion, desire, and even pleasure in religion and life.[14] Hays argues from reason and Scripture, the only authorities needed for discussing religious, theological, and ecclesiastical matters considered too difficult for women and 'common reasoners'. She takes up politics, denying Wakefield's concern that public worship leads to priestcraft and arguing that public worship unrestricted by the state produces social pluralism, toleration, and reconciliation—conventionally feminine values and practices but central to liberal Dissenting politics.

Hays also capitalizes on such themes in her twelfth and thirteenth pieces, on philosophical necessity and materialism, raising the possibility that the social and natural world 'produce' the individual, nullifying free will, moral and social duty, the deity, and life after death. This question divided liberal Dissenters just when they needed unity in their campaign for civic rights; by 1793 materialism and 'necessarianism' were also blamed for the French Revolution. Hays feminizes the question in several ways. In the twelfth piece, a letter to 'Amasia', she explains her acceptance of 'the doctrines of materialism and necessity' by stressing their consoling, inspiring, and edifying elements. She argues that God has endowed each individual with a sensibility upon which general and particular external circumstances impress a unique moral and intellectual being. She sees pleasure and pain as part of a divine system guaranteeing eternal pleasure through 'temperance, regularity, and self-denial'—virtues conventionally recommended to women but also required by professional men. Formally, Hays adopts a dialogical method, responding to points raised by her correspondent, writes clearly and directly, avoids digressions and scholastic intricacies, and uses references and quotations that would be within the compass of a literate woman—sermons, popular theological writing, poetry, and a translation of Erasmus. In the thirteenth piece she avoids her male correspondent's dismissive peremptoriness and suggests that a woman too may contribute to pursuit of truth. She uses authorities within the compass of a woman's education—poets, Wollstonecraft's

14 [Anna Lætitia Barbauld,] *Devotional Pieces, Compiled from the Psalms and the Book of Job; To Which Are Prefixed, Thoughts on the Devotional Taste, on Sects, and on Establishments* (London, 1775).

Vindication, and Hartley's *Theory of Man*—but insists that she has 'studied' the subject and is not arguing from mere 'inspiration' or '*intuitive* genius'. Against the objection that such a topic is inappropriate in a work of *belles-lettres* she argues that even the unlearned—many of whom are women—must consider all questions that bear upon their happiness. The feminized discourse of *belles-lettres*, popularizing learning, scholarship, and 'philosophy', is the appropriate way to do so.

Other pieces treat women's issues and concerns in relation to the public and political spheres. The second piece, an essay, develops her friend George Dyer's argument that women of sensibility are more in favour of political liberty than men are, and cites Catharine Macaulay Graham, Wollstonecraft, Barbauld, Ann Jebb, Helen Maria Williams, and Charlotte Smith. Hays argues that women are more detached from the present corrupt political system because they have no opportunity for public office. She goes on to consider Britain and the influence of the French Revolution, applying a conventionally 'feminine' line of practical optimism and opposition to extremes, conflict, and violence, while conducting Enlightenment criticism of social misery and 'the venal politics of the day', and citing a variety of 'philosophers' ancient and modern.

To justify this feminization of philosophy and politics, the following essay, on female education and domesticity, echoes Wollstonecraft in arguing that women kept in mental bondage will be seduced by court culture or contaminated by the vulgar, thus undermining bourgeois values and culture. Like Wollstonecraft, Hays aligns domestic and state politics, arguing that any arbitrary power creates 'helpless effeminacy'—a negative form of the feminine—for 'the only true grounds of power are reason and affection' (p. 23). Like Wollstonecraft, she denies that educating women unfits them for domestic duties and management. She closes by quoting Robert Robinson's claim in his *Political Catechism* that any 'science' may be 'reduced to a few first principles' for common readers; Hays extends this claim to include women.

Two other themes of women's education and influence are the novel and social converse. The novel was widely seen as a problem in social control of the increasing and unknown 'reading public', and especially women. Hays adopts the liberal argument that love of the marvellous is natural to the young and will lead from fiction to biography to philosophical, political, moral, and religious truth, and thus to the problems of real life. As part of the domestic economy and with parental guidance, novel-reading will reproduce not court culture but taste, understanding, and intellectual independence. The essay (XIV) on social converse deals with another field of cultural struggle and social conflict, often seen as a medium for enacting artificial social distinctions and power relations, and an obstacle to 'candour', or expression of the authentic self. Hays illustrates abuse of social converse with fictitious Theophrastan characters, such as the boring hypocrite, the superficial literary dictator, the pedantic sophist, the coxcomb, the cynic, and the newspaper politician, typifying a variety of professional men and their discourses. She represents the domestic affections, especially friendship, as the only escape from such abuses (pp. 199–200). True social converse, like true oratory in Hays's first letter, is domesticated and feminized.

On the other hand, the fiction in *Letters and Essays* is 'philosophical', like that written by men of the Enlightenment. The third piece, an essay on female education, is followed by three connected stories showing that love and rational religion, mediated by cultivated yet domestic women and feminized yet publicly useful men, can overcome the errors of courtly dissipation, petty bourgeois narrowness and hypocrisy, and excessive Enlightenment rationalism:

It is time for degraded woman to assert her right to reason, in this general diffusion of light and knowledge. The frivolity and voluptuousness, in which they have hitherto been educated, have had a large share in the general corruption of manners; this frivolity the sensible vindicator of our rights justly attributes to the entire dependence, in which we are trained. (p. 84)

Yet false subjectivity, or excessive 'sensibility', merely makes a woman selfish, as illustrated in the following two pieces, the essay on novel reading (VII) and its accompanying short story (VIII), in which a young woman developes Sentimental heroinism from reading too many novels and romances.

The following piece, another letter to 'Amasia', complements this story with 'portraits' of an ideally domesticated, professionalized, and complementary couple belonging to the gentry. Superior to 'vulgar prejudices', Hortensius educates his daughters and sons alike, while Hortensia is a female counterpart to her professionalized and feminized husband. This moral and social economy corresponds to the financial one: the family live within their income, thus avoiding recourse to courtly intrigue and patronage to offset extravagance. Their chief care is to train their children 'for the benefit of society, and for the glories of immortality'—a divinely sanctioned investment economy for the dissemination of bourgeois-genteel culture through society and the state, over time.

This vision of ideal cultural revolutionaries is followed by Elizabeth Hays's two stories, more narrowly didactic, socially conservative, and gloomy, with moralistic titles—'Cleora, or the Misery attending unsuitable Connections' and 'Josepha, or the pernicious Effects of early Indulgence'. 'Cleora' concludes that present society offers most women no career but marriage, yet youthful fancy creates delusions which actual husbands and married life cannot equal. By contrast, 'Josepha' concludes with a stirring exhortation to women of the Revolutionary decade:

In this age of light and liberty, may our bosoms be fired with a more worthy emulation! and in the reformation of manners so much talked about, and so loudly called for, let us catch the glorious enthusiasm, and take the lead!—If we could but unite in intention, great would be our power, and extensive our influence; the character of one sex has ever been found to affect that of the other . . . (p. 157)

The stories show two contrasting women—one in tune with Mary Hays's Revolutionary feminism, the other reminiscent of moralistic, conservative, and pessimistic conduct-books of previous decades.

The remaining pieces (XVII to XXII), two stories and four poems, are earlier work by Mary Hays, some of it already published. In 'A Fragment: In the Manner of the Old Romances', a baron's daughter has a premonitory dream-vision of the consequences of succumbing to desire. In 'The Hermit: An Oriental Tale', Zeibriel learns there is no domestic security and virtuous conduct under a despotic government, and he retires from society to instruct youth. The poems, 'An Invocation to the Nightingale', two sonnets, and 'Ode to a Bullfinch', are personal, expressive, and lyrical, representing the poet's sorrow, disillusionment with the world, and preference for reflective subjectivity and the domestic affections. Whereas the preceding pieces go beyond merely feminine Sensibility by feminizing philosophy, theology, and politics, these ones typify the Sentimental amateur belletrism found in magazines of the previous decades. They form a coda representing an earlier stage of their author's feminine consciousness—preliminary to Revolutionary feminism but subsumed in it, according to the pattern of intellectual and moral growth suggested in the pieces on female education and novel reading. Unlike the other pieces, the Sentimental ones are also monological, expressive, and lyrical rather than dialogical, so that the text as a whole suggests progress from the merely subjective and monological to the usefully social and dialogical, from pre-Revolutionary to Revolutionary consciousness, a dialectical relation of masculine and feminine in a class-based cultural revolution.

Readers recognized and appreciated this. George Dyer conveyed praise from William Frend and William Beloe.[15] The Hays' minister, Hugh Worthington, conveyed the approval of 'a *venerable* old critic'.[16] Another friend assured Hays that a hostile notice in the *English Review* must be by 'some narrow-hearted bigot, who is a sworn enemy to Mrs. Wollstonecraft and her disciples'.[17] Theophilus Lindsey, another leading Dissenter, praised it for combining masculine and feminine intellectual traits.[18] Her cousin the entrepreneur Benjamin Seymour, who had emigrated to America, showed the book to his friend Josiah Quincy in Boston, who saw Hays as one of a company led by Wollstonecraft in a general social and cultural reform.[19]

Reviewers were divided. The liberal *Analytical Review* praised Hays for 'exercising' the 'rights of woman, which have been of late so ably asserted by an enlightened female philosopher', and venturing 'beyond the boundaries which the tyranny of example and custom has prescribed to female writers' to explain 'to her female readers some of the leading arguments on philosophical or theological subjects' thereby helping them to the independence called for by Wollstonecraft. The *Critical Review* termed Hays 'a subaltern to Miss Wolstonecraft' and agreed that she 'has certainly the merit of having exercised her intellectual faculties with freedom, on important subjects not commonly studied by women', but dismissed her work as 'nothing more than a faint echo of the Priestleyan school'. Other critics were equally condescending. One told Hays not to disparage the feminine art of cookery—a point taken up in Elizabeth Hamilton's caricature of Hays in *Memoirs of Modern Philosophers*. Another warned that 'to be spinning webs of feeble reasoning' on philosophical subjects 'can neither make a woman valuable, nor amiable'. The *English Review* damned Hays for trying by her example 'to prove, that "woman possesses the same

[15] Letters from George Dyer to Mary Hays: 2 Dec. 1792 in the Pforzheimer Library, and 25 Aug. 1793 in *Love-Letters of Hays*, ed. Wedd, 226.

[16] Letters from Hugh Worthington to Mary Hays, 3 Sept. and 9 Dec. 1792, 21 May 1793, Dr Williams's Library.

[17] [John?] Evans to Mary Hays, in *Love-Letters of Hays*, ed. Wedd, 222–3.

[18] Theophilus Lindsey to Mary Hays, 15 Apr. 1793, Dr Williams's Library.

[19] Benjamin Seymour to Mary Hays, Boston, 21 Dec. 1795, Pforzheimer Library.

powers as man"—that (as she modestly expresses herself) "there is no sexual character"'. Thus 'the pupils of Mrs. Wollstonecraft actually invalidate, by these specimens of themselves, the very doctrines which they are labouring to establish'.[20]

Hays was already moving away from the liberal Dissent of Robinson, Worthington, and Disney (to whom she dedicated *Letters and Essays*) towards the rationalism and materialism of the 'English Jacobins', led by William Godwin. She wrote to him in October 1794, saying that she had been struck by a summary of his *Political Justice* in the *Analytical Review*, by Frend's opinion that the book would ' "in a few years operate as great a change in the political sentiments of our nation as Locke's famous treatise on government" ', and by Godwin's political novel, *Things As They Are; or, The Adventures of Caleb Williams*, which 'excited in my mind a sensibility almost convulsive!' Following Godwin's own condemnation of 'the artificial forms which have served but to corrupt and enslave society', she asked to borrow *Political Justice* because she could not afford to buy it.[21] Godwin was receptive to intellectual enquirers, men or women. Cautiously generous, he loaned her one volume at a time and opened a philosophical and personal correspondence with her.

As with Eccles, Robinson, Frend, and others, she adopted an attitude of feminine independence. She found his main principles 'demonstrative as the theorems & problems of Euclid, requiring only patience to follow the series, & comprehension to take in the result, to ensure conviction!' Yet 'the feelings of my heart sometimes revolted against the decisions of my judgement', and she resisted his condemnation of the domestic affections as an irrational prejudice. Following liberal Dissenters such as Disney and Price, she argues that the passions, rather than being an obstacle to happiness, are the source of desire for the good. She concedes that the passions cause moral conflict, but she argues that this is evidence for life after death and the doctrine of the fortunate fall. She apologizes for weak argument: 'The education of women, like the boasted polish of the ancients, extends not beyond the cultivation of the taste: This renders a habit of severe investigation & abstract attention difficult to be attain'd.' But she needed intellectual

[20] *Analytical Review*, 16 (Aug. 1793), 464; *Critical Review*, NS 8 (Aug. 1793), 433–4; *British Critic*, 1 (Aug. 1793), 463; *English Review*, 22 (Oct. 1793), 255–6.
[21] Mary Hays to William Godwin, 14 Oct. 1794, in *Love-Letters of Hays*, ed. Wedd, 227–9.

'exercise' to counter the 'too exquisite sensibility' that is 'foster'd by the delicacy of female education, & those habits of privacy & retirement which afford the imagination too much leisure to seduce by its enchantments, or subdue by its imperious tyranny!'[22] By the spring of 1795 she was taking a more personal tone, suggesting that Godwin, with all the advantages of the the 'wise *man*', can afford the philosophical optimism set forth in *Political Justice*. In May 1795 she had Godwin to tea with other 'English Jacobin' Dissenters, including Frend and Dyer, whetting her appetite for the larger public and political sphere available to them but closed to her.

She also identified with a woman who had entered that sphere to her cost. In July Hays wrote to Godwin echoing Wollstonecraft's sociology of women's oppression. She deplored restriction of women to 'domestic avocations & the vanity of varying external ornaments & hanging drapery on a smooth block', though she herself did not 'despise, & regularly practise, the necessary employments of my sex', 'But all these are insufficient to engross, to fill up, the active, aspiring, mind!' Excluded from professional and public life, women unwilling to marry for mere security 'remain insulated beings': 'The strong feelings & strong energies which properly directed, in a field sufficiently wide, might—ah! what might they not have aided?—forced back, & pent up, ravage & destroy the mind that generated them!' The last few sentences could apply to Wollstonecraft, by now a victim of her own feminist principles of Revolutionary vanguardist sexuality and conjugality. They could also apply to Hays's sense of being marginalized even by English Jacobin 'philosophy': 'Philosophy, it is said, should regulate the feelings, but it has added fervour to mine—What are passions, but another name for powers?'[23] Later the correspondence turned to issues of gender and sexuality. Hays condemns some of Godwin's favourite writers, such as Swift, Voltaire, Rousseau, and Sterne, for their courtly morality, arguing after Wollstonecraft that such ideas have produced 'two classes of victims', those for whom marriage is merely a form of prostitution in which sexual favours are exchanged for material security and those who reject marriage and are forced by social convention to remain celibate and deny their natural sexual desires. She gives herself as an example of the latter.[24] Accordingly, she has left her family home, where she had 'been sheltered too much like a hot-house plant',

[22] Letter of 7 Dec. 1794, Pforzheimer Library.
[23] Letter of 28 July 1795, Pforzheimer Library.
[24] Letters of 1 Oct. and 13 Oct. 1795, Pforzheimer Library.

to pursue an independent career as a writer. Later events suggest that she also hoped to join the sexual culture of the political and intellectual avant-garde.

Godwin was struck by Hays's ability to particularize 'philosophy' in her own experience and to generalize that experience in a critique of 'things as they are'. This was the form of novels written by himself and friends such as Thomas Holcroft, and he encouraged her to attempt such a work.[25] Just then Wollstonecraft re-entered Hays's life, recovering from an attempted suicide and about to publish a politicized autobiographical travel narrative, *Letters Written During a Short Residence in Norway, Sweden, and Denmark*. Hays brought her two literary-philosophical idols together at tea on 8 January 1796, with Holcroft. But soon she herself was disappointed in attempting to form the amorous egalitarian conjugality called for in her and Wollstonecraft's Revolutionary feminism. For some time she had secretly loved William Frend. Early in January she revealed her feeling to him, but it was not reciprocated. Hays immediately analysed for Godwin the nature of her passion and the social causes of its failure. She acknowledged that the opposition of reason and passion 'roused my mind into energy' and blamed the rejection of her love on the sexual double standard:

Men are by this means render'd sordid & dissolute in their pleasures; their affections blunted & their feelings petrified: they are incapable of satisfying the heart of a woman of sensibility & virtue—supposing such a woman has the power (which I believe is not often the case) of fixing, in any degree, their attentions!—Half the sex, then, are the infamous, wretched, victims of brutal instinct—the other half—if they sink not into mere frivolity & insipidity—are sublimated into a sort of—what shall I call them?—refined, romantic, unfortunate, factitious, beings, who cannot bear to act, for the sake of the present moment, in a manner, that should expose them to complicated, inevitable, evils—evils, that will, almost, infallibly overwhelm them with misery & regret![26]

She told Frend she intended to write fictional 'confessions' as self-therapy, 'to engage my mind, to sluice off its impressions', but also as social critique: 'A philosophical delineation of the errors of passion, of the mischief's of yielding to the illusions of the imagination, might be useful.'[27] She told Godwin she intended to write a 'philosophical

[25] Letter of 5 Nov. 1795, Pforzheimer Library.
[26] Letter partly dated 5 Feb., postmarked 6 Feb., Pforzheimer Library.
[27] Letter of 5 Feb., Pforzheimer Library.

romance' but thought that the model he proposed to her was beyond her powers:

I am a woman, I mean by this, that education has given me a sexual character.—It is true, I have risen superior to the generality of my sex, I am not a mere fine lady, a domestic drudge, or a doll of fashion, I can think, write, reason, converse with men & scholars, & despise [or 'despite'] many petty, feminine, prejudices. But I have not the talents for a legislator or a reformer of the world, I have still many shrinking delicacies & female foibles, that unfit me for rising to arduous heights.[28]

Yet she also claims that these restricted opportunities gave women knowledge of the psychology of love unavailable to 'philosophers'.

She was using writing—both fiction and letters—to create the kind of identity and relationship she felt unjustly denied to her by false social values and even by Godwin's 'philosophy'. For she felt frustrated by Godwin's 'philosophical' approach to her, her novel, and her letters, and took different tacks to make him more sympathetic. She fell into complaints of her reduced circumstances, revealed that she had been proselytized by some English Kantians, indulged in philosophical teasing and coquetry, assumed the familiar tone of confidante, and accused him of disliking Elizabeth Hamilton merely because she lacked youth and beauty.[29] She felt inhibited in company, flustered by attention, and incapable of chit-chat or repartee, even when she prepared carefully and really exerted herself. Like many of her class she could not express her sense of authentic subjectivity in available social customs, conventions, and practices. As a woman she blamed her difficulty on gender differences produced by decadent court culture and mistakenly appropriated by cultural revolutionaries—even those like Godwin.

By early May she completed her manuscript as a two-volume novel entitled 'Henrietta Courtney'. Godwin praised its 'energy of feeling, & ardor of expression' but thought it lacked 'story' and a plausible 'hero', resulting in the 'radical defect' of the narrator-heroine's subjectivity dominating the text and stifling the reader's interest.[30] Hays replied that 'my story is *too real*', that the 'hero' is addressed 'to the stubborn heart, which I sought in vain to melt, [by] a just, but far from an exaggerated, picture, of its own cruel & inflexible severity', and that to

---

[28] Letter postmarked 20 Feb. 1796, Pforzheimer Library.
[29] Letters of 23 Mar., 4 Apr., 29 Apr., and 3 May 1796, Pforzheimer Library
[30] Hays quoting Godwin, in her letter of 11 May, Pforzheimer Library.

interest the reader a novel had to portray authentic subjective experience.[31] When Godwin suggested readers would find the heroine's unrequited passion uninteresting, Hays replied that it 'is a proof of a lively & strong imagination, of a sanguine, an enterprising, an ardent, an unconquerable, spirit—It is strength, tho' ill directed'. She suggests that Godwin would see a man's unrequited passion, such as Petrarch's for Laura, as the basis of great literature, whereas a woman's passion is supposed to be insufficiently interesting: 'Its existence is in the imagination, rather than in the senses—I doubt whether fruition might not be its grave.'[32] Passion comes from the imagination, which flourishes, for good and ill, because of unnatural and unjust restraints on women's education, experience, opportunities, and sexuality. Yet these very restraints, by forcing the self inward, nourish 'creative powers'. Thus she is confident that her 'manner' rather than the 'story' will make her heroine's passion 'interesting'. In defending her novel Hays connects feminist politics and aesthetics by implying that women may not be disabled from sublime experience by 'retirement' in domestic life but rather empowered subjectively and thus artistically.

Memoirs of Emma Courtney came out from Godwin's own publisher, Robinsons, in November 1796. Janet Todd argues that in Hays and Wollstonecraft 'the literary nature of the feminine ideology of sensibility is clearest' and autobiography and fiction 'most scandalously intertwined'.[33] Yet Hays's novel, like Wollstonecraft's unfinished *The Wrongs of Woman; or, Maria* and most English Jacobin novels, generalizes the autobiographical into political critique, validated however by the sense of autobiography inscribed in the fiction. Not as overtly political as Godwin's *Things As They Are*, Holcroft's *Anna St. Ives* (1792), or Wollstonecraft's *The Wrongs of Woman*, Hays's novel is, like them, a 'philosophical romance', or fictionalization of 'philosophy'— the rationalist social and political criticism held by many to be responsible for the Revolution. 'Philosophy' in this sense was a masculine discourse and Hays aimed to novelize and thus feminize it, thereby resolving what she saw, from her correspondence with Godwin and her rejection by Frend, as a devaluing of women's intellectual culture and therefore a dangerous separation of masculine and feminine

---

[31] Letter of 11 May 1796, Pforzheimer Library.
[32] Undated letter, probably May 1796, Pforzheimer Library.
[33] Janet Todd, *The Sign of Angellica: Women, Writing, and Fiction 1660–1800* (London, 1989), 237.

discourses within the professional middle-class cultural revolution. As a Revolutionary feminist she aims to interfuse these discourses to create a more effective alliance of men and women 'philosophers' in the cultural revolution, anticipating a similar project by Romantic writers in the Revolutionary aftermath.

Accordingly, the Preface of *Emma Courtney* uses the language of Enlightenment materialism and quotes Helvétius to argue that the most 'interesting' and 'useful' fictions, such as those of Ann Radcliffe and Godwin, delineate strong passions, 'by which the philosopher may calculate the powers of the human mind, and learn the springs which set it in motion'. Yet a 'more universal sentiment', love, has been 'hackneyed' in novels and is 'consequently more difficult to treat with any degree of originality'. Doing so requires frank realism drawn from personal experience, representing 'a human being, loving virtue while enslaved by passion, liable to the mistakes and weaknesses of our fragile nature'. This is a 'hazardous experiment' but 'calculated to operate as a *warning*, rather than as an example'. Formal and thematic emphasis on the heroine requires 'a simple story' and subordinate hero—'it was not *his* memoirs that I professed to write'. In the political climate of 1796 such 'philosophical' and artistic aims would be viewed with suspicion or hope, and therefore 'this production of an active mind' is presented to the vanguard of cultural revolution—'the feeling and the thinking few'.

The novel's opening narrative frame presents a split in 'feeling and thinking', however, with two letters from the narrator-heroine showing her as woman of feeling one moment, 'philosopher' the next. In the first letter Emma protests at having her 'affecting narrative' torn from her heart in order to save her correspondent, the young Augustus Harley, from the mental torments she has suffered over love for his father. The letter's broken sentences, numerous dashes, and rhetorical questions textualize her distress. But the second letter calmly sets forth the necessitarian philosophy informing the narrative to follow, and exhorts Augustus to philosophize his experience and live his philosophy, after her example, for reason and passion are connected in a chain: 'Sensation generates interest, interest passion, passion forces attention, attention supplies the powers, and affords the means of attaining its end.' A similar concatenation forms the individual: 'Every man is born with sensation, with the aptitude of receiving impressions; the force of those impressions depends on a thousand circumstances, over which he has little power; these circumstances form the mind, and determine the future character.' But she rejects determinism: 'We are all the creatures of education' but 'chance, or accident', has a great role because 'one strong affection, one ardent incitement, will turn, in an instant, the whole current of our thoughts, and introduce a new train of ideas and associations'. Thus only a physically, emotionally, and intellectually emancipated life will expose the individual to the variety of 'impressions' and resulting passions and ideas necessary to attain the 'truth' that empowers the individual ethically and politically. This is the argument for the potential centrality of women's experience and 'philosophy' that Hays had worked out in her correspondence with Godwin. Appropriately, then, Emma's sentimental first letter is subsumed in the philosophical second letter as she declares, 'Learn, then, from the incidents of my life, entangled with those of his to whom you owe your existence, a more striking and affecting lesson than abstract philosophy can ever afford.' Feminine discourse, like female experience, not only has power of its own, but superior power.

The following 'memoirs' show how Emma's female experience made her the woman of feeling and 'female philosopher' of the opening letters. The only child of a 'dissipated, extravagant, and profligate' gentleman and the heiress of a 'rich trader'—the familiar union of rank and money—she lost her mother at birth and was raised by her aunt and uncle, mercantile middle-class people retired to the country. Mrs Melmoth's reading of 'old romances' made her sentimental and religiose, a trivial but decisive circumstance for Emma: 'the tenderness of this worthy woman generated in my infant disposition that susceptibility, that lively propensity to attachment, to which I have through life been a martyr' (vol. i, ch. 3). Her aunt's relation of oriental tales—widely considered extravagant and piquant—'excited vivid emotions' in Emma, making her 'vain and self-willed', the heroine of her own imagination as constructed by the romances she read. Consequently she found boarding-school, with its rules, petty competitiveness, and rote learning, an 'exile': 'home appeared to me to be the Eden from which I was driven', and she retreated to romantic fantasy (ch. 4). Return 'home' was clouded by her uncle's death, and her aunt's excessive mourning, due to lack of intellectual resources, left the children 'to run wild'. Emma's 'avidity for books' grew: 'I subscribed to a circulating library, and frequently read, or rather devoured—little careful in the selection—from ten to fourteen novels in a week' (ch. 5).

Emma's father became alarmed at her excessive 'sensibility' and brought her once a week to his town house to read and mix in society. He countered her 'passion for adventurous tales' (ch. 6) with history, beginning with Plutarch's *Lives* (ch. 7). This key text in eighteenth-century classical republicanism inspired her 'with republican ardour', 'a high-toned philosophy', and 'the virtues of patriotism'.[34] In contrast, she found her father's companions mere 'gallants', 'coxcombs', and free thinkers. Modern history further disgusted her with accounts of 'corrupt, luxurious, licentious, perfidious, mercenary' societies and governments and she sought refreshment 'in the fairer regions of poetry and fiction' (ch. 8). She then took up the unfeminine subject of controversial theology and found that her 'mind began to be emancipated . . . I reasoned freely, endeavoured to arrange and methodize my opinions, and to trace them fearlessly through all their consequences; while from exercising my thoughts with freedom, I seemed to acquire new strength and dignity of character'. Reading Descartes inspired her with 'a passion for metaphysical enquiries', but Rousseau's *La nouvelle Héloïse* 'fell into my hands' and 'the impression made on my mind was never to be effaced, producing 'a long chain of consequences, that will continue to operate till the day of my death' (ch. 8).

Emma's sense of subjective superiority was reinforced by her precocious sentimental and intellectual development and left unrestrained after the death of her aunt and her father. But her material resources did not match her sense of spiritual nobility and she was forced to live with a paternal uncle and his family:

Cruel prejudices!—I exclaimed—hapless woman! Why was I not educated for commerce, for a profession, for labour? Why have I been rendered feeble and delicate by bodily constraint, and fastidious by artificial refinement? Why are we bound, by the habits of society, as with an adamantine chain? Why do we suffer ourselves to be confined within a magic circle, without daring, by a magnanimous effort, to dissolve the barbarous spell? (ch. 11)

The 'magic spell' again stands for the invisible power of ideology over the mind and body of the individual. Emma found her relatives the Mortons indolent and supercilious, but two interesting if different men visited there—Mr Montague, the courtly son of a local 'medical gentleman', and Mr Francis, a 'philosopher'. Warned that Francis has no estate or ' "lucrative profession" ', Emma declared that she considered him ' "as a *philosopher*, and not as a *lover*" '. Their philosophical

---

[34] Harold T. Parker, *The Cult of Antiquity and the French Revolutionaries: A Study in the Development of the Revolutionary Spirit* (Chicago, 1937).

correspondence (using copious extracts from the letters between Hays and Godwin) awakened in Emma's mind 'a train of interesting reflections, and my spirits became tranquillized'.

This completes the first movement of the novel. The second opens with Emma's introduction to Mrs Harley, who treated her with the 'maternal love' she had never known (ch. 16). Montague complacently offered his hand but was rejected and vowed vengeance (ch. 17). Then Emma fell in love with Mrs Harley's absent son Augustus by contemplating a portrait miniature of him. Emma retrospectively analyses this extraordinary process:

> Cut off from the society of mankind, and unable to expound my sensations, all the strong affections of my soul seemed concentrated to a single point. Without being conscious of it, my grateful love for Mrs Harley had, already, by a transition easy to be traced by a philosophic mind, transferred itself to her son. He was the St Preux, the Emilius of my sleeping and waking reveries. (ch. 18)

The heroes of Rousseau's novels are read into real life by an imagination insufficiently anchored in that life. Ironically, Montague then brought Emma and Harley together, for courtly intrigue is self-defeating. In an episode from Gothic romance, Montague abducted Emma 'on a dark and stormy night'. But when the coach overturned Emma showed herself a philosopher by her coolness (ch. 19) and was aided by a stranger who turned out to be the injured Harley. Nursed back to health by her, he called her ' "My sister!—my friend!" ' and Mrs Harley considered her ' "the meritorious child of her affections" ' (ch. 21). Herself deprived of domestic affections, Emma is too susceptible to these appeals. For some months they all lived together in the kind of domesticity for which Emma had long yearned (ch. 22), but the Mortons considered Emma's reputation ruined and banished her (ch. 23). Montague offered to 'protect' her, but she rejected such chivalry (' "I should be mortified . . . by having it supposed, that I stood in need of a *champion*" ') and confessed that she loved Harley in mind and body: ' "I respected his virtues and attainments, and, by a too easy transition—at length—loved his person" ' (ch. 24). Moral attachment leads to sexual desire, the mind affects the body, in the erotic ideology of the political and cultural avant-garde of the 1790s. The same pattern is seen in the work of Wollstonecraft and the relationships in the circles she and Helen Maria Williams frequented in Paris and, to some extent, London.

Emma then confessed her love in a letter to Harley himself, asserting her right to desire despite social convention, quoting Wollstonecraft's *Vindication* and Holcroft's novel of revolutionary egalitarianism, *Anna St. Ives*, and claiming the sanction of ' "nature, reason, and virtue" '— the professional middle-class ideology of authentic selfhood legitimated by a transcendental order. But she learned that conditions on Harley's inheritance, standing for the power of property supporting ' "custom and prescription" ', prevented him from reciprocating (ch. 25). Emma found relief in writing for Francis a philosophical rationale for her declaration to Harley and demanding from Francis philosophical recognition and empowerment of her female 'nature' (based on Hays's letter to Godwin of 28 July 1795). After a vague answer from Harley, Emma repeated her confession of love, though admitting that this ' "*is not what I would recommend to general imitation*" ' (ch. 27). The italics register awareness of growing reaction in the mid-1790s against Revolutionary feminism and avant-garde amorous culture. Emma moved to London as tutor for her cousin, Mrs Denbeigh; with rooms and a profession of her own she now had social independence as well as independence of desire.

The second volume opens by reminding the reader of the novel's narrative frame with a note from Emma to young Augustus Harley restating her educative purpose: to trace her passions 'from the seeds by which they have been generated, through all their extended consequences', enabling him to learn 'to regulate and to subdue' his own. The following chapters analyse her situation in relation to the general condition of women, mingling autobiography with philosophy, echoing Wollstonecraft, quoting masters of Sensibility such as Richardson, Sterne, and Rousseau, and referring to English Jacobin political theory and fiction. She believed that, improved by philosophy, she could rise above the debased character of woman to be Harley's 'friend'. The reflections, dialogues, and letters in this part of the novel exemplify the Revolutionary feminist crusade to make 'philosophy' more humanly comprehensive, socially useful, and politically effective. Two letters illustrate Emma's struggle (vol. ii, chs. 3 and 4), and an extended dialogue with a number of courtly characters applies her 'philosophy' in a social critique of war, crime, slavery, social hierarchy, and the oppression of women (vol. ii, ch. 5).

Echoing Hays's correspondence with Godwin, Emma traces her plight to the divided society that has produced her divided being: ' "I am neither a philosopher, nor a heroine—*but a woman, to whom education has given a sexual character.*'' This does not mean, however, that she and other women are trapped in their socially produced subjection, able at best to philosophize about it: she can unite herself ' "to a man of worth" ' and have their offspring reproduce ' "our mingled virtues and talents" ', eventually encompassing, ' "like spreading circles on the peaceful bosom of the smooth and expanded lake— the whole sensitive and rational creation" '. Hays often uses water imagery to express female 'nature' and power, but the passage also merges her various intellectual and cultural influences. Hays's Dissenting background is seen in Emma's dedication to self-improvement and usefulness. The plot of romantic comedy, as appropriated by the Sentimental discourse of merit, is seen in Emma's wish to reproduce her and Harley's 'mingled virtues and talents' over time, through their children. Her Revolutionary feminism is seen in her insistence not only on women's right to intellectual and erotic desire but on the philosophic, and even revolutionary character of such desire. For Emma's declaration of rights envisages a global revolution originating in an authentic and avant-garde relationship of domestic affection. Emma can escape from oppression by using the very 'sensibility' that keeps women subject and that is used to justify such subjection. This escape relies on neither Godwinian 'political justice' nor Wollstonecraft's activist feminism but on the rational 'charity' of liberal Dissenters such as William Frend—the occasion of the novel and the actual addressee of Emma's letters to Harley. A further letter sets forth a feminist philosophy of love, combining philosophical argumentation with conventionally 'feminine' forms such as the lover's complaint and the self-vindication against what Emma suspected was a residual ideology of courtly woman in Harley's desire (vol. ii, ch. 7). She goes on to construct a Revolutionary feminist vision of progressive domesticity, with woman as custodian of the authentic domestic life that grounds the civic life conducted and experienced by men.

Emma herself had 'yet to learn', however, 'that those who have courage to act upon advanced principles, must be content to suffer moral martyrdom'. When told Harley had been married to another she turned again for a writing cure to Francis, based on letters between Hays and Godwin in early 1796. These are more emotional and stylistically disturbed than the letters to Harley, which exemplify the fusion of feeling and reason in feminizing an otherwise masculine discourse to serve women's experience, subjectivity, and knowledge. This revolutionary marriage of discourses then breaks down into the

expressivity of Emma's letter to Francis and the excessively philosophical tone and style of his reply. Emma admits, however, that his letter
'roused me from the languor into which I was sinking', and her long
reply is a closely argued feminist self-vindication (vol. ii, ch. 12). Like
Wollstonecraft and Hays, she attributes the 'miserable' condition of
women to the repression of female desire, 'from chastity having been
considered a sexual virtue'—for women, not men:

'Men are thus rendered sordid and dissolute in their pleasures . . . the simplicity
of modest tenderness loses its charm; they become incapable of satisfying the
heart of a woman of sensibility and virtue.—Half the sex, then, are the
wretched, degraded, victims of brutal instinct: the remainder, if they sink not
into mere frivolity and insipidity, are sublimed into a sort of—(what shall I call
them?)—refined, romantic, factitious, unfortunate, beings . . . '[35]

The letter goes on to justify female passion as a form of the same
energy that animates men in the public, political sphere. Passion is a
form of power, but in a society dominated by decadent court culture
women are rendered creatures of sensibility; sensibility generates passion; passion is (subjective) power; but society then denies women any
outlet for this power, while acknowledging and even encouraging
its destructive expression by men in political ambition, conflict, and
conquest.

This exchange between Emma and Francis ends the novel's second,
central movement and completes the novel's statement of Hays's
Revolutionary feminism. This differs from Wollstonecraft's feminism
in emphasizing less the professional and civic potential of women's
subjective being and more the expression of that being in erotic and
intellectual equality with men, as the basis for authentic domestic
relations. Henceforth the novel's emphasis shifts from subjectivity to
story.

This shift is signalled by Emma's illness. It was a novelistic cliché
that mental conflict produces bodily disease, but Hays gives the device
philosophical form according to the epistemology of Sensibility.
During the winter, emblematically 'severe and cold', Emma saw
Harley again when his mother contracted a fatal illness (vol. ii, ch. 14).
Again emblematically, Emma and Harley met by accident in the
library during a lightning storm, when she justified her ' "extravagance" ' and ' "false and romantic" ' views to him as ' "the ardent
excesses of a generous mind" ' (vol. ii, ch. 15). She pleaded for

<hr>

[35] Compare Hays's letter of 5 Feb. 1796, quoted above.

friendship but he left her. Montague reappeared but Emma clung to her narrow independence. While visiting London she was again shocked by the fate of women without means or protection, degraded by courtly erotic culture masquerading as modern chivalry; but when she lost her small financial independence she herself chose marriage as security and accepted Montague's offer. Experienced novel readers would recognize this as a false ending, and the next chapter tells how a man thrown from his horse was brought to Emma and turned out to be Harley. Emma, following Wollstonecraft's suggestion that women could practise medicine, had assisted her husband in his profession and learned enough to care for Harley. Absorbed in her task even to the exclusion of her own maternal duties, she heard a delirious Harley confess his remorse and consign his own son to her care. But Emma summoned the self-discipline gained from reflection: 'I banished the *woman* from my heart . . . *affection had converted me into a heroine!*' (vol. ii, ch. 21). In a conflict between the woman of sensibility and the professionalized consciousness constructed by 'reason' and 'virtue', the latter wins out. Appropriately, Harley then died confessing his love for Emma.

An illness again punctuated Emma's ensuing subjective struggle. She adopted Harley's son Augustus, angering her husband, and his character deteriorated. After seducing Emma's servant and possibly murdering her child he killed himself, leaving Emma a remorseful letter and his estate. Independent at last, she fondly watched her daughter Emma and young Augustus, who believed themselves brother and sister, turn into the ideal complementary man and woman of Emma's progressive social vision. Emma hoped their union would achieve the ideal domesticity she had longed for, but little Emma died just before becoming a woman. This event seems to contradict the stated revolutionary optimism of the novel, but the delay in realizing Emma's vision of avant-garde conjugality even beyond the children's generation could reflect Hays's doubts about the imminence of domestic and social revolution expressed in Wollstonecraft's *The Wrongs of Woman* and other English Jacobin works of the mid-1790s. Furthermore, her daughter's death leaves Emma in the position of mentor to young Harley, a reversal of the usual gendering of such a relationship and a situation Hays intended to represent as an intermediate stage between obsolete court society and a fully feminized civil society of the future, similar to that called for by Williams in her Revolutionary prose epic.

Thus the novel closes with Emma's last address to Augustus, whom she calls 'my more than son': 'I have laid bare my mind before you, that the experiments which have been made upon it may be beneficial to yours!' Because of systemic injustice rather than personal failings she has been disappointed in the 'passions of [her] youth', her 'rational plans of usefulness', and 'the darling hopes of maternal pride and fondness': 'Hitherto there seems to have been something strangely wrong in the constitutions of society—a lurking poison that spreads its contagion far and wide—a canker at the root of private virtue and private happiness . . . a Circean cup that lulls into a fatal intoxication.' Disease and poison were familiar figures for the invisible but deadly power of ideology as false consciousness, and the allusion to Circe gives a specifically erotic character to this power. Thus 'moral martyr-dom' may be the fate of the philosophical vanguard who, 'daring to trace, to their springs, errors the most hoary, and prejudices the most venerated, emancipate the human mind from the trammels of superstition, and teach it, *that its true dignity and virtue, consist in being free*'. Since Emma has carried out this project in her memoirs, she is implicitly of this vanguard. She has also contributed to the 'spread of truth' as the Godwin circle recommended and as they dramatized in their novels—by individual communication.[36] As a result of her risky experiment in confession Emma hopes to see in Augustus, 'the son of my affections', another Harley but one who has 'escaped from the tyranny of the passions, restored to reason, to the vigor of his mind, to self controul, to the dignity of active, intrepid virtue'—code words for progressive professionalized subjectivity. Emma looks forward to death with no hope of immortality except through her revolutionary legacy as an exemplary female philosopher.

Working with the materials of the Sentimental novel as developed by women novelists such as Charlotte Smith and reconstructed by English Jacobin novelists such as Holcroft and Godwin, Hays produced an experimental and powerful representation of a major issue in the cultural revolution—the social construction and reconstruction of the individual subject, as both subjectivity and subject of the state. The novel is 'autobiographical' but this is less important than Hays's use of the novel form to generalize, politicize, theorize, and finally revolution-ize her self and experience, not as raw data but already constructed by what she recognized years earlier, in her letters to Eccles, to be a novelization of self and society that served class and gender interests

---

[36] Gary Kelly, *English Fiction of the Romantic Period 1789–1830* (London, 1989), 41.

not hers, and thus profoundly self-alienating. For Hays and the other English Jacobins, 'philosophy', or the critical method intrinsic to professional work, along with a particular social critique, offered liberation from this reproduction of the hegemonic order in the individual self, often figured as the widespread cultural practice of novel reading.

Yet novel and philosophy were not only at opposite ends of the discursive order but differentiated by gender and class. To bring them together was a revolutionary act, a transformation of the discursive order, thereby enabling the subject in both senses to be rewritten. This was the task undertaken by Godwin and Holcroft in their novels; for Hays this move was doubly revolutionary since she would also be reconciling a gender difference retained—wrongly, according to Revolutionary feminism—by professional middle-class culture. Godwin joined novel and philosophy to disseminate his political thought more widely to the 'reading public', and he integrated his philosophical anarchism, materialist epistemology, and necessitarianism into the novel both by plotting a 'logical' connection between circumstances, character, and action and by using language that generalizes the individual situation to 'things as they are'—his novel's main title. Holcroft, who collaborated in the construction of Godwin's political theory, had the same aim in his epistolary novel *Anna St. Ives*, but he developed his 'philosophy' more through dialogue and epistolary exchange, thus producing a form more open and dialogical than Godwin's, and closer to genres and practices conventionally ascribed to women writers. Hays's novel combines Godwin's form of the pseudo-memoir with Holcroft's use of epistolary polyvocalism and philosophical dialogues.

In terms of conventional gendering of discourse, then, it could be argued that Hays feminizes Godwin's novel form and masculinizes Holcroft's to construct her own, Revolutionary feminist version of the English Jacobin novel, or 'philosophical romance'. To exhibit a 'female philosopher' as protagonist was already to go beyond Holcroft and Godwin, and doubly scandalous in relation to the gendering of discourse and culture. But Emma Courtney's career also shows how the construction of femininity according to court culture contains within itself the genesis of rebellion against it. Hays exhibits a woman constructed by circumstance and romance-reading to be a mere 'heroine', but whose experience of the gap between 'romance' and 'things as they are' then generates a new, political consciousness, reconstructing her as a social critic and social visionary, or 'philosopher' in the precise sense of the term used in the Revolution debate. This is the novel's message of revolutionary hope—that the internalization of 'things as they are' inevitably produces the conditions, first subjective and then social and political, for their revolutionary transformation.

Yet Emma remains powerless to change 'things as they are' and is left with only a transposed revolutionary hope that young Augustus, 'the son of my affections', will escape 'from the tyranny of the passions' intrinsic to court culture and return 'to reason, to the vigor of his mind, to self controul, to the dignity of active, intrepid virtue!'—or professional middle-class subjective autonomy and ethical practice. Hays's Revolutionary feminist vision seems to fail by leaving Emma's legacy as 'philosopher' to a man and not expressly to other women. But this feminism aimed for the emancipation of women as essential to the professional middle-class cultural revolution, for only if Revolutionary feminism were incorporated in the cultural revolution could that revolution purge its remaining courtly elements and thus succeed at some time in the future, precisely through works such as the *Memoirs of Emma Courtney*.

The novel's main formal problems are those of all English Jacobin novels—first to represent convincingly the necessary genesis and growth of revolutionary consciousness in a pre-revolutionary situation and, second, to suggest that this representation has general application. Yet convincing presentation of individual subjectivity, or psychological realism, conflicts with making this individual representative. Like the other English Jacobin novelists, Hays works hard to elaborate her protagonist's subjectivity, by several related devices. First there is the expressive first-person confessional narrative mode, as one side of a dialogue between a woman and a man she loves not erotically but with the 'domestic affections'. This dialogue is reinforced by letters to the same man and to another who has a different relationship to the protagonist. Then there is weakening of the plot of life-story centred on failed courtship, though the fact that the heroine does the courting defamiliarizes the hackneyed form and opens the way for a repetitive form of lover's complaint in the central movement of the novel. The relentless and deliberately painful expression of the heroine's frustrated subjectivity derives from that in Frances Sheridan's *Sidney Biddulph* and Charlotte Smith's novels and anticipates that of later novels of passion such as Mary Brunton's *Self-Control* (1810) and *Discipline* (1814) and Lady Caroline Lamb's *Glenarvon* (1816) through to late-Romantic novels such as Charlotte Brontë's *Villette*.

In *Emma Courtney* representation of subjectivity *in extremis* is relieved by occasional scenes of social satire and multiple dialogue, but these serve to diversify the characterization of the heroine and by contrast further emphasize the subjective power exhibited through her confessions. More important are the numerous passages of 'philosophic' subjectivity, showing the protagonist's ability to go beyond conventional limits of the feminine but indicating the cost of this transgression in divided selfhood. The division is clearly indicated in language and style, seen in difference between the opening two letters and in the recurring contrast between the heroine's language and style of personal complaint and those of her 'philosophizing'. To point this contrast Hays takes it to an excess that itself illustrates the dangers of such division. The heroine's language of feeling is almost hackneyed in its adoption of familiar tropes of Sensibility; her philosophical language, from Helvétius's and Godwin's materialism, verges at times on jargon. These extremes indicate a lack of self-coherence that is, the novel argues, the cultural revolutionary's inescapable condition in a pre-revolutionary situation. Furthermore, the heroine's extremes of language and reiteration of her misery hint at near loss of formal control by the author. With the evidently autobiographical character of the text this suggestion of precarious artistic coherence transfers the protagonist's self-division to her author, paradoxically validating rather than undermining the authority of the novel's argument about the irreconcilability of the feminine and the philosophical in unrevolutionized society.

Critical reaction was concerned at the novel's political implications but generally positive about its representation of subjective suffering as internalized social conflict. The liberal *Analytical Review*, not surprisingly, praised *Emma Courtney* as a contrast to 'the loose lascivious scenery, which imparts so dangerous a fascination to the pages of many a modern novel' and as 'the vehicle of much good sense and liberal principle', exhibiting the cultivation of its author's mind. The moderate *Monthly Review* also praised it for rising 'above the class of vulgar novels', displaying 'great intellectual powers', and exploring 'a moral problem which is eminently important': whether 'minds of a superior mould' should try 'to exempt themselves from the common delicacies or hypocrisies of life, and on all occasions to give vent to their wildest feelings, with conscientious sincerity;—or patiently to submit to the incumbent mountains of circumstance, without one volcanic effort to shatter the oppressive load into ruin'. Readers would recognize such imagery as common figures for the French Revolution. The conservative *Critical Review* was more explicit about the political implications of Hays's novel, and warned, 'Whenever great passions break out . . . there reason should direct its more immediate attention; and our conduct must, in a great measure, be regulated by the welfare and good order of society.' The *British Critic* declared, 'The lady's head seems to be full of the sophistries of Rousseau, Helvetius, and writers of that class', whom readers would recognize as 'philosophers' often accused of preparing the way for the Revolution and adopted by the English Jacobins.[37]

Meanwhile Hays herself was writing, though anonymously and without pay, as a female philosopher, setting forth the philosophical underpinnings of *Emma Courtney* in several letters to the *Monthly Magazine*, a new periodical for liberal Dissenters. Discussion of a pressing political issue of the mid-1790s, 'Ought the Freedom of Enquiry to be Restricted', turned into a debate on women's education. 'M. H.' and 'A Woman' (almost certainly Hays) defend the materialist epistemology of Helvétius in order to deny that men and women have different 'natural powers, aptitudes and dispositions'. Hays argues that since 'all knowledge is conveyed through the medium of the senses', 'bodily as well as mental powers are principally attributable to education and habits'.[38] For when advancing 'civilization', or the rise of court society, ended domination by brute strength, men deprived women of education and duped them with courtly 'gallantry' in order to keep them ideologically and culturally subject. Yet Hays names many women of the past who overcame these circumstances, anticipating the aim of her *Female Biography* a few years later.[39] In fact, she argues, the historical record suggests that women could hardly have produced 'wilder theories, absurder conclusions, greater perversity of manners, more pernicious mistakes in morals, and errors in legislation' than men have. The subjection of women is thus associated with other forms of 'tyranny' and injustice that must be overthrown: 'Sexual distinctions respecting chastity' masquerade as 'chivalry' but are 'deeply entangled with the system of property', 'one of those evils flowing from feudal institutions, the baneful effects of which can only cease with the

[37] *Analytical Review*, 25 (Feb. 1797), 174, 178; *Monthly Review*, NS 22 (Apr. 1797), 443–9; *Critical Review*, NS 19 (Jan. 1797), 110–11; *British Critic*, 9 (Mar. 1797), 314–15.
[38] *Monthly Magazine*, 1 (June 1796), 386–7.
[39] Ibid. 2 (July 1796), 469–70.

renovation of civil society'. Excluded from trades and professions, women make 'mercenary' marriages, fall into some kind of prostitution, or accept life-long celibacy and dependence—themes of Hays's recent novel and her next one.[40]

Turning to the related question, 'Are Mental Talents productive of Happiness?', Hays then develops a sociology of revolutionary change based on subjective traits conventionally ascribed to women. She argues that women's sensibility, supposed to be the sign of their intellectual inferiority and justification for their subjection by men, is a source of revolutionary change because 'strong mental powers appear to be connected with acute and lively sensation, or the capacity of receiving forcible impressions', thus empowering the individual subjectively. Like the revolutionary, the individual so empowered then transcends temporality and creates new worlds in imagination, thereby becoming politically conscious and even rebellious. Society has been and is uncongenial to such 'mental talents', however, producing unhappiness for the individual: commercial societies favour 'pecuniary gain' over 'mental improvement'; 'aristocratical and feudal institutions . . . deprive merit of its encouragement, and talents of their just and natural reward'; 'monarchical and despotic governments, by their splendour, their allurements, and their terrors, have a tendency to debauch the taste, corrupt the heart, and fetter the mind, and afford a temptation to the prostitution of talents'; and whether or not 'republics' foster revolutionary 'mental talents' remains to be seen. But such 'talents' have revolutionary potential because they are thwarted and produce individual unhappiness: 'when pent up and oppressed, the whirlwind and the torrent are not more wild and destructive'—familiar images for the Revolution itself.[41]

These letters stake Hays's claim to a Revolutionary feminism more 'philosophical' than Wollstonecraft's, but they brought no money and Hays began reviewing novels for the *Analytical Review* in late 1796 or early 1797, under Wollstonecraft's direction.[42] The disclosure of Wollstonecraft's secret affair with Godwin sharpened Hays's sense of failure to join in the avant-garde domesticity she believed her 'talents' and 'powers' entitled her to, in accordance with the sociology of revolutionary consciousness sketched in her *Monthly Magazine* letters. This

[40] Ibid. 3 (Mar. 1797), 193–5.
[41] Ibid. (May 1797), 358–60.
[42] *Letters of Wollstonecraft*, ed. Wardle, 375–6.

desire began to cause a rift with her sister Eliza. When Eliza read one of her sister's favourite sources of revolutionary sensibility, Rousseau's *La nouvelle Héloïse*, she was so 'charm'd' and 'enervated' by it that she planned to read Helvétius as an antidote, and then complained:

You sometimes reproach me with want of sensibility—in this you do me injustice—I much doubt whether my feelings are not equally strong with your own—though various circumstances may have rendered them less irritably acute,—the only difference between you, & me, is this.—that terrified by your example, it has been the business of my life, to repress sentiments, which it has been too much yours, to indulge—in avoiding one extreme, I may sometimes have run into the other,—& vainly boasted of a philosophy which in an hour of temptation would have avail'd me nothing—you know my heart to be capable both of love, & friendship—though a more indiscriminate mixture with society than you experience may have made me less romantic—I am neither cold—nor selfish—I am only more cheerful—more rational & not quite such a maniac as my unfortunate favourite sister.[43]

The last reference echoes a letter of 6 February 1796 from Mary Hays to Godwin (inserted in *Emma Courtney*) referring to herself as a 'reasoning maniac'. Eliza's letter acknowledges sexual desire as frankly as Mary's letters to Godwin or *Emma Courtney* does, but the sisters continued to drift apart. Like other Revolutionary feminists and English Jacobins, Hays was becoming marginalized as counter-Revolution and counter-feminism gathered strength and as many former Revolutionary sympathizers turned to disguised forms of political action, such as the emergent Romantic movement. Hays quarrelled with Elizabeth Hamilton, whose *Letters of a Hindoo Rajah* (1796) contains a comprehensive attack on the English Jacobins, and early in 1797 Wollstonecraft passed on one Dissenting minister's opinion: 'you are *stigmatized* as a Philosophess—a Godwinian' whose novel *Emma Courtney* was thought to 'undermine religion'.[44] Robert Southey typified an incipient movement away from English Jacobinism by young Romantic writers in condemning Hays's letters in the *Monthly*

---

[43] Undated letter, Pforzheimer Library, addressed to Mary Hays at 30 Kirby St., and thus written sometime between Oct. 1795 and Nov. 1798 when Hays lived at that address. The end of the second to last sentence originally read 'a more indiscriminate mixture with society than you experience may have cured my romantic expectations'.

[44] *Letters of Wollstonecraft*, ed. Wardle, 382; the minister was A. L. Barbauld's husband.

Magazine as 'nonsense' and dismissing her as 'a Godwinite', though 'an agreeable woman'.[45]

Meanwhile, George Dyer suggested that Hays and another woman in the Godwin circle, A. Cristall, might together 'fabricate an excellent *poetical novel*, I mean a novel with occasional poetical effusions introduced', which would be good in its 'principles' and 'productive' of good.[46] The use of the novel in the Revolution debate had revived discussion about the genre's artistic and ideological potential, and Hays summarized her views in the *Monthly Magazine*.[47] Rejecting Samuel Johnson's well-known warning against depicting wicked or morally mixed protagonists, which had been invoked against English Jacobin novelists, she argues for social and psychological realism: 'The business of familiar narrative should be to describe life and manners in real or probable situations, to delineate the human mind in its endless varieties, to develope the heart, to paint the passions, to trace the springs of action, to interest the imagination, exercise the affections, and awaken the powers of the mind.' Prose fiction may do so in two distinct ways, or sub-genres. The 'romance' displays 'a picturesque fancy, and the creative powers of a fertile and inventive genius', while the novel proper shows 'an attentive observance of mankind, acute discernment, exquisite moral sensibility, and an intimate acquaintance with human passions and powers'. The romance demands 'a luxuriant and poetic style'; 'the language of the novelist should be simple, unaffected, perspicuous, yet energetic, touching, and impressive' (p. 181). By placing these two sub-genres on an equal footing Hays implicitly justifies romance, the kind she practised herself and which was usually condemned precisely because it was thought to license subjectivities disruptive of the established cultural, social, and political order. But she also argues that the aim of all 'fictitious histories' should be to address those uninterested or untrained in 'philosophy', or social critique. An artistic and revolutionary vanguard ('persons of talents and observation') can use psychological and social realism to promote social harmony, toleration, and reform through portrayal of common human errors and failings and evocation of the 'common sympathies'

---

[45] *The Life and Correspondence of Robert Southey*, ed. Charles C. Southey (New York, 1851), 96, quoted in Burton R. Pollin, 'Mary Hays on Women's Rights in the Monthly Magazine', *Études anglaises*, 24 (1971), 271.

[46] Letter endorsed 6 Feb. 1797, Pforzheimer Library, and in *Love-Letters of Hays*, ed. Wedd, 238–9.

[47] *Monthly Magazine*, 4 (Sept. 1797), 180–1, signed 'M.H.'

pervading 'all ranks', unifying the nation in the cause of 'truth and reform'. Thus a genre long associated with women and therefore regarded as sub-literary can contribute to cultural and social revolution as the feminization of civil society.

The feminist basis for this social vision is implied in another article in the same issue of the *Monthly Magazine*—Hays's obituary of Wollstonecraft.[48] It portrays Wollstonecraft as the woman cultural revolutionary combining masculine and feminine traits, 'no less distinguished by admirable talents and a masculine tone of understanding, than by active humanity, exquisite sensibility, and endearing qualities of heart', commanding 'respect' yet 'winning the affections' (p. 232). Unlike most women, Wollstonecraft was not enfeebled but empowered by her sensibility in the way Hays had already outlined in her earlier letters to the *Monthly Magazine*. Because Wollstonecraft was 'quick to feel' she became 'indignant to resist the iron hand of despotism, whether civil or intellectual', by awakening 'in the minds of her oppressed sex a sense of their degradation' and desire for 'the dignity of reason and virtue'. At the same time, 'her philosophic mind, taking a wider range, perceived and lamented in the defects of civil institutions, interwoven in their texture, and inseparable from them, the causes of those partial evils, destructive to virtue and happiness, which poison social intercourse and deform domestic life'. Thus she became a feminist cultural revolutionary and 'by her impassioned reasoning and glowing eloquence, the fabric of voluptuous prejudice has been shaken to its foundation, and totters towards its fall'. Moreover, she exemplified her own 'philosophy': 'A victim to the vices and prejudices of mankind, her ardent, ingenuous, unconquerable spirit, resisted their contagion, contemned their injustice, rose superior to injury, and rested firmly on its own resources and powers' (p. 233). Unfortunately, Godwin's *Memoir* of Wollstonecraft, published in the spring of 1798, frankly discussed her exemplification of Revolutionary feminism in her private life and she became the focus of attacks by Anti-Jacobin periodicals on the social and political vanguard.[49] Hays, as a well-known follower and defender of Wollstonecraft, was implicated in this notoriety. Meanwhile she was ignored by the Godwin circle and even banished

[48] *Monthly Magazine*, 4 (Sept. 1797), 232–3.
[49] See R. M. Janes, 'On the Reception of Mary Wollstonecraft's *A Vindication of the Rights of Woman*', *Journal of the History of Ideas*, 39 (1978), 293–302; repr. in Mary Wollstonecraft, *A Vindication of the Rights of Woman*, ed. Carol H. Poston, 2nd edn. (New York, 1988).

by Godwin, who wrote in October 1797 declining further 'intimacy', though not friendship, with her.[50]

Nevertheless, Hays may have had additional claim to participation in Wollstonecraft's feminist project at this time. In September 1796 Wollstonecraft had read what she called Hays's 'Sisters M.S.' and commented, 'It has merit; but displays more rectitude of mind than warmth of imagination'; she returned the work a week or so later 'with some observations'.[51] This may have been the *Appeal to the Men of Great Britain in Behalf of Women*, published in the spring of 1798 by Wollstonecraft's publisher, Joseph Johnson. The only claim for Mary Hays's authorship was made in 1825 in William Thomson and Anna Wheeler's *Appeal of One Half of the Human Race, Women, Against the Pretensions of the Other Half, Men, to Retain Them in Political and Thence in Civil and Domestic Slavery*, and though Gina Luria thinks there is 'every internal evidence' that it is by her, some passages seem characteristic of her views and style while others do not.[52] Hays may have pretended the book was by her sister while seeking advice from Wollstonecraft, yet much of the *Appeal* resembles the even tone, straightforward style, didactic bent, and pious seriousness characteristic of Eliza Hays's contributions to *Letters and Essays*, and she would be more likely than her sister to prefer anonymous publication of such a book in the late 1790s.

The 'Advertisement to the Reader' claims that the greater part of the book was written 'some years ago' but set aside when Wollstonecraft's *Vindication* appeared. The failure of *A Vindication* to overcome readers' 'prejudices' then induced the author to resume the work. These circumstances would fit the experience of Hays and her sister in the early 1790s, and the *Appeal* resembles their liberal Dissenting values of the early 1790s rather than Hays's Revolutionary feminism of the mid-1790s. The 'Introduction' argues that the political tradition of the eighteenth-century 'commonwealthmen' and liberal Dissent should be extended to women, 'whom heaven having in its wisdom formed their equals, could never surely, save in its wrath, doom to be the slaves of man' (pp. i–ii). The author also affects the modesty and moderation characteristic of an earlier eighteenth-century feminism, appearing 'not in the garb of an Amazon' and not 'as a fury flinging the torch of

---

[50] Letter of 22 Oct. 1797 from Godwin to Hays, Shelley MSS, Bodleian Library; *Love-Letters of Hays*, ed. Wedd, 10.

[51] *Letters of Wollstonecraft*, ed. Wardle, 351, 353.

[52] Gina Luria, 'A Note on the Authorship', in the reprint of *Appeal to the Men of Great Britain in Behalf of Women* (New York, 1974).

discord and revenge amongst the daughters of Eve; but as a friend and companion bearing a little taper to lead them to the paths of truth, of virtue, and of liberty' (pp. v–vi).

The following three sections sustain the impression of connections to rational religious Dissent. 'Arguments Adduced from Scripture Against the Subjection of Women' methodically considers the fall from Eden and Eve's punishment as allegorical, shifting emphasis away from Paul's restrictions on women (a major problem for Christian feminists) to the Saviour's tolerant, forgiving, and positive attitude, and concludes that 'reason goes hand in hand with religion in opposing the claims of the one sex, to a right of subjecting the other' (p. 25). 'Arguments Adduced from Reason Against the Subjection of Women' adopts the liberal Dissenting view that the oppression of women is one aspect of the broader context of social conflict and injustice. The section 'Of the Erroneous Ideas Which Men Have Formed, of the Characters and Abilities of Women' takes a rationalist and historicist line, conceding that greater physical (and consequently mental) delicacy is the only essential difference between women and men, but insisting that comparison of abilities is impossible because women have never had equal opportunities in equal numbers with men and there is no comprehensive history of women and their achievements.

The next two sections come closer to Wollstonecraft's *Vindication* in sarcasm and critical edge, signalled by the epigraph to the section 'What Men Would Have Women To Be', from the working-class poet Ann Yearsley: 'Implicit faith, all hail! Imperial Man | Exacts submission!' Conduct-book prescriptions for the education of women are condemned as contradictory and 'chivalry' is dismissed as compensation for actual oppression. The following section, 'What Women Are', again has an epigraph from Yearsley and recapitulates central points of Wollstonecraft's *Vindication*. The author then concedes that women properly exercise their social influence 'in the sweet circle of domestic life' where 'the seeds of every virtue publick and private, and in both sexes, are planted and nourished to best advantage' (p. 81). By contrast, court society allows women only 'that kind of back stair influence' of mingled sexual and political intrigue, and to serve this system women are kept 'in a state of PERPETUAL BABYISM' (p. 97).

The next section, 'What Women Ought To Be', is the longest, comprising about half the book, and in certain respects goes further than *A Vindication*. Its epigraph indicates the difficulty of speaking for women from within a discursive order dominated by men: *Chi mi darà la voce e le parole* | *Convenienti à si nobil soggetto* (Who will give me the voice and the words suitable to such an elevated subject). Women are excluded from professional and public life, mere drudges in the lower classes, ornaments in the upper ranks, and in all classes assigned the role of biological and cultural reproduction within the home. The so-called 'masculine woman' simply 'emulates the virtues and accomplishments' that are 'common to human nature' and thus 'to both sexes'. Most women have to exercise more resistance to physical pain and denial of physical pleasure than men do—a reference to the sexual double standard and 'scientific proof' of women's incapacity for sexual pleasure. Women may be physically incapable of war or heavy labour and 'common sense' may exclude them from such public professions as law and divinity. But 'Nature' has not 'denied them the necessary talents': 'The natural flow of eloquence, and command of language,—the glow and warmth of imagination,—the nice discrimination with which they are so generally gifted,—leave little room for doubting of their capacity for reasoning and disputation' if they should receive the necessary intellectual training (pp. 194–5). Yet this is denied them and they are always subject to men, 'husbands taking up the authority, when parents leave it off' (pp. 257–8)—a reference to the legal fiction of 'feme covert', by which a woman's legal identity was 'covered' by her father's until her marriage and by her husband's thereafter. The section concludes with consideration of marriage, the major profession available to women at the time, and the basis of a long-standing analogy between the family and the state. Like *A Vindication* and the writings of eighteenth-century 'commonwealthmen', the *Appeal* argues that patriarchy in domestic and public life are similar and mutually supporting, and should be limited to the power to do good (p. 289).

The six-page conclusion promises that if 'this sketch' enjoys public 'approbation' there will be a second, consisting of 'A chapter on Religion—One on Politics—One on Old Maids—A short one of Queries—And a Recapitulation of the main subject of the Appeal'. The author apologizes, tongue in cheek, for excessive use of 'I' and unwarranted use of 'we', but it was not until the book was written and 'multiplied by the gossiping, though respectable art of printing', that she thought it might seem 'incorrect', 'ridiculous', or vain. Perhaps, she notes slyly, these are faults only in 'the feminine gender' (p. 299).

Critical reaction was, not surprisingly, divided. The review in Joseph Johnson's *Analytical Review*, probably by Alexander Geddes, a liberal intellectual Catholic and friend of Wollstonecraft, is favourable but not entirely free from a tone of 'gallantry', portraying the author as the 'champion of her sex, more wily but not less urgent' than Woll-stonecraft, coming 'forward with a feminine grace' and 'a sportive air' to assail 'us with no unskilful weapons'.[53] By contrast, the *British Critic* condemns the *Appeal* as a force for revolutionary subversion, part of the present 'spirit of speculation' in 'modern philosophy' that declares 'whatever is, is wrong' and blames 'the *incorrect organization* of society, and the abuses of established institution' rather than the 'real cause, the wickedness and mischievous passions of human nature'. The reviewer anticipates Hannah More's *Strictures on the Modern System of Female Education* by insisting 'that woman possesses the sovereign empire of the heart, an influence and authority greater than laws and regulations could possibly sanction or establish as her right', but 'reason is generally thrown away upon *system-makers* and *visionary reformers*, for where the heated imagination misleads the understanding, argument loses its effect'. And once again the author's intellectual deficiencies are suppos-edly revealed by her incompetence in written discourse, as the reviewer finds that the *Appeal*'s language is 'slovenly and incorrect, the reasoning weak and frivolous, and . . . it abounds with grammatical errors'.[54]

By the time the *Appeal* was published Hays was drifting away from the Godwin circle: she met Godwin less than half a dozen times in 1798, and their acquaintance ceased in 1800. She was associating more with young Romantic writers such as Southey, Coleridge, and Charles Lloyd, and writing a new novel, published in 1799 as *The Victim of Prejudice*. It adopts the figure of the 'fallen woman' used in the Revolutionary feminist critique of the property system and courtly 'chivalry'. According to this critique, women were duped by 'chivalry' and denied 'exercise' of mind and body so that they could be excluded from the professions and dispossessed by the property system, leaving them only prostitution in some form—marriage, the 'mistress system', or outright sale of their bodies. Prostitution was thus a figure for seduction of middle-class woman by glamorous upper-class culture resulting in a fall to worse than lower-class status—the social non-being of the commodified or 'common' woman. This is the experience recounted by Jemima in Wollstonecraft's *Wrongs of Woman* and by the mother of the narrator-heroine in *The Victim of Prejudice*.

---

[53] *Analytical Review*, 28 (July 1798), 25.
[54] *British Critic*, 13 (Feb. 1799), 205–6.

There was growing concern over prostitution during the mid-1790s, as crop failure and wartime economic dislocation caused unemployment, broke up families, loosened the power of social convention, and drove rural labouring men and women into towns in search of work or welfare. Patrick Colquhoun's *Treatise on the Police of the Metropolis* (1796) estimates the number of prostitutes in London at many thousands, and treats prostitution as the cause of breakdown in social bonds between parents and children, employers and employed. Like other commentators, he sees it as 'noxious and dangerous to the peace and good order of society' but attributes it not to economic or social factors, let alone systemic injustice, but to 'human passions', or emulation of court culture by other classes, manifested as 'license' and 'crime'. To control this social disorder he advocates policing, 'asylums' for the fallen, and control of what could not be suppressed. By the late eighteenth century many cultural revolutionaries were similarly treating aspects of historic upper- and lower-class culture as linked manifestations of false ideology, to be criminalized and policed, regulated, or reformed.

During the 1790s this attitude was sharpened by fear of lower-class revolution, and prostitution and other 'crimes' were politicized in complex, often contradictory ways.[55] Revolutionary sympathizers often saw prostitution as symptomatic of a decadent court regime requiring radical reform if not revolutionary overthrow. Revolutionary feminists saw prostitution as both the product and the real character of courtly 'gallantry' toward women. Burke and other anti-revolutionists saw prostitution as a sign of lower-class moral and social instability, a characteristic of selfish and decadent British and French aristocrats trying to exploit lower-class discontent to serve their own political ends, and a product of Revolutionary subversion of 'order and good government'. This view was strengthened during the mid-1790s by the increase of prostitution and related 'crimes' pointed out by Colquhoun and others, and by lurid accounts of sexual licence in France under the Directory.[56] Counter-feminists in France and Britain treated Revolutionary feminism as a cover for free expression of women's sexuality,

---

[55] E. P. Thompson, *The Making of the English Working Class*, rev. edn. (Harmondsworth, 1968), 61; for later attitudes to prostitution see Judith Walkowitz, *Prostitution and Victorian Society: Women, Class, and the State* (Cambridge, 1980); Paul McHugh, *Prostitution and Victorian Social Reform* (New York, 1980); Linda Mahood, *The Magdalenes: Prostitution in the Nineteenth Century* (London, 1990).

[56] Patrick Colquhoun, *Treatise on the Police of the Metropolis* (London, 1796).

equated with prostitution, and thus a direct threat to the foundation of the state in domesticity.

The Victim of Prejudice is a reaction against such attitudes. Whereas the *Memoirs of Emma Courtney* argued for women's equality of desire with men, denied by court culture as well as the professional middle-class cultural revolution, Hays's new novel calls for the readmission into society of 'fallen' women or victims of courtly erotic culture. Aware of counter-feminist criticism, Hays admits in her 'Advertisement to the Reader' that she may be accused of glamorizing the evil she portrays, for such charges had been laid against *Emma Courtney*. But her present purpose is to describe 'the mischiefs which have ensued from the too-great stress laid on the *reputation* for chastity in *woman*', and 'no disrespect is intended to this most important branch of temperance, the cement, the support, and the bond, of social virtue'. This sexual double standard has produced 'the corruption of our youth', 'the dissoluteness which . . . has overspread the land', and 'the sacrifice of hecatombs of victims' as part of the decadence and corruption that caused the French Revolution and were enfeebling Britain. Thus the announced theme of *The Victim of Prejudice* is central to the Revolution debate and Revolutionary feminism and, like Godwin's *Things As They Are* and Wollstonecraft's *The Wrongs of Woman*, it has a politically suggestive title. Like those novels and *Emma Courtney*, it is a confessional pseudo-memoir generalizing from personal experience to social critique, it is narrated retrospectively from a situation of crisis necessarily 'produced' by the events of the story, it is addressed to a revolutionary posterity, it attacks the denaturing effects of property and rank on individual identity and domestic affections, it uses a Gothic plot of flight and pursuit to dramatize oppression, it deploys Gothic settings of prisons and tribunals to represent the operation of ideology as *force majeure*, it dramatizes social conflict through 'philosophical' dialogue, and it broadens the social critique by inset or parallel narratives. Unlike *Emma Courtney*, it is not dialogical, nor is it as richly allusive, referential, concerned with 'facts', or systematically researched as *Things As They Are* and *The Wrongs of Woman*. But it gains intensity by concentrating on the emotional and bodily experience of victimization, as both the internalization of false social values ('prejudice') and the mental and physical suffering that results (the experience of 'the victim'). *The Victim of Prejudice* narrates the political body of woman as victim of 'things as they are'.

Like other English Jacobin novels, this one opens *in medias res* and recounts in retrospect the events leading to the 'fallen' condition in which the narrator-protagonist (her name is not revealed until the third chapter) now finds herself: 'A child of misfortune, a wretched outcast from my fellow-beings, driven with ignominy from social intercourse, cut off from human sympathy, immured in the gloomy walls of a prison, I spread my hands and lift my eyes to the Moral Governor of the Universe!' (p. i). Only such a being, 'who searcheth the heart, [and] judgeth not as man judgeth', could see her true subjective worth. But as in *Emma Courtney* the narrator addresses not only a transcendent being above social conflicts and relativities but also her political heir on earth, implicitly the reader:

And thou, the victim of despotism, oppression, or error, tenant of a dungeon, and successor to its present devoted inhabitant, should these sheets fall into thy possession, when the hand that wrote them moulders in the dust, and the spirit that dictated ceases to throb with agony, read; and, if civil refinements have not taught thy heart to reflect the sentiment which cannot penetrate it, spare from the contemplation of thy own misery one hour, and devote it to the memory of a fellow-sufferer, who derives firmness from innocence, courage from despair; whose unconquerable spirit, bowed but not broken, seeks to beguile, by the retrospect of an unsullied life, the short interval, to which will succeed a welcome and never-ending repose. (pp. ii–iii)

It is only the victim of 'despotism', 'oppression', and 'error' who would have the subjective qualifications to recognize the truth and validity of this narrative. Yet there seems no hope that such recognition will lead beyond itself, just as the narrative itself was undertaken only 'to beguile' the time before death.

By contrast, the narrator's 'retrospect' then opens with her memories of happy childhood in Wales—during the 1790s a refuge for several English Jacobins from government spies and reactionary politics—where Mary is raised by Mr Raymond, who 'cherished notions somewhat singular respecting female accomplishments': 'I was early inured to habits of hardiness; to suffer, without shrinking, the changes and inclemencies of the seasons; to endure fatigue and occasional labour; to exercise my ingenuity and exert my faculties, arrange my thoughts and discipline my imagination' (i. 6). According to the principles of Wollstonecraft's *Vindication*, bodily and mental 'exercise' together create the independent self, manifest in Mary's appearance: 'Tall, blooming, animated, my features were regular, my complexion a rich glowing brunette, my eyes vivacious and sparkling; dark chestnut hair shaded my face, and floated over my shoulders in luxuriant profusion; my figure was light and airy, my step firm, my aspect intelligent, and my mind inquisitive' (i. 7). This is the first of many such self-representations, insisting on the interrelationship of body and mind and giving greater moral and intellectual significance to the later violation of Mary's body, foreshadowed just after this passage.

Mary's youthful harmony of circumstance and subjectivity, mind and body, is soon jarred. First the poison of class difference is introduced when William and Edmund, the sons of the rich, noble, and proud Mr Pelham, are entrusted to Raymond to be educated as gentlemen. Mary now hears that she is an adopted orphan, weeps for no apparent reason, and for the first time feels embarrassed in company. Social difference and alienation have entered her consciousness, affecting her bodily. But she nevertheless emulates and even surpasses the brothers in both their studies and adventures. Her deeds of heroism endear her to the impetuous and romantic William, but her misadventures draw the unwanted attentions of Peter Osborne. Raymond is alarmed by the growing attachment of Mary and William and 'began to doubt whether, in cultivating my mind, in fostering a virtuous sensibility, in imbuing my heart with principles of justice and rectitude, he had not been betraying my happiness!' (i. 57–8).

He tells Mary she must separate from William, for merit and social rank are not equivalent. Paradoxically, Raymond's moral teaching makes Mary aware of the very feeling from which he intends to guard her, and she cannot promise Raymond 'heroism' in ceasing to love William, but once alone her gratitude to her benefactor inspires her:

A generous heroism nerved my mind, throbbed in my bosom, glowed on my cheek, a spirit congenial to artless youth, by whom the veil of society, behind which corruption and contradiction lurk, has not been rent. My eyes regained their lustre, and my features their wonted spirit. (i. 96–7)

Again her subjectivity is expressed bodily, moving from 'mind' to 'bosom' to 'cheek'.

She finds herself appropriately if ironically banished to a domestic paradise with a country curate, Mr Neville, and his family:

Through this happy family, perfect harmony and tenderness reigned: Mr. Neville loved and entirely confided in his wife, of whose value he was justly sensible; while her affection for him had in it I know not what of tender solicitude, of exquisite softness, of ardent devotion, which, to hearts less susceptible, would appear excessive or inconceivable. Their children, lovely and promising, were equally their delight and care: they formed, between their parents, a new and more sacred bond: their expanding faculties and budding graces authorized and justified a parent's fondest hopes. (i. 111–12)

Mary now understands society well enough to contrast this Eden of bourgeois domestic happiness with courtly society on one hand and plebeian life on the other:

Happiness, coy and fair fugitive, who shunnest the gaudy pageants of courts and cities, the crowded haunts of vanity, the restless cares of ambition, the insatiable pursuits of avarice, the revels of voluptuousness, and the riot of giddy mirth, who turnest alike from fastidious refinement and brutal ignorance . . . thou art only to be found in the real solid pleasures of nature and social affection. (i. 112)

The three-class model of Enlightenment and pro-revolutionary social criticism locates 'happiness' in the middle rank and legitimates it as 'nature'. The lyrical apostrophe expresses the cultural revolutionary's self-validating politicized sensibility. In Hays's novel such outbursts often close chapters, linking the novel's narrative of individual experience to the political and social reality in which the novel aims to intervene.

Yet the Nevilles' domestic happiness only makes Mary feel more sharply her social isolation, promptly dramatized when she is cut off by the ocean tide while out walking to relieve her melancholy. She is rescued by the nefarious Osborne, however, who again forces his attentions on her. This episode prefigures Mary's discovery of her 'original sin' as social outcast. For absence has made William recognize his own feelings and he comes to see Mary; enchanted by the daily spectacle of the Nevilles' domesticity he declares his love. Mary writes to Raymond for advice, but his reply encloses an account of her parentage that shows her she can never be united with a man of William's social standing.

This account is the inset autobiography of Mary's mother, who once rejected marriage to Raymond only to be seduced by a man of rank and fortune and then abandoned with her illegitimate child—Mary. Once fallen she was barred from respectability and chose a life of delusive pleasure. But the widening circle of observation then opened to her produced a critical awareness of systemic social injustice: ' "by enlarging the circle of my observation, though in the bosom of depravity, my understanding became enlightened: I perceived myself the victim of the injustice, of the prejudice, of society, which, by opposing to my return to virtue almost insuperable barriers, had plunged me into irremediable ruin"' (i. 162). She became the sworn enemy of society and rejoiced to spread disease and vice among others—symbolically returning to society the physical and moral corruption that denatured her. An accidental meeting with Raymond reawakened her conscience, however, and she implored him to save her daughter. Raymond did so, but warns Mary, '"In the eye of the world, the misfortunes of your birth stain your unsullied youth: it is in the dignity of your own mind that you must seek resource"' (i. 170–171).

This marks another turning point in Mary's consciousness and her internalization of social division, but to no avail against systemic injustice. The more rapid succession of events now represents the fact that her situation is beyond her control. Symbolically, she is caught in a storm and contracts a violent fever, but recovers with a renewed determination to merit her benefactor's confidence, agreeing to marry William only with his father's consent. Meanwhile Osborne's machinations destroy the basis of Mary's independence, causing the loss of Neville's curacy and Mary's small inheritance. Osborne renews his licentious proposals, Raymond dies, and Osborne reveals that William is about to be married to a wife chosen by his father. When Mary goes to be domestic companion with a family in London she is abducted by Osborne and, after a week's resistance, 'I suffered a brutal violation' (ii. 79). She escapes into the street only to encounter William, who blames paternal power for forcing him to abandon her and argues that their bond of 'nature' should outweigh the merely social one of marriage. Mary rejects this argument and sets about establishing her own independence by selling paintings of flowers. Osborne discovers this resource, however, and threatens Mary's employer into cutting her off. She realizes that 'the fatal tale of my disgrace pursued and blasted all my efforts', like Caleb Williams in Godwin's novel, and describes her mental anguish and consequent physical sensations in painful detail.

Arrested for debt she finds herself again in Osborne's hands, but rejects his dishonourable offer and is sent to prison to break her spirit. There she accidentally meets James, Raymond's former servant, who bails her out and takes her to live on his farm, where she helps run the dairy, studies botany, and teaches the village children. Social usefulness, rural pursuits, and nature revive her, but 'I was destined once more to be dashed on hidden shoals, and swallowed up in an unfathomable abyss' (ii. 191). Natural misfortunes force her into debt, Osborne again besets her, a creditor makes indecent proposals, and friends avoid her. She considers revealing her plight to the village leaders, but realizes her oppression is systemic, not personal:

what credit has the simple asseverations of the sufferer, sole witness in his own cause, to look for against the poison of detraction, the influence of wealth and power, the bigotry of prejudice, the virulence of envy, the spleen and the corruption engendered in the human mind by barbarous institutions and pernicious habits? (ii. 200–1)

Oppression is not only external and institutional, but internalized in individuals as their daily 'reality'. The Gothic figure of 'poison' again represents the invisible operation of ideology, naturalizing humanly constructed injustice. With this realization Mary's will, her subjectivity as a power, is paralysed: 'I sunk into listless, stubborn sadness' (ii. 202).

Paradoxically, Osborne is now impressed by her heroism and implores her to accept 'a *legal* title to his hand and fortune'—apart from the moral 'title' she has as his victim (ii. 204). She refuses and sets off to start her life again, 'a sentiment of mingled heroism and despair still sustaining me' (ii. 209). But she is arrested for debt and imprisoned. She takes up her pen to soothe her woes by tracing their origin and progress, thus returning to the point from which the narrative began. But even writing cannot console: 'I sink beneath a torrent, whose resistless waves overwhelm alike in a common ruin the guiltless and the guilty' (ii. 213). Systemic social injustice now seems a force of nature, and she addresses herself to a force beyond it:

O God of truth! (if priests belie thee not;) O God of truth and love!—I can no more; my quivering fingers drop the pen!—Posterity, receive my last appeal!
     *   *   *   *   *   *   *   *   (ii. 214–15)

The asterisks indicate simultaneous breakdown of self and writing, and abandonment of both to powers beyond the narrator's control—posterity and God, historical continuity and transcendence of history—that are to take over where the text breaks off, vindicating and thus validating both narrator and text.

Narrator and text resume, only to prepare for the final silence and 'asylum' of death. She has a final meeting with Mrs Neville, who dies with Mary at her side reflecting that '*I have lived in vain!* unless the story of my sorrows should kindle in the heart of man, in behalf of my oppressed sex, the sacred claims of humanity and justice' (ii. 231). The phrasing recalls the title and aims of the *Appeal to the Men of Great*

Britain in Behalf of Women, but 'the victim of prejudice' closes her narrative pessimistically: 'Ignorance and despotism, combating frailty with cruelty, may go on to propose *partial* reform in one invariable, melancholy round; reason derides the weak effort; while the fabric of superstition and crime, extending its broad base, mocks the toil of the visionary projector' (ii. 232).

Hays's novel is clearly indebted to Wollstonecraft's *The Wrongs of Woman*. Its heroine too recounts her 'fall' while inside a prison and traces the same process of social rebellion springing from the encounter of a fine sensibility with a world divided by class and gender. But whereas Wollstonecraft's novel, imitating the autobiography of the Revolutionary victim of sensibility Marie Roland, is addressed to posterity as the heroine's daughter, Hays's novel incorporates the mother's narrative in the daughter's and addresses the latter's tale to a general posterity, a revolutionary vanguard. Whereas Wollstonecraft embodies the narrative of sexual harassment and exploitation in the inset tale of the lower-class Jemima, Hays assigns this material to the heroine herself. Hays's novel subsumes the Sentimental novel of education in the English Jacobin novel of social protest, just as her earlier works had subsumed the politics of Sensibility in Revolutionary feminism.

By the time Hays published *The Victim of Prejudice* she was well known as a Revolutionary feminist, and the reviewers treated the novel accordingly. The *Analytical Review* struggled to praise it, finding 'amidst even the imperfections of the present work, a mind apt at moral description, fertile in sentiment, and considerably skilled in the science of the feelings', and representing the 'imperfections' as aesthetic rather than political—principally the heavy reliance on coincidence to justify the heroine's vicissitudes, thus undermining the 'philosophical' or systemic implications of her fate. The *Monthly Review* associated Hays with the other 'English Jacobin' novelists and complained that 'the novels which issue from this school' elevate love, 'a transient passion' but subjective absolute, above 'the regulations and institutions of society'. The *Critical Review* appreciated Hays's artistic and intellectual ability but condemned them as 'employed in a manner highly danger-ous to the peace and welfare of society'. The reviewer praised Hays's psychological realism as 'scarcely inferior to the effusions of Rousseau', but also found the heroine's case not convincingly generalized to support the novel's 'indiscriminate imputations on society and the laws'. The *Anti-Jacobin Review* attacked both of Hays's novels for undermining domestic woman, asking whether 'it is most for the advantage of society that women should be so brought up as to make them dutiful daughters, affectionate wives, tender mothers, and good Christians, or, by a corrupt and vicious system of education, fit them for revolutionary agents, for heroines, for Staels, for Talliens, for Stones, setting aside all the decencies, the softness, the gentleness, of the female character, and enjoying indiscriminately every envied privilege of man?' The references here are to leading political women *salonistes* of the Directory and late 1790s—Mme de Staël, Mme Tallien, and Helen Maria Williams.[57]

Shortly after *The Victim of Prejudice* was published Hays discovered how the growing condemnation of Revolutionary feminism could affect her personally. For some time she had carried on a 'sentimental' correspondence with the poet and novelist Charles Lloyd, who pretended to his friends that she had offered herself to him in accordance with what was assumed to be her feminist sexual permissiveness. When Hays reproached him for this he replied that she deserved such treatment because of the principles exhibited in her writings and behaviour.[58] Lloyd's conduct was condemned by his friends, but they were unclear as to whether or not Hays had indeed brought the insult on herself by her feminist 'speculation'. The danger of being misread and misrepresented, textually and personally, had obviously increased greatly by the late 1790s, and in the Revolutionary aftermath feminism of any kind would have to take more acceptable forms.

[57] *Analytical Review*, NS 1 (Mar. 1799), 329; *Monthly Review*, NS 31 (Jan. 1800), 82; *Critical Review*, NS 26 (Aug. 1799), 450–2; *Anti-Jacobin Review and Magazine*, 3 (May 1799), 55.

[58] Lloyd's letter to Hays is quoted in Charles Lamb's letter to Thomas Manning of 8 Feb. 1800; see *The Letters of Charles and Mary Anne Lamb*, ed. Edwin W. Marrs, Jr., (Ithaca, NY, 1975), i. 181–2, 183–4 nn. 1–3.

4

Elizabeth Hamilton and Counter-Revolutionary Feminism

AT the end of the Revolutionary decade Mary Hays and Helen Maria Williams faced an uncertain personal and political future. For Elizabeth Hamilton the prospect was more promising. Though little different from Williams and Hays in social background, education, and upbringing, Hamilton took the 'anti-Jacobin', counter-feminist line during the 1790s. Yet she too operated as a woman writer within the professional middle-class cultural revolution. She was born in 1758 in Belfast, the third child and second daughter of a merchant and his wife, both of whom died shortly afterwards.[1] She was then raised near Stirling by her aunt and uncle Marshall in an upper-middle-class home permeated by the values of the cultural revolution—she later compared it to the Wolmar household in Rousseau's *La nouvelle Héloïse*. She helped the neighbouring poor, played much outdoors, 'was indifferent to her doll', read avidly, and revered 'national' heroes such as William Wallace and classical heroes of the *Iliad*. She was educated in conventional 'feminine' subjects, became passionately fond of dancing, and later studied science, but always regretted receiving no classical education.

With the Marshalls she also experienced class and cultural difference. Her aunt had 'married down' and was a Presbyterian, while her uncle was an Episcopalian; yet there was domestic harmony and commitment to professional middle-class meritocracy. Hamilton later reported that

[1] Biographical information from Elizabeth Benger, *Memoirs of the Late Mrs. Elizabeth Hamilton, with a Selection from Her Correspondence, and Other Unpublished Writings*, 2nd edn., 2 vols. (London: Longman, Hurst, Rees, Orme, & Brown, 1819). The second edition differs from the first in reordering some of the letters, eliminating certain eulogistic passages, excising or moderating some passages critical of the strictness of the Presbyterian church attended by Hamilton as a girl, identifying some of the names earlier represented by initials or blanks, explaining Pestalozzi's educational system (to which Hamilton became an adherent), giving more extracts from Hamilton's journal concerning her religious beliefs, inserting additional letters, deleting some periodical essays incorrectly ascribed to her previously, showing more of her 'human' and emotional side, and giving more emphasis to her personal struggles.

her aunt 'wished me to be self-dependent; and, consequently, taught me to value myself upon nothing that did not strictly belong to myself, nor upon any thing that did, which was in its nature perishable'.[2] Nevertheless, she felt socially superior and had a turn for 'ridicule', tempting a family friend to make her a religious sceptic, but Bible study prevented this. Like Williams and Hays, she had a male mentor—her brother Charles, who was 'not merely a companionable friend, but an object of enthusiastic attachment,—a director for her studies,—an oracle to whom she was proud to yield implicit obedience'.[3] He had entered business in Dublin but sought a more genteel career in the army, leaving for India in 1772.

Hamilton's schooling ended in her mid-teens and she became her aunt's companion. She was warned that her learning would seem 'unfeminine', and studied in secret. Her aunt died in 1780 and Hamilton's brother invited her to India, teasingly suggesting that she would find a husband there—India was already recognized as a marriage market—but she rejected the prospect as unlikely to produce the new model domesticity.[4] She turned to writing as an alternative to marriage. 'Like many other solitary thinkers' she 'was irresistibly impelled to become a writer' and her early work indicates how she was positioning herself in relation to conflicts of class and gender within the professional middle class. Like Williams and Hays she tried out acceptably feminine *belles-lettres*, including a journal of a Highland tour, some verse, and a historical novel based on the life of Lady Arabella Stuart. The novel contained some dialogue in Scots, which Hamilton also used playfully in her letters, indicating a self-conscious distance from lower-class language and culture. An essay published in the *Lounger* (no. 46, 17 December 1785) takes up the contrast between women's intellectual 'accomplishments' and the fashion system and courtly amorous culture. 'Almeria', daughter of a model country clergyman, finds that the attention of suitors depends on her assumed social status rather than her subjective merit and she gladly finds refuge and happiness in returning to rural domesticity.[5] Hamilton's poem 'Anticipation' looks forward to being an 'old maid' as refuge from the same experience.[6] As in

[2] Benger, *Hamilton*, i. 43.
[3] Ibid. 47.
[4] See Percival Spear, *The Nabobs: A Study of the Social Life of the English in Eighteenth Century India*, rev. edn. (London, 1963), 36–7; Pat Barr, *The Memsahibs: The Women of Victorian India* (London, 1976), 11–12.
[5] Benger, *Hamilton*, i. 297–311.
[6] Ibid. 95–6.

much Sentimental literature, class conflict is transposed into gender conflict, but then used to advance the claims of women to some form of the moral and intellectual training thought necessary for professional men.

At this time 'a happiness dearer than [literary] distinction appeared to invite her acceptance'—apparently a prospect of marriage—but 'the vision passed away, happily, without casting an invidious shade over her future existence'.[7] She seemed destined for a secure if dependent domestic life as her uncle's housekeeper and companion, with little time for the study that she loved, but her brother's return from India opened new opportunities. His sister later ascribed to him 'the development and almost the creation of her mind', for 'he taught her to explore her own latent and hitherto unappropriated treasures: it was for his penetration to discover, in the beautiful flowers that embellished the surface, the qualities of the soil beneath'.[8] For in India Charles Hamilton had become involved in a particular branch of the professional middle-class cultural revolution, led by Sir William Jones and his fellow Orientalists in the Asiatic Society at Calcutta, and dedicated to reform of both colonial administration and the empire's subject peoples.[9] Charles Hamilton had participated in the Rohilla war and was preparing a history of it. He had also studied Oriental languages and was given five years' leave in England by Warren Hastings to translate the Persian code of Islamic law for use by the colonial administration. In London in 1788 the Hamiltons associated with supporters of Warren Hastings, then being tried before Parliament in a struggle for control of the East India administration. They also became close friends of the Revd Dr Gregory and his wife, who came to represent Hamilton's ideal of 'female excellence'—both cultured and domestic, and supporting her husband's professional and public work as cultural revolutionary.[10] After several years Charles Hamilton was appointed British resident at Oudh in India, probably as part of Henry Dundas's programme to break the power of the 'India Interest' in British politics.[11] Before he left England, however, he died of tuberculosis, in March 1792.

---

[7] Benger, *Hamilton*, i. 96–7.

[8] Ibid. 108–10.

[9] Garland Cannon, *Oriental Jones: A Biography of Sir William Jones (1746–1794)* (Bombay, 1964); S. N. Mukherjee, *Sir William Jones: A Study in Eighteenth-Century British Attitudes to India*, rev. edn. (London, 1987).

[10] Benger, *Hamilton*, i. 113.

[11] Cyril H. Philips, *The East India Company 1784–1834*, corr. edn. (Manchester, 1961), 43–4.

Hamilton was devastated. She wished to continue her brother's work as cultural revolutionary, but since his profession was barred to her and his studies were gendered masculine, she did so in one of the few ways open to her as a woman, a fictionalized version of him, his career, and his work as an Orientalist. She knew even this might be judged an 'unfeminine' transgression into men's discourse, and submitted the first part, set in India, to her advisor Mrs Gregory. Though Mrs Gregory urged her to complete the work, Hamilton still hesitated. She finally joined her satire on courtly society and empire to a satire on courtly-revolutionary politics in England, but she knew that both subjects would be considered unsuitable for a woman and even when she decided to publish she remained loath to put her name to it, 'sensible that the woman, who has once been brought before the public, can never be restored to the security of a private station', and repelled by 'a measure which might seem to imply a dereliction of that delicacy which was her peculiar characteristic'.[12] But her brother's memory legitimized the project. Alluding to the ink of the manuscript but punning on the race of her main character, an Indian rajah, she referred to the work as 'my black baby'; since she acknowledged her brother's central role in fertilizing her intellect, he is implicitly the father of this 'child of my brain'.[13] She finally published her novel in 1796, with her name on the title-page, as *Translation of the Letters of a Hindoo Rajah; Written Previous to, and During the Period of His Residence in England; To Which is Prefixed a Preliminary Dissertation on the History, Religion, and Manners of the Hindoos*. Its material, viewpoint, and political purpose show the influence of her brother, as reflected in his published Orientalist work, *An Historical Relation of the Origin, Progress, and Final Dissolution of the Government of the Rohilla Afghans in the Northern Provinces of Hindostan; Compiled from a Persian Manuscript and Other Original Papers* (1787), and a translation and edition of *The Hedaya, or Guide: A Commentary on the Mussulman Laws* (1791). The aim of these works is to justify British intervention in India and reform of colonial administration, led by the Orientalists, as an attack on court government both in the empire and at home.

Charles Hamilton's account of the Rohilla war claims to be taken from a Persian manuscript and describes the defeat of the Rohilla

---

[12] Benger, *Hamilton*, i. 129–30.
[13] Ibid. 127.

Afghans, largely thanks to the British, as a 'revolution' transforming into peace, security, and prosperity the situation of anarchy brought about by the decadence of feudal Muslim rule in northern India. Underlying this account and justifying British intervention in Indian affairs is an Enlightened historicist critique of feudalism and decadent court government in Europe. Hamilton's edition of the *Hedaya* continues this project, with the advantage of hindsight resulting from the Revolution in France, which is alluded to, though cautiously, as an overthrow of feudal despotism and anarchy similar to that being effected by the British in India. Charles Hamilton's 'Preliminary Discourse', with its rational, analytical, 'objective', and historicist method, implicitly subordinates the Islamic law code itself to the superior viewpoint of an implied reader who will be applying the code mitigated by the reason and moderation of the benevolent imperialist. In accordance with the Orientalists' Enlightened cultural relativism the code is respected for having something to teach Europeans, for example the rights enjoyed by Muslim women, contrary to the common European view of them as virtual slaves. Nevertheless, the 'Preliminary Discourse' portrays Islamic law as the remains of a primitive, oral, and autocratic society that must be understood so that it can be applied with European reason, justice, and benevolence until it is inevitably superseded, as is happening with similarly outmoded societies and cultures elsewhere, as 'new empires' rise, and 'old' ones throw off 'the long rivetted chains of despotism'. America and France required a revolution to throw off 'despotism' and 'superstition', but Britain had long done so and now must revolutionize her empire under divine aegis, partly as a way of restraining 'Oriental' forces of despotism at home.

This mission is partly validated by differences of language and style, manifesting differences of culture, to which Hamilton's texts draw attention. He claims that his translation of the Indian manuscript account of the Rohilla war had to be subsumed into British accounts of the event, implying that the Indian view was incomplete and inferior to the British one. For similar reasons he draws attention to the relation of language and culture seen in the *Hedaya*. The Islamic law code is, as he says, a 'dry' work, but its language is straightforward and informal because the code was originally oral, embodying customs known to all Muslims through their common culture. English law had a different origin and development and therefore a different language, employed in the 'Preliminary Discourse' and sustained throughout the text by the glossing of words, customs, and institutions that have no equivalent in Britain. The Islamic law and the society it reflects are 'translated' into British terms and thereby preserved insofar as they still have a use, but otherwise subordinated. The same effect is achieved by the contrast of language and style between Hamilton's 'Preliminary Discourse' and the preceding 'Introductory Address' by the Muslim scholars who compiled the Persian text. This 'Address' is, as one reviewer put it, 'in the true Eastern manner' of extravagance and hyperbole European readers then expected from Orientals.[14] Yet both 'Address' and 'Preliminary Discourse' express the hope that the translation will facilitate benign British intervention in India: subjects and ruler have a common aim, which is that of the Orientalist programme in India; this aim is also that of the cultural revolution in Britain and even the early Revolution in France.

For Charles Hamilton's translating and editing colonize Oriental texts while appearing to preserve and disseminate them, subsuming them in an Orientalist imperial project designed to supersede the culture, society, and state that produced them. Similarly, the Orientalists aimed to translate and subsume 'oriental' values and practices abroad and at home, in order to subvert and supersede the culture and state that produced them, in a non-violent or cultural revolution, accompanied by professionalization of society and the state. In this project, revolution at home and abroad were intertwined, though the Orientalists thought the process had to begin in the empire. By reforming colonial administration and Indian society and government, the Orientalists aimed to cut off exploitation of India by those British administrators and traders who encouraged Indian courtly decadence in order to enrich themselves and return to Britain to use the same methods there. *Letters of a Hindoo Rajah* picks up this project as Charles Hamilton had developed it to the early 1790s, and joins it to a mid-1790s concern with the dangerous turn taken in the mean time by the Revolution in France and the cultural revolution in Britain.

Like Charles Hamilton's published work, *Letters of a Hindoo Rajah* claims to be a 'translation' and covers every aspect of society from property and family relations to government, laws, religion, and culture. Both use a double perspective: the account of the Rohilla war and the edition of the *Hedaya* appropriate Eastern culture for the use of the West and reform of the East, while *Letters of a Hindoo Rajah*

[14] *Monthly Review*, NS 7 (Apr. 1792), 427.

defamiliarizes the West by portraying it through Eastern eyes, implying that there are 'oriental' elements in Britain which should be purged, just as Britain's Orient should be occidentalized for its and Britain's good. Both contrast the language and style of East and West, both have historical introductions, both are dedicated to or praise Warren Hastings, and both bear the imprint of publishers of the English Enlightenment.[15] Elizabeth Hamilton does seem to accept the gendered hierarchy of discourse by referring to her own work as a 'trifle', yet it is more ambitious than her brother's: it gives as comprehensive a representation of British society as the latter does of Indian society, it offers a critique of both pre-Revolutionary British society and the Oriental society observing it and contrasted with it, and as a novel it could reach a far wider readership. Hamilton's novelization of her brother's Orientalist project does aim to serve his memory by disseminating his work beyond the narrow circle of professional and political men to the entire 'reading public'. At the same time, she characterizes the work of her brother and the Orientalists as a feminized form of culture and politics, thus placing their work and hers on paths converging in a shared model of civil society.

Her strategy is to blend discourses conventionally differentiated hierarchically by gender. The novel was widely considered a 'women's' genre and therefore sub-literary, yet it typically served to exemplify broad public and political issues in private life, especially in the Revolution debate. Hamilton masks the fictional character of her work: the title could pass for non-fiction and women were well known as translators of learned and literary works from modern European languages, if not Oriental ones. One reviewer even thought it advisable to assure readers 'that this is a work of fiction and fancy'.[16] Furthermore, Hamilton uses a form of the novel historically practised by men—the satirical travel narrative such as Swift's *Gulliver's Travels*, Montesquieu's *Lettres persanes*, Goldsmith's *Citizen of the World*, or Johnson's *Rasselas* that uses actual or fictitious alien cultures to defamiliarize European culture and society. Hamilton both bolsters her defamiliarization and reclaims her novel from the 'merely' feminine by appropriating discourses conventionally gendered masculine—the Enlightened learned disciplines practised by her brother and his colleagues—in her 'Preliminary Dissertation', glossary, and notes. The

[15] George Kearsley and the firm of Robinsons, respectively.
[16] *Monthly Review*, NS 21 (Oct. 1796), 176.

result is an early footnote novel of the kind developed in the Revolutionary aftermath by women writers, including Hamilton herself, to practise learned discourses and engage in political issues conventionally closed to them. It is true that Hamilton claims only the acceptably feminine task of popularizing this knowledge, especially for 'those of my own sex', but she also feminizes the Orientalists' work by characterizing it as pacific and sympathetic, recovering 'more permanent' treasures than the loot obtained by other imperialists' characteristically masculine rape of the Orient. Finally, Hamilton gives the Enlightened critique of imperialism a bent some would have seen as 'feminine' by using it as Williams did in her poem *Peru* and by insisting on its divine validation through Christian faith.

Hamilton's aim in this compositional work is to find an acceptably 'feminine' way of carrying on her brother's Orientalist project. Like his works, *Letters of a Hindoo Rajah* has an editorial apparatus that appears to serve and to mediate the text it surrounds and 'translates'. But this apparatus is informed by the authoritative Western and 'masculine' discourse of Enlightened 'philosophical history', with its interest in the life cycle of civilizations, its comparative and relativist approach to different cultures past and present, its linking of social, cultural, and political forces of change, its ideology of 'progress' and 'improvement', its demystification of 'despotism' and 'priestcraft', its rationalism and materialism. The Enlightenment perspective and method implicitly contain and subject the Oriental text and place the culture that the text embodies within an Enlightened order of values and plot of history. At the same time, this textual colonization of the Orient can be read as an analogy to reform of 'oriental' elements in Britain and the West.

For example, Hamilton's 'Preliminary Dissertation' first invokes an Enlightenment figure of primitive innocence in describing Hindu culture and society before the Moghul conquest, under a benign ruler and stable caste system, unlike ancient and modern Europe: 'The turbulence of ambition, the emulations of envy, and the murmurs of discontent, were equally unknown to a people, where each individual, following the occupation, and walking in the steps of his fathers, considered it as his primary duty to keep in the situation that he firmly believed to have been marked out for him by the hand of Providence' (vol. i, pp. xvi–xvii). This reads like a description of medieval European society, and the Enlightenment law of historical progress ordains that such a society cannot continue. Its very tranquillity caused decline into

religious idolatry and intellectual stagnation, according to the Enlightenment argument that progress is generated by conflict:

> In the struggle of contending interests, though peace is sometimes lost, intellec-
> tual energy is roused, and while the strife of emulation, and restlessness of
> ambition, disturb the quiet of society, they produce, in their collision, the
> genius that adorns it: it is accordingly pronounced, by one [Sir William Jones]
> who must be allowed competent to the decision, that 'Reason and Taste are
> the grand prerogatives of European minds, while the Asiatics have soared to
> loftier heights in the sphere of Imagination.' (p. xxxv)

Hamilton goes on to argue that because Hindu society lacked intellectual energy it was subjugated by a martial Muslim culture, and readers
would notice that Hamilton's description of this conquest resembles
accounts of Revolutionary violence—an implied warning that an
effete Britain could be overcome by a martial Revolutionary France
just as the Revolutionaries had overcome an effete court monarchy at
home. But salvation is at hand for both India and Britain. When the
Moghul empire in turn broke down into local despotisms, the British
were compelled to save the people from their rulers, restore their laws,
reform commercial and state administration, and pacify social and
religious conflict, guided by a feminized masculine culture in the form
of the sympathetic but paternalistic understanding of India found in
the work of the Orientalists, which now includes Hamilton's own popularization.

For in Hamilton's 'Preliminary Dissertation' the Orientalists represent both the ideal toward which Indian history is moving and the
cultural and political force that intervenes in Indian history to attain
that goal. Hamilton is associated with their work in acceptably feminine
ways both as a popularizer and through a tie of domestic affections
expressly referred to in her text. This association enables her to justify
her own work, which some readers may censure 'as a presumptuous
effort to wander out of that narrow and contracted path, which they
have allotted to the female mind' (p. lvii). But she was taught 'that
toward a strict performance of the several duties of life, Ignorance was
neither a necessary, nor an useful auxiliary'. In domestic life books
were her only instruction, and when India became a subject of public
debate she studied the works of the leading Orientalists and would
have gone on to acquire Indian languages had there not occurred 'a
fatal event, which transformed the cheerful haunt of domestic
happiness'—an allusion to her brother's death. Her studies were 'inter-

woven' with 'ideas of past felicity' and she reverted to them for consolation: 'The letters of the Rajah were sought for, and the employment they afforded was found so salutary . . . that the study of them was resumed, as an useful relaxation, and, being brought to a conclusion, they are now presented to the world' (pp. lix–lx). Her work not only contributes to reform of India and Britain, but is part of a self-reform from mourning to usefulness, a 'proper' course for a woman to take.

The fictitious letters show what has to be reformed and how that reform may be carried out, again through the intervention of individuals, be they men or women, imbued with the kind of feminized Enlightened critical consciousness attributed to the Orientalists and exhibited by the author in her 'Preliminary Dissertation'. Most of the letters, supposedly written in the mid- and late 1770s, are between Zāārmilla, Rajah of Almora, descendant of the petty Moghul rulers now controlled or pensioned off by the British, and his friend Kisheen Neêay Māāndāāra, a Zimeendar or landed 'gentleman' of Cumlore in Rohilcund, a region recently pacified by the British expedition which Charles Hamilton had participated in and had described in print. These disturbances arose from the breakdown of court government into anarchy, a situation that many thought had occurred in France and was threatening Britain in the mid-1790s. The novel's principal correspondents are exiles from this breakdown, Indian equivalents of the French *émigrés*, and they now have the leisure and motive to learn how they and their country could have avoided this fall by adopting the programme of the Orientalists. Hamilton's 'Translation' presents the pre-Revolutionary consciousness of an Orientalized court society as warning and instruction to Britain by 'translating' British culture and society into Oriental terms, tracing in the Rajah's letters a rapprochement of East and West at a time of deep social and cultural divisions within Britain and increasing external threat to Britain and its empire.

This translation has a tripartite structure and Hamilton may have intended the novel to be a typical triple-decker. The Rajah first approaches the West as he emerges from the chaos of the Rohilla wars. His early impressions of the British are offset by reactions from his friend Māāndāāra and the learned Brahmin Sheermaal, who has already visited Britain. Some years pass before the Rajah's second encounter with the West, travelling through Indian states under British protection, into East India Company territories, to England. The third section describes his impressions of Britain: from initial awe and admiration he achieves a more complex view and concludes that folly is universal because the passions are everywhere the same. He returns home critical of Oriental elements remaining in Britain but appreciative of its cultural revolution. At the end of the novel he is partly occidentalized, though since he has not (yet) become a Christian the process remains incomplete—a merely secular, temporal, and relative 'enlightenment'. The de-orientalization of the Rajah represents not so much the transformation of the East, however, as an ideological and cultural revolution in the still courtly West, especially Britain.

The correspondence opens with a long letter from Zāārmilla, in the flowery style conventionally attributed to Orientals, describing unrest in the Rohillas and the Rajah's meeting with a wounded British officer, Captain Percy—based on Charles Hamilton—who revolutionizes Zāārmilla's view of life. Zāārmilla's previous study of Oriental history had left him pessimistic about human nature: 'I beheld the few, whom fortune had unhappily placed in view of the giddy eminences of life, putting the reins of ambition into the bloody hand of cruelty, lash through torrents of perfidy and slaughter, till, perhaps, overthrown in their career, they were trampled on by others who were running the same guilty race' (i. 14). This common Enlightenment critique of the origins and nature of feudal monarchies makes Zāārmilla doubt that a benevolent deity rules the universe—a familiar problem in Enlightenment theodicy. But Captain Percy argues that 'In Europe man has not always, as in Asia, been degraded by slavery, or corrupted by the possession of despotic power. Whole nations have *there* acknowledged the rights of human nature, and while they did so have attained to the summit of true glory' (i. 16). Zāārmilla replies that the Romans ruled the world as long as they 'performed Poojah to the Goddess of Liberty' but they were seduced by 'Wealth and Luxury, the enemies of the Goddess'. Percy insists that the benefits of liberty were 'unknown in the world, till taught by the religion of Christ'.

When Percy further explains the tenets of Christianity, the lack of a caste system in Britain, the principles of the British constitution, and the values of British society, Zāārmilla shows he still has an Oriental mind lacking professionalized critical consciousness when he takes the theory for reality, exclaiming, 'It is not there as in the profligate court of Delhi, where great riches, a supple adherence to the minister, and a base and venal approbation of the measures of the court can lead to titles and distinction' (i. 21). One thing that disturbs Zāārmilla, however, is that Christianity considers women 'in the light of rational beings! free agents! In short, as a moiety of the human species; whose souls are no less precious in the eye of the Omniscient than that of the proud lords of the creation!' (i. 28–9). Captain Percy explains that the natural physical superiority of men had enabled them to tyrannize over women in a primitive state of society, and though advancing civilization gave the advantage to reason, in which the sexes were equal, men were reluctant to give up their now illegitimate power (i. 33–4). The same sociogenesis of women's subjection is found in Enlightened social critics and Revolutionary feminists.

The first letter, from the Rajah, sketches a comprehensive critique of Indian and British society. The next five letters illustrate this critique from different perspectives. Māāndāāra's reply represents what British readers would take to be the Oriental's naïve credulity as he considers Zāārmilla bewitched by the infidels but modifies the Rajah's account by recounting his experience of British hypocrisy and immorality. He also sends Zāārmilla three letters from the Bramin Sheermaal, just returned from England, challenging Zāārmilla's view of the British and describing British vices, including cruelty to slaves, upper-class irreligion, clerical worldliness, fashionable dissipation, injustice to the lower classes, obsession with rank, contempt for the middle class, regional prejudices, the use of Oriental wealth for social emulation, and degradation of women leading to prostitution.

Like Zāārmilla's idealized view of Britain, Sheermaal's view is defamiliarized by his comparisons with his own culture. Card-playing is described as a form of idolatry, prostitutes are compared to ancient Hindu blood sacrifices to the goddess Calee, and the British class system is described as three 'castes'—'People of Family, People of No Family, and People of Style, or fashion' (i. 118). Sheermaal's view that these prove 'the Braminical origin of the English nation' illustrates a commonplace of Enlightenment cultural relativism, that all cultures see others in their own terms. Yet Sheermaal also presents an idealized picture of the virtues, culture, civility, and forbearance of the common people in Britain. Adapted from pre-Revolutionary Sentimental ruralism, this was a middle-class social fantasy widely disseminated during the mid-1790s, depicting the common people as a diminutive version of the virtuous middle class, both freed from ideological and cultural subjection to the decadent and courtly upper class and protected against contamination by 'Jacobinism'.

Zāārmilla's next letter to Māāndāāra discusses their impending exchange of sisters as wives; the Rajah declares that he will treat his wife with Western liberality. He also rejects Sheermaal's picture of Britain: himself devoutly religious he cannot believe that Christians would so disregard the teachings of their Shaster, or holy book. This marks the end of the first part of the novel, which would itself make a coherent and complete text. But the correspondence resumes five years later around 1779 or 1780 with another letter from Zāārmilla to Māāndāāra, recording the birth of his son, various episodes of the Rohilla wars, and the clemency of the British toward the defeated. Zāārmilla travels around British India, and though he meets virtuous men such as Dr Denbeigh and Captain Grey, he sees that there is some truth in Sheermaal's account of the British. This section offers another layer of the novel's doubled critique of unreformed East and West. A further layer is promised when Zāārmilla decides he must see Britain himself; the voyage and tour of Britain fill the second volume of the novel, and offer a variant of the critique presented earlier.

On the voyage the Rajah meets characters representative of the society he is to investigate, including a young woman addicted to novels. Zāārmilla's defamiliarizing account of the conventional novel (ii. 18–24) is itself conventional, but a central set-piece here. Orientals, like children and women in the West, were supposed to have a taste for the fabulous, but even the Rajah finds novels too extravagant and fantastic, with especially bad effects on women readers, and in need of the renovation that *Letters of a Hindoo Rajah* aims to provide, precisely by defamiliarizing the taken-for-granted. The point is not only to distinguish *Letters* from most examples of the genre in which it participates but to reform novel reading as the main exercise in critical thought for women, who are the basis of domestic and thus public life.

Once in England the Rajah carries this outlook through a variety of encounters and incidents, raising a variety of topics, including the evils of the pew system in churches, the absurdities of modern architecture, the state of the theatre, the benefits of science, snobbery in advertising, the role of charity, the benefits of enclosing common lands, the unreliability of newspapers, the injustice of imprisonment for debt, the ignorance of critics, the nature of British rule in India, the growth of religious scepticism, the futility of melancholy, the pleasures of nature, the virtues of the professional middle class, the importance of moral and intellectual merit, the superiority of simple over elaborate dress (especially for women), the proper way to manage an estate, the uses of travel, the character of marriage East and West, the excesses of fashionable society, the absurdities of modern 'philosophy', and a great deal about the education, character, and role of women. Many of these topics, characters, and incidents are common in late eighteenth-century literature, but topics peculiar to the mid-1790s are introduced, including the debate over Tom Paine's *Age of Reason* (1794), the arguments of Burke's *Letter to a Noble Lord* (1796), growing resistance to Revolutionary feminism, the increasing crisis of political conscience and commitment among the middle classes, use of conspiracy theories to explain the French Revolution, growing professional middle-class criticism of the ruling-class's moral, social, and political leadership in the face of domestic and international crisis, and related emphasis on 'woman', domesticity, and national unity, ideologically reinforced by religious renewal and the Church.

The Rajah encounters these issues through two contrasting groups of characters. One includes Zāārmilla's friends from India and the voyage—Charlotte Percy, Captain Grey, Denbeigh, the virtuous widow, and Delomond—with the addition of their friends the virtuous philosopher and scientist Dr Severan, Lady Grey and her daughters, the good steward Trueman, the virtuous labourer Gregory Grub, the professionalized landed gentleman Mr Darnley, and Denbeigh's wife and family. The other group centres around the titled English Jacobin, Sir Caprice Ardent, and includes his insipid wife and novel-reading feminist daughter and his hangers-on, the metaphysical and political philosophers Puzzledorf, Axiom, Vapour, and Dr Sceptic. This part of the novel uses such familiar satirical devices as the Theophrastan Character, the philosophical dialogue, the inset narrative of a character's life, and bathos, which became commonplace in anti-Jacobin novels of the late 1790s.

Sir Caprice, his family, and followers represent three important and interconnected themes of the mid-1790s Revolution debate—the pervasiveness of the fashion system, even in the domain of art, philosophy, and politics; the decadence and incapacity of some of the upper classes; and the transmuted courtly character of 'Jacobinism'. Women are mediators of these evils. Dr Severan's inset narrative explains the Ardents' character for caprice in somewhat Godwinian terms as the product of miseducation, especially of Lady Caprice (ii. 95). Like the mere courtly coquette, she works on her husband's vices for her own narrow interest. Not surprisingly, she despises both her sex's 'weaknesses' and their domestic virtues, and her daughter is both a 'philosopher' and utopian feminist:

She pants for that blessed period, when the eyes of men shall no longer be attracted by the charms of youth and beauty; when mind, and mind alone, shall be thought worthy the attention of a philosopher.

In that wished-for æra, the talents of women, she says, shall not be debased by household drudgery, or their noble spirits broken by base submission, to usurped authority. The reins will then be put into the hands of wisdom; and as women will, in the age of reason, probably be found to have the largest share, it is they who will then drive the chariot of state, and guide the steeds of war! (ii. 216–17)

This burlesques Revolutionary feminism, like 'Jacobinism', as merely disguised lust for power. Readers would see an obvious analogy between such feminism and the court 'mistress system' it claims to reject.

Miss Ardent's feminism is based on the Godwinian materialism and revolutionary millenarianism of the novel's 'philosophers', bathetically exposed in Letter XVI (misnumbered XV) when Puzzledorf and Axiom testify at the trial of a robber by delivering a dissertation on identity and claiming in Godwinian fashion that crime is only error; the thief says he stole only after hearing Axiom's views on property and justice (ii. 197). The scene burlesques both Godwin's treatise *Political Justice* and his novelization of it in *Things As They Are; or, The Adventures of Caleb Williams*. Later at Ardent Hall the philosophers attack religion, though Zāārmilla finds that they worship idols of their own, called 'Systems', with an intolerance that would disgust a Hindu. This comparison suggests a parallel between the passionate speculation of the 'philosophers', the too-eager credulity of the Rajah and other Orientals, and the fantasizing of women novel readers.

Characters suffering from these intellectual extremes lack the proper balance of reason and imagination, become unnatural, impractical, or dupes of pseudo-reasoners, and undermine social order. Sceptic practises the supposedly Godwinian theory of impartiality, but according to the Rajah, 'It seems to have been the endeavour of his life, to eradicate from his bosom, those social feelings and affections, which form so great a part of the felicity of common mortals' (ii. 208). Sceptic's philosophy leads to atheism, which in turn leads to immorality, which undermines society's central pillar—'domestic woman'. Zāārmilla observes, 'I am told, that the female converts seldom fail to make an offering to Atheism of their peace, purity, and good fame; and that of its worshippers, among the lower orders of men, numbers every year suffer martyrdom, at a place called Newgate; which I suppose to be a temple dedicated to this superstition' (ii. 209).

According to Hamilton, atheism purveyed to the middle classes by Godwin and to the lower classes by Paine undermines social order by seducing society's intellectually weak elements—women and the common people—leading them not to revolution but to crime. Vapour advocates free love: ' "By destroying the domestic affections, what an addition will be made to human happiness! And when man is no longer corrupted by the tender and endearing ties of brother, sister, wife, and child, how greatly will his dispositions be meliorated!' " (ii. 212). But when Sceptic's nephew uses these arguments to seduce his cousin, she kills herself, and the nephew follows suit (ii. 267–73). Undeterred by this example, at the end of the novel another female convert, Miss Ardent, elopes with Axiom to the Continent.

The contrast to these 'philosophers' is a significantly more diverse group of characters, for 'philosophers' form cabals and conspiracies but virtuous professional middle-class people form friendships and families. The younger sister of Sir Ardent, Lady Grey, and her daughters represent ideal domestic woman who will triumph over the Ardents' feminism because Lady Grey is educating Sir Ardent's daughter Julia (named after Rousseau's reformable 'nouvelle Héloïse'). Lady Grey warns Julia particularly against false Sensibility, in the mid-1790s being blamed for social and political vanguardism, as ' "too often another word for selfishness' " when it does not lead to ethical action. Axiom attributes her views to ' "Hume's Principles of General Utility' " and Puzzledorf attributes them to Godwinian necessitarianism; but she declares, ' "I have taken them . . . from the doctrines and examples of Jesus Christ and his Apostles" ' (ii. 258–9). Such put-downs are characteristic of anti-Jacobin novels, but Hamilton here advances an Anglican doctrine of faith and works against movements seen to be linked in a proto-revolutionary coalition, including lower-class Methodism, middle-class Dissent, and the political disaffection they were thought to encourage during the 1790s.

Not surprisingly, the Rajah then learns that Lady Grey is a good estate manager, looks after the poor and distressed, supervises her children's education, and was the intellectual equal and advisor as well as domestic companion of her late husband. Mrs Denbeigh, the daughter of a Dissenting minister, also educated her daughters to be learned yet feminine and domestic. Though such women have little power over their own lives—the young widow, Lady Grey, and Charlotte

Percy all lost ideal companions through the accidents of mortality—
their religion and passive virtues enable them to carry on, unlike the
'philosopher' Vapour, who believes that the 'age of reason' will
conquer death—a favourite idea of English Jacobins. The novel's
virtuous domesticated women do not entertain such fantasies but
practise faith and works in their domestic sphere or, like Lady Grey,
extend these 'duties' into local society, as envisaged by the Bluestocking
feminists and middle-class Evangelicals such as Sarah Trimmer. In the
comic universe of this novel such feminine virtues receive social,
public, and divine recognition in a marriage of true minds, or what the
wise Mr Denbeigh calls ' "such an union of minds as includes a
similarity of taste and sentiment' " and ' "such a degree of esteem as is
essential to mutual confidence' " (ii. 306). Marriage is the proper role
for the professionalized woman, analogous to the collegial 'partnership'
of professional men. Such matches are made between Lady Grey and
Dr Severan, and Darnley and Emma Denbeigh. This ideology of courtship and marriage was found in more novels as the cultural revolution
was reformulated to resolve the conflicts of the 1790s; it would
become central to post-Revolutionary novels such as Jane Austen's.

For exceptional women there might be alternatives. The elder
Denbeigh counsels Charlotte Percy (a self-portrait of the author) to
overcome grief at her brother's death with active duties. When she
protests that her 'power to be useful' is 'circumscribed' he replies that
she has enough 'powers' of 'mind' to become a writer:

'Ah! Sir,' returned Charlotte, 'you know how female writers are looked down
upon. The women fear, and hate; the men ridicule, and dislike them.'
    'This may be the case with the mere mob, who receive every prejudice
upon trust,' rejoined Mr. Denbeigh; 'but if the simplicity of your character
remains unchanged—if the virtues of your heart receive no alloy from the
vanity of authorship; trust me, my dear Charlotte, you will not be the less dear
to any friend that is deserving of your love, for having employed your leisure
hours in a way that is both innocent and rational.' (ii. 329)

The novel itself demonstrates how this may be so, and the statement
is a rejection of recent attacks on women's writing in such satires as
William Gifford's *Mæviad* and *Baviad*. *Letters* embodies a feminism of
the Revolutionary decade distinct from and partly rejecting the Revolutionary feminism of Wollstonecraft and Hays, but overlapping with it
and drawing on a common intellectual and literary inheritance in
Enlightenment and Sentimental culture. Hamilton's more domestic

and religious feminism was more acceptable in the 1790s and anticipates the Romantic feminism of the Revolutionary aftermath and varieties of Victorian feminism that grew from it. At the same time, Hamilton's feminism gave her a public and even political identity without sacrificing her feminine and domestic one, as seen in critical reaction to her novel. The anti-Jacobin *British Critic* concluded that she had displayed masculine powers without sacrificing her femininity, and a lead article in the conservative *Critical Review* praised her in similar terms, but the liberal *Analytical Review* accused the novel of promoting the dogmatism it condemned, showing 'little knowledge and great presumption', and wasting its satire on such subjects when 'a wide field of fashionable follies, which might have yielded an abundant harvest' was neglected. But the reviewer also praised Hamilton's critique of courtly woman and 'the barbarous, sensual prejudices, which have hitherto been indulged respecting the female mind and manners'. Only the *Monthly Review* took a patriarchal view, dismissing Hamilton's Orientalist scholarship, preferring her 'delineations of scenes at home, where she is better acquainted', and questioning her command of standard English.[17]

One consequence of *Letters*, however, was a quarrel with Mary Hays. Before it was published Hays had talked to Hamilton of her personal affairs and friends. After the book came out, Hays felt betrayed and complained to Hamilton, who replied in March 1797 that Hays paid 'a strange sort of a compliment' to Godwin 'in taking it for granted' that he was the chief object of attack in *Letters of a Hindoo Rajah* and 'that it is impossible to laugh at any thing ridiculous without pointing at him'.[18] In her next novel Hamilton would satirize Godwin and his circle even more comprehensively, and include a cruelly comic portrait of Hays.

Hamilton's success now promised independence and a role in burgeoning counter-revolutionary literature. Her sister went to Ireland and Hamilton took single lodgings, spending her mornings in study and her evenings meeting the Gregorys and other friends. One of their conversations suggested a satire on modern 'philosophy', Hamilton wrote a preliminary sketch, and Gregory approved. 'Almost wondering at her own temerity', she retired with a friend to Gloucestershire to

[17] *British Critic*, 8 (Sept. 1796), 238, 241; *Critical Review*, NS 17 (July 1796), 242; *Analytical Review*, 24 (Oct. 1796), 431; *Monthly Review*, NS 21 (Oct. 1796), 177–9.
[18] Elizabeth Hamilton to Mary Hays, 13 Mar. 1797; letter in Pforzheimer Library.

carry on with the novel.[19] Just before completing it she became ill—perhaps a sign of self-doubt—but returned to London, finished the novel, and had it published in the summer of 1800.

Memoirs of Modern Philosophers carries forward the counter-revolutionary element of *Letters of a Hindoo Rajah*, formalized in its textual structure, authoritative narrative mode, characters representing the contending parties within the professional middle-class cultural revolution during the 1790s, 'philosophic' dialogues, and triple plot of seduction, quixotic errantry, and romantic courtship. This structure novelizes the Revolution debate of the late 1790s, yet its deliberately old-fashioned techniques recall an earlier, more genial, and less dangerous kind of ideological conflict and reinforces the novel's defence of tradition and convention against 'innovation' and transgression. Moreover, the novel's formal structure and thematic repertory together construct the 'author' as a model consciousness representing the coming ruling class as it emerges from the Revolutionary decade's dangerous internal conflicts, including that of gender. For Hamilton reaffirms the centrality of 'domestic woman' to the ideology and practice of the professional middle-class cultural revolution, but in a way that could be seen as transgressing the limits of 'domestic woman'. Consequently she kept her name off the title-page of the first edition, though she claimed that this was to give 'effect' to the novel's 'humour'.[20] But the 'humour' was of a kind conventionally associated with men's writing and it is directed at intellectual and political discourses conventionally barred to women. Although *Memoirs* partly feminizes the 'masculine' discourses and topics it reworks, it also gives its narrator a masculine identity and constructs its 'author' as a paternalistic political commentator. Furthermore, like its predecessor, *Memoirs of Modern Philosophers* uses elements conventionally associated with men's genres, including satire, burlesque, the learned quasi-novel, the social survey, the Quixote tradition, the *roman-à-clef*, and the philosophical dialogue, historically used to satirize 'false' ideologies. In redeploying them against the attack of 'modern philosophers' on domestic woman, Hamilton has to become something like the kind of 'female philosopher' she deplores.

The novel conveys a social, cultural, and political critique of upper-class decadence, middle-class emulation, and lower-class subversion in three main stories and a number of supporting inset stories. The main

---

[19] Benger, *Hamilton*, i. 132.
[20] Ibid. 141.

stories concern quixotic pursuit, intrigue or seduction, and sentimental courtship—principal forms of eighteenth-century fiction. *Memoirs* appropriates these for its own public, political ends, using the novel, conventionally a 'woman's' genre, to demolish 'modern philosophy', conventionally men's discourse, though practised and novelized in the 1790s by what Hamilton would see as unfeminine 'female philosophers' such as Mary Hays.

The quixotic pursuit is conducted by Bridgetina Botherim (a caricature of Hays), whose reading of novels and 'philosophy' has made her despise domesticity and conventional feminine conduct. She persuades herself that she loves the virtuous young professional man Henry Sydney (an allusion to William Frend) and pursues him openly and relentlessly, until disappointment and the fate of her friend Julia Delmond make her realize the value of domesticity, tranquillity, and respectability. Though the Quixote was usually a male character, there were several female versions. Bridgetina's co-Quixote and pathetic counterpart is Julia Delmond, named after Rousseau's 'nouvelle Héloïse' and thus a critique of the domestic subversion effected through the classic novel of Sensibility by the author widely viewed as a 'father' of the French Revolution. Julia is the daughter of a too-genteel military officer and an insipid heiress; novels and 'philosophy' open her to seduction by Vallaton, a Frenchified, Jacobin, plebeian ex-hairdresser. Her fate shocks her co-Quixote and Julia delivers the novel's moral against Revolutionary feminism to a chastened Bridgetina (iii. 345–6). The pathetic Quixote cures the comic one.

Bridgetina and Julia are Quixotes in the sense of enthusiastic but unrealistic and impractical pursuers of visionary ideals. Quixotes misread the world and act inappropriately because their ideology or 'system' is false, derived from the wrong books, such as chivalric romances (satirized in *Don Quixote*), Dissenting religious and political literature (satirized in Samuel Butler's *Hudibras*), or Methodist 'new light' (satirized in Richard Graves's *Spiritual Quixote*). This long literary tradition was associated with men's writing but an emergent women's tradition included Charlotte Lennox's *Female Quixote* (1752) and later novels of manners. These 'Quixotes' are figures for the hitherto merely domestic and private individual of either sex trying to read and negotiate the public and social world dominated by the social 'other', especially in the form of courtly intriguers. Such protagonists often set out with false expectations derived from romances and novels purveying courtly ideology and culture or their transmuted form of

Sensibility. The 'Quixote' falls or is led into repeated errors of misreading, comic or pathetic, until false consciousness is purged by a shocking revelation or a wise mentor (usually male) who re-educates the protagonist in professional middle-class critical consciousness of self and society. Revelation is a figure for demystification of court power, and re-education a figure for ideological and cultural reproduction. Cultural conflict is plotted as false and true courtship, threatened seduction or contamination of the protagonist, terminated by marriage to a professionalized gentleman or (less often) a gentrified professional. This version of the Quixote story was dominant from Frances Burney to Jane Austen at least.

Hamilton's version is more politically explicit in order to engage directly in the novelistic aspect of the Revolution debate. English Jacobin novels such as Robert Bage's *Man As He Is* (1792) and Thomas Holcroft's *Adventures of Hugh Trevor* (1794–7) show an idealistic young man pursuing virtue in a society corrupted by court government and culture, and suggest that only revolution can make the world fit for such 'Quixotes'. But anti-Jacobin novels such as William Beckford's *Azemia* (1796), Isaac D'Israeli's *Vaurien* (1797), Charles Lloyd's *Edmund Oliver* (1798), George Walker's *The Vagabond* (1799), and Jane West's *A Tale of the Times* (1799) show the Quixote as an impractical dupe of 'Jacobin' intriguers, conspirators, and seducers.[21] Accordingly, these novelists usually gender the Quixote female, since 'woman' had long been a figure for the subvertible, seducible element in a social class and since the villain in anti-Jacobin novels aims to subvert the state by subverting 'domestic woman' and domesticity.

Anti-Jacobin novels adapt the Quixote story to satirize two particular forms of ideology as false consciousness—imaginative fantasy and 'metaphysical' speculation—along with the means of disseminating them—novels and 'philosophy'. These two discourses were conventionally gendered feminine and masculine respectively and ranked at opposite ends of the discursive order. But anti-Jacobin contributors to the Revolution debate portray them as variants of merely theoretical, unrealistic, impractical, impulsive enthusiasm that produced the Revolution in France and motivated Revolutionary sympathizers in Britain. In anti-Jacobin novels they are represented by the female Quixote who has been indulged in excessive novel reading and the subversive male 'philosopher' who combines upper- and lower-class vices, often with

[21] Marilyn Butler, *Jane Austen and the War of Ideas* (Oxford, 1975), 133–4.

an alien, especially French connection. He attempts to seduce the 'fair enthusiast' by undermining her principles with 'philosophy', either to obtain her property or simply to exercise social power—for centuries the main element in plots of seduction.

In anti-Jacobin novels such as *Memoirs of Modern Philosophers* the Quixote story is an allegory of class conflict in the 1790s. The villain's 'philosophy' is both the manifesto and the mask of a lower-class upstart who infiltrates the courtly upper class and uses what he learns to subvert the professional middle class, taking woman as the conventional figure for the class's weakest element. In pre-Revolutionary versions of this plot woman is seduced by courtly glamour and her own desire for upward social mobility because she is subordinated in her own class and has little to lose in going over to the class enemy. But once used by the social 'other' to exploit or infiltrate her class, she is abandoned to lower-class contamination or absorbed into the lower class as a prostitute. 'Woman' is reduced to her desirability and desiring and then transformed into a commodity, powerless and dehumanized. This plot helps to account for increasing concern over prostitution during the 1790s, seen in Mary Hays's *The Victim of Prejudice*. In the fate of the 'fallen woman', middle-class women and men could read their individual and collective disaster.

The inset story of Vallaton, the Jacobin intriguer in *Memoirs of Modern Philosophers*, adapts another familiar form of eighteenth-century fiction and the counterpart to the Quixote story—the picaresque narrative of the lower-class anti-hero who resists the hegemonic order by learning how to use the weaknesses of his 'betters' against them. Born and raised in the criminal underworld of London, Vallaton was taken in by a well-to-do patroness and learned how to ape and court her upper-class friends. But in France he picked up 'modern philosophy' and a mistress, a vulgar woman who played the Goddess of Reason at a Revolutionary festival—the great ceremony held in the de-Christianized Paris cathedral of Notre-Dame on 10 December 1793. Vallaton fixes on Julia as his prey, seduces and abandons her, escapes to France with the Goddess of Reason, and is eventually guillotined.

This plotting of class conflict advances several topics of the professional middle-class social critique—the ideological and cultural hegemony of upper class over lower, dissemination of courtly decadence throughout society by economic patronage and social emulation, and therefore the need to separate the lower orders from their historic masters, confer on them a diminutive version of bourgeois culture, and supervise them more closely. Otherwise the result, as in France, will be revolution replacing one corrupt despotism by another, both decadently courtly and vulgarly plebeian—a dangerous coalition of the professionals' class rivals. Hamilton's versions of the Quixote story as allegory for class conflict reappear later in Amelia Opie's *Adeline Mowbray* (1804), Elizabeth Le Noir's *Clara de Montfier* (1808), E. S. Barrett's *The Heroine* (1813), and even Jane Austen's novels, where the explicitly political content is dropped. In other post-Revolutionary novels by Walter Scott, Lady Caroline Lamb, and Mary Shelley, the anti-Jacobin version of the Quixote story, like other elements of the Revolution debate, is subsumed into an ambivalent Romantic critique of excessive individualism on one hand and society's incommensurability with aspiring individuality on the other.

The alternative to the Quixote story and the resolution of social conflict are represented in the third story of *Memoirs of Modern Philosophers*—the courtship of Henry Sydney and Harriet Delmond, the novel's model professional man and domestic woman. The courtship is occasionally and comically disrupted by Bridgetina's pursuit of Henry, and he and Harriet try to save Julia Delmond. But in comparison to the farce or melodrama in the female Quixotes' stories, the courtship of Henry and Harriet is deliberately low-key, impeded mainly by her modesty and his diffidence and need to establish a career, and thus it is a critique of the dramatic and improbable stories involving (or written by) 'modern philosophers'. This kind of story is used by Jane Austen and others in the Revolutionary aftermath to insist on the danger of quixotism in private life and the superior value of Arminian ethics relying on providential justice rather than a merely secular 'system'. Appropriately, the marriage of Henry and Harriet closes *Memoirs* and, like the form of sentimental comedy that inspires it, implies wider social benefits to follow from such unions.

The moral of the main stories—Henry and Harriet's success, Julia's failure, and Bridgetina's defeat—is reinforced and amplified by inset stories, including the 'History of Captain Delmond', the account of Vallaton's early life and career, and the story of the failed courtship of Henry Sydney's patron, Miss Fielding, and his father. The novel switches from one principal story to another or stops for one of the insets, creating for the reader the impression of a loose, complex, but interconnected structure of stories. This pattern contrasts with the comic reversals or pathetic denouements experienced by Quixotes guided by their 'systems', and also foregrounds free will and providential opportunity in the individual life, in contrast to English Jacobin novels' 'necessitarian' form, showing the necessary construction of character by social circumstances. 'Necessitarianism' was often seen as a secular version of Calvinist predestination. To counter it, anti-Jacobin novelists, most of whom were associated with the Established Church, assume Anglican and Arminian doctrines of free will and providentially assisted ethical action, overcoming personal frailties and imperfect knowledge in a comic novelistic universe with a benevolent deity dispensing narrative justice not by some abstract 'system' but by local charity and domestic virtues. Such a form counters not only the secular materialism and rationalism of the 'modern philosophers' but also the Arian, Socinian, and Calvinist theology of Dissenters, seen by many critics as sectarian bases for pro-Revolutionary rationalism and materialism.[22] Hamilton draws attention to these ideological differences by making her novel a political *roman-à-clef*, though this again transgresses gendered bounds of discourse. In particular, *Memoirs* attacks the 'modern philosophers' of the Godwin circle who, Hamilton thought, gave subversive practices of unreason and false philosophy a dangerously seductive glamour. Godwin, Holcroft, Wollstonecraft, and Hays are caricatured and their works are mentioned, quoted, and burlesqued, but Mary Hays is made the principal butt; even her short stature and slight squint are ridiculed.

Paradoxically, in mounting her satire Hamilton has to use 'philosophical' devices already developed by English Jacobin novelists. One of these is the Theophrastan Character embodying specific values or dispositions and named accordingly. Bridgetina Botherim, the pestering 'female philosopher' and man-chaser ('bother-him'), is a diminutive Bridget or Bride, alluding to Bridewell, the house of correction for prostitutes and 'fallen women'. Bridget here means Mary Wollstonecraft, pilloried in the anti-Jacobin press as no better than a prostitute after her husband William Godwin's *Memoirs* of her revealed her sexual transgressions; Bridgetina represents Mary Hays, Wollstonecraft's follower, or 'little Bridget', perhaps an allusion to Hays's short stature. Less complexly allusive are Myope, the 'philosopher' of short views (both Godwin and Holcroft wore spectacles), and the sloganizing Glib, circulating-library proprietor and Myope's Sancho

---

[22] In fact many leading Revolutionary sympathizers in the 1790s, such as Joseph Priestley and William Godwin, were or had been Socinians or Calvinists. See J. C. D. Clark, *English Society 1688–1832: Ideology, Social Structure and Political Practice During the Ancien Regime* (Cambridge, 1985), 330, 331–2, 342–6.

Panza. Alphonso Vallaton is so named by his novel-reading patroness from mishearing 'funny vagabond', his nickname as a street beggar. Vallaton is also a variation on the villain of Isaac D'Israeli's anti-Jacobin novel *Vaurien* ('worthless'). 'Val', the root of 'value', combines with the French 'ton', in English usage as 'fashion' or 'mode', in a pejorative sense. Vallaton's worth depends on fashion, be it intellectual, social, or political. Association with foreignness is also found in the too-worldly Delmonds, from 'le monde', an appropriated French expression for fashionable society, and in the snobbish Villers family, whose name indicates that their values are merely those of the fashionable 'Town' (French '*ville*').

Characters with Theophrastan names are treated as burlesque and one-dimensional; those receiving more 'realistic' treatment are named accordingly, though their role is no less allegorical. The Dissenting Sydneys and Anglican Orwells are model professional middle-class characters and thus their names suggest good English stock and mainstream culture, though 'Sydney' has historical associations with Algernon Sidney, the seventeenth-century nobleman, commonwealthman, and martyr to court government and religious persecution, who remained a hero for eighteenth-century Dissenters and who was often cited in the 1790s as a model for modern patriots.[23] Mr Sydney and the Anglican vicar Dr Orwell represent different religious and political traditions and cultures, yet they are similar in character and close friends (i. 18–19). Their friendship and the marriage of Henry Sydney and Harriet Orwell represent the mutual toleration, respect, and co-operation of different religious, political, and cultural communities within the professional middle class, communities that were once opposed in civil war, and during the 1790s threatened to be so again.

Hamilton purposely presents individual characters in terms of family membership and resemblance, playing them off against egregious and disruptive individualists of the kind supposedly instigating Revolution in France and social conflict in Britain. Emphasizing the familial also counters Godwin's notorious attack on the domestic affections as irrational. Not all family forms are approved in *Memoirs*, however. Sir Anthony Aldgate, representing the City's commercial interest (hence his name) as supporter of autocracy, is a domestic tyrant. The Gubbles, senior and junior, seem limited to merely cosy, petty bourgeois domes-

[23] Caroline Robbins, *The Eighteenth Century Commonwealthman*, repr. (New York, 1968), 46.

ticity. The widow Botherim and her daughter lack the guiding presence of the late vicar Botherim and so have deteriorated into extremes—the mother a mere 'notable woman' (skilled housewife) and the daughter a feminist 'philosopher' despising the work her mother does. There are also admirable singletons, such as Mrs Fielding, a late version of the Bluestocking feminist, engaging in philanthropic activities and encouraging the career of Henry Sydney.

Nevertheless, *Memoirs* is built on family histories, as may be seen in the fate of the Delmonds. The inset 'History of Captain Delmond' (i. 12) recounts his adventures during the American Revolution and his return home only 'to be fattened for fields of future glory'. In enforced idleness he took up reading romances, moved on to free-thinking philosophers, and developed both a false code of 'honour' and a sceptical outlook. Accordingly, he managed a 'romantic' elopement with an insipid heiress and fought a duel. His daughter Julia was allowed to read whatever she wished and, intoxicated by novels, she developed an ungoverned imagination and became 'an adept in the art of castle-building' (i. 147). Her 'ruin' by Vallaton causes her father's death from grief, her mother's death from bitterness, and her own death from remorse. The fate of the Delmonds traces the moral and intellectual corruption initiated by professional middle-class emulation of upper-class values, disseminated by fiction and 'philosophy', leading to seduction by plebeian ambition dressed in upper-class glamour and masquerading as revolutionary 'reason' and 'virtue'. Lacking the ideological, cultural, and social support of religion, proper patriarchal authority, and maternal domestic affections, the Delmonds' weakest element is subverted by class enemies, destroying the entire family.

By contrast, the triumph of the professional bourgeoisie is figured in the Sydneys and the Orwells. Mr Sydney senior was unable to marry the virtuous and rational heiress Miss Fielding when his religious principles prevented acceptance of a Church living. Educated for the Dissenting ministry at Glasgow University (unlike Oxford and Cambridge, Scottish universities did not require subscription to the tenets of the Church of England), he married an orphan and educated their son Henry for the medical profession. Henry is helped in his profession by the still unmarried Mrs Fielding (the title 'Mrs' was conferred on a woman after a certain age, regardless of marital status). Mindful of her own disappointment in love, she requires that he earn £500 a year before marrying, though he finds that professional success depends too much on upper-class patronage (iii. 46–7). Once again, social values and class relations are inscribed in the history of the individual family. But Henry needs a proper wife to reproduce these values in his turn, and he finds her in the domestic but cultured Harriet Orwell. Guided by Mr Sydney, Henry and his inexperienced sister Maria achieve marriages of true minds, the necessary basis of the professional middle-class hegemony that the novel's conclusion foretells and that the novel aims to bring about.

Memoirs conducts its anti-Jacobin argument mainly by plotting affective relationships between characters representing factions within the professional middle-class cultural revolution. But like other 'philosophical novels', it also dramatizes its political content through dialogue, including individual characteristic 'speech' and dramatic interchange between these diverse 'voices'. The novel opens with Mrs Mapple praising 'Biddy's' pudding, but 'Biddy' protests that she is 'Bridgetina' and making puddings is a waste of time. Mrs Botherim defends her daughter's domestic heterodoxy:

'You will find, if you converse with her a little, that she is far too learned to trouble herself about doing any thing useful. Do, Bridgetina, my dear, talk to your cousin a little about the *cowsation*, and *perfebility*, and all them there things as Mr. Glib and you are so often upon. You have no ideer what a scholar she is . . . she has read every book in the circulating library, and Mr. Glib declares she knows them better than he does himself.'

'Indeed, mamma, but I do no such thing,' cried Bridgetina, pettishly; 'do you think I would take the trouble of going through all the dry stuff in Mr. Glib's collection—history and travels, sermons and matters of fact? I hope I have a better taste! You know very well I never read any thing but novels and metaphysics.' (i. 3–4)

Mrs Botherim's malapropisms are deformations of key Godwinian terms, conveniently italicized for the reader. Later, when Mrs Botherim praises their manservant for being a 'good' cowherd, Bridgetina rebukes her mother:

'It appears, madam, that you know very little of the nature of goodness. What is goodness but virtue? *Considered as a personal quality, it consists in the disposition of the mind, and may be defined [as] a desire to promote the benefit of intelligent beings in general, the quantity of virtue being as the quantity of desire. Now desire is another name for preference, or a perception of the excellence, real or supposed, of any object; and what perception of excellence can a being so unenlightened possibly possess?'* (i. 182)

The commonplace that 'modern philosophers' are impractical is reinforced by the passage italicized to indicate a quotation from Godwin. As the narrator observes, Bridgetina speaks 'for the press' (i. 191).

Between the extremes of Mrs Botherim's vulgarisms and Bridgetina's jargon is the standard English used by the narrator and 'spoken' by characters like the Orwells and the Sydneys. When Bridgetina praises Rousseau, hoping to arouse sentimental interest from Henry Sydney, he condemns the master of Sensibility and cites Wollstonecraft:

'The inconsistency and folly of his system,' said Henry, 'was, perhaps, never better exposed than in the very ingenious publication which takes the Rights of Women for its title. Pity that the very sensible authoress has sometimes permitted her zeal to hurry her into expressions which have raised a prejudice against the whole. To superficial readers it appears to be her intention to unsex women entirely. But—'

'And why should there be any distinction of sex?' cried Brigetina, interrupting him; 'Are not moral causes superior to physical? And are not women formed with powers and energies capable of perfectibility? Ah! miserable and deplorable state of things in which these powers are debased by the meanness of hous[e]hold cares! Ah! wretched woman, restrained by the cruel fetters of decorum! Vile and ignoble bondage! the offspring of an unjust and odious tyranny, a tyranny whose remorseless cruelty assigns to woman the care of her family! But the time shall come when the mind of woman will be too enlightened to submit to the slavish task!' (i. 196–7)

Bridgetina declares her feminism and enacts it by interrupting Henry—a small but significant transgression of the social decorum against which she rails. Her Godwinian jargon, orotund hyperboles, and stilted apostrophes burlesque the style of English Jacobin declamation, and her argument is further undermined by her oblique yet transparent hint, in 'the cruel fetters of decorum', of an undeclared passion for Henry.

Bridgetina is challenged first by another woman, Harriet Orwell, in what is meant to be a contrastingly courteous, calm, rational, and kindly style:

'Indeed, Miss Botherim,' said Harriet, 'I do not think that there is any thing either slavish or disagreeable in the task: nor do I think a woman's energies, as you call them, can possibly be better employed. Surely the performance of the duties that are annexed to our situation, can never be deemed mean or ignoble?'

Harriet notes Bridgetina's jargon ('energies, as you call them') while herself avoiding Bridgetina's artificial parallelisms, elevation, and exclamations. Harriet's views and voice are then validated by paternal authority in her father's condemnation of 'all the system-makers who have taken upon them to prescribe the duties of the sex': 'One philosopher, and one only, has appeared, who, superior to all prejudices, invariably treated the female sex as beings who were to be taught the performance of duty, not by arbitrary regulations confined to particular parts of conduct, but by the knowledge of principles which enlighten the understanding and improve the heart.' When Bridgetina declares she has never heard of this philosopher, Dr Orwell replies, 'Very probably not . . . his name was JESUS CHRIST' (i. 199). As Christ's earthly vicar Dr Orwell assumes divine and institutional authority for such remarks; as the successor in office to Bridgetina's late father he assumes the right to rebuke her 'philosophical' feminism with a Christian version of it. Shortly afterwards the political implications of Bridgetina's 'philosophy' are exposed when she tries to persuade some labourers that they are unhappy, discontented, and rebellious. But a good old man, of the kind favoured in fantasies of plebeian complaisance such as Hannah More's Cheap Repository tracts, expresses contentment with his lot and loyalty to Henry Sydney for saving his son from the smallpox.

A more elaborate display of false 'voices' occurs when Julia Delmond accompanies Vallaton to Villers-Castle (vol. i, ch. 18). A variety of pretentiously fashionable and courtly individuals are assembled, including Miss Mushroom, daughter of an army agent who made his fortune from government funds; the effete Colonel Goldfinch; and the fashionable Lady Page, who recognizes Vallaton as a former hairdresser and society gigolo. Each speaks a different fashionable cant while gossiping about the sexual intrigues of the day, and they consume a luxurious dinner while insensitively discussing the plight of the poor. The 'normal' voice in this group belongs to Miss Mordaunt, whose mordant critiques of the others' pretences are more a reminder than an enforcer of discursive and thus cultural and political order. Julia is not yet lost and like the reader can see through the false language of the others; yet she becomes entangled in a dialogue at cross-purposes when discussing Vallaton with her hostess, whom she imagines, as if in a novel, to be his long-lost mother.

Hamilton does show that women may join the authoritative paternal chorus, as seen in Mrs Fielding, who both moralizes like Mr Sydney and Dr Orwell and criticizes sharply like the narrator. As she tells a gourmandizing baronet, ' "Within a hundred yards from where you now sit, have I this morning seen a family of eight souls, to whom the price of that very dish you have spurned from your table would have afforded luxuries for a week. . . . to misery such as theirs your conduct is an insult" ' (iii. 71). This echoes the common criticism of the upper classes for abdicating their social 'duties' and thus contributing to the economic distress behind the potentially revolutionary situation in Britain. Mrs Fielding's main work is in rescuing female victims of such distress from prostitution. By the kind of coincidence anti-Jacobin novels rely on, one of those in her 'Asylum of the Destitute' turns out to be the fallen Julia Delmond. Mrs Fielding moralizes on woman's fate in a style echoing the authoritative fathers, and Julia takes up that style in her repentant peroration, reinforcing Bridgetina's decision to abandon 'philosophy' and completing dissemination of the paternal chorus's wisdom to the younger generation (iii. 12–14).

Together the main elements of 'story' in *Memoirs of Modern Philosophers*—plot, character, dialogue, and description—represent the defeat of one element of the professional middle-class cultural revolution by another. The victorious faction is also embodied textually in the novel's 'discourse', including third-person authoritative narration, authorial 'voice' or characterization of the 'author' in the text, and certain elements of textual structure. Although Hamilton had used epistolary first-person narration in *Letters of a Hindoo Rajah*, she offset its immediacy by devices including the 'Preliminary Dissertation', factual footnotes, and narrative irony distancing the reader from the Rajah's viewpoint. Even in 1796, first-person narration was strongly associated with English Jacobin novelists, who use it to gain readers' sympathy for condemnation of 'things as they are'. Consequently, anti-Jacobin novelists use authoritative, often satirical third-person narration to formalize their ideal of a hierarchical but not autocratic society; thus *Memoirs* burlesques English Jacobin narrative, particularly Mary Hays's *Memoirs of Emma Courtney*, in Bridgetina's account of the progress of her passion for Henry Sydney (vol. ii, ch. 3).

First-person narration was also associated with women's writing. By choosing authoritative, learned, and satirical discourse, Hamilton and other anti-Jacobin novelists were implicitly rejecting feminization of culture and literature now associated with Revolutionary sympathy in such writers as Helen Maria Williams and Mary Hays. In the context of the Revolution debate, third-person, satiric, learned narration reaffirms patriarchy and paternalism, though not that of the courtly upper class. For anti-Jacobin novelists modify third-person narration by sympathetic representation of subjectivity through reported inward speech (or 'free indirect discourse') and especially by the incorporation of characters' letters—ways of setting character before the reader that are momentarily unmediated by narratorial intervention. These devices are found in Hamilton and novelists with similar politics from Frances Burney to Jane Austen.

Nevertheless, Hamilton also reinforces authoritative, objective third-person narration in *Memoirs of Modern Philosophers* by various devices. Like its predecessor, *Memoirs* is an oblique narration, framed not as a 'translation' but as a found manuscript, not from a social margin ouside Britain but from one within—the Grub Street world of 'men of letters' condemned by Burke as instigators of revolution. In a prefatory letter to the publisher, the book's 'Editor', Geoffry Jarvis, describes retrieving a manuscript tossed from a garret in Paternoster Row, the booksellers' quarter in London. The first fifty pages had been used as fire-lighters (a figure for the 'incendiary' power of print?), but Jarvis publishes the MS on the advice of a gentleman of worth and knowledge—perhaps an actual letter from Hamilton's adviser Dr Gregory, and thus a counter to Mary Hays's inclusion of letters from Godwin in *Memoirs of Emma Courtney*. The accidental, highly mediated process by which the book is supposed to have come to the public also represents the accidental, social, and contingent nature of authorship and publishing, in contrast to the view of 'modern philosophers' that 'the spread of truth' is inexorable.

The letter from the gentleman of worth and knowledge also suggests a rapprochement with what the text condemns. He expresses concern for consensus in the professional middle-class cultural revolution, and praises *Memoirs* for 'supporting the cause of religion and virtue' without the rancour shown by recent opponents of 'the *New Philosophy*'—a reference to other anti-Jacobin novels and the *Anti-Jacobin Magazine* (vol. i, p. xiii). The author protests that the villain uses 'some of the opinions promulgated in Mr. Godwin's *Political Justice*', not 'to pass an indiscriminate censure on that ingenious, and in many parts admirable, performance, but to expose the dangerous tendency of those parts of his theory which might, by a bad man, be converted into an engine of mischief, and be made the means of ensnaring innocence and virtue'. Furthermore, 'it is opinions, not persons, at which the shafts of ridicule are in the present work directed', and especially 'philosophical novels' that present the dangerous 'new philosophy' in its most seductive form. *Memoirs* even uses its material form to seem above the fray of the novelistic Revolution debate, being in elegant octavo rather than the usual shoddy duodecimo and printed by the fashionable Bath publisher and circulating-library proprietor R. Cruttwell for the London firm of Robinsons, publisher of Godwin, among others.

For like English Jacobin novels, *Memoirs of Modern Philosophers* claims superiority to the mere 'fashionable novel' by incorporating a range of factual, public, and political material, suggesting that it be read as a quasi-novel, dominated by material other than mere fiction.[24] Like *Letters of a Hindoo Rajah, Memoirs* is a footnote novel, for the same reasons—to redeem the novel from mere narrativity while steering between the discursive extremes of fictional fantasy and 'philosophical' speculation it condemns. For example a death-bed scene, a stand-by of Sentimental novels politicized by English Jacobins, here has a footnote asserting that the scene is drawn 'from *real life*' (ii. 121). Material dealing with public and political issues of the day is assigned to particular characters and dramatized by novelistic techniques, but most readers would see it as expressing the author's point of view. Henry Sydney's comprehensive cultural, social, and economic account of contemporary Scotland (vol i, ch. 17) is enlivened by the diverse interventions of other characters, but readers would see it as the author's version of the *embourgeoisement* of rural society also represented in Sentimental tales, Hannah More's Cheap Repository tracts, and political economists such as Arthur Young. The description of Mrs Fielding's asylum for destitute women (vol iii, ch. 3) resembles Bluestocking feminist projects to soften agrarian capitalism, prevent its victims from becoming a discontented proletariat, and extend women's domestic role into forms of social control.

Hamilton further reinforces authorial characterization and control by quotations from the emergent institution of 'national' literature, especially in chapter epigraphs.[25] As in other novels, these indicate the nature of the events to follow, guide the reader to the tone of a particular chapter, suggest cultural and political affiliations, and advertise the author's command of literary culture. For example, a quotation from Butler's *Hudibras*, the seventeenth-century mock epic of social

---

[24] See Gary Kelly, *English Fiction of the Romantic Period 1789–1830* (London, 1989), 253.

[25] These cite Horace's *Ars poetica*; the 'classic' English authors Shakespeare, Milton, Dryden, and Pope; earlier minor writers such as Samuel Butler, Prior, Cotton, Thomson, Goldsmith, Young, and Lyttelton; a verse burlesque by Ralph Broome called *The Letters of Simpkin the Second*; and Hamilton's contemporaries Southey, Hannah More, Cowper, Samuel Rogers, and Burns.

rebellion, suggests that the 'English Jacobins' were political descendents of Puritan rebels and regicides. Milton is cited several times, and though he was associated with the regicide Commonwealth, by the late eighteenth century he was seen as a religious epic poet appealing to all sects and thus a force for national cultural unity under Christianity. Particularly prominent, and not just as chapter epigraphs, are quotations from Burns and Cowper, the former used to celebrate virtuous ruralism and the latter to heroize domesticity and quotidian life. The use of quotations and epigraphs in *Memoirs* implies that the author, unlike the 'modern philosophers', speaks for the 'national' culture.

This 'author' is more overtly characterized in the narrator's addresses to the reader, comments on issues raised, and reflections on the process of narration. These addresses and the novel's prefatory letter imply an author–narrator who is male. There is dry though not bitter sarcasm in the narrator's comment on Mrs Botherim's skill at cookery:

> Though the science of cookery was the only one with which Mrs. Botherim was acquainted, it may be doubted whether it did not sometimes produce attractions as powerful as the metaphysical knowledge of her daughter.
>
> Even Mr. Myope himself has been suspected of this preference; and has been actually known to leave his free-will opponent in possession of the last word, from the *necessity* he felt himself under of devouring the good things set before him on Mrs. Botherim's table. (i. 8–9)

A trope familiar in anti-philosophical satire from Lucian to Peacock shows the inescapably physical nature of humanity and thus the pretentiousness of 'metaphysics'. A different tone is struck when the narrator addresses the reader, especially the 'fair reader', as in answering imagined protests at 'his' ignorance of domestic economy (i. 108) while avoiding both 'gallant' condescension and paternalistic didacticism. Manly indignation, not feminine sympathy, informs the narrator's comment on the soldiers surviving the American war and returned home, 'some to languish out their lives in hospitals ... some to a wretched dependance on the bounty of their families, or the alms of strangers; and the few whose good fortune it was to escape unhurt ... either disbanded to spread habits of idleness and profligacy among their fellow-citizens, or sent into country quarters to be fattened for fields of future glory' (i. 120). The passage also reflects the strong anti-war feeling uniting both Jacobins and anti-Jacobins in the late 1790s. A literary and cultural knowingness is exhibited when drawing the reader's attention to the novel's own discourse, as in comments on

Captain Delmond's recourse to reading from boredom: 'The important discovery made by this young soldier, we should here strenuously recommend to the serious attention of those whom it particularly concerns; did we not apprehend, that to recommend books, through the medium of a book, to those who never look into one, would not probably be attended with any great effect' (i. 122). Here the reader is made aware of belonging to the 'reading public' and elsewhere alerted to novel conventions or philosophical abstractions being adapted, burlesqued, or rejected.

This is not formal reflexivity, problematizing conventions that enable certain kinds of writing or any writing, but a device for inducing in the reader a critical consciousness resistant to 'modern philosophers' and their kinds of writing. The reader so implied is the counterpart to the author characterized through the narrator's 'voice' as variously knowing, sympathetic, drily humorous, analytical, and cultivated (rather than learned); somewhat formal; detached and superior in relation to the characters in the story; and polemical and moralizing. But it is never notably a woman's 'voice', unlike the various 'voices' constructed by writers of Revolutionary Sensibility such as Helen Maria Williams or Revolutionary feminists such as Wollstonecraft and Hays. Hamilton is not writing or constructing the authorial persona of an 'honorary man' but constructing an 'author' deliberately different from those of English Jacobin novels by women or men. The 'voice' of this character is similar to but broader than that of the novel's paternal chorus, which does accommodate women. The authoritative cultural voice constructed in and by the text of *Memoirs* may be claimed by women, exceptional though they might be. The novel's 'story' mounts a comprehensive critique of what was seen as the avant-garde pro-revolutionary coalition in Britain and presents alternatives to this vanguard in the professional middle-class paternal 'chorus' and their virtuous, active, and romantic younger generation, and their loyal and contented dependants. So too, the novel's 'discourse' presents the same alternative in its textualization of narrator and 'author'—an anti-courtly, anti-vulgar, non-plebeian, but also anti-Jacobin version of the professional middle-class cultural revolutionary.

This version appealed to many readers: *Memoirs* quickly went into a second edition, to which Hamilton added her name, a third edition appeared in 1801, and a fourth in 1804. Critical reaction was mixed, however. The *Anti-Jacobin Review* called *Memoirs* 'the first novel of the day', proof 'that all the female writers of the day are not corrupted by the voluptuous dogmas of Mary Godwin, or her more profligate imitators', such as 'M[ary] H[ay]s'. Moreover, 'the same means by which the poison is offered' are 'the best by which their antidote may be rendered efficacious' for it would then 'find its way into the circulating libraries of the country, whence is daily issued such a pestiferous portion of what are termed enlightened and liberal sentiments'. By condescending 'to the irksome, though meritorious, labour of plucking up and burning the weeds', Hamilton deserved 'the thanks of her country, and the honour of being classed with the most unexceptionable female writer of the times'—Hannah More.[26] Other reviewers were less enthusiastic. The *Critical Review* praised the 'domestic scenes' and the virtuous characters but found Vallaton and Bridgetina overdone. The conservative *British Critic* heard *Memoirs* was by Richard Graves, author of *The Spiritual Quixote*, but also thought that Vallaton and Bridgetina were overdone and compared *Memoirs* unfavourably to John Walker's anti-Jacobin novel *The Vagabond*. The *Monthly Review* praised 'the intentions and the abilities' of the 'fair author' but thought there was only 'futility in this method of exposing the principles of a writer' because 'the crimes of a hypocrite cannot be fairly imputed to the nature of any moral or religious system'.[27] These reviewers felt that such satires were keeping alive controversies that now had to be transcended.

In a prefatory 'Advertisement' to the second edition (November 1800), Hamilton tries to meet these criticisms. She had remained anonymous until the new edition because 'prejudice against the known opinions, or even the *sex*, of a writer may unwittingly bias the reader's mind'. The burlesque characters were mere creations of 'fancy' whereas the virtuous characters were drawn from the circle of 'her own acquaintances'. Her intention was to divest 'certain principles' of 'the adventitious splendour they had received, from the elegance and pathos that distinguish the language and sentiments of the authors by whom they have been chiefly promulgated'—Godwin, Wollstonecraft, and Hays. To Hamilton it was as important to oppose the 'discourse' as the contents of 'modern philosophy'. Nevertheless, she did not repeat the experiment. In *Letters of a Hindoo Rajah* and *Memoirs of Modern Philosophers* she constructed a counter-revolutionary feminism in texts fusing 'feminine' and 'masculine' discourses to resist Revolutionary

---

[26] *Anti-Jacobin Review and Magazine*, 7 (Sept. 1800), 39; 7 (Dec. 1800), 375–6.

[27] *Critical Review*, NS 29 (July 1800), 311, 313; *British Critic*, 16 (Oct. 1800), 439–40; *Monthly Review*, NS 34 (Apr. 1801), 413–14.

feminism without denying women a place in public, political discourse and the cultural revolution. Like the Revolutionary feminists, however, she found that resisting the gendering of discourse was not only difficult but liable to misinterpretation.

PART II

Women, Writing, and the
Revolutionary Aftermath

5

Introduction

B Y the late 1790s the terms of the Revolution debate in Britain were shifting decisively. The earlier phase of the debate had been preoccupied with interpreting the Revolution in relation to past history, its likely outcome, and its significance for Britain. In the late 1790s the debate was concerned with the decadence of the French Directory, consolidation of the Revolutionary state under Bonaparte, spread of the Revolution to other parts of Europe, and France's turn to imperial expansion. The course of the Revolution debate was also affected by legal harassment and suppression of British Revolutionary sympathizers, increasing press censorship, economic and social dislocations of wartime, and widespread belief that increasing luxury, vice, and irreligion would bring divine retribution in the form of defeat by France. Furthermore, there was growing concern that Britain was about to disintegrate, as France had in the early and mid-1790s, in conflicts of culture, religion, class, region, and even gender. Rebellion in Ireland, lower-class disaffection in Scotland, and political demonstrations and 'riots' in various parts of England seemed to challenge metropolitan power and central institutions. Naval mutinies, the 'discovery' of 'Jacobin' plots, and the emigration of leading reformers to France and America seemed to indicate the spread of revolutionary impulses. The rise of Revolutionary feminism and even the prominence of women writers, whatever their politics, seemed to challenge paternalist and patriarchal power. Yet many who abandoned faith in the French Revolution during the mid- and late 1790s remained highly critical of Britain's ruling élites, blamed them for deterioration in 'order and good government', and looked for alternatives to both the Old Regime and 'Jacobinism'. Some cultural revolutionaries blamed themselves for precipitating social conflict by 'premature' demands for reform, and began emphasizing the need for national consensus among themselves, *embourgeoisement* of the lower classes, and ideological conversion rather than political overthrow of the ruling classes.

Many observers sought to explain the unprecedented and rapid

succession of Revolutionary events by conspiracy theories, the operation of long historical cycles, or Providential design. Samuel Kenrick
wrote to his friend James Wodrow in March 1799:

What could possibly be more unexpectedly astonishing than the rapid downfall
of civil & religious tyranny, wch we have been witness to?
. . . The contest is between light & darkness—knowledge & ignorance—rational
religion & superstition or if you will—virtue & vice. . . . light, knowledge & (I
hope) religion & virtue have been gradually gaining ground for 3 centuries, in
active exertions—while despotism & superstition are proportionably giving
way—& as if by a sudden explosion have almost instantaneously vanished
together at their two foundation heads in Europe—France & Rome . . . What
strikes me is, the visible hand of an over ruling Providence . . .

Many in Britain saw Bonaparte as an instrument of this process and
followed his rise with fearful fascination. The liberal-minded Kenrick
saw him as the embodiment of the Revolution and the instrument of
Providence in overthrowing 'Feudal tyranny & popish bigotry', but
Wodrow disagreed. He felt that the Revolution itself gave the 'fatal
blow' to Popery and feudalism and that Bonaparte 'has rather propt up
the tottering fabrick' of the Catholic Church and 'is doing every thing
in his power to revive in France, at least the honours & trap[p]ings' of
the feudal system (3 Nov. 1803).

Interest in Bonaparte was connected to concern for the moral and
political condition of Britain and its effect on the nation's ability to
withstand French imperialism.[1] In 1798 Kenrick read Helen Maria
Williams's *Tour in Switzerland* and thought it showed that Switzerland
had been 'as ripe for a revolution as ever France was'. In the following
years Kenrick and Wodrow continued to debate whether or not
Britain was in the same condition. Kenrick felt that Revolutionary
France, led by Bonaparte, was such an external force, toppling the
decadent regimes of Europe and the world, perhaps including Britain
and its empire. Wodrow disagreed:

every free nation wishing to preserve her Liberty must be able and prepared to
defend it from dangers both from within & from without; otherwise she must
soon become a prey to some more poor but more warlike nation. [N]ow for
this purpose she must cultivate & not only the peaceful virtues Industry
sobriety &c, by means of which her Freedom will soon raise her to wealth &
opulence, but also the military spirit . . .

---

[1] See John Dinwiddy, 'England', in Otto Dann and John Dinwiddy (eds.), *Nationalism in the Age of the French Revolution* (London, 1988), 53–70.

Kenrick read Helen Maria Williams's *Sketches of the State of Manners and Opinions in the French Republic* (1801) and thought it showed that France now had a more advanced civil society than Britain. Yet he too expressed the new and widespread sense of divinely sanctioned nationalism and imperialism and envisaged the English language and culture spreading around the world.

Nevertheless, there was increasing concern over Britain's domestic problems, especially the economic and social distress caused by war, poor harvests, and the rise of rents and prices. In April 1800 Kenrick described a 'riot' at Worcester in which hungry people took over the market and sold the food at what they considered a fair price, turning over the proceeds to the merchants. At the same time, he denounced Pitt's new income tax as a 'frenchified requisition'. When a French invasion seemed imminent gold and silver coin disappeared due to hoarding and upper- and middle-class men formed local voluntary military units designed to intimidate any 'Jacobin' fifth column. Wodrow approved of the aim of the newly formed British and Foreign Bible Society to Christianize both Britain and its empire. Many welcomed the formation of the Whig-led 'Ministry of All the Talents' in 1806 as a move to national reconciliation and salvation. Kenrick wrote in February 1807, 'I cannot help anticipating already important consequences from their first victory, in the abolition of the slave trade—wch I hope will be followed up wth the wise & liberal emancipation of the Irish Catholics, wth meliorating the laws of Scotland wth respect to juries, & allowing your clergy a just & decent support.' He also hoped for a reform in the poor laws by which 'the sober & industrious are most cruelly oppressed, to encourage & support idleness & profligacy, without affording relief to the really indigent & unfortunate'. But he feared that the death of the Ministry's mainstay, Charles James Fox, and the known hostility of George III to the government would bring it and these reform measures down.

By now many had come to see Bonaparte as a 'destroyer of kings and kingdoms' and emergent British Romantic nationalism was inspired by Spanish popular resistance to him. In October 1808 Wodrow joined enthusiastically 'with all the inhabitants of Britain & the friends of Liberty in every country in ardent wishes' for the success of the 'Spanish Patriots' who through 'Divine Providence' might be the 'unlikely' means of 'checking the carreer [*sic*], & humbling the pride of a mighty conqueror'. Kenrick thought Britain now led the war of liberty against court government and religious 'superstition': 'instead of being the tyrant of the seas as her envious neighbours call her, behold she steps forth to protect the oppressed & humble the oppressor. Formerly we shed our best blood about disputed imaginary titles & family squabbles. But now it is the cause of Man, & Liberty.' After French victories in the Peninsula, however, there was widespread feeling that Britain's ruling class was not equal to the contest, with localized but nation-wide political violence, revelations that the Duke of York's mistress had been using her influence to sell army commissions, the fall of the Portland government in 1809, attempts to diminish Parliamentary corruption, the assumption of the Regency by the Prince of Wales in 1811, the assassination of Prime Minister Spencer Perceval in 1812, and his succession by Lord Liverpool, widely considered a political nonentity. Relief at Wellington's gradual achievement of military supremacy in Spain from 1811 to 1813 and Napoleon's catastrophic Russian expedition in 1812 was offset by new threats to the Empire, including the outbreak of war with the United States in 1812.

Shaken by a decade of popular political protest and violence, concerned at increasing class alienation, and determined to exercise power wherever they could, the middle and upper classes turned in the Revolutionary aftermath more purposefully to control of the 'lower orders'. The rising cost of poor relief led to reform of charitable foundations and the poor law, creation of new philanthropic and educational programmes, and establishment of institutions to rescue and reclaim the 'fallen'. Many of these projects aimed to pacify lower-class political disaffection and had the additional benefit of bringing together upper- and middle-class people of converging social and political interests, though they often developed into local power struggles along class and religious lines.[2] Middle-class women in particular, following the advice and example of Sarah Trimmer, Hannah More, Elizabeth Hamilton, and others, organized charitable projects and institutions, usually with some connection to conventionally feminine domains, such as education, healing, and consoling, and projects relating to girls and women.[3] 'Houses of industry' supported by voluntary

---

[2] See Betsy Rodgers, *Cloak of Charity: Studies in Eighteenth-Century Philanthropy* (London, 1949), ch. 1; David Edward Owen, *English Philanthropy 1660–1960* (Cambridge, Mass., 1964), chs. 4–5; Derek Fraser, 'The Poor Law as Political Institution', in *The New Poor Law in the Nineteenth Century*, ed. Derek Fraser (London, 1976), 111–27; see also Richard Tompson, *The Charity Commisssion and the Age of Reform* (London, 1979).

[3] Anne Summers, 'A Home from Home—Women's Philanthropic Work in the Nineteenth Century', in Sandra Burman (ed.), *Fit Work for Women* (London, 1979), 33–

subscriptions were set up in various towns and cities to offer work-for-welfare and ideological retraining to the unemployed, those too old to find other work, abandoned children, and women without work or family support. The fall into prostitution among the latter was an increasing concern and various 'magdalene asylums' were set up, often in conjunction with or near to 'houses of industry'. Literacy drives and distribution of tracts to the poor, criminals, and the young were organized on local and national scales, supported by such societies as the Royal Lancasterian Institution, founded in 1808 and dedicated to the monitorial education system devised by Joseph Lancaster and others. At the same time the moral, economic, and political debate over poverty, social welfare, and social control became more intense, led by the new kind of professional administrator such as Patrick Colquhoun, various followers of Malthus and his *Essay on Population* (1798, expanded 1803), Church of England Evangelicals such as J. B. Sumner and Edward Copleston, 'political economists' such as Ricardo, Utilitarians such as Bentham and James Mill, and socialists such as Robert Owen.[4]

Despite the disruption of trade caused by war, the growth of the factory system, manufacturing towns, wage-labour, and cultural changes gave workers a new sense of distinct social identity and economic independence. The landed gentry and agricultural interest, who also formed the basis of both rural administration and national government, were increasingly suspicious of the manufacturing interest, a hostility shared by professionals, who identified more with their historic patrons than with the commercial and manufacturing bourgeoisie. The latter saw Parliamentary support for high grain prices, embodied in the Corn Law of 1815, as 'class legislation' favouring the landed gentry. Concern over external affairs diminished with the revocation of international trade restrictions by the 1812 Orders in Council, the curtailing of the East India Company's monopoly in 1813, peace with the United States in 1814, and defeat of Napoleon by the Allies in 1814 and 1815. But post-war economic dislocation, political protest, and government repression further intensified social conflict.

63; Frank K. Prochaska, *Women and Philanthropy in Nineteenth-Century England* (Oxford, 1980), Introduction.

[4] See J. R. Poynter, *Society and Pauperism: English Ideas on Poor Relief, 1795–1834* (London, 1969), ch. 4; R. A. Soloway, *Prelates and People: Ecclesiastical Social Thought in England 1783–1852* (London, 1969); R. A. Cage, *The Scottish Poor Law 1745–1845* (Edinburgh, 1981); Mitchell Dean, *The Constitution of Poverty: Toward a Genealogy of Liberal Governance* (London, 1991).

The conflicts helped to crystallize, advance, and consolidate an emergent, distinctively industrial and urban working-class culture.[5] The language of 1790s artisan protest still circulated, alarming the 'privileged orders' and alienating middle-class reformers who would otherwise be sympathetic. The government attempted systematic suppression of workers' organizations and political activities from the late 1790s, leading to strikes. Acts of economic resistance such as the machine-breaking or Luddism of 1811 and 1812 were seen by many in the middle and upper classes as portents of revolution. Urged on by an increasingly vigorous reformist press, led by Cobbett's *Political Register*, Wooler's *Black Dwarf* (1817–24), Richard Carlile's *Republican* (1819–25), a number of provincial newspapers, and the satires of William Hone, many working-class people turned to self-education, self-reliance, and autonomous political organization. They founded reading clubs for self-education, 'friendly societies' to insure members against sickness, unemployment, and old age, and political societies such as the Hampden Clubs (1816). They organized political demonstrations such as the Spa Fields meeting of 1816, the march of the 'Blanketeers', or unemployed handloom weavers, from Manchester to London in 1817, and the large demonstration at St Peter's Fields, Manchester, that led to the 'Peterloo Massacre' in 1819. In these protests women were both present and active in significant numbers. Some working-class radical men even planned revolution, such as the risings at Pentrich, Derbyshire, in 1817 and near Huddersfield in 1820, and the Cato Street Conspiracy of 1820 designed to assassinate the Cabinet and inspire a national revolution.

As in the 1790s, autonomous lower-class identity and aspirations were viewed by the upper and middle classes with incomprehension, fear, and hostility. The government, its supporters in the provinces, and those who feared a revival of 'Jacobinism' more than they feared the government resorted to legal repression, censorship, intimidation, spies, *agents provocateurs*, and even force. There were reprints of propaganda published in the 1790s, especially Hannah More's Cheap Repository tracts, denounced in William Hone's *Reformist's Register* for 5 April 1817:

[5] E. P. Thompson, *The Making of the English Working Class*, rev. edn. (Harmondsworth, 1968), pt. 3; S. Maccoby, *English Radicalism 1786–1832: From Paine to Cobbett* (London, 1955); John Clarke, *The Price of Progress: Cobbett's England 1780–1835* (London, 1977).

The false whining hypocritical papers of this canting crew, are issued from the shop of Mr. HATCHARD, Bookseller to the *Society for bettering the Condition of the Poor*, in Piccadilly, where the society holds its meetings; and the general tenour of the *trash* is, 'work, if you can get any thing to do, and if not, apply to the [parish] overseers; and if they cannot provide for you, you will do your utmost to starve with as much propriety as the most respectable amongst your neighbours.' (i. 325–6)

During episodes of plebeian political agitation and economic resistance many in the middle classes were alarmed into suspending or modifying their own political demands. In other circumstances, such as the 'Queen Caroline Affair' of 1820–1, artisans and marginalized middle-class groups, including many professionals, joined in calls for a thorough national reform, amounting to overthrow of the ruling class, as the only way to realize their political and economic aims.

The 'Queen Caroline Affair' marked a turning point in political language, consciousness, and culture between the Revolution debate and its aftermath on one hand and the reform movements of the 1820s and 1830s on the other. It was also a spectacular public demonstration of the politics of gender and the gendering of politics. Caroline had become a focus for these issues ever since her alienation from the Prince of Wales shortly after their marriage in the 1790s, for as with the political opposition between the Prince of Wales and his father George III, political factions formed around conflicts within the royal family. The monarch's considerable powers of patronage were important in sustaining the government, and the Opposition gathered around his sons, especially if the heir apparent had personal disagreements with his father, expecting that the accession of their political patron would result in their forming the new government. Such expectations rose during the 1790s and 1800s because of the mental instability of George III and the possibility of the Prince of Wales becoming Regent. But when this finally happened in 1811 the Prince disappointed his long-time followers, many of whom turned to his alienated wife. The Prince feared that his untimely death would bring his daughter to the throne before her majority, giving his wife considerable political influence or even powers of regency. Furthermore, the Prince, unlike his wife, was unpopular because of his notorious extravagance and association with unpopular governments and in reaction he imposed restrictions on her public and private life, including relations with their daughter.

In public opinion the relations of the royal family became a political drama of 'domestic woman' overborne by the familiar evils of court politics and government, and analogies were drawn with the fatal factionalism and intrigues of the French royal court before and during the Revolution. When George III died Caroline returned from abroad to claim her 'rights' as queen. The Prince ordered the government to investigate her conduct while on the Continent, hoping to have her tried for treason as an adultress and thus depriving her of political influence or power. Caroline portrayed herself as a 'wronged' woman, wife, and mother, the victim of court intrigues, a figure in whom many in the middle and lower classes could see themselves. Women in particular saw her as a symbol of their own powerlessness and aspirations.[6] The Revolutionary feminist Mary Hays portrayed Caroline as an example of the oppression of women that she, Wollstonecraft, and others had protested against in the 1790s. Men saw Caroline as the victim of an unchivalrous, ungentlemanly, even 'un-English' system of court patriarchy. Popular resentment over her 'trial' in the House of Lords and rejoicing over her 'acquittal' constituted 'a massive, unprecedented political mobilization against an incumbent government, against the venality and corruption of an unreformed parliament, and against the character and honor of a reigning monarch'.[7] The government's supporters saw Caroline's politicized popularity as a potentially revolutionary feminization of politics, similar to that made infamous by Burke over thirty years earlier in his description of the attack on Versailles by the women of Paris on 6 October 1789. For the 'Queen Caroline Affair' revived political language and imagery from the Revolution debate, revealed the importance of 'domestic woman' in focusing social, political, ideological, and cultural conflicts in the Revolutionary aftermath, and marked a turning point toward the reform debate of the 1820s and 1830s.

During the 1820s the intensity of popular protest diminished and the threat of revolution seemed to recede, thanks largely to a degree of economic prosperity and the decision of many lower-class leaders and middle- and upper-class reformers to support reform of Parliament and political representation as a key to all grievances and to the restoration of social harmony. Nevertheless, there was increasing criticism of the capitalist system itself as the source of economic inequality and social misery, in the work of writers such as Robert Owen and Thomas

[6] Thomas W. Laqueur, 'The Queen Caroline Affair: Politics as Art in the Reign of George IV', *Journal of Modern History*, 54 (Sept. 1982), 443.
[7] Ibid. 464–5.

Hodgskin. At the same time there was continued movement to self-reliance among working people, with increase in union organization, mutual benefit societies, co-operatives, and so on. Deterioration of the economy in the late 1820s revived militant popular protest, however, and the emancipation of Roman Catholics from their civil disabilities and the inclusion of a certain proportion of the middle classes in the electorate came to seem inevitable if revolution were again to be forestalled. Other reforms included criminal law, public welfare, labour laws, public health, municipal government, public education, and colonial administration. These changes, largely designed, effected, and administered by men in public debate and office, enabled the state to mediate between old and new interests in the 'political nation' and support the various volunteer efforts led by the middle classes and often by women, as seen in the post-Revolutionary career of Elizabeth Hamilton, to revolutionize public and private life and head off social protest and rebellion ranging from trade-unionism to prostitution.

Though women did play an important role in unofficial operation of the state, they continued to be not only excluded by law from all aspects of civic life, including the electorate, civic office, professions, universities, and so on, and subordinated by law to men in terms of legal identity and their sexual, maternal, and property rights, but restricted by social convention in many aspects of cultural activity. Yet women were increasingly defined as the ideological and cultural foundation of society, state, nation, and empire, in fact serving the interests and identity of the professional middle class and their allies in other classes. The reformers of the late 1820s and 1830s assumed that the interests of women were identical to those of their social class, an assumption most women accepted. Late-Romantic and Victorian feminists, like earlier post-Revolutionary writers such as Williams, Hays, and Hamilton, exploited this figure of domestic-state woman to advance the social position and educational opportunities, if not—at least until the second half of the century—women's civil and electoral rights. The tactics worked out by Williams, Hays, Hamilton, and other women writers in the Revolutionary aftermath continued to be major resources for feminisms of various kinds until well into the twentieth century.

Not surprisingly, a major consequence of the Revolution debate was a movement to remasculinize culture and literature against the claims of Revolutionary feminists and feminization by women writers of conventionally masculine discourses to reach a wide readership. As with other historical 'progressive' movements, feminisms of various kinds were encouraged or tolerated by male cultural revolutionaries until the movement encountered strong opposition or secured important gains. Though the Revolution debate revealed dangerous divisions within the professional middle-class cultural revolution, the Revolutionary aftermath saw this revolution make increasing gains while encountering increased resistance from elements of 'Old Corruption' and increased rivalry from lower-class political movements. The result was that many cultural revolutionaries became less tolerant and more suspicious of feminisms within the cultural revolution, more insistent in excluding women from the public and political sphere, and more determined to appropriate the feminization of culture and politics achieved by women writers in the few decades before 1800. Though 'women's' genres continued to have lower status than those practised by men, for example, their power in cultural reproduction had been clearly demonstrated in the Revolutionary decade, and continued to be expanded afterwards. As a result, women writers in the Revolutionary aftermath became even more reluctant to assume a professional public identity, undertake professional literary work such as editing and journalism, or attempt the learned discourses and noble genres.

Certain learned discourses, such as the sciences, continued to be an almost exclusively male preserve. Women who overcame the great difficulties in their way to acquiring scientific knowledge and training tended to practise science in ways that would have seemed characteristically 'feminine' at the time, including minute observation, exhaustive cataloguing and compilation, and a pragmatic and improvisational approach to learning what was necessary in order to do such work.[8] Women who did original work did not necessarily publish it. Women who did publish on science, such as Margaret Bryan and Jane Marçet, tended to do educational and popularizing work. Some women participated in science by translating men's work, as Helen Maria Williams did with Aimé Bonpland and Alexander von Humboldt's travels in America. Women's main contribution to science was through acceptably feminine roles of mediator and popularizer, especially for children.

Hester Piozzi produced an experiment in feminizing historiography

---

[8] See 'Caroline Lucretia Herschel', in Marilyn Bailey Ogilvie, *Women in Science: Antiquity through the Nineteenth Century; A Biographical Dictionary and Annotated Bibliography* (Cambridge, Mass., 1986).

with her *Retrospection; or, A View of the Most Striking and Important Events, Characters, Situations, and their Consequences, which the Last Eighteen Hundred Years Have Presented to the View of Mankind* (1801). Her anti-Enlightenment, anti-materialist, and anti-Jacobin historiography uses a relentlessly personal 'voice', carefree disregard of learning, and refusal to be awed by the scope of the subject or the high cultural status of the discourse. Ellis Cornelia Knight attempted another experiment in feminizing history and antiquities in her modestly titled *A Description of Latium . . . with Etchings by the Author* (1805). Part travelogue, part guidebook, part museum catalogue, and part essay, it too treats history as culture rather than politics while periodically alluding to the recent, Revolutionary history of Europe and Italy. Most of the women who feminized history and related subjects such as geography, travels, and biography in the Revolutionary aftermath did so through novels such as Elizabeth Hamilton's *Memoirs of the Life of Agrippina, the Wife of Germanicus* (1804), Jane Porter's 'biographical romances' *Thaddeus of Warsaw* (1803) and *The Scottish Chiefs* (1810); narrative verse such as Felicia Hemans's *Tales and Historic Scenes* (1819) and the young Elizabeth Barrett's *The Battle of Marathon* (1820); and writing for children, such as Priscilla Wakefield's *The Juvenile Travellers: Containing the Remarks of a Family During a Tour through the Principal States and Kingdoms of Europe* (1801).

One form of history women could essay without transgressing gendered limits of discourse was biography. The culture of Sensibility, with its emphasis on the authenticity of the private and domestic self, encouraged biographical and autobiographical writing. The Revolutionary decade focused interest on the lives, backgrounds, and motivations of individuals in order to explain the unprecedented events of the time. There were political biographies of Burke, Paine, Wollstonecraft, and other figures in the Revolution debate. Mary Hays's biography of Wollstonecraft in the *Annual Necrology for 1798* (published 1800) led to her six-volume *Female Biography* of 1803, and after years of infrequent hack-work Hays was recalled to political biography again at the time of the 'Queen Caroline Affair' with her *Memoirs of Queens* (1821). Lives of public and historic individuals were counterbalanced by lives of heroines in private life; memoirs of several seventeenth-century noblewomen were published for the first time, and letters and other biographical materials of late eighteenth-century 'Bluestockings', such as Elizabeth Montagu, Mary Delany, and Elizabeth Carter, were published. Biographies of women authors such as Mary Robinson, Ann

Jebb, and Elizabeth Hamilton were published to show the compatibility of intellectual and literary life, domesticity, and public spirit in oblique response both to Revolutionary feminism of the 1790s and to post-Revolutionary counter-feminism.

Many women wrote autobiographies but few were published (usually after the writer's death) and others were converted to more acceptable genres. There were many religious autobiographies, especially by women from Methodist and Quaker communities whose egalitarian tradition endowed women with spiritual authority denied them in the established Church. Semi-fictionalized autobiographies of transgressive or criminal women such as Eliza Fenning the murderer, the prostitute Phebe Phillips, and the female soldier Susannah Cope reaffirmed gender boundaries by illustrating the extraordinariness of transgression.[9] Another acceptable form of female autobiography was travel writing, especially with the Sentimental emphasis on the personality of the traveller rather than mere observation, learning, or connoisseurship. In the Revolutionary aftermath women such as Anne Grant, Frances Wright, Mariana Starke, and Anne Plumptre used travels for textual construction of a unique self, authenticating their excursions into learned, social, antiquarian, critical, and political discourse. But the commonest way to publish the self while respecting feminine decorum was still through fiction such as the post-Revolutionary autobiographical novels of passion by Amelia Opie and Lady Caroline Lamb.

One expression of this attitude was sharper criticism of the 'learned lady', 'bluestocking', or woman writer of any kind but the narrowly utilitarian. The 'learned lady' had long been ridiculed but the figure was recontextualized and politicized in the Revolution debate both by claims of Revolutionary feminists to be 'female philosophers' and by participation of women writers in the Revolution debate. In the Revolutionary aftermath 'bluestocking' acquired a sharper edge and became more distinctly pejorative, applied 'sneeringly to any woman showing a taste for learning, a literary lady', and 'much used by reviewers' of the first quarter of the nineteenth century (*Oxford English Dictionary*). Many Romantic social critics saw 'Bluestockings', 'learned ladies', and women writers as extremes of woman—symptoms of courtly effeminacy, potential Revolutionary feminists, or representatives of the new puritanical utilitarianism—inimical to the gentrified

---

[9] Dianne Dugaw, *Warrior Women and Popular Balladry 1650–1850* (Cambridge, 1989), 213.

professionalism that was becoming the mainstream of Romantic culture.

Post-Revolutionary resistance to feminization of politics, culture, and writing was also expressed through remasculinization of topics, genres, tropes, and schemata developed by women writers in recent decades. Before the Revolution women writers developed genres such as the personal lyric, verse narrative, and the novel and techniques such as expressivity, desultory form, a non-learned range of allusion and quotation, and domestic realism. In the Revolution debate women writers used these genres and figures to participate in politics, even when apparently refusing to do so. But men such as Wordsworth, Coleridge, Southey, George Dyer, and Charles Lamb remasculinized some of these forms as early as the mid- and late 1790s in their 'conversation poems', 'lyrical ballads', sonnets after those of Charlotte Smith, verse narratives of heroism in everyday life such as Wordsworth's 'The Ruined Cottage', loco-descriptive poems such as 'Tintern Abbey', the occasional prose tale such as Lamb's *Rosamund Gray*, and Wordsworth's autobiographical epics *The Prelude* and *The Excursion*. Literary coteries such as that around Wordsworth and Coleridge were centred in domesticity and the domestic affections, produced plans for retired communal living such as 'Pantisocracy', and established loose communities of cottage rusticity in the bosom of sublime nature in the Lake District. Their work and correlative way of life may be seen as a reaction against the confrontations, conflicts, heroic hyperbole, and theoretism of the Revolution debate.[10] Through the 1800s and early 1810s women led innovation in the novel and dominated the form as never before, and it was not until the work of Walter Scott that this genre too was captured by masculinized literary culture and considered worthy to enter the emergent institution of the 'national' literature. Significantly, Scott thought it no disgrace for a successful professional man to publish best-selling narrative poems, but refused to acknowledge his authorship of the Waverley Novels until forced to do so in 1827.

In the central topics of cultural revolution, including subjectivity, domesticity, the local and particular, and quotidian life, women writers continued to be leaders, innovators, and even best sellers in the Revolutionary aftermath. But the remasculinization of literature and

[10] See, e.g., Nicholas Roe, *Wordsworth and Coleridge: The Radical Years* (Oxford, 1988).

culture steadily appropriated, marginalized, or subordinated this work. Representations of subjectivity and silent suffering in everyday life continued to be a prominent literary topic in writers such as Maria Edgeworth, Amelia Opie, Mary Brunton, Mary Tighe, Barbara Hofland, Felicia Hemans, and many others. But 'romantic', sublime, and especially transgressive or criminal subjectivity were generally regarded as unsuitable for women or beyond their experience and capacity, the province of men such as Coleridge, Byron, Maturin, and Hazlitt. Domesticity of a sentimental, socially nurturing, and ameliorative kind was also considered 'proper' matter for women writers and some, such as Edgeworth, Elizabeth Le Noir, and Elizabeth Hamilton, went to the extent of representing national moral and social reconstruction engineered by women. The poet Felicia Hemans celebrated heroic domesticity and the quotidian or 'trivial' sublime, but these topics were appropriated and increasingly dominated by men such as Wordsworth, Coleridge, and Charles Lamb.

The extension of the acceptably feminine topic of domesticity to include representing the nation was pursued by many women writers in various ways, but this too was resisted and eventually appropriated by the remasculinization of culture. Representing the nation through the local and particular, especially in the novel, was pursued through the 1800s and 1810s by writers such as Maria Edgeworth, Lady Morgan, Christian Isobel Johnstone, Susan Ferrier, and Mary Mitford. National history and culture were made to seem a particularly feminine domain by Mme de Staël's *Corinne; ou, l'Italie* (1807), widely read, discussed, and imitated in Britain. Jane Porter novelized historical national resistance in Poland and Scotland, Lady Morgan developed the 'national tale', Lady Caroline Lamb created another female national bard (and political leader) in *Glenarvon* (1816), Anne Grant wrote a critical study of Scottish Highland folklore in *Essays on the Superstitions of the Highlanders* (1811), and Felicia Hemans, who was influenced by de Staël before taking up German Romanticism and the example of Wordsworth, produced several major historical narrative poems of national resistance as well as scores of translations and imitations of folk-songs.

But these developments too were increasingly resisted or appropriated by men. In *The Heroine; or, Adventures of a Fair Romance Reader* (1813), Eaton Stannard Barrett (who had hymned domesticated femininity in *Woman*, 1810) adopted the method of Elizabeth Hamilton's *Memoirs of Modern Philosophers* to burlesque 'Corinnism', the 'female

Gothic', Revolutionary feminism, the 'national tale', and the feminization of literature, culture, and history.[11] But Scott, who had already
appropriated folk ballad in his best-selling poems, decisively masculinized the 'historical romance' in his Waverley Novels, thereby making
it fit for the emergent institution of 'national' literature. His work was
modified by other men, such as John Galt, James Hogg, and Edward
Bulwer Lytton, but his example was followed by inventors of 'national'
culture and literature, throughout Europe and beyond, into the twentieth century.

Thus the post-Revolutionary remasculinization of culture not only
increased pressure on women to promote and conform to the domestic
ideal in the 'national' interest but also appropriated or marginalized
women writers' initiatives, themes, genres, and individual works. The
increasing professionalization of writing and consolidation of Literature
as a central institution of national culture, identity, education, and
power gave professional men an even tighter grip on print culture, as
editors, critics, publishers, patrons, and 'gatekeepers' of various kinds.
There continued to be a market for the acceptably shocking and
outrageous woman writer, exploited by publishers such as Henry
Colburn, especially if, like Lady Morgan and Lady Caroline Lamb, the
writer mixed in fashionable and upper-class society, or like Mary Anne
Clarke and Harriette Wilson, she was already 'ruined'. Most women
writers who wished to challenge the heightened post-Revolutionary
idealization of 'domestic woman' and elude the remasculinization of
culture and literature had to learn new ways of resistance in the
interstices of power-knowledge, new arts of writing in a double sense.

For women writers continued to exploit conventional associations of
femininity in order to explore the central themes of the professional
middle-class cultural revolution in its new, post-Revolutionary phase.
But as these topics had been recontextualized by the French Revolution
and its impact in Britain so they were redefined, restructured, and
redirected again in the Revolutionary aftermath. Representation of
subjectivity as a personal absolute and culture of merit was transformed
by anxiety over transgressive, anti-social individualism, crime and
madness, or the cult of the 'great man'. After the Revolutionary
decade domesticity and the domestic affections were represented as

---

[11] See Gary Kelly, 'Unbecoming a Heroine: Novel Reading, Romanticism, and
Barrett's The Heroine', Nineteenth-Century Literature, 45 (Sept. 1990), 220–41.

even more fragile havens from a social and political domain irretriev-
ably divided and embattled, even more decisively 'feminine' as a
refuge and inspiration for the heroized and professionalized man.
Women's extended forms of domesticity were expanded further to
include preserving and disseminating the 'national' history, culture,
and identity and domesticating the racial and cultural 'other' in the
empire.

Representing and celebrating subjectivity continued to be a major
preoccupation of women writers. In her essay on 'The Origin and
Progress of Novel-Writing' (1810), A. L. Barbauld argues that women
writers focused on subjectivity because of their oppressed condition:

> Why is it that women when they write are apt to give a melancholy tinge to
> their compositions? Is it that they suffer more, and have fewer resources against
> melancholy? Is it that men, mixing at large in society, have a brisker flow of
> ideas, and, seeing a greater variety of characters, introduce more of the business
> and pleasures of life into their productions? Is it that humour is a scarcer
> product of the mind than sentiment, and more congenial to the stronger
> powers of man? Is it that women nurse those feelings in secrecy and silence,
> and diversify the expression of them with endless shades of sentiment, which
> are more transiently felt, and with fewer modifications of delicacy, by the
> other sex?[12]

Barbauld's rhetorical questions imply that in representing subjectivity
women are superior to men because of their restricted domestic lives.

But in the Revolutionary aftermath most women novelists avoided
representing the passions as they had been during the 1790s by Mary
Hays, Mary Wollstonecraft, Elizabeth Inchbald, Charlotte Smith, Mary
Robinson, and others. Joanna Baillie's anonymously published closet
dramas, *A Series of Plays on the Passions* (1798), caused a sensation, but
their subject-matter induced many readers and critics to believe they
were written by a man. Few women novelists represent transcendent
or transgressive 'Romantic' individualism in female protagonists, despite the example of de Staël's *Corinne* (1807) and with the exception
of Gothic romances such as Charlotte Dacre's *Zofloya; or, The Moor*
(1806), late Sentimental tales such as Amelia Opie's *The Father and
Daughter* (1801) and *Adeline Mowbray* (1804), and novels of passion
such as Lady Caroline Lamb's *Glenarvon* (1816) and Mary Shelley's
Frankenstein (1818).[13] Most women writers combined the didactic

---

[12] *The British Novelists*, i. 48.
[13] On novels of passion see Gary Kelly, *English Fiction of the Romantic Period 1789–1830*
(London, 1989), 184–95.

realism of Maria Edgeworth with representation of tormented subjectivity as internalized social conflict and contradictory social codes, especially for women. Examples include the novels of Maria Edgeworth, Mary Brunton's *Self-Control* (1810) and *Discipline* (1814), Barbara Hofland's *History of an Officer's Widow, and Her Young Family* (1809) and *Patience and Perseverance; or, The Modern Griselda: A Domestic Tale* (1813), Amelia Opie's *Temper* (1812) and *Valentine's Eve* (1816), Frances Burney's last novel, *The Wanderer; or, Female Difficulties* (1814), and Jane Austen's novels.

Austen began writing novels during the Revolutionary decade but only began publishing in the 1810s. Even her titles indicate the post-Revolutionary emphasis on the relation of female subjectivity to reproduction of ideology and culture in quotidian domestic life. Titles such as *Sense and Sensibility*, *Emma*, and *Mansfield Park* are common in earlier novels representing the construction of 'character' as predominantly subjective but sustaining a social culture based on agrarian *rentier* capitalism, or the landed estate. But this interrelationship had never seemed so fragile as in the Revolutionary decade and its aftermath. Austen shows this fragility and proposes solutions characteristic of the cultural revolution but with particular point in the Revolutionary aftermath. A central female consciousness has to negotiate her way through the social temptations of courtly emulation on the one hand and contamination by bourgeois vulgarity on the other, but she also has to avoid the subjective moral pitfalls of pride or humility. This central consciousness is alternately placed in scenes of social relating within the family or the wider social sphere of the local and county gentry or left alone to interpret the actions she has just been party to. The novels are laced with a hermeneutic terminology—'understand', 'believe', 'credit', 'perceive', 'know'—that is almost philosophical but remains a language of interpretation in everyday life, for devices of psychological 'realism' developed by Austen and others were designed in part to naturalize the philosophical or theological underpinnings of their novels.

The heroine's activity of 'mind', a word then encompassing intellect *and* feeling, constitutes her subjectivity in response to a social world that is 'other': unfamilar (often when seeming most familiar), alien, and even hostile to her moral and rational self. The heroine's subjective grappling with this world is filtered through 'free indirect discourse', or inward speech and thought 're-presented' by the narrator with degrees of sympathy, detachment, or critical irony that fluctuate and

vary often and quickly, forcing on the reader a test in interpretation
like that challenging the heroine, and establishing the narrator's powers
of 'mind' as those toward which the heroine strives. In a way muted to
conform to post-Revolutionary aversion from Revolutionary feminist
rhetoric, the Austen narrator possesses and the Austen heroine strives
for a subjectivity called for by that feminism. In one sense the Austen
heroine, like those of many Sentimental novels, strives to perform the
task of criticism as defined by one of Austen's favourite moral writers,
Samuel Johnson: 'to improve opinion into knowledge' as the basis for
aesthetic and moral choice and ethical or political action. But criticism
so defined is also the basis of professional practice of many kinds,
especially in the élite 'learned' professions to which Austen's father
and brothers belonged. In another sense the Austen heroine exemplifies the plight of the oppressed in general, according to liberal Dissenters in the Revolution debate, and the plight of oppressed woman
excluded from men's professional culture, according to Revolutionary feminists.

The Austen heroine uses her critical thought through her choice of a
proper partner in marriage, rejecting both the merely courtly or
merely bourgeois and furthering a coalition of learned professions and
landed gentry in the national interest. Such a choice implicitly rejects
that suggested by some Revolutionary feminists—a fierce, militantly
professional independence from gentry society and culture and rejection
of marriage as its central institution of cultural and economic reproduction. But the Austen heroine also clearly rejects the dangerous excesses
to which the gentry and emulative professionals are liable because of
their privileges and power. These excesses were understood by every
reader in the Revolutionary aftermath as dangerous not only to the
continued hegemony of those classes but to the continued existence
and imperial hegemony of Britain. Thus the Austen heroine could
speak to the interests of male as well as female readers, for the situation
of the young woman just entering 'the world' (or fashionable society)
had long been a paradigm for young men just entering professional,
public, and political life, intellectually and morally tested, tempted, and
possibly exploited by social and economic superiors or moral and
cultural inferiors.

It is true that the subjectivity of the Austen heroine is compatible
with Austen's Anglican Arminianism—her emphasis on true knowledge as the basis for proper ethical action in a fallen and divided world
that is nevertheless presided over by a benevolent deity who will, even

in this life, reward Christian virtues, which turn out to resemble those passive virtues conventionally recommended to women. Austen's novels plot the wedding of 'masculine' and 'feminine' aspects of gentry-professional culture, though these are not necessarily distributed entirely to male and female characters. Implicitly or explicitly, Austen's novels also envisage the extension of this culture into the local community and thence into the character and destiny of the nation and empire. Her novels represent the centrality of a certain kind of subjectivity or 'mind', here figured as a feminine version of professional culture, to both a post-Revolutionary coalition of professionals and gentry in the 'national' interest and the ideological and cultural reproduction of that coalition through domesticity.

The centrality of domesticity to the national interest and imperial destiny became a major topic of women's writing in the Revolutionary aftermath, enabling women writers to retain a 'feminine' and domestic character while discoursing on the great political concerns of the day. In Felicia Hemans's poem *The Domestic Affections*, published in the crisis year 1812, domesticity is represented as at once a refuge from social conflict, an inspiration in imperial enterprise, a rejection of the courtly, and divinely validated. In later works Hemans treats the domestic affections with greater subtlety, complexity, and power. In *Tales and Historic Scenes* (1819), published in another year of social and political crisis, she reaffirms the centrality of the domestic affections to national unity and imperial destiny as well as their transcendent authenticity against the vicissitudes of time, history, and empires, the relativity of social identities such as class and race, and the inevitability of death and oblivion.

Many other women writers extended domesticity into major areas of social and political concern in the Revolutionary aftermath, especially 'weak' elements in class, nation, and empire—women, children, the lower classes, and the peoples Britain seemed destined to protect and 'civilize'. In the late eighteenth-century cultural revolution these groups were often treated in the same way or made figures for each other as intellectual inferiors, social dependents, and moral wards of a professional middle class figured as a professional European or British man. The post-Revolutionary preoccupation with social order and control of potentially rebellious or disloyal elements in the home, the nation, or the empire made cultural revolutionaries turn again to print, their favourite technology for social reconstruction precisely because it was supposed to work through the subjectivity of the reader, transforming the individual from within, as professional middle-class people knew from their own education and experience. Thus women and children became the targets of increasing numbers of moralistic tales and novels, while the lower orders and colonized peoples were addressed by an increasing number of societies promoting literacy and distributing Bibles and tracts.

Hannah More herself established the basis for such a comprehensive programme of print during the Revolutionary decade. This work was recognized with an edition of her collected *Works* (1801), a rare honour for a woman author, living or dead. Here More reorganized her Cheap Repository tracts into two groups, 'Stories for Persons in the Middle Ranks' and 'Tales for the Common People'. Significantly, the latter group is given an epigraph from Burke. In 1805 More published another manifesto for evangelical cultural revolution, in the form of an education manual ostensibly addressed to the person charged with educating the heir presumptive to the throne, Princess Charlotte, as a responsibility of national importance. In fact, *Hints towards Forming the Character of a Young Princess* addresses the reading public and envisages the *embourgeoisement* of the monarchy to make it the model for a professionalized and united nation dedicated to its own reproduction around the globe and through history. Since readers would recognize the contrast between this vision and the notorious courtliness of the Princess's father and his political followers, More's book was politically provocative while wearing the aspect of a woman author's proper concern with domestic education and religion.

Other women writers extended domesticity to include the 'national' identity, culture, history, and destiny, as well as the domestication of the racial and cultural 'other' in the empire. 'Identity' here meant both unique individuality and oneness, despite differences of gender, class, and region. During the Revolutionary decade local interests and identities, reinforced by conflicts of class and religion, threatened civil war in parts of Britain and produced rebellion in Ireland and in the Vendée and elsewhere in France. In the Revolutionary aftermath national identity was a continuing cause of political and cultural anxiety. A single 'national' identity had to be created without provoking local rebellion. This was done by celebrating and even inventing local and regional identities but subsuming them in a larger 'national' identity and interest, defined not so much from within the 'nation' but from external, global and historical, Revolutionary and post-Revolutionary struggles against France, America, Russia, and other rivals. The 'nation' was constituted as its 'destiny' to rule and civilize alien peoples throughout the world, to 'protect' them from themselves and from predatory neighbours. This imperial 'mission' was not separate from the 'national' identity and interest or an extension of them, but essential to inventing and sustaining them.

The Revolutionary decade had revealed the power of the 'people' as a historical force in a spectacular and unprecedented way, though interest in and anxiety about them had been growing among the upper and middle classes for some time.[14] Local history, 'popular antiquities', and even botany and zoology were used by professional middle-class cultural revolutionaries to redefine rural Britain, undermining popular culture's definitions of rural nature, economic structure, and social relations while countering the economic proprietorship and social pre-eminence of the gentry. But representing the 'national' identity created ambiguities for women. Women, children, the lower classes, and less 'civilized' peoples were seen as similarly given to orality, fictionality, and narrativity. Thus popular culture was to professional culture as child was to parent and woman was to man in the domestic ideology of the time. On the other hand, middle-class women writers could be seen to have a 'natural' sympathy with lower-class women who preserved popular culture, and the lower classes could be seen as children of a larger growth for whom middle-class women writers would have a 'natural' understanding within extended domesticity. Furthermore, antiquarianism (now folklore) and related ways of inventing the nation were considered learned discourses and thus convention-ally gendered male. Consequently, women writers did not practise 'popular antiquities' directly, though even before the Revolution they too imitated popular ballads and wrote narrative poems illustrating and annotated with antiquarian lore. But in the Revolutionary aftermath such writers as Maria Edgeworth, Lady Morgan, and the Porter sisters dominated the novelization of popular culture, and Anne Grant produced an important treatise of Romantic folklore in *Essays on the Superstitions of the Highlanders of Scotland*.

They were better able to do so because of recent developments in use of the 'mother tongue', where women could, again, be supposed to have a 'natural' expertise. The professional middle class completed the

---

[14] See Robert W. Malcolmson, *Popular Recreations in English Society 1700–1850* (Cambridge, 1973); Bob Bushaway, *By Rite: Custom, Ceremony and Community in England 1700–1880* (London, 1982).

formation of its own written dialect, or 'standard English', before the Revolution, and then used it as the basis for a spoken dialect of their own that would be of no particular place. Once established, this 'standard' subordinated all other class-based or regional varieties of the language; the same pattern was extended through the empire as a whole.[15] Furthermore, 'standard' written and spoken English were of no particular place or region, but a 'national' dialect enabling its users to assume the character, if not the power, of a new 'national' class. The best way to display this new form of power-knowledge was in writing that contrasted particular dialects or contained them by 'standard' English. Most kinds of professional writing, from sermons to law briefs, had to be in 'standard' language, but literature, especially the novel and drama, had licence to be dialogical—not the democratic and relativist polyglossia envisaged by Mikhail Bakhtin but an assertion of the power of the 'standard' language and its owners. For this reason literature, or writing ostensibly as an end in itself rather than for professional ends, was gaining importance and power; in the Revolutionary aftermath literature using language to represent the 'nation' as diversity-in-unity became especially powerful.

The rise of 'standard' English again placed women writers in an ambiguous position. Historically, men mastered ancient and foreign languages to enter the 'learned' élite professions, whether or not these languages were necessary to their work. Most women were excluded from these languages, as from the professions, and limited to the vernacular or 'mother tongue', long associated with woman's role in domestic education. The rise of 'standard' English was also accompanied by insistence of cultural gatekeepers—most of whom were men— that most women had a weak grasp of grammar, spelling, and lexicon, and limited literary competence. But in the Revolutionary aftermath women writers exploited the expertise in the 'mother tongue' conventionally and historically attributed to them in order to participate in the new power-knowledge of the 'national' language.

Maria Edgeworth was one of the first and most active in seizing this opportunity. In *Castle Rackrent* (1800) she has a lower-class Irish

---

[15] On standardization see Dick Leith, *A Social History of English* (London, 1983), 54–5. On the usefulness of 'standard' language to professionals, see James Milroy and Lesley Milroy, *Authority in Language: Investigating Language Prescription and Standardisation* (London, 1985), 42–3. On linguistic imperialism see Bill Ashcroft, Gareth Griffiths, and Helen Tiffin, *The Empire Writes Back: Theory and Practice in Post-Colonial Literatures* (London, 1989), 7–8.

narrator use a muted written form of dialect to describe the decline and fall of his employers, the Rackrent family, due to their courtly extravagance. The story itself contains no character capable of resolving this dangerous social contest. Such a character is represented only in the 'editor's' explanatory notes purporting to explain popular Irish language and culture to the English reader. Since the characters in the story all use some form of 'non-standard' English and only the 'editor' uses the standard, the reader is invited to share the editor's perspective. *Castle Rackrent* was followed by other 'Irish Tales', including 'Ennui' in *Tales of Fashionable Life* (first series 1809), 'The Absentee' in *Tales of Fashionable Life* (second series 1812), and 'Harrington' (1817), representing local and regional language and culture as plebeian while the gentrified professionals, professionalized gentry, and narrators use 'standard' English and exhibit a supra-local, national consciousness. In her Burneyesque novels and tales, including *Belinda* (1801), most of the *Tales of Fashionable Life*, and *Patronage* (1814), Edgeworth mainly employs idiolect and sociolect rather than regional dialect to differentiate limited characters from authoritative ones and the omniscient narrator.

Edgeworth novelizes the moral and intellectual philosophy, social critique, and political economy of the Enlightenment that had also been deployed in the Revolution debate, especially by the English Jacobins. But by embodying these ideas in denser and more variegated local and domestic detail, avoiding overt 'philosophy', and focusing on the issue of social and regional cohesion of Britain and its empire she feminized English Jacobinism, making it palatable to many in the post-Revolutionary reading public. Edgeworth subsumes local language, history, culture, folklore, economic structure, and social relations into the consciousness of a 'national' class, represented by her narrator and implied reader. This pattern was followed by other writers of 'national tales' and 'historical romances', including Walter Scott, from whom the pattern was taken into other emergent national literatures.

Edgeworth contributed little to the feminization of history. Historiography was conventionally reserved for men, and women usually practised it obliquely, in 'feminine' forms such as prose fiction. Seventeenth-century courtly novellas and heroic prose romances by women and men validate a moral and social vision of the present by 'finding' it in some ideal or partly fictionalized past. Eighteenth-century women writers continued this project. Clara Reeve's *The Champion of Virtue* (1777), reissued as *The Old English Baron* (1778), projects late eighteenth-century professional middle-class virtues back into the social and political conflicts of late-medieval England, showing their triumph over courtly intrigue and plebeian 'superstition' and implying their suitability for a similar triumph in the present. Sophia Lee's *The Recess; or, A Tale of Other Times* (1783–5) represents the oppression of women by court society and politics in the fate of two daughters by a secret marriage of Mary Queen of Scots. Ann Radcliffe developed the 'historical romance' further in her Gothic romances of the 1790s, establishing a vogue lasting at least until the 1820s.

Novelizing classical antiquity also went back to courtly heroic dramas and romances and in the eighteenth century was appropriated to professional middle-class values by such works as Sarah Fielding's *Lives of Cleopatra and Octavia* (1757). In 1792 the second-generation Bluestocking Ellis Cornelia Knight published *Marcus Flaminius; or, A View of the Military, Political, and Social Life of the Romans: In a Series of Letters*, perhaps inspired by Barthélemy's *Voyage of Young Anacharsis in Greece* (1788). But discovery of the present in classical times was tainted during the 1790s by the Revolution's adoption of Greek and Roman civism, institutions, names, and even styles of furniture and dress. While finding antecedents of modern professional middle-class virtues in ancient times, Knight argues that these virtues could only be perfected with the advent of Christianity, giving her novel a counter-revolutionary edge and anticipating the mid-1790s debate over the 'rise of infidelity' and Paine's *Age of Reason*. In the Revolutionary aftermath Elizabeth Hamilton attempted a similar project in *Memoirs of the Life of Agrippina, the Wife of Germanicus* (1804). Again, it was not until the appropriation of historical fiction by men that novelized antiquity began to appeal to the reading public, with such novels as J. G. Lockhart's *Valerius: A Roman Story* (1821), George Croly's *Salathiel* (1829), and Bulwer Lytton's *The Last Days of Pompeii* (1834).

Eighteenth-century historical and Gothic romances also reinforced and popularized the *embourgeoisement* of chivalry by the 'philosophical history' of the Enlightenment, tranforming it from an aristocratic culture of social rank and status to a subjective attribute in the professional discourse of 'merit'. In writers such as Jane Porter and Felicia Hemans chivalry is a feminized extension of domesticity into the public sphere as the motive force in the 'national' and imperial history and destiny, rather than a merely masculine and martial culture. In Porter's *Scottish Chiefs* (1810) the historical hero William Wallace is roused to the national cause against English aggression by the murder of his wife and destruction of his home. Unlike the English aggressors, who are courtly and selfish, Wallace is inspired by patriotism, the domestic affections, and Christian faith, embodying the ideal of 'antient chivalry' in Burke's *Reflections on the Revolution in France*. Porter's novel also speaks to wars of national resistance in Switzerland, Italy, Spain, Poland, and elsewhere—Porter had already novelized recent Polish national struggles in *Thaddeus of Warsaw* (1803). Sir Walter Scott continued this work and made it a European literary sensation in *Ivanhoe* (1819). Post-Revolutionary chivalry was adopted publicly and politically by all classes during the 'Queen Caroline Affair'; thereafter it mediated the coalition of gentry and professional culture through the nineteenth and into the twentieth century.[16]

In *England and Spain; or, Valour and Patriotism* (1808) Felicia Browne (later Hemans), whose brother and future husband were officers in the Peninsula, linked the war there to the two countries' chivalric past and Britain's imperial destiny. Hemans transforms chivalry from a social to subjective culture, from history to the transcendent. She apostrophizes the 'Genius of chivalry! whose early days, | Tradition still recounts in artless lays', whose 'transient pageantries are gone' but whose 'firm, exalted virtues yet remain'. These virtues turn out to be partly feminized, partly professional, and partly patriotic: 'Fair truth arrayed in robes of spotless white', 'Warm emulation', 'purest love', 'Ardour', 'generous courage', loyalty, 'Untainted faith, unshaken fortitude', and 'patriot energy'. Browne then surveys the history of Spanish resistance to and eventual triumph over the Oriental Moorish tyranny. In this paradigm France is energetic and militant Islam threatening to destroy the decadent and therefore weakened 'England and Spain', unless they are roused again by 'artless lays'—poems such as *England and Spain*. Browne fulfils her role as woman author by hymning the pleasures of peace that will ensue once the 'valour and patriotism' she has helped to rouse have done their work. In doing so she retains her feminine character while discoursing on Britain's worst international military crisis since the American Revolution.

After the defeat of Napoleon and in the developing social crisis of post-war Britain, Hemans's attitude to history became increasingly ambivalent and even pessimistic. *The Restoration of the Works of Art to*

---

[16] See Mark Girouard, *The Return to Camelot: Chivalry and the English Gentleman* (New Haven, Conn., 1981); Girouard describes the Brass Founders' parade as knights come to defend Queen Caroline on 12 Jan. 1821, and its connection to professionalized gentry culture (pp. 68–9).

Italy (1816) exploits an acceptably feminine interest in 'taste' and the aesthetic to reflect on the entire historic span of Western civilization just saved from the Revolution. She equates Italy's political and imperial grandeur with the historically transient and relative and Italy's trans-historical importance with its works of art, thus feminizing both Italy and history, and mediating between time and eternity. The poem is elegiac and abandons history as made by Napoleon and other 'great men'. In *Modern Greece* (1816) Hemans responds to Wordsworth's masculinization of domesticated wisdom and Byron's masculinization of Greece, history, and politics. She exploits the feminine sensitivity to landscape established in Radcliffe's Gothic novels and Mme de Staël's *Corinne* to have the Wanderer of Wordsworth's *Excursion* find in Greece's historicized landscape a 'blest control' and 'high power' that override Greece's historic vicissitudes and present enslavement. This inspiration has passed to Britain, where works such as the Elgin marbles, installed in the British Museum in 1816, will inspire a new cycle of greatness and eventual decline. The historical process seems pointless and futile contrasted to the permanence of art and nature and transcendence through the divine. History made by 'man' inevitably becomes merely 'fallen records of his power' while feminized nature ever returns and the beauty of the Elgin marbles endures with an implicitly superior 'power'. The feminized consciousness of Hemans's Wanderer and the author implied in the text can recognize this and communicate it to the modern power, Britain, which will in turn become 'fallen records' to inspire 'nations unborn'. *Modern Greece* was published just after a long war of national and imperial survival but amidst social and economic crisis in Britain and search for a new international role. Despite its feminine version of patriotism, the poem registers profound ambivalence about the widespread view of Britain as the embodiment and favourite of history. The poem suggests that feminine virtues and feminine consciousness offer, if not a way to resolve this crisis then a way to transcend it.

Tales and Historic Scenes, published in the year of Peterloo, is no longer ambivalent but pessimistic. Each of its nine poems is set at a time when a historic power was about to end. Against imminent historic oblivion the poems celebrate various subjective absolutes inspiring acts of self-abnegation and domestic heroism. In 'The Abencerrage' romantic love transcends political divisions among the Spanish Moors that led to their downfall. In 'The Widow of Crescentius' a woman steps out of her domestic character to avenge her betrayed husband. In

'The Wife of Asdrubal' a woman defies her husband's betrayal of his people and dies with them. Here transcendent human subjectivity rather than art or nature reveals the hopelessly relative nature of history as the public, political sphere. The volume addresses the crisis of the late 1810s as its two predecessors addressed the end of the Napoleonic era. All three works address the Revolutionary aftermath by proposing two solutions to the historical process that has, in its most recent and spectacular cataclysm as in each preceding epoch, been dominated by men and therefore violent, cyclical, and futile. Hemans first feminizes, domesticates, and civilizes history to make it embody the permanent and transcendent rather than the temporal and temporary. This approach resembles Williams's feminization of the Revolution during the 1790s. Then Hemans leaves even feminized history behind, abandoning it as a product of human action for cultivation of subjectivity, domesticity, art, and nature in a Romantic 'wise passiveness'. This approach would be fully developed in Hemans's major poems of the 1820s, *The Forest Sanctuary* (1826) and *Records of Woman* (1828), and made her the most popular English Romantic poet after Scott and Byron and an author of international importance.

But by then the remasculinization of culture and literature was well advanced, relegating women writers to the margins of the emergent 'national' literature and culture that they had done so much to construct as a way out of revolutionary crisis during the Revolutionary aftermath. By then, too, the remasculinization of literature and culture had transferred to men writers authority in the domains of subjectivity, domesticity, and extended domesticity that women writers had exploited for half a century or more in order to participate in the public, political sphere and in the professional middle-class cultural revolution, without abandoning their identity as 'domestic woman'. Nevertheless, women such as Helen Maria Williams, Mary Hays, and Elizabeth Hamilton continued to develop the arts of resistance in literature and culture as they had to in everyday life.

6

Helen Maria Williams in Post-Revolutionary France

IN the late 1790s Helen Maria Williams was secure and well off in Paris, at the centre of intellectual, literary, and political life. Despite continuing war with Britain, Bonaparte's military victories and over-throw of the Directory seemed to stabilize the Revolution at last, apparently guaranteeing the values of feminized civil society that Williams claimed to be the 'true' character of the Revolution, and she argues this view for British readers in *Sketches of the State of Manners and Opinions in the French Republic, Towards the Close of the Eighteenth Century, in a Series of Letters* (1801). Since she aims to feminize the Bonapartist Revolution, which otherwise would seem to have an excessively masculine, martial, and autocratic character, she again takes up the 'feminine' rhetorical techniques she had used in the 1790s. The title of *Sketches* suggests the desultory, personal, belletristic form suited for a 'mere' woman involved in a man's sphere, and it is again dialogical, ostensibly addressed to a Swiss correspondent. But after so many false new dawns of Revolutionary optimism, celebrated or anticipated in successive volumes of *Letters* from France and her *Tour* of Switzerland, she aims to give this latest phase of the Revolution more convincing finality by the structure of her narrative, which is that of a Revolutionary romance journey from war and crisis—conven-tionally masculine domains—to peace, prosperity, and cultural progress—conventionally feminine concerns. The first volume resumes the Revolutionary narrative from *A Tour in Switzerland*, deals with the Swiss revolutions of 1798, goes on to the political turbulence in France, the revolution and counter-revolution in Naples, and closes with Bonaparte's return from Egypt in October 1799. The second volume opens with his *coup d'état* of Brumaire (November) 1799, goes on to the social and cultural state of France after this new Revolutionary cycle, describes the renewed warfare of 1800, Bonaparte's victories, and the resulting hope for peace in early 1801, and closes with consideration of Revolutionary public culture and the place of literature in it—the cultural basis for a stable Revolutionary future. Thus the text is again constructed as a narrative of crisis and resolution, as the Revolutionary struggles of volume one give way to Bonaparte's Revolutionary mastery in volume two and a concluding renewal of Revolutionary hope.

Throughout this narrative Williams again emphasizes the feminization of civil society, through cultural revolution, as the only sound basis for revolutionary transformation of society and the state. She contrasts the vicissitudes and relativities of the public, political sphere with permanent, subjectively inspiring nature and the socially secure, morally inspiring, subjectively fulfilling, and even heroic domestic affections. She correlates domestic virtue and heroism with true revolutionary values and presents false revolutionary movements as destroyers of such domesticity. Anticipating a major theme of Romantic literature, she defines heroism less as aristocratic martial glory and 'chivalry' and more as bourgeois subjectivity and domesticity. She emphasizes the cultural transformation brought about by the Revolution, including both new public institutions and the social psychology of revolutionary transformation within each individual. Thus she again insists on the importance of women in society, culture, and politics, and conceives of the state as an internalized, quotidian, and domestic reality, and not merely an external, public, institutional one.

These issues raise the question of her own contribution, as a woman, to the Revolution, and she rejects both 'the censure which has been thrown on writers of the female sex who have sometimes employed their pens on political subjects', including herself, and the 'Anti-Jacobin darts' aimed at her political views: 'The political system I most abhor is the system of terror, whether it be jacobin terror in France, or royalist terror at Naples' ('Preface'). In her earlier work she characterized the Jacobin Revolution as brutally masculine; anti-Jacobin anti-feminism now enables her to claim a middle ground of feminized professional middle-class ideology and culture between extremes. This ground, she claims, is about to be established in Switzerland, her correspondent's homeland, by the Revolution's embodiment, Bonaparte. She situates true 'equality' between demagoguery and despotism and defines it in terms of the professional middle-class ideology of 'merit', based on intellectual and moral capital ('knowledge', 'wisdom', and 'virtue'), accumulated as 'the fruits of ... honest industry', and rewarded according to 'right' by social 'distinction' and political 'power'.

Unfortunately, Switzerland repeated the mistakes of the Revolution in France, when 'philosophy' was used to justify a 'wild and chimerical equality': 'if, however, this be philosophy, my heart is still at a remote distance from its elevated heights—I have not yet learnt to wipe away the bitter tears which fall for actual, positive miseries, by speculations of future probable good; and to reason with those cold calculators in the presence of their bleeding victims' (i. 7, 12–13).

Williams's feminization of the Revolution also explains her otherwise surprising turn to religion to answer her correspondent's question whether the Revolution has been good or bad for the majority. She assigns the Revolution a Christ-like role of ameliorating 'the lot of the unfortunate, as the great teacher of mankind preached his gospel to the poor'. Revolutionary secularization went too far, but that is now being corrected, 'for surely religious influence, well directed, is among the cheapest, and best supports of the state'. This influence requires suitable economic and social conditions, however, so the Revolution rightly improved the peasant's material lot:

He is now become in many instances the proprietor of that soil which he heretofore was accustomed to till for another . . . His moral situation has undergone a revolution no less favourable. In the commune where he once dragged his reluctant steps to bend before some arbitrary mandate of seigniorial vexation, or do fealty and homage for some privileged exactions, he now stands erect, a free citizen; he finds none superior to himself, but such as the law, which is the same for the whole, allows; and in the appointment of those persons, whether municipal, magistrate, or legislator, he has a direct, or primary decision. (i. 53–4)

A new subjectivity, to which religious belief is relevant, is being built on the new economic, social, and political order, thereby guaranteeing the Revolutionary state. Just as important, 'the Revolution has done much' for women of the peasant class (i. 54).

From the interconnected political, economic, social, and ideological gains of the Revolution Williams turns to consider its international success. She condemns the decadence and corruption of the Directory, but claims that the spirit of freedom is now too strong to be crushed, though temporarily suppressed in Poland and Naples. Her extended account of 'the revolution and counter-revolution at Naples' illustrates this optimism. Jacobin excesses within and outside France produced counter-revolutionary excess, balancing the account book of political terror and clearing the way for Revolutionary renewal and stability.

She is disappointed that her native country has aligned itself with counter-revolutionary terror by failing to prevent the monarchist repression at Naples. For the Neapolitan 'patriots' admired Britain's 'laws, her manners, her customs, her remote [i.e. ancient] and hereditary love of liberty, that proud pre-eminence, that lofty distinction above the other nations of the earth, which it is devoutly to be wished she may ever continue to deserve, and to secure!' (i. 199–200). The passage deliberately and ironically echoes Burke's impassioned defence of 'antient chivalry' in his *Reflections*.

Williams next considers the intellectual and cultural gains of the Revolution, praising new institutions 'for the civilization and refinement of the people' that will thereby secure the Revolution from further turmoil. She illustrates this topic with her familiar device of a 'true tale', 'The History of Perourou; or, The Bellows-Mender; Written by Himself'. She claims to have received a copy of this story from a representative Revolutionized character—a former *abbé* and *philosophe* who practised religious tolerance and who was transformed by the Revolution into a man of business. But Williams also offers the story as relief from Revolutionary turmoil and war: 'I felt pleasure in turning from the change of Empires, the rise and fall of Kingdoms and Republics, to copy the humble revolutions of domestic life' (i. 247). Domestic revolutions succeed where political ones fail, suggesting that political revolutions must be based on domestic ones if they are to succeed. This was Williams's argument since the early 1790s.

The tale has its own title and is set apart from Williams's account of the public, national, and international dimension of the Revolution. The first-person narrative tells of a humble village bellows-mender used by some gentrified artisans of Lyons to gain revenge on Aurora, the haughty daughter of an art dealer, for thinking herself above a marriage with one of them. These men transform Perourou into a gentleman outside and in. He is bathed two hours morning and afternoon for a week 'to get rid of my tinkering-skin, and complexion', and his patrons give him a genteel education: 'One taught me to read, another to write; another some notions of drawing, a few lessons in music, a little in short of every thing' (i. 256). Calling himself the Marquis of Rouperou, a capitalist proprietor of mines, he pretends to be collecting pictures, meets the dealer's daughter, and they fall in love. He experiences an internal revolution, and is inspired by 'the new emotions which animated my bosom' (i. 259). His acquisition of bourgeois subjectivity is complete. But each evening he dutifully reports the progress of his courtship to his employers. Once married, he takes his wife to his native village and his parents' miserable hut, where his patrons assemble to witness Aurora's humiliation. Here Perourou experiences a further revolution, a sense of having triumphed personally but failed in domestic and social sympathy (i. 272). Aurora flees to a convent and seeks an annulment of the marriage, but she is granted only a separation when it is revealed that she is pregnant by her husband.

Meanwhile, Perourou is offered the means to enrich himself through the new capitalist opportunities opened by the Revolution, but he finds such success meaningless without the domestic affections (i. 288–9). He visits his wife and child in disguise, and when his son is drawn to him by a natural feeling he reveals himself and successfully pleads for reconciliation. Their reunion is marked by a public festival on the theme 'Pride Conquered by Love', and includes Aurora's reconciliation with Perourou's former patrons. The story shows the subjective, ideological, and cultural transformation of a son of the people that is possible in the post-Revolutionary era. This transformation in sensibility is later validated by external, financial, and social ones, also made possible by the Revolution, but 'natural' domestic affections are then shown to overcome both the merely social distinctions and the rampant commercial spirit of the Revolutionary aftermath. One reviewer found the tale hard to credit: 'had it been found in a novel, it would have been thought rather too improbable ever to have occurred in real life'.[1] Nevertheless, the story became one of Williams's most popular works, being quickly republished in various chapbook editions (Dublin, 1801; London, 1803; Edinburgh, 1810) for the urban lower-middle-class or artisan readership interested in cheaper versions of the fashionable reading-matter of their 'betters'. Later the story became the basis of Bulwer Lytton's successful play *The Lady of Lyons* (1838), performed into the twentieth century.

Further anecdotes in *Sketches* show how much the Revolution still has to do. Accordingly, volume one closes with the expected return of Bonaparte from Egypt and volume two opens with the coup of Brumaire 1799, enabling him to carry out this work. Williams witnessed this new beginning and, as in her account of the Festival of the Federation in 1790, she insists that her immediate and subjective response to the coup may be more perspicuous than analyses that are merely

[1] *Critical Review*, NS 31 (Feb. 1801), 188.

political and philosophical. She assures her correspondent, 'Do not be alarmed—I am not going to play the part of an analyser of constitutions, and act the lofty politician. My flights are always very near the surface' (ii. 39), implying that her conventionally feminine interest in the immediate, the subjective, the local, and the quotidian achieves a political understanding superior to that achieved by the detachment necessary for abstract and theoretical views, conventionally the domain of men. Accordingly, her letter 'On the State of Women in the French Republic' claims that women's way of understanding politics has enabled them to stay apart from the rage of party which had almost destroyed the Revolution: 'Women, who are in general more accurate calculators of good and evil from sentiment, than reasoners from abstract principle to remote consequences, have kept aloof from the contest' (ii. 50). This letter was thought of sufficient interest to the post-Revolutionary situation to be reprinted in the liberal *New Annual Register* for 1801.

In view of this letter Williams has to explain the Revolution's failure to grant women full equality. She argues that women have gained from the Revolution only at second hand, by the ending of patriarchal feudal rights. She denies that women want full political rights in the Republic, but suggests that the Revolution would have been better off with direct female participation (ii. 51–3). She points out the contradiction between the Revolution's exclusion of women from national education and its ideology of woman, family, and domesticity as foundations of civic virtue and the state:

What claim has the Republic to the attachment of that part of the human race from whom it witholds the first privilege of our nature, the first gift of Heaven—instruction and knowledge? . . . She to whose forming care the first years of the Republican youth are confided, is expected to instil principles which she has never imbibed, and teach lessons which she has never learned— She who exerts over man an empire which, being founded in nature, is as immutable as her laws, and beyond the reach of his imperious institutions, is treated as a being merely passive in the important interests of the State, while she has power to fix the Republic on an immoveable basis, or shake it to its very foundations . . . (ii. 53–5)

Wollstonecraft advanced the same argument in *A Vindication of the Rights of Woman*.

Like Wollstonecraft, Williams argues that women should be allowed into professions so that they can achieve independence, and she rejects the argument that only men should have the vote because husband and wife 'are but one political person', for 'it is not clear how from this union women can remain civilly single, and politically married' (ii. 58–9). But she maintains her earlier, somewhat courtly view of women and the state when she insists that they can be trusted to support the new form of the Revolution because 'love of glory is natural to the sex' and the Revolution is now led by the hero Bonaparte. Furthermore, French women have proven their own capacity for heroism during the Terror—'that fatal epocha of the Revolution, during which, the courage of so many of the other sex shrunk back appalled'.

It was women, who, in those days of horror, proved that sensibility has its heroism—and that the affections of the heart can brace the nerves with energy, that mocks the calculations of danger.—It was women who penetrated into the depths of dungeons, who flew to the abodes of despair—who were the ministering angels that whispered hope and comfort to the prisoner . . . it was women, who, in defiance of captivity and death, sought the dwellings of tyrants covered with the blood of innocence, and pleaded the cause of the captive, with that irresistible eloquence which belongs to the inspiration of the heart. . . . What Roman virtue was displayed by Charlotte Corday!—what more than Roman fortitude dignified the last moments of Madame Roland! (ii. 63–4)

Women are qualified for political life not only by their Revolutionary heroism but by their intellectual capacity, as Williams demonstrates herself by analysing the Republic's judicial system and religion and Bonaparte's military campaigns and imperial mission in the East. She goes on to more conventionally 'feminine' interests, describing Bonaparte's humane character, denying that the Revolution is atheistic, mourning the domestic yet intellectual Mme Helvétius, centre of the 'idéologue' circle, hoping for peace, applauding the decline of party politics, and describing the advance of literature under the Republic. Since her own writings, though in English, are part of this literature, she closes *Sketches* with a lyrical exemplification of this claim:

It is difficult indeed to believe, on the authority of any critics whatever, that the Revolution, that stupendous event which has awakened all the energies of the human mind, which has unfolded the most lofty subjects of speculation, the most animating themes of wonder, which has shaken ancient systems to their foundations, and seems to have called into existence a new universe, that such an event can prove unfavourable to the interests of science and of literature; or that the cheerless darkness of superstition, the iron-reign of despotism, and the debasing influence of error, are more auspicious to the emanations of genius, than the clear light of philosophy, the genial spirit of freedom, and the immortal principles of truth. (ii. 298–9)

The achievements of the feminized Revolution, now guaranteed by the manly hero Bonaparte, are not only defended in *Sketches* but exemplified in its author's way of doing so.

Sketches was received in England with interest, for as the *Critical Review* asserts, Williams's 'admirers are not confined to this island, nor indeed to this quarter of the globe'. The reviewer praises her appropriation of the epistolary form and rhetorical exploitation of 'feminine' discourse to feminize the Revolution. The *Monthly Review* acknowledges Williams as a leading English commentator on the Revolution: 'Few English women, or even English men, have enjoyed a more ample opportunity of observing' the Revolution, 'and though she betrays an evident partiality' for the present government there, 'she manifests knowledge and penetration in her remarks on the scenes and characters passing before her'. Nevertheless, her writing also exhibits 'feminine' weaknesses, including mistaken facts, 'too strong and too poetical colouring', 'an affectation of sentiment and sensibility', reliance on (if not plagiarism from) the researches of others, and especially a devotion to her country's enemy that was unbecoming in an 'English woman'. The *British Critic* went further, including Williams 'among the most active labourers in the cause of France', the 'desperate exiles' and 'profligate men' and 'abandoned shameless women' from all over Europe who have gathered in Paris 'to promote the views of France against their respective countries', subsisting by 'the wages which they have received from the successive tyrants of France' or, 'having become stigmatized and infamous at home', employing 'themselves most industriously to excite a revolution subversive of the manners and morals of their native country, which, as long as they prevail, must exclude such wretches from all hope of returning into society'.[2]

Defiantly, Williams published an 'Ode to Peace' to honour the treaty of Amiens, negotiated in October 1801 and signed the following March. This agreement was in fact a victory for France, confirming all political and territorial gains of the Revolution, but it was greeted with popular rejoicing even in Britain. Williams may have been emboldened by this anti-war attitude to reaffirm her own assertion of

---

[2] *Critical Review*, NS 31 (Feb. 1801), 183–4; *Monthly Review*, NS 35 (May 1801), 82–3; *British Critic*, 17 (June 1801), 582–3.

the Revolution's achievements in *Sketches*, and not incidentally to cast herself as a consistent advocate of feminized politics, in the face of accusations that she had turned her coat politically too many times to be a credible commentator. For this reason the 'Ode to Peace' of 1801 echoes her earlier *Ode on the Peace* of 1783, celebrating the end of war between Britain and the American colonies—another struggle between her native land and a country whose cause she preferred. In both poems she faces the difficult task of chiding Britain and approving a former foe without relinquishing her authority as a voice for opinion in Britain. In both poems she does so in part by associating her cause with transcendence of recent conflict. In both poems, for example, she equates peace with a sudden burst of light—familiar figure for enlightenment and the progress of civil society. In 'Ode to Peace' she also equates the Revolution with Nature and 'feminine' virtues and pursuits and echoes her earlier justification of Revolutionary war by declaring that only 'Freedom' 'can spread a moral charm | O'er war's fell deeds'. In passages that would have galled British anti-Jacobins she hails the 'Republic' 'whose independent power | All earth contested once, all earth confesses now', laments that her native country had joined 'the impious league against mankind', rejoices that these 'misguided efforts' have failed, and calls on Britain to emulate France by chasing 'from your shores the abject vices' of court government—'Ambition', 'Corruption', and 'Servility'.

The poem would have seemed outright treason in Britain after the resumption of war in 1803, and apparently did Williams little good in France: according to Stone, Williams's failure to include Bonaparte in her poem left him harbouring a resentment against her. Williams and her friends were already turning against Bonaparte's regime, however, seeing it as a form of court government and a return to 'masculine' politics, and her 'Ode to Peace' reflects that attitude by its glaring omission of any reference to Bonaparte, who proclaimed himself the Revolution's embodiment and saviour. Furthermore, Williams and Stone were well off and kept up a prominent cosmopolitan salon; by 1802 an Irish visitor described it as 'chiefly composed of liberal republicans and anti-Bonapartists'.[3] In August 1802 Hester Piozzi heard from 'profess'd Democrates' just returned from Paris that Williams's house 'is the resort of a Literary coterie, all *malecontents*, who

---

[3] Valentine Browne Lawless, 2nd Baron Cloncurry, *Personal Recollections of the Life and Times, with Extracts from the Correspondence* (Dublin, 1849), 185–6.

tell those that get into their circle what a short duration the present order of things will be granted, and what happy days await France when the next change takes place'.[4] Most of Williams's Girondin friends were dead, but in her salon, reputed to be 'le plus intéressant' in Paris, she recreated the political and cultural life of her feminized Revolution of 1792–3.

Her salon included foreigners such as Irish political refugees and acquaintances of Stone, the Polish patriot Kosciusko, the American ambassador, the Dutch scientist and representative of the Batavian Republic, Jan van Swinden, and Philip Stapfer, Swiss intellectual, revolutionary, and diplomat. Foreign visitors included the actor Kemble, Fox the Whig politician, Italian princesses and German princes, the American poet Joel Barlow, Benjamin West, President of the Royal Academy, and several Italian writers. Leading French intellectuals and politicians included Chevalier de Boufflers, former *abbé* and soldier, 'philosophe', and one-time favourite of Napoleon; J.-A. Esménard, world traveller, political journalist, defender of the King in 1792, refugee from the Jacobin Terror, member of the disastrous French expedition to Santo Domingo, head of the bureau of theatres under Napoleon, and author of operas and the poem *La Navigation*; and Charles de Pougens, the blind natural son of the Prince de Conti, diplomat, essayist, scientist, novelist, linguist, and mythographer. Artists and belletrists included J.-F. Ducis, court favourite before 1789, successor to Voltaire in the Académie Française, playwright and adapter of Shakespeare, dedicated family man, who declined Napoleon's offers of patronage; Louis Vigée, cousin of the painter Elisabeth Vigée-Lebrun, author of stage comedies and light verse, editor of the *Alamanch des Muses*, refugee from Jacobin Terror, and the most famous public reciter of the time; the dramatist and political poet Chénier; Bernardin de Saint-Pierre; the painter Gérard; and the dramatist, critic, and political writer Ginguené. Scientists and political economists included the naturalists von Humboldt and Bonpland; the Comte de Lasteyrie du Saillant, world traveller, agricultural economist, and promoter of social, cultural, and moral improvement; and J.-B. Say, Protestant, businessman, follower of Adam Smith, associate of Brissot, editor of the *Décade philosophique* from 1793 to 1800, and translator of Williams's *Tour in Switzerland*. Protestant intellectuals included P.-J. Bitaubé,

---

[4] *The Intimate Letters of Hester Piozzi and Penelope Pennington 1788–1821*, ed. Oswald G. Knapp (London, 1914), 248.

translator of Homer, critic, poet, and fellow victim with Williams of imprisonment in 1793; and P.-M. Marron, Protestant pastor, victim of Robespierre (his published account of the ordeal was addressed to Williams), and man of letters. Leading opposition politicians included Carnot and Grégoire. Carnot was a former army engineer, friend of Robespierre, reorganizer of the Revolutionary armies and architect of the military victories of 1792–3, member of the Committee of Public Safety, survivor of the Thermidorean reaction, member of the Directory, briefly Minister of War under Bonaparte, and opposition leader during the Consulate and Empire. Grégoire was the son of a tailor, ecclesiastic member of the Third Estate, supporter of religious toleration, founder of the Amis des Noirs (which Williams joined on moving to Paris), elected bishop of Blois, member of the Committee for Public Instruction, Senator under Bonaparte, but leader of political opposition.

More important, Williams's salon connected with the circle of 'idéologues' that met at the house of Mme Helvétius, widow of the Enlightened materialist philosopher, lamented by Williams in Sketches.[5] Their ideas resembled those of both the English Nonconformist Enlightenment and the Girondin-led salons of the early 1790s that Williams knew well. They claimed to have perfected the sensationist epistemology of Condillac and others into a comprehensive system of knowledge based on four intellectual faculties—sensibility, which enabled the individual to receive impressions from the outside world or from self-reflection; memory, which reproduced past sensations and mediated between past and present ideas; judgement, which made connections between various sensations and ordered them into understanding or knowledge; and will, which was produced by judgement, motivated bodily and mental actions, brought knowledge of the non-self through resistance, and thereby proved the freedom of the self as autonomous willing identity. The 'idéologues' also had a theory of signs as the necessary means of communicating such a subject's knowledge of the world and itself to others, and a comprehensive system of knowledge emphasizing scientific method.[6] Their central ideas could be readily subsumed in Williams's feminization of culture and politics and their friendship kept her close to the centre of political and cultural life in

---

[5] Antoine Guillois, Le Salon de Madame Helvétius (Paris, 1894).
[6] See Sergio Moravia, Il tramonto dell'illuminismo: Filosofia e politica nella società francese (1770–1810) (Bari, 1968); Emmet Kennedy, A Philosophe in the Age of Revolution: Destutt de Tracy and the Origins of 'Ideology' (Philadelphia, 1978).

the Revolutionary aftermath. They were already prominent and active under the Directory and, like Williams, sympathized with Bonaparte's consolidation of the Revolution through appropriate political, cultural, and educational institutions. They dominated the journal *Décade philosophique* and the important section of moral and political sciences in the *Institut national*. Several were in the Senate and on such policy-making bodies as the Committee of Public Instruction. But Bonaparte soon found them less malleable than he wished and by 1802–3 many were in political opposition. He shut their *Écoles centrales* and replaced them with his own Imperial University, removed many of them from public office, dissolved the section of moral and political sciences in the *Institut national*, and turned their key term, 'idéologie', into a synonym for impracticality and false philosophy, an association it retains to the present.

Under the Napoleonic regime, then, Williams's salon was imbued with the Sentimental feminized politics she had found in the pre-Revolutionary coteries of London in the 1780s, the Girondin salons of 1792–3, and again in the 'idéologue' circles of the Revolutionary aftermath. She received about sixty guests in a 'large and beautiful' room; the women sat in chairs along the walls and the men gathered in the centre of the room. When the theatres let out there was a new influx of people. On one occasion Louis Vigée recited his work, with Williams seated at his feet, exclaiming enthusiastically at particular passages.[7] But the prominence and the political character of Williams's salon brought her and Stone under police surveillance and harassment even before the resumption of war between Britain and France in May 1803. Furthermore, Napoleon disliked political women, was irritated by the ostentatious Anglophilia of the political opposition, and was later said to have resented this celebrated English writer for failing to eulogize him in her 'Ode' on the Peace of Amiens.

In 1803 she made an oblique return to political writing and the Girondin epoch with a three-volume translation entitled *The Political and Confidential Correspondence of Lewis the Sixteenth; with Observations on Each Letter*. This project was designed to exploit a recent public controversy in Britain between the French counter-revolutionary writers Bertrand de Moleville and Mallet du Pan on one hand and the Whig Opposition leader Charles James Fox on the other. At issue was

[7] Reichardt, *Un hiver à Paris sous le Consulat*, quoted in Lionel D. Woodward, *Une anglaise amie de la Révolution française: Hélène-Maria Williams et ses amies*, repr. (Geneva, 1977), 151–2.

the policy of Louis XVI toward the Revolution and whether or not he had betrayed it by secret intrigues, thereby meriting his death at the hands of the Revolution.[8] The controversy had centred on the authenticity of a document supposed to be from the hand of the French king, and it was of more than historical or academic interest because the character and fate of Louis XVI was very pertinent to the political standing of the royalist party in the Revolutionary aftermath. A manuscript edition of what were supposed to be Louis's secret letters was prepared by royalists to arouse sympathy for him and thus for the royalist party. The manuscript was drawn to Williams's attention by Bonaparte's secretary of police, who later claimed to have suggested ways to reverse its royalist aims.[9] Williams translated and published it with additional letters and her own commentary criticizing the king and supporting the conduct of the Revolutionaries. She assures her readers that the authenticity of the letters had been warranted by men of authority, but in fact the letters were forgeries.

According to Williams, the editors of the original manuscript claimed that the king's letters show him in his authentic, private, and domestic character. She replies that her version will better meet the post-Revolutionary desire in Britain and France for national unity and reconciliation after the controversies and conflicts of the Revolutionary decade (vol. i, pp. v–vi). She agrees that the king's private letters show his true character: not the saintly yet heroic image that the French editors construct but rather the enemy of the Revolution and betrayer of his people. She then reviews the various subjective responses to the king that observers would have experienced through the successive stages of the Revolution and concludes that the Revolutionary experience has made possible the subjective consciousness or ideological self necessary to read the Revolution and its leading characters, including *their* subjective consciousness, correctly. In order to show that she has that Revolutionary consciousness she embarks on one of her lyrical flights:

And what period in the annals of mankind more calculated to awaken solemn, rapt attention, to seise [*sic*] every faculty of the soul, to call forth every feeling excited by the sublime and the terrible, than the epocha of that revolution which, in its effects, will change the condition, and almost the destinies, of

---

[8] Hedva Ben-Israel, *English Historians on the French Revolution* (Cambridge, 1968), 30–2.

[9] Details of the affair are found in Woodward, *Williams*, ch. 12.

man? How long will posterity pause on the solemn page which marks its mighty records! In reading history, we pass rapidly over the common flight of years and ages, like the traveller, who diligently pursues his way through a country which presents only ordinary objects: but, when this astonishing æra unfolds itself to the intellectual view, the reader will feel a sensation similar to that of the same traveller, when, suddenly bursting on his sight, he beholds scenes of overwhelming majesty, and finds himself surrounded by images of nature, the beautiful, the sublime, the terrific, the stupendous, which fill his mind with astonishment, or swell his bosom with enthusiastic emotion. (vol. i, pp. xxiii–xxiv)

The articulate energy of syntax enacts the sudden revelation of the Revolutionary sublime that the passage describes. But the revelation comes about through an act of the mind, characterized as 'posterity' in the process of 'reading' the 'solemn page' of 'history', which is yet again characterized as a natural landscape, simply there to be discovered and responded to immediately. Revolution as progressive experience arouses political feelings, as Louis XVI did at various moments from 1789 to 1793 and as he continues to do afterwards upon reflection. But once Revolution has become historic and written, it is no longer political but natural and yet subjective, external to yet within those who, like the narrator-author, can feel it right and write what they feel.

As in all Williams's writings on the Revolution, sensibility manifest in the text validates the text's politics. Here, however, Williams feminizes politics and the Revolution in a new way. She appropriates an absolute monarch and one of the Revolution's protagonists, not only translating him from French to English but, through her commentary, translating him for the Revolutionary aftermath and for her feminized Revolutionary politics—a threefold supererogation, yet presented with what would seem becoming feminine modesty, as a service to the Revolution, 'in the same manner as an obscure individual may be remembered, who carves his name upon an immortal monument which mocks the destruction of time' (vol. i, pp. xxiv–xxv). The French editors intended the letters to be a 'monument' to the king and thus an inspiration to the royalist cause, but Williams's intervention makes them part of the greater monument that is the Revolution. This monument, unlike Louis, is 'immortal', and on it Williams has 'only' inscribed her name, thereby making it hers.

The main body of the *Correspondence* is shaped accordingly. Williams not only displaces the commentary of the French editors with her own but makes her commentary into a history of the Revolution, with the mixture of narrative, analytical, and lyrical styles that marked her earlier writings on the Revolution, thus assimilating this work to her long-running project of vindicating the Girondin Revolution. Williams also adds a section of 'Supplementary Letters' not found in the manuscript, showing Louis's plans to organize a counter-revolution, thus reinforcing Williams's portrayal of him as an enemy of the Revolution. Her comments on individual letters suit her preference for desultory form and enable her to present the Revolution with the same immediacy of an unfolding event that had characterized her *Letters*; occasionally she even slips into the narrative present tense. Throughout she contrasts the private and domestic character of the king with the ceremony and policy required of him in his public and political capacity, implying that the king and the man, like court government and domesticity, were at odds; and while many saw Louis's personal weaknesses as the cause of his downfall, she claims that it was the monarch who could not sustain the character of man of feeling, husband, father, and friend. In short, the *Correspondence* is directed to keeping alive the spirit of the feminized Girondin Revolution as the Revolution was in the process of being appropriated to individual masculine ambition once again, under Bonaparte.

This aim, and the possibility that royalist sympathies would be aroused despite Williams's intentions, made the book an object of suspicion to Bonaparte's police. Further sales were banned and remaining copies were impounded. Williams wrote letters to the presiding judge, professing her affection for France, the present government, and the 'great man' who formed and guided it, and claiming that no one had contributed more than she to removing British prejudices against the Revolution, for which she had been calumniated by the hired propagandists of the British government. Friends in official posts validated the good intent of the publication and the copies were eventually released, though Williams claimed to have incurred considerable financial losses. Bonaparte ordered censorship of books tightened up; Williams did not test the government again, publishing nothing in English of her own until 1814.

Nevertheless, the book made her enemies among counter-revolutionaries in both France and Britain. The *Edinburgh Review* described her translation as inadequate and careless, either affectedly paraphrased or 'meanly literal', and her commentary characterized by 'tawdry bombast' and 'chilling affectation', 'flaunting in all the colours and flowers

that she can collect', and showing 'cold-hearted petulance' and unfeel-
ing indifference to Louis's heroic and domestic character and tragic
fate.[10] A. F. Bertrand de Moleville's book-length attack was quickly
translated into English by the government writer R. C. Dallas as *A
Refutation of the Libel on the Memory of the Late King of France, Published
by Helen Maria Williams* (1804). Williams's sex is related to her
political crimes and she is described in terms that recall Burke's
unnatural and monstrous political women, or 'revolution harpies': 'she
pretends to shed tears for his [Louis's] death, and yet delves to the
bottom of his grave to spit upon him that venom which her lips and
pen distil', and she is 'this doting, superannuated fondler of the
revolution', who is 'big', or pregnant, 'with revolution' (pp. 6–7, 11).
The author suggests that Williams's private 'life and adventures' are so
scandalous that were they published readers would think them 'a libel,
or at least a novel', and he accuses her of being ignorant of politics, an
incompetent translator, and an inaccurate historian—the kind of charges
often levelled at women who ventured into discourses conventionally
reserved for men.

In France Williams continued to be regarded as a friend of the
Revolution, an important British writer, and an asset to the regime's
opponents. Williams disliked the regime's militaristic character and
Napoleonic cult of the warrior, its perpetuation of the Jacobins'
exclusion of women from the institutions and processes of the state,
and its restoration of the pre-Revolutionary subordination of women
to patriarchal domestic authority in the Civil Code of 1804. The
political culture of the regime treated women as merely domestic,
serving the nation as dutiful wives, fertile mothers, and frugal house-
keepers, and it was widely known that Bonaparte's own relations with
women were not much different from those of any monarch of the
ancien régime.[11] Legally, politically, and culturally, Napoleonic France
was increasingly inimical to the egalitarian, Sentimental, feminized
Revolution Williams had celebrated since 1790. She was now effectively barred from political writing but in 1808 a selection of her
lyrical poems was translated and published by her anti-Bonapartist
friends Boufflers, Esménard, and Pougens as a flourish of the opposi-
tional Anglophilia that infuriated Bonaparte. She turned more to

[10] *Edinburgh Review*, 3 (Oct. 1803), 213–15.
[11] For a brief overview, see the article 'Femme' by Yvonne Knibiehler, in *Dictionnaire
Napoléon*, ed. Jean Tulard (Paris, 1987).

domestic life, taking responsibility for her late sister's two sons, Charles and Athanase Coquerel, and she and Stone enjoyed their affluence, touring Normandy in 1810. But her mother died in 1812 and Stone's business speculations led to the loss of his fortune. She turned to her literary and scientific interests in order to make some money, translating the work of her friends Alexander von Humboldt and Aimé Bonpland as *Personal Narrative of Travels to the Equinoctial Regions of the New Continent, During the Years 1799–1804* (1814–21) and *Researches, Concerning the Institutions & Monuments of the Ancient Inhabitants of America, with Descriptions & Views of Some of the Most Striking Scenes in the Cordilleras!* (2 vols, 1814).[12]

In her Preface to the *Personal Narrative* Williams signals a change of direction from political writing, but this is misleading, as seen in her characterization of the explorer as a lover rather than a philosopher or a conqueror:

Happy the traveller, with whom the study of Nature has not been merely the cold research of the understanding, in the explanation of her properties, or the solution of her problems! who, while he has interpreted her laws, has adored her sublimity, and followed her steps with passionate enthusiasm, amidst that solemn and stupendous scenery, those melancholy and sacred solitudes, where she speaks in a voice so well understood by the mysterious sympathy of the feeling heart. . . . How often will posterity also turn from the terrible page of our history, to repose on the charm of a narrative, which displays the most enlarged views of science and philanthropy! (vol. i, pp. vi–viii)

The allusions to Robespierrian reason and Napoleonic imperialism are obvious and Williams implies that nature and travel writing offer a feminized, erotic yet sublime refuge from the horrors perpetrated by such different though related forms of narrowly 'masculine' culture. 'What sympathy does the traveller excite', she declares, 'while he imprints the first step, that leads to civilization and all its boundless blessings, along the trackless desert, and, struggling with the savageness of the untamed wilderness, obtains a victory that belongs to mankind' (vol. i, p. viii). The image of wilderness would remind readers of the recent and pointless horrors of Bonaparte's Russian campaign. Whereas Bonaparte tries to remake the world using military force, von Humboldt is more like the Revolutionaries of the early 1790s, raising 'the

---

[12] *Researches* and the first three volumes of the *Personal Narrative* were published by a conger of fashionable booksellers including Longman & Co., Colburn, and Murray; vols. iv and v (in two parts) of the *Personal Narrative* were published in 1819 and 1821 by Longman & Co., suggesting that the other partners backed out of a loss-making project.

mind to general ideas, without neglecting individual facts; and while he appears only to address himself to our reason, he has the secret of awakening the imagination, and of being understood by the heart' (vol. i, p. ix). Thus von Humboldt is a scientist for a post-Revolutionary age, feminizing his subject with feeling and imagination to give it a fully human character and appeal.

Williams responds as a woman, and as she once mediated the Revolutionary political vision for English readers so she now mediates von Humboldt's revolutionary scientific vision for the same readers, who are, like her, supposedly glutted with Revolution. This is acceptably feminine intellectual work and Williams seems like von Humboldt's dependant, since his writing gives her access to discourses from which she would normally be excluded by convention and education. But as von Humboldt has feminized scientific travel, making it greater than mere science, his writing has been shaped accordingly, and she points out that he has generously enabled her to complete the process by advising her and by writing in a way accessible to all, 'even' women. Furthermore, she avoids calling her work a 'translation', except on the title-page. She is an 'interpreter', and the text is 'my pages'.

Bonaparte's fall brought crowds of British tourists to Paris and Williams's salon again became one of their meeting-places. But the years had taken their toll. Henry Crabb Robinson found Stone to be an invalid and Williams with no 'traces' of her reputed 'former beauty', though she talked politics 'without restraint'. Stone told him that 'Buonaparte was their enemy' because Williams refused 'to write in his favour'. She also seemed out of touch with literary life in Britain, having never heard of Wordsworth, for example.[13] But she could now resume her work as leading British commentator on the Revolution and its aftermath, and in 1815 she published another collection of letters in her familiar style, entitled *A Narrative of the Events which Have Taken Place in France, from the Landing of Napoleon Bonaparte, on the 1st of March, 1815, till the Restoration of Louis XVIII; With an Account of the Present State of Society and Public Opinion.*

Again the designated genre—'a narrative'—indicates a 'feminine' discourse rather than the kind of reflective analysis readers might

---

[13] *Henry Crabb Robinson on Books and Their Writers*, ed. Edith J. Morley, 3 vols. (London, 1938), i. 147–8.

expect a man to write. To reassert her sentimental connection with Britain Williams addresses her (again unnamed) English correspondent as 'the friend of my youth', but she also establishes the difference between their political experience: 'Although divided from each other by a geographical space of only a few short leagues, at what an insurmountable distance were the two countries which we inhabit separated by the ascendancy of that Implacable Will, which had placed a barrier between the nations more insurmountable than the wall of China!' Williams represents her political experience, and thus her authority, as historical, for during her residence in Paris she has 'witnessed all the successive phases of its revolutions', but her authority is also subjective, warranted by the sensibility many readers would know from her earlier work. That very sensibility has, however, forced her into silence during the Napoleonic regime, for 'the iron hand of despotism has weighed upon my soul, and subdued all intellectual energy' (p. 5). Thus her silence authenticates her representation of Bonaparte's regime as an embodiment of the merely masculine Revolution that had previously silenced her during the Jacobin government of 1793–4. Though political oppression has now ended, a subjective oppression remains: 'those who have witnessed the Revolution' feel a 'weariness of the memory of what is past', and she can deal only with Bonaparte's 'hundred days', or the 'second volume' of what Mme de Staël calls 'Bonaparte's adventures' (pp. 7–8). This phrase novelizes the history of the Napoleonic era, bringing it within the scope of women's writing. In fact, she insists, it was her sensibility that once made her a 'Bonapartist': 'Yes, I admired Bonaparte; I admired also the French revolution. To my then youthful imagination, the day-star of liberty seemed to rise on the vine-covered hills of France, only to shed benedictions on humanity' (p. 7). But just as her feminine Revolution was succeeded by a repressively masculine Jacobin Revolution, so the anti-Jacobin Bonaparte was succeeded by the repressively masculine Emperor who revived court culture and politics, accommodated that supporter of despots, the Catholic Church, and renewed wars of imperial conquest.

The rest of the book treats Bonaparte's 'hundred days' as a return of masculine Revolution. His landing from Elba again divided both the country and individual families: 'The division in families is not one of the least evils of civil discord. Its serpents writhe upon the calm bosom of domestic life, and transform all its joys to bitterness' (p. 20). The women of France, except for a few courtiers, opposed Bonaparte's 'tyranny' as an enemy of the domestic affections:

Who had not wept for a brother, an affianced lover, a husband, or a son? . . .
Conscription—what a terrible word!—How little you can feel, or comprehend
all its meaning!—Oh no! it has drawn no tears from your eyes—it has
awakened no anguish in your bosom! They only understand it well, whose
children have been exposed to its savage grasp. (pp. 65–6)

The exclamations signal immediacy of emotional expression, and Williams explains that her adopted nephews would have been drafted into
the army had not Bonaparte fallen. Many readers would recall her
earlier enthusiasm for the Revolution because it freed her friends the
du Fossés from patriarchal tyranny. Such readers would also recognize
an implied contrast between France and Britain, but now reversed,
with Britain the positive term and France the negative one. Yet the
spirit of feminized Revolution has remained alive even under Bonaparte, appropriately enough in the 'bosoms', or sensibility, of 'the
women of France', for whatever the government of the day or
structure of the state, and though women are excluded from the public
and political sphere, they constitute the true state because they preside
over subjectivity and the domestic affections, thereby influencing 'the
great as well as the little interests of society'. This Revolutionary spirit,
she claims, was kept alive by women of all classes (p. 69).

The *Narrative* then details Bonaparte's attempt to revive his popularity after he had alienated the people, and especially the women. But
the people 'saw nothing but slavery in the revival of jacobinism, and
its junction with imperialism' (p. 83). As a result, Bonaparte's manliness
was undermined. He wore body armour against assassination, according
to one of Williams's informants he acted the coward on the field of
Waterloo, and he lacked courage to make a hero's exit after defeat.
Williams's heroes now are Wellington and the English troops who,
unlike their Continental allies, avoid unnecessary bloodshed and do not
pillage. The arrival of the heroic yet benevolent—and thus
feminized—British troops and Louis XVIII's promulgation of the
'Charter' seem to guarantee the gains of the feminized Revolution,
capped by a symbolic female reclamation of a site drenched in Revolutionary blood, the Tuileries gardens, where 'Ladies formed their own
sets for country-dances, and bringing their own music with them,
danced light as nymphs, and crowned with lilies, before the windows
of the Château; where the king stood, sometimes gracefully kissing his
hand, and sometimes wiping his eyes, while he witnessed all these
testimonies of enthusiastic affection' (pp. 273–4). Bonaparte, by

contrast, now belongs to history, and Williams accordingly provides a summary of his character and career.

She seems to conclude the *Narrative* by asking if the French people are going home at last, after years of wandering. Such figuring of political history in domestic terms was becoming increasingly common in the new Romantic literature. Similarly, the question is more than a 'speculative investigation' to Williams: 'it comprehends all that can awaken solicitude, all that can interest the heart; all chance of personal tranquillity towards the evening of a stormy life, and all hope of felicity for the objects most dear to me, and to whom life is opening'—another reference to her nephews (p. 303). A quarter of a century of the vicissitudes of Revolution come down to personal and family matters. Yet this, Williams suggests, is the fundamental character of politics and she predicts that France will now return to the principles of feminized Revolution: 'her energies, no longer wasted on the crusades of ambition, but directed towards intellectual attainments, in eternal alliance with the first feelings of our nature', will influence 'the general amelioration of the human race' (pp. 307–8). The attribution of feminine gender to France is deliberate, and the prophecy makes a fitting conclusion to the *Narrative* and her Revolutionary prose epic. But as in the 1790s her hopeful prophecies prove ill-founded and she has to add two further letters dated October 1815, discussing the Congress of Vienna, which restored the power of court despotism over Europe: 'of all the consequences of the French revolution, this was the most fatal to the liberty of mankind' (p. 378). The main text does close on another hopeful note, but darkened by a sense that masculine militarism and despotism have once again prevailed.

Williams's work continued to rouse differing responses. In a long review of several books on Napoleon's 'hundred days', the Tory *Quarterly Review* found Williams's *Narrative* the 'best', and though 'occasionally affected' in its style, 'written with accuracy, with a free and, we had almost said, an impartial spirit'. The *Monthly Review*, however, returned to old charges, accusing Williams of moral laxity in private life, tergiversation in politics, impious religious principles, sentimentality in her opinions, and writing mere journalism that will not 'pass current fifty years hence'.[14]

Shortly afterwards British opinion became alarmed at mistreatment of Protestants during the power vacuum after Bonaparte's fall, and there

---

[14] *Quarterly Review*, 14 (Oct. 1815), 69; *Monthly Review*, NS 78 (Nov. 1815), 300, 309.

were calls for British military intervention. Williams was well connected to the Protestant community in France and in a letter *On the Late Persecution of the Protestants in the South of France* (1816) she discusses the matter in relation to the history of the Revolution and its aftermath. Toleration for Protestants had been an important Revolutionary measure and many British Dissenters, such as Samuel Kenrick and James Wodrow, welcomed the Revolution for that reason. Despite Bonaparte's Concordat with the Papacy, Protestantism continued to be protected by the state. With the Restoration of the monarchy there was concern that the old alliance of Church and State would lead to renewed persecution of Protestants, for religious differences had become entangled in Revolutionary politics at an early stage, with bloody consequences. In southern France Protestant support for the Revolution was resented by Catholics and royalists, leading to reprisals during counter-revolutionary uprisings and after Bonaparte's fall.[15] The vicissitudes of the French Protestants both paralleled those of the Revolution and indicated what could happen if the nation disintegrated. In 1816 there were many in Britain besides Dissenters who were interested in this question.

Williams's pamphlet, again in the familiar letter form, is written for them. It concentrates on the treatment of the Protestants under the Revolution and Bonaparte and explains recent massacres at Nîmes in the context of Protestant sufferings since the seventeenth century. Williams personalizes the subject, using it to meet charges that she has 'confessed' to the 'transgression' of supporting the Revolution. She argues that it was protection of Protestants by the Revolution and Bonaparte that earned her support for both. Her brief but moving account of the sufferings of the Protestants under court absolutism prepares for her expression of sympathetic joy with French Protestants freed from such horrors by the Revolution, and she insists that 'Amidst all the various phases of the French Revolution, the star of religious liberty had moved calmly in its majestic orbit, and cheered despairing humanity with a ray of celestial radiance' (p. 5).

Nevertheless, she draws a parallel between the September Massacres of 1792 and the recent massacres at Nîmes, presenting the latter in terms of the domestic affections, as reported by a personal friend, Mme Juillera, who describes what happened when a Catholic mob tried to

---

[15] Adrien Dansette, *Religious History of Modern France*, trans. John Dingle, 2 vols. (Freiburg, 1961), i. 57.

enter the Protestant church and massacre its congregation:

'I held my little girl in my hand, and approached the foot of the pulpit,—my husband rejoined us,—I thought of my nursling boy, whom I had left at home, and should embrace no more! I recollected that this day was the anniversary of my marriage—I believed that I was going to die, with my husband and my daughter—It was some consolation that we should die together; and it seemed to me that this was the moment in which we were best prepared to appear in the presence of God—the victims of a religious duty . . .' (pp. 49–50)

Readers familiar with Williams's work would see a parallel between this scene and those during the Terror, reported in *Letters* (1795). Williams uses the event now, however, to associate both Catholic and Jacobin terror with the Bonapartists by pointing out that the latter 'alone exulted in' the outrage at Nîmes, for 'the placid blessedness of ordinary life, when it flows in its calm and equal current, is hateful to those, whose hopes are only buoyant amidst the disturbance of the tempest' (p. 54).

In *A Narrative* Williams argued that Bonaparte was hostile to feminine, domestic virtues; now she resumes that claim and represents Britain as the repository of those virtues. News of the persecutions made 'Indignation beat high in every British bosom' and 'associations, which watch with wakeful jealousy over the civil and religious rights of mankind', condemned the outrages in France. She then gives way to one of her familiar apostrophes, here addressed not to the feminized Revolution but to a feminized yet heroic England:

Favoured and glorious England! How poor are the trophies of other nations compared with those which encircle her brows! She has ever the pre-eminence in all the counsels of philanthropy; the arbitress of moral action—the guardian of the wronged, whatever region they inhabit, with whatever colour they may be tinged. (pp. 55–6)

France's Revolutionary and Napoleonic 'trophies' contrast with Britain's philanthropic ones. These feminine yet armed virtues have a global mission of legitimate imperialism extending even into France. Yet the British government was party to the restoration of 'despotism' deplored by Williams in *A Narrative* and so she attributes only to the people of Britain the 'unwearied vigilance' necessary to prevent the recrudescence of Catholicism, for Williams the historic prop of court government.

A different aspect of Williams's post-Revolutionary interests is expressed by her next work, *The Leper of the City of Aoste: A Narrative*
(1817), a translation of Xavier de Maistre's *Le Lépreux de la cité
d'Aoste* (1811). The tale is representative of the post-Revolutionary
and Romantic spirit of religious devotion and quietism and Williams
may not have known who the author was; de Maistre had served in
the Russian army against Bonaparte and his better-known brother
Joseph was a leading conservative political philosopher. Williams offers
the book specifically as an alternative to Revolutionary turmoil, arguing that the Revolution induced writers to devote 'to politics those
powers of mind, which, in calmer periods of human history, would
have been devoted to more soothing meditations'. Most of the tale
itself is in highly expressive dialogue between the leper and an unnamed
army officer. The latter implicitly represents the world of politics,
revolution, and the struggles of empires while the leper represents the
victim of nature and society, consoled briefly by the domestic affections
and more permanently by the sublime nature visible from his isolated
tower, the beauty of his garden, his intense sensation of mere existence,
and simple piety. The tale represents domestic heroism in the face of
unmerited misfortune—the parallel to Job is explicit—and relativizes
the issues and events of the Napoleonic period by portraying the
heroic yet feminized capacity for suffering of the victims of the 'great'
men of the day.

Williams wrote the tale for money, and it was published by a
bookseller (George Cowie in the Poultry, London) who catered for
the urban market in sentimental and sensational chapbooks. For as the
Revolution was being transformed from politics into history Williams's
importance as a commentator declined. Henry Crabb Robinson
thought her *Narrative* 'not historical enough' and 'too much in the
style of a party-writer', though one 'whose love of justice and truth are
still pure'. She and Stone were now in financial difficulties and in 1817
Crabb Robinson tried to persuade the editor of *The Times* to employ
her.[16] In the same year an American visitor, George Ticknor, found
her Sunday evening salons pleasant and frequented by 'literary English-
men, with several Frenchmen, well known in the world'. He found
Williams 'an uncommon woman' who talked 'sensibly', 'except when
she gets upon politics'. Nevertheless, he thought she was 'evidently
waning': 'Her conversation is not equal to her reputation, and I suspect

---

[16] *Crabb Robinson*, ed. Morley, i. 176, 182.

never was brilliant; since, as I should think, it must always have been affected.'[17] Stone died in May 1818 and a friend cheated Williams out of the remains of their fortune. Crabb Robinson visited her in Paris a few years later and found her looking ill and unhappy, yet liked 'everything about her, but her rather fulsome compliments'. Williams's Sentimental culture and manners, which had always struck others forcibly, now seemed odd or even absurd to those who had not seen that culture at its height in the 1780s and 1790s. Faced with poverty she wrote yet another political book, dealing with the Restoration of the French monarchy. Crabb Robinson helped to sell it but found London publishers uninterested; he eventually placed it with the relatively new firm of Baldwin, Cradock, & Joy.[18]

Letters on the Events which Have Passed in France since the Restoration in 1815 (1819) was one of several books by women describing post-Napoleonic France and Europe, including Anne Carter's *Letters from a Lady to Her Sister During a Tour to Paris in the Months of April and May, 1814* (1814), Lady Morgan's *France* (1817), and Mary and Percy Bysshe Shelley's *History of a Six Weeks' Tour through a Part of France, Switzerland, Germany and Holland* (1817). Williams's *Letters* is short, returns to the main points of *A Narrative*, repeats the material in Williams's pamphlet on the French Protestants, and uses the same Sentimental devices—epistolary form, expressive style, and personal perspective—found in her earlier books on the Revolution. Yet she thought the book was new and more balanced than its predecessor. She told Crabb Robinson that in her previous book she had been 'too glad to be delivered from Napoleon and too glad of what followed', but had since been 'cured' of those feelings and had now written not only a more 'liberal' work—too much so for her previous publisher—but her 'best' so far.[19]

At the outset of the book she reclaims her Revolutionary heritage, rejecting charges that her 'prolonged silence' means that she has abandoned her former principles: 'the enthusiasm I once felt for the cause of liberty still warms my bosom', otherwise she would defend herself like a woman 'by reverting to the past, and recapitulating a small part only of all I have seen, and all I have suffered', for 'where the feelings and affections of the mind have been powerfully called forth by the attraction of some great object, we are not easily cured of

[17] *Life, Letters, and Journal of George Ticknor*, 2 vols. (London, 1876), i. 130.
[18] *Crabb Robinson*, ed. Morley, i. 224–5.
[19] Quoted in Woodward, *Williams*, 184.

long cherished predilection' (pp. 1–2). The immediacy of her response to the Revolution left an impression still felt, like a great love. This, she implies, is a domain where women may claim to be experts, and again she measures political change by its effect on the women of France. Bonaparte's policy of conscription 'made all the women of France his enemies, and their influence being sufficiently powerful in this country, their resentment, no doubt, contributed to his overthrow' (pp. 123–4). Like the women of France, Williams claims political authority from personal response, for she has witnessed 'all the stupendous events that usually fill the lapse of ages, and resound through the spaces of creation . . . interwoven with every thing around me, linked with all my hopes or fears, connected with my very existence, and fixing irreparably my destiny' (pp. 3–4). Because of her intense response to the Revolution she is its product, and even speaks of 'we' meaning 'the French'. Because the Revolution encompassed 'the lapse of ages' and 'the spaces of creation' it equals the whole of time and space and transcends it; thus her ability to grasp the Revolution through her feminine sensibility makes her the measure of both the Revolution as it recedes into history and history itself. She transcends both in a feminization of time and space that resembles Felicia Hemans's in *Tales and Historic Scenes*, published the same year.

Yet there are those who wish to undo the Revolution as a feminized historical experience. The counter-revolutionaries 'believed that the moment was arrived when the revolutionary principles of equal rights, independence, toleration, and whatever else belonged to that order of things, might be crushed for ever' (p. 5). But Revolutionary history as subjective experience has left its mark on the new generation as on Williams:

they are too well read in modern history, of which their country has been the great theatre, to seek for liberty where it is not to be found. They do not resemble that misled and insensate multitude who, in the first years of the revolution, had just thrown off their chains, and profaned in their ignorance the cause they revered. (pp. 8–9)

Revolutionary historiography, to which Williams has contributed largely, fixes the Revolution as subjective experience, thereby ensuring its transmission over generations and preventing Revolutionary error from being repeated. Indeed, the lessons of Revolutionary history may be disseminated by the very agents who brought that history to an end in defeating Bonaparte:

The crusades that so long devastated Europe roused the human mind from its long lethargy, and unfolded its intellectual powers. Who shall say that the armies of the north have not imbibed new ideas of freedom and independence while they sojourned in France? (p. 73)

It was a commonplace of Enlightenment historiography that despite the fanaticism, war, destruction, and misery caused by the Crusades, they were a major cause of the Renaissance; Williams projects that commonplace on to the Revolution and turns it into a political hope.

This hope is linked to an important thematic and structural device. As in her writings of the 1790s, Williams often compares France with her own native land; but now she distances herself from Britain, which has been accused of considering 'freedom as an home-production, chartered for her own use', while consigning the rest of Europe to the conquerors and despots of the Congress of Vienna, which was seen by liberals throughout Europe as an attempt to reverse history. Thus Williams devotes most of her text to describing political, religious, and intellectual rights now enjoyed by the French because of the Revolution and Louis XVIII's 'Charter', but still being denied to the British people by their government. Much of this description responds to French and British critiques of the Revolution. Replying to the claim that the Revolution stifled literature, she argues that 'polite literature' has little chance to flourish in constant Revolutionary turmoil followed by prolonged militarization of society. Yet in France politics have almost become a cultural activity, with large audiences following Benjamin Constant's lectures at the Paris Athenée. Moreover, the French have now allied the sciences to 'patriotism' and made them 'an essential part of modern education'—a reminder of her own claim to science as translator of von Humboldt. She admits that in disseminating religion Britain surpasses France, and singles out the British and Foreign Bible Society for praise, but 'we'—the French—'shall learn to imitate what we admire' (p. 113). Williams also praises the 'general respect for religion' that 'now prevails' in France, in contrast to the irreligion of the Revolution. It is not surprising, then, that elsewhere in *Letters* (1819) she quotes Chateaubriand, for the note of piety here is consistent with that of early French Romanticism, manifested in her translation of *The Leper of the City of Aoste*.

Letters was welcomed by the *Monthly Review*, which was glad to see Williams again 'as an original writer, after having seen her in the less dignified capacity of a translator'. The reviewer found her account authoritative and enlightening and wished it were longer. But the *British Critic* denounced her as 'an ex-jacobin' who 'took as active a part' in the French Revolution 'as a *woman* could take', sneered at 'the undiminished interest which this profound lady still takes in the welfare of all the nations of the earth', and ridiculed her expressive, personal style: 'she obviously can hardly write without the tears streaming down her cheeks; notes of admiration conclude every sentence; Oh!'s and Ah!'s choke her utterance before she can begin them.' *Letters* itself is 'full of all the stuff and nonsense, and cant and slang, of French jacobinical philosophy', composed in 'extremely bad taste', and dependent on others' opinions, with 'no sort of authority whatever': 'Jacobinism is a disease, and not an error; it is a leprosy in the understanding, for which there is no cure; a sin against the welfare of mankind, for which, there appears to be no repentance.'[20] A generation after the Revolutionary decade Williams could still be made a figure for all that was seen as transgressive about the Revolution.

Williams's interest in Romanticism, apparent in *Letters* (1819), made her aware that Sensibility, which had sustained her career as a writer since the 1780s and her feminization of politics for three decades, was being subsumed in a new form of the professional middle-class cultural revolution. In 1823 she explored this relationship in a collection of her verse going back to the 1780s, *Poems on Various Subjects; With Introductory Remarks on the Present State of Science and Literature in France*. It was designed to make money, but she used the occasion to situate her life, career, and writing in relation to the political and cultural revolutions of her time and to claim a place in the new cultural vanguard of Romanticism. In the 'Introduction' she admits that she has long had more important work than poetry, 'confining my pen almost entirely to sketches of the events of the Revolution' and 'treading on the territory of History' (pp. ix–x). She claims to have united poetry and politics in only four poems—*Peru* (revised into a series of six 'Peruvian Tales' resembling Hemans's *Tales and Historic Scenes*), her poem on the abolition of the slave trade, 'The Bastille: A Vision', and her 'Ode to Peace', which incurred Bonaparte's displeasure at the time of the treaty of Amiens. Significantly, these poems resemble her Revolutionary prose epic in feminizing public and political events.

[20] *Monthly Review*, NS 90 (Sept. 1819), 32, 36; *British Critic*, NS 12 (Oct. 1819), 392–4, 399.

Accordingly, she then considers the relation of the Revolution to literature. Many thought that the Revolution eclipsed literature, but she argues that literature was subsumed and transformed by the Revolution as 'eloquence', which had been 'shackled in a thousand ways before the Revolution' but 'burst at once into splendour, when the delegates of the people were permitted to proclaim their rights'. It was especially 'the immortal members of the Gironde' who showed 'that the purest source of eloquence is found in the love of liberty' (p. xvi). The same thing happened after the fall of Bonaparte. By equating literature with eloquence, conventionally the art of persuasion in the public and political forum, Williams politicizes it, for society, subjectivity, and literature form a circuit that is political: 'From the natural connection that exists between our feelings and our situation, a new state of society must have led the vivid imagination of the poet to new images, and his heart, tremblingly awake to every human sympathy, must have felt new emotions' (p. xix). When these are expressed they constitute literature as eloquence because it intervenes in other subjectivities and thus brings about 'a new state of society', which constitutes new subjectivities in a permanent revolution. Therefore she disagrees that France's literature was greatest under Louis XIV, its most absolute monarch, and argues that had a writer such as Racine lived during the Revolution 'his mind would have taken a different tone, and feeling; he would have written more after his own heart; far from the ceremonial of a court by which he was sometimes shackled, he would have seized the philosophic spirit of the times, and allied the fervour of the patriot with the pathetic tenderness of the poet' (p. xx). That is, he would have written like Williams herself.

The same revolutionary process applies to the material of literature—language. The French Revolution has introduced 'many new words' because of new social, political, and cultural 'circumstances', though the French admit this 'with reluctance' as a kind of 'innovation' analogous to and supporting political revolution: 'Those upstart words seem despised like the people, by the privileged orders, for having no ancestry. The French Academy steadfastly persist in excluding many parliamentary terms which the Chamber of Deputies have resolutely adopted' and the 'new denomination of *romantic* in literature, gives a French critic the same kind of shivering fit, as that of *liberal* in politics produces on the nerves of an *ultra*' (p. xx n.). The literary and political vanguard are one, opposed by a united front of political counter-revolutionaries and conservative institutions of language (the French Academy) and literature (the critics). Williams clearly sides with the former by naming several writers of the literary vanguard as friends and pro-revolutionaries, thereby uniting her politics of literature and her domestic affections once again. Thus she denies both the counter-revolutionary claim that Revolution and literature are incompatible and the Bonapartist claim that literature, like everything else, has degenerated since the Restoration. And just as the Revolution transformed literature, so literature as she defines it now embodies, preserves, and disseminates the Revolution.

From the argument of this 'Introduction' all of Williams's poems, not just the four she acknowledges to be overtly political, may now be read as expressions, products, and contributions to the Revolution, in the past, through the present, and into the future. Pre-Revolutionary poems such as *Peru*, *Edwin and Eltruda*, 'The Morai', and 'An American Tale' can be read as anticipating the Revolution. Her few poems of the Revolutionary decade and Napoleonic period, such as her verse epistle to Dr John Moore, her translations and imitations of French poets, her elegy to Joel Barlow, and her address to the anti-slavery campaigner Clarkson, now seem vindicated by history. Some poems, such as the sonnets, seem to have gained new significance in the context of Romantic literature—as she explains that her sonnet to Hope has become especially important to her because during a recent visit Wordsworth recited it to her 'from memory, after a lapse of many years' (p. 203 n.). Finally, some recent poems overtly link the political and the domestic in a way she has suggested was characteristic of Romanticism. 'The Charter; Addressed to My Nephew Athanase C. L. Coquerel, on his Wedding Day, 1819' calls for the kind of egalitarian and companionate marriage celebrated in the literature and culture of Sensibility and compares it to the constitution and political life of the state:

> Ah! may no *ultra* thirst of power
> Embitter life's domestic hour;
> No principles of feudal sway
> Teach without loving, to obey;
> The heart such joyless homage slights,
> And wedlock claims its Bill of Rights—   (p. 268)

Such a marriage would be abrogated only by death and transcended only in the life hereafter:

> Thus be the charter'd Code imprest,
> With all its statutes, on your breast;
> No duty it enjoins forsook,
> Till Time at length shall close the book;
> And hope shall frame, for worlds to come,
> A treaty that survives the tomb.   (p. 272)

Readers familiar with Williams's Revolutionary prose epic would recognize her favourite device of validating the Revolution by appeal to the domestic affections. Readers familiar with the French writers she mentions or with contemporary English writers such as Felicia Hemans would recognize the post-Revolutionary Romantic transcendence of history in the subjective, domestic, and eternal. *Poems on Various Subjects* subsumes both Williams's pre-Revolutionary poems and those of the Revolutionary decade and Napoleonic period to her post-Revolutionary situation and Romantic sympathies, just as she argues that post-Revolutionary politics and culture subsume those of the feminized, Girondin Revolution of which she was a part.

Poems received little critical notice and had little or no impact in Britain for several reasons: Williams was no longer a figure of interest to the reading public or to controversialists, and poetry by women was already marginalized within Romantic literature and criticism. The *Monthly Review* welcomed the *Poems* but found the recent ones not up to those published earlier and the quality 'always above mediocrity though wanting in some of the higher characteristics of genius'—a commonplace in reviews of women's poetry during the 1820s. The reviewer did find the value of the book 'considerably enhanced by the force and elegance of its prefatory remarks' on the state of French literature and thought her prose writings in general to be far superior to her poetry, but Williams is treated as a figure once controversial and still well known but belonging to the past.[21]

By the time she published her next and last work, Williams was virtually forgotten. This epilogue to her Revolutionary prose epic was not even published in English, but in a French translation by her nephew Charles Coquerel as *Souvenirs de la Révolution française* (1827), which he claims to have performed out of respect for her and as an eyewitness contribution to the history of 'l'événement le plus influent des temps modernes' ('the most influential event of modern times',

---

[21] *Monthly Review*, NS 102 (Sept. 1823), 20, 23.

p. v).[22] The title suggests that this is a work of retrospection and Williams again defends herself against charges of political apostasy and vindicates the view of the Revolution she had maintained through a quarter of a century, but she gives contemporary relevance to her work in two ways—by claiming that the gains of the Revolution are being undermined by royalists, Bonapartists, and Jesuits, and by attacking recent historians of the Revolution. These two aims are related because, as Williams recognized, conflicting historical interpretations of the Revolution had become a major factor in the political debates of the Revolutionary aftermath, in both France and Britain. Her aim was to intervene in these debates by insisting again on the value of the feminized Girondin Revolution as model of national transformation without resort to violence. In order to effect her intervention she has to insist again on the validity of her kind of feminized Revolutionary historiography against others that had developed in the Revolutionary aftermath, especially after the fall of Napoleon.[23]

Both her argument and her method are exemplified in anecdotes such as her account of a dinner with Pétion, mayor of Paris, at the height of the Girondon Revolution:

La conversation fut vive et animée au dernier point. On parlait peu des causeries ordinaires de la société. Les femmes paraissaient oublier le soin de plaire, et les hommes songeaient moins à les admirer.

Il y avait dans ce salon-là quelque chose de mieux que la galanterie. Une estime mutuelle, un commun intérêt pour les grandes questions du jour, étaient ce qui paraissait le plus. On parlait de la liberté avec des accens profonds et sincères, qui approchaient de l'éloquence. La joie de ce repas patriotique était augmentée plutôt que distraite par la foule immense qui encombrait la place de Ville, et mille voix confuses faisaient parvenir jusqu'à nous le cri répété de: 'Pétion ou la mort.'

[The conversation was lively and animated to the highest degree. There was little of the commonplace society chitchat. The women seemed unconcerned about pleasing, and the men thought less about admiring them.

In that salon there was something better than gallantry. What appeared most was a mutual esteem, a common concern for the great issues of the day. Liberty was spoken of in fervent and sincere tones, which approached eloquence. The joy of this patriotic dinner was increased rather than diminished by the huge crowd that filled the Place de Ville, and a thousand mingled voices came to us with the repeated cry of 'Pétion or death.' (pp. 19–20)]

---

[22] Quotations are my own translations from the French, corrected by Marianne Krajicek.
[23] Ben-Israel, *English Historians on the French Revolution*, chs. 3–4.

This symbolic event represents the feminized Revolution as a harmonization of gender and class differences that had divided the nation under the *ancien régime*, but Williams goes on to show how that harmony was broken by the Jacobin Terror, then partially restored after the Thermidorean reaction of 1794, only to be submerged during the Bonapartist regime. She presents the Restoration as another revival but sees the rise of the ultras and the Jesuits in the 1810s and 1820s as yet another attempt to destroy the feminized Revolution.

In the face of this threat Williams feminizes the Revolution in several ways and more thoroughly than before. She again celebrates the Revolutionary heroism of Marie Roland, Charlotte Corday ('ce Brutus féminin', p. 59), and other women, however obscure, inspired by their domestic affections as wives, mothers, daughters, friends. She describes in fresh detail her own influence on the Revolution, such as persuading Bancal des Issarts to vote against death for Louis XVI, assisting Miranda to embark on a military career, and dissuading a young woman from entering monastic life after the Restoration, for through such apparently small acts, within any woman's power, public life is transformed, revolutions brought about, and counter-revolution foiled. Her earlier works also emphasized women's Revolutionary roles as leaders, heroines, victims, or a powerful force in public opinion, but she now treats with feminist sarcasm the remasculinizing of culture, politics, and the state under Bonaparte and the Restoration. Women are 'shut up within the confines of the home' and 'given permission to soothe the cares and troubles of life' once they have lost the beauties that 'embellish' existence. But they are not allowed 'to leave the narrow circle where men have enclosed them' or use their influence in 'those great issues where the interests of humanity are debated and decided'.

En général, les devoirs et l'activité des femmes sont renfermés dans l'enceinte du foyer domestique. On nous octroie en effet la permission d'adoucir les soins et les inquiétudes de la vie humaine; et même, quand nous avons perdu les grâces qui embellissent l'existence, on nous permet de déployer encore ces vertus, qui la consolent. Mais il n'est pas accordé aux femmes de sortir du cercle restreint où les hommes les ont enfermées, et d'intervenir dans ces hautes questions où les intérêts de l'espèce humaine se débattent et se décident. (p. 72)

Not surprisingly, then, although women too may feel 'patriotic fervour' they abstain from public affairs, except for the exceptional 'woman of masculine spirit' ('une femme d'un mâle génie'), such as

Mme Roland, who loved France 'with passion, because women do not love by halves' ('avec passion, parce que les femmes n'aiment point à demi'): 'I never tired of her enspiriting brilliance of conversation, of that eloquence which came from the bottom of her heart. She delighted in my sentiments, and our friendship became closer' ('Je ne me lassais pas d'éclat entraînant de sa conversation, de cette éloquence, qui partait du fond du cœur,' p. 73). The initial sarcasm of this passage culminates in the redirected courtly cliché that women are devoted to love, but gives way to the feminine sympathy that validates Williams's feminization of the Revolution. Williams then draws Roland into the present by comparing her to the heroic women of the modern Greek struggle for liberty, sanctified by her poem 'Lines on the Fall of Missolunghi', appended to the end of Souvenirs.

In her earlier writings Williams insisted that the Revolution was based on domains conventionally gendered female, but she now goes further, arguing that revolutionary times produce a particularly close connection 'between public affairs and private destinies' ('entre les affaires publiques et les sorts privés', p.4) and since 'a woman's political principles always derive from her feelings' ('les principes politiques d'une femme dérivent toujours de ses sentimens', p. 199) she is especially in tune with such times. By contrast, she argues, merely theoretical politics disguised the merely personal ambition of the Jacobins and Napoleon, resulting in the sacrifice of thousands of individuals and families. Accordingly, she claims that her 'sentiments' and 'impressions' are more accurate and reliable than the 'general views' of either politicians or historians, and she celebrates the feminized Revolution with unprecedented detail, fervour, and nostalgia in order to show how it was lived through personal relations and feelings within women's culture, rather than through merely public, political, or military events dominated by men. She places those who participated in feminized Revolutionary culture—the Girondins and Marie Roland, and thus herself—at the centre of the Revolution, between extremes of court and mob despotism, as an example to the post-Revolutionary age. In this way she aims to transform what might be considered 'merely' feminine and sentimental nostalgia into both Revolutionary history and a revolutionary future. She aims to insert 'her' Revolution of the past into the present by exemplifying its living presence in her text, or feminizing Revolutionary historiography.

For example, although Souvenirs is not in epistolary form but a continuous narrative, it uses a loose chronological structure with much personal observation and anecdote to represent the Revolutionary experience with the immediacy that might be expected of a woman writer. Williams retells, often in greater detail than before, the du Fossés' story, the attack on the Tuileries of 10 August 1792, the Girondin Revolution, her imprisonment in 1793, her accidental meeting with Bonaparte during his coup of 18 Brumaire, and the Allies' siege of Paris in 1814. These anecdotes and their new particularity are meant to prove that she had continuous direct knowledge of the Revolution and its aftermath and that this knowledge often came through the converging intellectual, political, social, and personal relations that inspired and even constituted the Revolution. This inspiration is located in the Girondin circle.

She further feminizes Revolutionary historiography by affecting a 'feminine' modesty about her own work, presenting herself as 'a simple witness' ('moi, simple témoin', p. 96) 'whose aim is to retrace here the impressions of those remarkable times as they occurred' ('dont le but est de retracer ici les impressions contemporaines de ces jours remarquables', p. 89) and her text as 'this very light sketch' and 'less a piece of writing than a description of the feelings and opinions of my contemporaries' ('le tableau très-léger que je trace ici . . . moins un écrit qu'une description des sentimens et des opinions des comtemporains', p. 143). Yet these 'feelings' live powerfully in her memory. She exclaims at one point:

Combien Paris m'environne et m'assiége d'images lugubres des temps passés! Combien il m'est arrivé de fois, en indiquant à des voyageurs anglais le théâtre des événemens mémorables de la révolution, de rapprocher le sentiment d'étonnement léger qu'ils éprouvaient, de ces émotions profondes que je ressentais moi-même, en présence de tant de souvenirs, et tant de maux qui n'ont pas été réparés.

[How Paris surrounds and besets me with gloomy images of past times! How often, in pointing out to English travellers the scenes where momentous Revolutionary events took place, have I had to reconcile the mild astonishment they felt with my own deep emotions in the presence of so many memories, of so many wrongs which have not been redressed. (p. 37)]

The past lives in the present, and history is immediate, conferring a unique authority on her account, for the reader of *Souvenirs* stands in relation to the text as the English travellers stood to Williams, their guide through the 'theatre of memorable Revolutionary events'. Williams's task in both cases is to communicate her 'profound feelings' to

others. Here the culture of Sensibility, which formed her as an intellectual and writer, converges with a major theme of the Revolution
debate and the Revolutionary aftermath—the relation between feeling
and reason, experience and theory in Revolutionary politics. Yet there
remains a gap between herself and her English guests, between her
experience and theirs, and between what the Revolution aimed to
achieve and what remains undone, even if only as 'wrongs which have
not been redressed'. Thus self-authorizing memory, as lived history
mediated by the individual sensibility—a 'feminine' intellectual
discourse—may yet have power, as expressed in Williams's text, to
alter the present and future according to 'her' Revolution. 'Feminine'
discourse once again turns out to have revolutionary potential.

Williams further elaborates feminized history by representing the
Revolution through the vicissitudes of individuals personally known
to her, following them to their end, be it the courageous martyrdom
of Mme Roland, the miserable death of Pétion, or the dishonourable
reward of Barère. For according to Williams individuals acting in a
concert of culture and feeling constitute a 'nation' and a revolution,
not social classes, as argued by François Mignet in his *Histoire de la
Révolution française de 1789 à 1814* (1824), according to whom 'one part
of the Revolution was carried out by the aristocracy, a second by the
middle class, and a third by the mob'. Williams declares:

Les grands mouvemens dans lesquels l'esprit humain s'agite ne sauraient se
subdiviser en portions aussi régulières. La révolution ne se fit point par l'effort
successif de masses spéciales, mais bien par le vœu unanime de tout le peuple
français. . . . Nos opinions et nos principes ne sont point le résultat de notre
place dans ce monde, mais bien de notre caractère et de nos dispositions.

[The great movements in which the human spirit stirs cannot be subdivided
into such regular portions. The Revolution was not carried out by the
successive efforts of distinct groups, but indeed by the unanimous will of the
entire French people. . . . Our opinions and principles are not at all the product
of our station in life but rather of our character and attitudes. (pp. 104–5)]

Williams has to deny Mignet's interpretation in order to sustain her
own representation of one professional middle-class faction, the feminized Girondins, led by a woman and Williams's friend, as the embodiment of both 'liberté' and 'nation'.

Thus her own account of the Revolution necessarily has a polemical
edge directed against rival accounts, especially those that attack or
ignore 'her' Revolution, as the Girondin-led period from 1791 to

1793. She conducts this polemic, however, not according to the 'new' historiographical methods of her rivals but by her own feminized method, implicitly in tune with the feminized Revolution she defends and promotes. For example, she rejects the Comte de Ségur's attempt to exculpate Bonaparte's conduct in the Russian campaign by reference to her own feelings at the time: 'How can I banish from my memory the image of those whom I knew, whose deaths were recounted to me by those who had seen them die' ('Comment pourrai-je banir de ma mémoire l'image de ceux que j'ai connus, dont la mort m'a été racontée par ceux qui les ont vus mourir'). Even the opinion of many cannot outweigh hers alone when her feelings are strong: 'The most general agreement cannot be as strong as these personal recollections' ('Tous les sentimens généraux ne peuvent être aussi forts que ces souvenirs individuels', p. 170). Consequently she rejects the impartiality affected by recent historians of the Revolution such as Mignet, a leader of what she calls 'the neutral faction', or those who equate coldness of feeling with 'justice': 'One must remain calm when one writes history; but even so one must not blame those whose hearts throb at the sight of good fighting evil' (p. 104). By denominating writers like Mignet a 'faction' Williams insists that their pretence of being above Revolutionary politics is only another way of being political, and another kind of Revolutionary—or counter-revolutionary—politics.

She herself does not hestitate to write as a woman by taking a personal and practical view of other Revolutionary historians. For example, she accuses some Revolutionary historians of mere partisanship. She dismisses de Ségur's *Mémoires; ou, souvenirs et anecdotes* (1824) and de Montholon's *Mémoires pour servir à l'histoire de France sous Napoléon* (1823–5, claimed to be dictated by Bonaparte at St Helena) as apology for the Emperor. She condemns Bertrand de Moleville's *Mémoires particuliers pour servir à l'histoire de la fin du règne de Louis XVI* (1816) as apology for the King. She sneers at the *Anti-Jacobin Magazine*, which attacked her personally, as required reading in the tea circles of London but utterly unknown in Paris (p. 44). She rejects criticisms of her supposed to have been made by Bonaparte and reported in Barry O'Meara's *Napoleon in Exile; or, A Voice from St. Helena: The Opinions and Reflections of Napoleon* (1822). Yet she takes an open and eclectic approach to varieties of historical writing, as long as they have practical use. She mentions Louis-Benoît Picard's historical novel *Gilblas de la Révolution* (1824), thereby suggesting that fiction may get at the historical truth as well or better than historiography can. She praises Léon Thiessé's *Résumé de la Révolution* (1826) for supplying invaluable details, appreciates *Mémoires de Mme la marquise de La Rochejaquelin* (1817), approves Louis-Adolphe Thiers's pro-Girondin *Histoire de la Révolution française* (1823–7), and praises the 'historical school' of François Guizot as a defence against what she sees as the mystifications of the Jesuits.

Further reinforcing the authority of her account and 'her' Revolution, she also attacks Revolutionary histories that might seem similar to her own. She dismisses the *Collection des Mémoires relatifs à la Révolution française*, published in over sixty volumes from 1820 to 1826, most of which favoured the Girondins, though a few were royalist and one was pro-Jacobin.[24] She calls these 'titillating books' ('livres piquans') that retail 'vulgar court intrigues' ('les intrigues vulgaires des cours') and reveal intimate details that should be kept sacrosanct, thus feeding a taste for mere details that readers may skim lightly, untouched by the melancholy incidents described therein (pp. 4–5). She distinguishes *Souvenirs* from this 'fashion of the moment' and claims to speak of herself only in self-defence, as a sign of authenticity, for 'one thinks little of one's own adventures after coming through tempestuous times. Revolution is a radical cure for egotism' ('on songe peu à ses propres aventures, quand on a traversé des temps orageux. Une révolution guérit radicalement l'égoïsme', p. 6). She implies that, unlike other eyewitnesses, her feminine sensibility was deeply stirred by her immediate experience of the Revolution, thus validating her personal account in the face of those others, especially the women. She suggests, for example, that her former friend Mme de Genlis's *Mémoires inédites . . . sur le dix-huitième siècle et la Révolution française* (8 vols, 1825) is merely a work of female vanity and therefore makes false accusations against Williams and Stone.

The most prominent rival, however, was Mme de Staël's *Considérations sur les principaux événements de la Révolution* (1818). Published just after de Staël's death, it sold sixty thousand copies in the first edition, went through three editions by 1820, and became the subject of an intense political debate on historical representation and interpretation of the Revolution. De Staël's situation was similar to Williams's: she came from a Protestant Enlightenment background, had an inside view of early Revolutionary politics, witnessed major Revolutionary

---

[24] Edmond Bire, *La Légende des Girondins* (Paris, 1881), 7.

events, led an opposition salon after the Revolution, and was harassed by Bonaparte's government. Her history of the Revolution also resembles Williams's: she praises 'liberté', denounces Jacobin and Napoleonic 'tyranny', defends the Protestants, gives personal recollections of events, praises the example of England, and denounces abstract theories as a basis for social reform and the constitution of the state. Williams attacks de Staël's history for being inaccurate, and for being inaccurate because of false feminine sensibility—a theme on which a woman author could reasonably claim unique authority. The reasons for Williams's attack on de Staël are revealed by the fact that Williams praises precisely what de Staël condemns—the early Revolution, the Girondins, and Pétion—and accuses de Staël of confounding Girondins and Jacobins 'in the manner of Burke and Mallet du Pan' (p. 19). However obliquely, Williams attributes such errors to de Staël's false femininity, characterizing her as the kind of woman she condemns elsewhere in *Souvenirs*—a 'bas bleu' or masculinized woman, too intellectual to be moved as she ought (as Williams shows herself to have been) and moved by the wrong things, such as the fall of Marie Antoinette. Williams even challenges the accuracy of de Staël's memory of scenes they both witnessed, leading to her self-authenticating outburst, 'How Paris surrounds and besets me with mournful images . . . !'

If de Genlis's *Mémoires* is merely self-centred and de Staël's *Considérations* incorrectly feminine or unfeminine, Jeanne Louise Henriette Campan's *Mémoires sur la vie privée de Marie Antoinette* (1823) is too weakly feminine. Campan was not only Marie Antoinette's maid but an adviser on etiquette at Napoleon's court, linking two court despotisms. Like de Staël she sympathizes with the late Queen of France, but as Williams sees it, whereas de Staël does so from misplaced sentiment Campan misguidedly attempts to vindicate her former mistress by revealing domestic details that in fact furnish 'an almost complete critique of the conduct of this unfortunate Queen'. History 'may be enriched and its truth increased' by such memoirs, but Campan has doubly betrayed the woman she served, in implied contrast to Williams, who vindicates Marie Roland but reveals only enough of her private life and character to verify the vindication. Williams's critique of the Revolutionary histories of de Staël and Campan situates her own *Souvenirs* between these extremes, neither falsely nor weakly feminine, neither too intellectual nor too gossipy, in an implicitly true middle ground of historical discourse.

While attacking 'false' Revolutionary history Williams vindicates and develops her own through an immediacy related to but distinct from that of her earlier work. Whereas that work was in epistolary form, supposedly written 'to the moment' at a personal and private level, the address of *Souvenirs* is public and general, and past response to the Revolution is now mediated through memory from a point in time 'produced' by the Revolution. Though she is decorously feminine in hoping only that 'perhaps sometimes the voice of my heart made itself understood to the hearts of those who read me, for sincerity is not without some force' ('peut-être quelquefois la voix de mon cœur s'est-elle fait entendre au cœur de ceux qui me lisaient, parce qu'une conviction sincère n'est pas sans quelque puissance', p. 199), this 'heart' first made her an 'enthusiast' for the Revolution, kept her faithful to it despite charges of apostasy, and now authenticates her feminized history:

Dans les graves annales de l'histoire, tout est raconté avec calme et avec méthode; mais je ne suis pas historien, j'ai seulement hasardé dans les pages précédentes mes propres sentimens pendant le cours de la révolution, de présenter son influence sur l'existence domestique, et de la peindre, d'une touche mal assurée sans doute, mais dont les traits laissent une certaine impression de vérité.

[In the serious annals of history everything is recounted calmly and methodically; but I am not a historian, and in the preceding pages I have merely tried to express my own feelings during the course of the Revolution, to present its influence on domestic life, and to depict it with a touch no doubt unsteady but whose strokes leave a certain impression of truth. Many others will look for the Revolution in books, but I instead recount it; the events of the narrative are in my memory, and the emotions they produced are still in my heart. (pp. 199–200)]

Memory as she presents it here and illustrates it in passages such as the tribute to Pétion is a feminine form of history, thereby superior to other forms in authenticity and power.

She defends such history against the common charge that it is necessarily biased and thus unreliable:

On craint qu'ils [contemporains] ne se soient laissé égarer par leurs sentimens et leurs impressions; comme si ces mêmes sentimens ne sortaient pas des faits qu'ils avaient eus devant les yeux, et de ce qu'ils avaient éprouvé, et de ce qu'ils avaient souffert. Quel guide meilleur l'historien peut-il prendre que l'impression des contemporains? C'est peut-être parce que les impressions, dans beaucoup de cas, ne sont pas venues jusqu'à nous, que bien des tyrans, dans l'histoire antique et moderne, ne se présentent point chargés de tout l'odieux qu'ils méritent.

[There is a fear that they [contemporaries] may have been carried away by their feelings and impressions, as if these very feelings were not the result of the events they saw before them, of what they experienced, and by which they suffered. What better guide can the historian take than the impressions of those who were there? It is perhaps because so many of these personal impressions have been lost to us that so few tyrants, ancient and modern, are depicted in the odious light they deserve. (p. 103)]

If there had been more feminized history, tyranny would be more detested and avoided than it has been; if the feminized Revolution had reached fulfilment, history such as Williams's would no longer be needed. The fact that her history exists validates its claim to be needed, and by treating the Revolution as it does, it prepares for the Revolution's triumph in the future:

Tel est le vœu de tous les amis de la dignité humaine, et surtout d'une personne attachée comme moi à cette France, par tous les souvenirs d'une longue habitation, par la mémoire des calamités publiques dont j'ai eu ma part, et des malheurs privés dont je n'ai pas été exempte; ce pays où tout me retrace les images des temps qui ne sont plus, où je passerai le peu d'années de la vie qui me reste, et auquel je demanderai enfin l'hospitalité d'un tombeau.

[Such is the wish of all the friends of human dignity, and especially of one attached as I am to this France by all the recollections of a long residence, by the memory of the public calamities in which I had my part, and by the private sorrows which I was not spared—this country where everything brings back images of yester-year, where I will spend the few years that remain to me, and of which I will request at last the hospitality of a grave. (p. 201)]

Having escaped Revolutionary death—symbol of the Revolution's futility for Romantic culture, Williams concludes this epilogue to her Revolutionary prose epic with a wish for the grave that was the Romantic alternative to and transcendence of Revolutionary action.

Her wish was soon granted. The year *Souvenirs* was published, she died, on 15 December 1827, and was buried as she wished next to John Hurford Stone in Père Lachaise cemetery—one of the Revolution's lasting institutions of a feminized civil society of subjective individualism, equality, and toleration.[25] A month after her death the *Monthly*

---

[25] Philippe Ariès, *The Hour of Our Death*, trans. Helen Weaver (Harmondsworth, 1983), 518, 533–4.

Review published the following notice in its 'Literary and Miscellaneous Intelligence': 'Miss Helen Maria Williams died lately in Paris, where she had resided since 1790. She wrote several works connected with France, which obtained for her a considerable degree of popularity in that country, as well as in this; but they have been already forgotten.'[26] This was true, but misleading. Williams's representation of the Revolution as a struggle between good and evil, 'feminine' and 'masculine', became the predominant way of representing and explaining the Revolution during the 1790s, the Revolutionary aftermath, and long after. But in the post-Revolutionary remasculinization of culture and literature, Williams's work, like that of other women writers, was marginalized, trivialized, and excluded from the history and the historiography it had helped to make.

[26] *Monthly Review*, 3rd ser., 7 (Jan. 1828), 139.

7

Mary Hays: Women, History, and the State

MARY HAYS continued writing feminist critique after 1800, though like other women writers she diverted this into forms acceptable to the post-Revolutionary move beyond the confrontations of the earlier 1790s. Her major project was the feminist biographical history of women that she had called for in 1796[1] and announced in the *Monthly Magazine* for 1798 as forthcoming. In fact it was not published until 1803, though what seems part of it, a biography of Wollstonecraft, was published in 1800 in Richard Phillips's *The Annual Necrology, for 1797–8*, apparently intended as the first of a series. The Preface argues that history is for statesmen while biography is accessible to all, and points out that annual obituaries were being published in both France and Germany, implying that the aim of the book was to popularize politics and history; since its publisher was known as a 'Jacobin' this implication would itself have a political edge. Most of the contributions to *Annual Necrology* were by the unnamed editor, but a few, including Hays's biography of Wollstonecraft, were by anonymous 'correspondents'.

Though certainly a piece of hack-work, Hays's biography continues her feminist discourse of the Revolution debate in several ways. It applies Hays's version of Enlightenment materialism to account for Wollstonecraft's character and fate as illustrations of the general condition of women. It attributes Wollstonecraft's strong passions to her domestic and social experience and her desultory education, and sees them as the source of her feminist protest and the cause of both the admiration and condemnation she and her works inspired. Hays intimates that she herself has similar experience as the basis for her judgement and exhibits the mind of a 'female philosopher', at some points writing expressively of Wollstonecraft's feelings, especially her religious devotion, her indignation at the treatment of women, her early exclusion from domestic and conjugal 'affections', her sympathy for the Revolution, her torment over Imlay, and her happiness with

[1] *Monthly Magazine*, 2 (July 1796), 470.

Godwin, and at other points adopting a transcendent, philosophical tone, with authoritative maxims, general principles, and expressions such as 'Experience teaches us that . . .'. In particular, Hays writes passionately of Wollstonecraft as a victim of society's denial of 'natural' female sexuality (pp. 454–5), implicitly rejecting the post-Revolutionary association between intellectual, social, and sexual transgression by women: 'vigorous minds are with difficulty restrained within the trammels of authority; a spirit of enterprise, a passion for experiment, a liberal curiosity, urges them to quit beaten paths, to explore untried ways, to burst the fetters of prescription, and to acquire wisdom by an individual experience' (p. 411). Hays accepts some criticisms of Wollstonecraft, including her sexual transgressions, the 'disorganization' of *A Vindication*, her lack of 'science' or 'learning in its appropriate sense', and even her supposed inattention 'to grammatical propriety', yet she insists that it is to such 'speculative and enterprising spirits, whom stronger powers and more impetuous passions impel forward, regardless of established usages, that all great changes and improvements in society have owed their origin' (p. 412). Thus Wollstonecraft 'has not laboured in vain: the spirit of reform is silently pursuing its course. Who can mark its limits?' (p. 459). Hays treats Wollstonecraft and Revolutionary feminism as things of the past, still cherished but now considered critically by those, such as Hays herself, able to see the relevance of this past for the Revolutionary aftermath.

She also knew its cost. She was pained by the misunderstanding with Charles Lloyd and being ridiculed in Elizabeth Hamilton's *Memoirs of Modern Philosophers*, and in February 1801 her sister Eliza wrote deploring 'the unmerited calumny' Hays had incurred but suggesting that she indulged her suffering.[2] A few weeks later Eliza wrote again, agreeing that 'celibacy' harms a woman's virtue and happiness: 'Her affections like a stream impeded in its course either run into irregular channels, or return into her own bosom where pent up, they ravage & destroy the soil they ought to have adorned & fertilized.' Eliza confessed that since 1798 or 1799 she herself had struggled to retain 'the sweet illusions of youth'—a loving relationship and possibly marriage—but was now resigned to a single life.[3] In fact, two years later, in 1803, she accepted an unexpected offer of marriage to a widower with several sons.[4]

[2] Letter endorsed 4 Feb. 1801, Pforzheimer Library.
[3] Letter of 24 Feb. 1801, Pforzheimer Library.
[4] Letter of 14 Aug. 1803, Pforzheimer Library.

Hays was now committed to writing as a professional, and in 1803 published *Female Biography; or, Memoirs of Illustrious and Celebrated Women, of All Ages and Countries*, again with Richard Phillips. Biography had become increasingly interesting to the reading public with the development of professional middle-class subjectivity, including the theme of 'genius', Sentimental and Enlightenment epistemology, psychological 'realism' in the novel and drama (including acting), the elevation of lyric over narrative poetry, the rise of autobiography as a distinct genre, and techniques of expressivity in painting and music. Major biographies and autobiographies concerned with uniqueness of character appeared before the end of the century, including Boswell's life of Johnson and Rousseau's *Confessions*. The Revolution debate focused intensely on subjectivity, largely to explain the seemingly unprecedented nature of the Revolution as a conspiracy led by excessive individualists. There were political biographies of leading figures in the Revolution debate such as Burke and Paine, autobiographies by Revolutionary leaders such as Mme Roland, collections of the lives of French political figures such as Stewarton's *Revolutionary Plutarch*, and 'philosophical' biographies such as Godwin's *Memoirs of the Author of a Vindication of the Rights of Woman*. Miscellany magazines ran series of short biographies of prominent public figures. Phillips's *Annual Necrology* was a similar, though short-lived venture.

Hays's *Female Biography* was designed both to further her English Jacobin political philosophy and her Revolutionary feminism and to cash in on both the vogue for biography and interest in the social, cultural, and political roles of women. Hays was to be paid ten shillings and sixpence per sheet. It was an ambitious task and almost got out of control. Hays produced a longer work than Phillips wanted, and the material is unevenly distributed. The work is arranged in alphabetical order but the first three volumes go only as far as 'c', almost half the alphabet is crammed into the sixth and last volume, and a supernumerary section of seventy pages with starred numbers is inserted into volume one between pages 238 and 239. The method of alphabetical listing is also erratic, sometimes based on the subject's first name, sometimes on her last, and sometimes on her title. Some of the lives, such as those of Catherine II and Elizabeth I, occupy most of a volume, while others are a few lines long. The thoroughness of the work also varies. For example the entry on Arnaude de Rocas is simply a translation of one from Jean François de La Croix's *Dictionnaire historique portatif des femmes célèbres* (1769), one of Hays's principal sources, many of the entries differ little from those found in other sources, while others skilfully amalgamate several different sources in a brisk narrative with sharp 'philosophical' comments of Hays's own.

Hays admits that *Female Biography* is mainly a compilation, 'intended for women, and not for scholars' (vol. i, p. vii). Yet it ambitiously aims to synthesize the varieties of biographical literature from the past in relation to the debate on women in the post-Revolutionary era. Accordingly, its variety of sources is broad, including classical historians and biographers such as Tacitus, Suetonius, Plutarch, and Josephus; general histories such as William Robertson's history of Scotland, Gabriel Daniel's *History of France*, Gibbon's *Decline and Fall of the Roman Empire*, Rollin's *Ancient History*, and Hume's *History of England*; scholarly archives such as James Granger's *A Biographical History of England*; 'secret court histories' such as Anquetil's *Memoirs of the Court of France*, Françoise de Motteville's *Memoirs for a History of Anne of Austria*, and C. F. P. Masson's *Secret Memoirs of the Court of Petersburg*; earlier biographical compendiums and dictionaries such as Pierre Bayle's *Historical Dictionary*, *Biographia Britannica*, Jean François de La Croix's *Dictionnaire historique portatif des femmes célèbres*, *Biographium Fæminium: The Female Worthies; or, Memoirs of the Most Illustrious Ladies of All Ages and Nations*, Thomas Gibbon's *Memoirs of Eminently Pious Women*, de Serviez's *Les Femmes des douze césars* (translated as *The Lives and Amours of the Empresses*), the *Biographical Magazine*, and Ann Thickness's *Sketches of the Lives and Writings of the Ladies of France*; biographies and memoirs of individual women such as John Toland's *Hypatia*, J. P. Siebenkees's *Life of Bianca Capello*, Marie Roland's *Appeal to Impartial Posterity*, Rachel Lady Russell's letters, Stuart's life of Mary Queen of Scots, Mme de Sevigné's letters, Sarah Fielding's novelized *Lives of Cleopatra and Octavia*, John Batchiler's religious biography *The Virgins Pattern: in the Exemplary Life, and Lamented Death of Mrs. Susannah Perwich*, and the memoirs of Mme de Maintenon; and even the historical notes to Mme de Genlis's *Knights of the Swan; or, The Court of Charlemagne: A Historical and Moral Tale*.

These sources reflect not only diverse genres but different social and political cultures, including classical writers enlisted by eighteenth-century 'classical republicans' and 'commonwealthmen', Enlightenment 'philosophical history', courtly 'secret histories' and biographies of chivalric heroes and dames of court culture, biographies of scholars and humanists, court memoirs and epistolary literature, pious biography, Sentimental biography, the newer 'national' biographies, and feminist biography. With the increasing importance of 'domestic woman' in the latter half of the century there were also more biographies and biographical dictionaries devoted to women, constituting a biographical form of conduct literature. Ballard's *British Ladies* (1752) was dedicated to Catherine Talbot, a leader of the mid-century upper-class 'Bluestocking' circle, and other collections emphasized the moral and intellectual, if not physical equality of the sexes. The editor of *Biographium Fæminium*, for example, noted that 'nature has been no less indulgent to the female sex than to the male, with respect to those noble faculties of the mind, which distinguish the rational from the animal and brute part of the creation', and went on to argue, as Hays had in the *Monthly Magazine*, that if there were not as many distinguished women as men, it was because of women's more limited education, circumstances, and opportunities.

Hays's Preface states her feminist purpose as 'the happiness of my sex, and their advancement in the grand scale of rational and social existence', redeeming them from their enslavement in court culture and their exclusion from learned and professional culture by a fusion of otherwise narrowly feminine or masculine traits, of 'graces and gentleness' with 'knowledge and fortitude', of reason with domestic affections. Hays carefully if disingenuously denies any political or sectarian motive, however:

Unconnected with any party, and disdaining every species of bigotry, I have endeavoured, in general, to serve the cause of truth and of virtue. . . . the reflections, sparingly interwoven, have been such as naturally arose out of the subject; nor have I ever gone out of my way in favour of sects or systems. (p. vi)

She makes other concessions to post-Revolutionary political circumstances in emphasizing domestic woman as national conscience and inspiration, 'finding' women in the past who would meet the needs of the present in which Hays writes. Yet in doing so Hays also sustains her feminist critique of the 1790s, first by attacking court culture's construction of woman, showing how exceptional women may overcome that limitation, and contrasting courtly woman with domestic woman; secondly by explaining the subjection of women as the internalization of false ideology, culture, and politics; thirdly by reclaiming intellectual and domestic women of the past as models for a revolutionary vanguard in the present and future; and fourthly by reflecting critically on written discourse as an instrument of female subjection or emancipation. Furthermore, by illustrating history through individual lives Hays advances a post-Revolutionary resiting of politics from the state and society to subjectivity. Finally, Hays's use of history in this way implies a progressive continuity between past, present, and future that ignores recent Revolutionary rupture and seems to obviate future revolutionary upheaval.

Hays's most prominent theme is the historic corruption and trivialization of women in court culture. Isabella of Bavaria, wife of Charles VI of France, is one of many examples in *Female Biography*. She 'was skilled in the arts of intrigue' and pursued pleasure and power 'without restraint', in the process becoming 'violent, implacable, and vindictive', and involving 'the kingdom in war and tumult': 'She lived to become odious and despicable, even to the party for which she had sacrificed humanity and the public good' (i. 223 *–4*). Like Wollstonecraft, Hays believes that some gender differences are 'natural', for example observing in her life of Mary Beale, the seventeenth-century painter, that 'The profession of the elegant and imitative arts, appears to be singularly appropriate to the delicacy of the female frame, to the sedentary habits of female life, and the culture of the taste and imagination, to which the education of women is peculiarly directed' (i. 250). But Hays objects to the way this 'natural' difference is perverted in court culture, which deprives women of autonomous subjectivity by making them slaves to their senses and their passions, or 'sensibility'. For example Hays attributes the celebrated piety of Berenice, Jewish mistress of the Emperor Titus, to her courtliness and the character of Jewish worship: 'a religion addressed to the senses will always be popular; the profligate life of Berenice rendered her not less scrupulous in the practice of the Jewish observances' (i. 293). Similarly, Queen Christina of Sweden's rejection of conventional femininity did not protect her against Roman Catholicism, 'that grand and affecting superstition', 'so fitted to allure the senses, to captivate the imagination, and to triumph over the affections of the human mind' (iii. 301–2).

The most notorious aspect of court culture, however, was its association with ungoverned and illicit female sexuality. Though Hays had defended female sexuality since *Memoirs of Emma Courtney*, she insists here that court culture trivializes it rather than liberating it, as commonly supposed. For example Ninon de l'Enclos was highly educated and financially independent, but her courtly epicureanism destroyed her capacity for the highest pleasures and she considered love 'as the mere caprice of the senses, a compact of animal gratification, or of mutual pleasure, free from duty, and subject to no restraint'. She was ignorant of 'that union of sentiment' in which sexual desire and friendship 'are exquisitely blended, in which the former loses all its grossness, and the latter acquires a more touching charm' (iv. 300). This argument resembles Wollstonecraft's philosophy of avant-garde sexuality in her letters to Imlay (in *Posthumous Works*, 1798), but the reader would conclude that Hays must herself have experienced what she describes here, implicitly validating her account of women's subjection by court culture and suggesting that such subjection continues still. It is true that a few women of intellectual ability could manipulate the court system rather than becoming its victims. Bianca Capello, for example, used 'the powers of her mind' to maintain 'that ascendancy which her personal charms had first given her over the affections of a capricious prince'. This admittedly immoral purpose may be extenuated by considering 'the Italian character, the circumstances of the times', and 'the disadvantages attending her entrance into the world, subjected to artifice and entangled in fraud' (ii. 143–4).

For construction of the individual by social and political circumstances, according to principles of Enlightenment sociology, is a central theme of *Female Biography*, supporting its Revolutionary feminist argument that, in order to resist seduction by court culture, women need both intellectual and moral training, 'reason' and 'virtue', comparable to those thought necessary for men. A woman with such qualities was Cecilia de Gonzaga, who was thus able to resist 'temptations to splendor and voluptuousness' and 'all the luxuries of her rank and situation' in order to devote money 'usually expended in pomp and ornament to feeding the poor', providing dowries for poor women, and maintaining churches (iv. 343–4). A different example is the courtesan Aspasia, mistress of Pericles, who not only achieved a high level of intellectual cultivation but was enlightened thereby to use her amorous influence for the public good. Some women of professionalized subjectivity may even surpass men in ability to master the court system: 'If the question respecting the equality of the sexes was to be determined by an appeal to the characters of sovereign princes, the comparison is, in proportion, manifestly in favour of woman' (iv. 70–1). This statement opens Hays's life of Queen Elizabeth of England, whose moral discipline and intellectual training enabled her to resist the seductions of court culture and even her 'natural' female desires: 'as a *woman*, cut off by the peculiarities of her situation from the sympathies of nature, and the charm of equal affections', Elizabeth's strong 'sensibility' acquired 'additional force and acuteness', but her 'reason' conquered 'her passions', 'and the struggles which her victories cost her, served but to display the firmness of her resolution, and the loftiness of her mind' (iv. 290). Hays then defends Elizabeth against the charge of male historians that the queen destroyed the woman:

Those who require more softness of manners, greater lenity of temper, and more feminine graces, to form the character of a woman, to whom they could attach themselves as a mistress and a wife, must be reminded, that these amiable weaknesses, which arise out of a state of subjection and dependence, are utterly incompatible with the situation of an absolute sovereign, and with the exercise of those qualities by which only such a situation can be maintained. (vii. 292)

Few women have found themselves in Elizabeth's 'situation', however, and Hays presents professionalized domesticity as an alternative to court culture's construction, subjection, and denaturing of women. A few powerful women, such as Mary Queen of Hungary, Frances d'Amboise, and Julia Mammea, retained their feminine character by ruling from the domestic position of wife and mother; others, such as Madame de Maintenon, found that the pleasures of court society could never equal those of domesticity (v. 383).

Female Biography contrasts the many women corrupted by court culture with women notable for intellectual struggles and achievements, yet these too had to resist and overcome a social culture dominated and controlled by men. For the gendering of culture and discourse has denatured, trivialized, and marginalized women just as court culture has. Anna Comnena, for example, 'renounced, in her youth, the amusements and occupations of her sex' in order 'to deliver up herself to a passion for study and letters' (iii. 431–2). The learned and artistic nun Juana Inez de la Cruz eventually gave way to 'superstition' and sold her library to raise money for charities, and Hays comments, 'the cultivation of the mind, with its consequent influence upon society, is a more real benefit to mankind than the partial relief of pecuniary exigencies' (iii. 442). Hays quotes Feijoo's opinion that de la Cruz's style excells 'in ease and elegance, rather than in energy and strength' because of the gendering of literary discourse and genre in her time.

Hays also meets the growing hostility to 'bluestockings' in the Revolutionary aftermath, suggesting that in the past women found marriage and intellectual pursuits incompatible. Lady Elizabeth Hastings was a 'female philosopher' whose 'fortune, beauty, and amiable qualities, procured her many solicitations to change her state, but she preferred, in a single and independent life, to be mistress of her actions, and the disposition of her income' (iv. 401). Similarly, Mary de Jars 'determined on a single life, that her devotion to letters might receive no interruption from family cares' (iv. 458). Yet in tacit protest against caricatures of herself, Wollstonecraft, and other Revolutionary feminists, Hays also insists that history shows talents and intellectual acquirements are not incompatible with moral virtue and domestic life. Hypatia the Alexandrian was so learned that she 'was emphatically termed *the Philosopher*', yet 'the purity of her manners, and the dignified propriety of her conduct, commanded general reverence and regard' (iv. 447, 449). The learned Madame Dacier translated the classics and though she pursued intellectual tasks separate from her husband's, they collaborated on a translation of Marcus Antonius and enjoyed a harmonious marriage.

Hays finds the reign of Elizabeth I to have been particularly favourable to intellectual yet domestic women. She opens her life of Thomas More's daughter Elizabeth Roper:

at no period of the English history does there appear to have been greater attention paid to the culture of the female mind, than during the age of Elizabeth; and at no time has there existed a greater number of amiable and respectable women. Even the domestic affections and appropriate virtues of the sex, modesty, prudence, and conjugal fidelity, far from being superseded by study and the liberal sciences, are, on the contrary, both strengthened and embellished. The habits of reflection and retirement which grow out of the exercise of the understanding, are equally favourable to virtue and to the cultivation of the heart. While the mind, by seeking resources in itself, acquires a character of dignity and independence, a sentiment of grandeur and generosity is communicated to its affections and sympathies. Dissipation and frivolous pursuits, by enfeebling the understanding, have a tendency to harden and to narrow the heart. If the concentrated passions of stronger minds, and these examples among women, are rare, have sometimes been productive of fatal effects, an impressive and affecting lesson, as in the sublimer devastations of nature, may be derived even from their failures. But the being, restless in the pursuit of novelty, irritable, dependent, unstable, and vain, who lives only to be amused, becomes necessarily selfish and worthless, the contempt and burthen of society, the reproach of one sex and the scorn of the other. (vi. 90–1)

This precis of Revolutionary feminist economy of mind, culture, and society not only claims that intellectual cultivation and domesticity are mutually beneficial, but also assimilates to Hays's feminism the growing interest in the Elizabethan age as a model for modern Britain in its crisis of national unity, international conflict, and imperial destiny. Finally, the passage again characterizes the narrator or 'author' of the passage as one who knows from experience the vicissitudes of which she writes.

In this way Hays associates herself with women of the past whom she casts as harbingers of Revolutionary feminism. For example Elizabeth Bury, the seventeenth-century Dissenter, regretted 'the disadvantages of her sex, who, by the habits of their education, and the customs of society, were illiberally excluded from the means of acquiring knowledge. She contended, that mind was of no sex, and that man was no less an enemy to himself than to woman in confining her attention to frivolous attainments' (ii. 69). Damaris, Lady Masham, is made a forerunner of the civic-minded wives and mothers called for by Wollstonecraft: 'expostulating with one sex, and endeavouring to inspire the other with a generous emulation, she exhorts women to assume their true dignity, and, by the instruction of their children, to raise the character of the age; reminding them of Cornelia the mother of the Gracchi, and of Aurelia the mother of Julius Cæsar; who, by their care in the education of their sons, rendered eminent service to their country' (v. 495). Several women, such as Aspasia, Hypatia, and Elizabeth Hastings, are designated 'female philosophers', a phrase made infamous in the Revolution debate. In the face of post-Revolutionary remasculinization of literature Hays praises earlier 'bluestockings' and emphasizes the mutual support and inspiration offered to each other by women in the past, forming a historical network of the feminist vanguard. Hays also singles out predecessors who called for or carried out female and feminist intellectual co-operation in the interests of society as a whole, such as the seventeenth-century writer Mary Astell, who envisaged a female academy to 'raise the general character of women' (i. 214), Harriet Eusebia Harcourt, who established two such institutions (iv. 388), and Ann Clifford, Countess of Pembroke, who pursued learning and philanthropic social projects from within and as extensions of conventionally feminine domesticity.

Hays's own project is implicitly continuous with these, for she uses the lives and works of historic women not only to validate her version of Revolutionary feminism for the Revolutionary aftermath but also to reflect on the historic construction of woman by literary discourse. The ostensible purpose of *Female Biography* is the modest one of teaching middle-class women readers to accept their lot and not envy their 'betters'—a message of social quietism derived from Hays's intellectual origins in liberal Dissent, but also in harmony with post-Revolutionary aversion to social conflict:

In reviewing the misfortunes of those who, by their natural advantages, or elevated rank in life, appear, on a superficial view, to be exempted from the common ills of humanity, she who, with less pretensions, and in an inferior station, repines at the fortune which has fallen to her lot, may learn to derive consolation, and to acquire fortitude. (i. 204★)

Thus *Female Biography* counters the glamorization of courtly woman in earlier courtly romances, histories, and biographies and the later Sentimental novel, thereby countering the influence of court culture which, many thought, had produced the French Revolution and was dividing and weakening Britain in the early 1800s. Hays suggests several times that the lives of courtly women and their emulators have the qualities of 'romance', or extravagant fiction. The miracle by which the Anglo-Saxon courtesan Emma was supposed to have proved her innocence 'savours, it must be confessed, of romance and fable' (iv. 313), and the life of Susannah Centlivre, actress and courtesan, has 'an air of romance'. The association of courtly women and romance is appropriate because court culture both produced and was reflected in romance literature, the descendant of which was the despised 'modern novel' that Revolutionary feminists such as Wollstonecraft and Hays had tried to reclaim from its association with court culture. Along with 'romance and fable' as false representations of reality goes 'superstition', a false or 'romantic' perception of reality, to which intellectually untrained and morally undisciplined women are also susceptible. For example Johanna de la Mothe Guyon, friend and teacher of Fénelon, was seized with religious enthusiasm and, 'under the delusions of a heated imagination, abandoned the common affairs of life, with the duties and occupations of her sex and station, to deliver herself up to sublime chimeras' (iv. 379).

But, Hays argues, women themselves progressively developed the literature of court culture. Thus the 'short gallant novels and stories' of Mary Catherine de Jardins 'superseded the ancient heroic romance. This style of fiction, more amusing, but less favourable to virtue and elevation of mind, than that which it displaced, became popular, and continued to prevail' (iv. 456–7). Madeleine de Scudéry made further progress by reforming romance, and disseminated her reforms to all classes, as the Revolutionary feminists aimed to do:

Romances were the taste of the age, to which [she] gave a new and more refined turn. Sentiments of honour, of heroism, and of virtue, were substituted for dissolute scenes and descriptions of intrigue; female manners were pourtrayed with delicacy and chasteness, and the passions refined from their grossness. Her books, which formed a new era in that species of writing, were bought with avidity, and read eagerly by persons of all ranks. (vi. 388–9)

De Scudéry also had to write for money, anticipating Hays's own generation of professional women writers. Then 'Madame de la Fayette substituted for the extravagant fictions of her predecessors, stories full of nature, of sentiment, and of that delicacy of passion, which moves the affections and touches the heart' (iv. 330), anticipating Hays's own form, the novel of passion. Thus the history of the novel embedded in *Female Biography* continues the work of Clara Reeve's *The Progress of Romance* (1785) and Hays's essay in the *Monthly Magazine* and serves several connected aims. It gives the pre-eminent 'women's' genre a literary history and full literary status and thus contributes to establishing the cultural, intellectual, and literary importance of women in the past. But it also implies a continuity between this past and the work of Revolutionary feminists and thus denies that the latter was a break with the past, justifies it in retrospect, and facilitates its insertion into the cultural politics of the present.

Hays's history of the novel brings her argument full circle, from a critique of courtly woman as product and victim of 'romance', through recovery of 'female philosophers', domestic heroines, civilizers, and national leaders in the past, to reaffirmation of woman as domestic yet rational, imaginative yet principled, carrying out cultural revolution through the discursive and literary means appropriate to her 'natural' role in society and culture. This is a self-vindication of Hays and Revolutionary feminism, not as an end in itself but in order to gain acceptance of that feminism in the post-Revolutionary debate on woman's role in 'national' culture and destiny. Many women writers who were not burdened with a Revolutionary feminist 'past', such as Maria Edgeworth, Elizabeth Hamilton, the Porter sisters, and Lady Morgan, were also turning the 'woman's' genre of the novel to those issues, historicizing fictional narrative and novelizing 'national' history and culture in verse and prose. Their efforts indicate the extent to which the polemical, political aims of *Female Biography* were widely shared in the Revolutionary aftermath.

Reviewers recognized Hays's aims. The *Critical Review* thought that the controversy 'concerning the comparative superiority or inferiority of the two sexes' might now be resolved by reference to Hays's 'compilation' of 'experience and the evidence of facts'. But the reviewer criticized the length of some lives and the omission of Mary Wollstonecraft 'who, according to the obvious intention of the author, ought to have been admitted as the champion of her sex, and the reviver of the sexual controversy'. Worse still, Hays included details and language 'with which we are surprised that any lady should ever have contaminated her pages', gave unnecessary attention to immoral women such as Mme de Maintenon, Ninon de l'Enclos, and Catherine of Russia, and in general searched 'for heroines—a species of beings, who, with us, stand in no higher favour than heroes, seldom the benefactors, and frequently the disturbers, of the peace of mankind'.[5] The *Monthly Review* also praised 'the fair editor' for 'this laudable attempt to bring under one view the scattered narratives of many celebrated characters in the walks of female life', but 'as this publication is principally intended for the use and instruction of young persons, we should have preferred to have seen the vicious and defective traits of several females ... more shaded from the view'.[6] The *British Critic*, hostile to Hays's writing in the 1790s, found *Female Biography* 'composed of entertaining and interesting materials' but marred by 'the same unfortunate bias' found in her earlier work and 'often impaired and discoloured by fantastical opinions, drawn from the school in which *one* Helen Maria Williams has distinguished herself with equal vanity and folly'.[7] Attempting to assert the relevance of Revolutionary feminism to the issues of the Revolutionary aftermath, Hays ran into the increasing hostility toward women thought to transgress ever-narrower bounds of femininity.

Female Biography offered Hays opportunities to practise feminist social criticism, but it was hack-work, and even before it was published she was engaged in similar work. Social criticism of any kind had to recognize the commercial nature of publishing, and writing for children offered women opportunities to sustain a writing career and serve the professional middle-class cultural revolution while retaining a 'femi-

---

[5] *Critical Review*, NS 37 (Apr. 1803), 415–24.
[6] *Monthly Review*, NS 43 (Jan. 1804), 92–3.
[7] *British Critic*, 22 (July 1803), 93–4.

nine' character as domestic nurturer and educator. Hays was one of many in the late eighteenth and early nineteenth century to turn to this form, and in 1804 Joseph Johnson published her first effort in this area, *Harry Clinton: A Tale for Youth*, dedicated to her nephew and adapted from Henry Brooke's *The Fool of Quality* (1765–70). Brooke was one of many writers in the mid-eighteenth century who, as self-styled 'patriots', attacked court government's corruption and patronage and called for independence for the professions and professionalization of the hegemonic class and government. *The Fool of Quality* was Brooke's best-known work and one of the most widely read of English Sentimental novels, reprinted into the twentieth century. In the Revolutionary aftermath of corrupt and unreliable aristocratic leadership, criticism of the kind mounted by Brooke gained new relevance, but it was seen as still tinged with upper-class values. *The Fool of Quality* had already been rewritten by John Wesley in 1781 and evoked imitations with sharper polemical edge, including Thomas Day's *Sandford and Merton* (1783–9), Elizabeth Inchbald's *Nature and Art* (1796), and Maria Edgeworth's children's stories of the 1790s and early 1800s.

Like Wesley, Hays claims in her Advertisement that Brooke's novel 'abounds with real genius and genuine feeling, but so obscured by fanaticism and extravagance, that it has sunk into neglect'. She also claims to attend to 'the practical education and culture of the *heart*', something she feels Maria and Richard Lovell Edgeworth neglected in their treatise *Practical Education* (1798), though she praises Maria Edgeworth's *Parent's Assistant* (1796–1800) and *Moral Tales* (1801). Thus Hays implies that her work participates in the new movement of moral and rational children's literature, much of which (including Edgeworth's) was put out by Joseph Johnson, publisher of *Harry Clinton* and Wollstonecraft's publisher in the 1780s and 1790s. Hays suggests a post-Revolutionary perspective in claiming that 'in the general principles of morality, with which the story is replete, care has been taken to avoid the narrowness of system, or the language of a party'. To make the work more popular she shortens it by about half. The story concerns two brothers, Richard and Harry, sons of the Earl of Moreland, a courtly landed gentleman, and a rich merchant's daughter—the familiar marriage of land and money, country and City. Richard is raised as a gentleman while his younger brother Harry, who is taken for a fool by his parents because he does not understand courtly manners and language, is put out to be raised by a farmer and his wife. He is then taken in, educated, and sent into the world by the benevolent Mr Fenton to speak truth, resist courtly tempters, and do good to the fallen, victimized, and erring. This story of contrasting destinies is set in the reign of William III, after the Revolution of 1688—supposed by many reformers to mark the foundation of the modern British constitution. Fenton turns out to be the Earl's long-alienated brother and Harry returns to his father to find that his mother and brother are dead; he reconciles his father and uncle and assumes the position of heir, signalling the fusion of gentry and bourgeois values in the national interest—a dominant post-Revolutionary theme.

By now Hays had accepted a less ambitious public and literary career. In 1805 her friend Henry Crabb Robinson reported that she was living 'in retirement' and 'highly respected' but pursuing 'literature as a profession' and 'content to be a useful writer', retaining 'feminine excellence and virtues while she seeks literary fame'.[8] She was then doing another piece of hack-work for Richard Phillips, completing a work for children begun by Charlotte Smith and published in 1806 as *The History of England, from the Earliest Records to the Peace of Amiens; in a Series of Letters to a Young Lady at School*. The title page gives the author as Charlotte Smith and Hays's name is not mentioned, but the third and last volume has a 'Prefatory Advertisement' in which Smith acknowledges that the work was originally designed as one volume but expanded to a length she had neither the health nor leisure to complete, and therefore 'undertaken by a lady, who, I have no doubt, has proved herself competent to her task'. Smith corrected many of the proof sheets, but declined 'to be considered as entirely responsible for more than the first eight hundred pages of the work'. She originally planned to stop at the death of George II, but 'in conformity' to other works of a similar kind 'it has been judged proper to continue it to the present period'. Thus the first two volumes are Smith's and the third Hays's. Smith wrote to Hays about the work as early as July 1800 and promised to help get books for her. But Hays did not do the work entirely as assigned, producing too much material and not covering 'the state of manners and society' to Phillips's satisfaction, and she had to get John Aikin, then editor of Phillips's *Monthly Magazine*, to mediate.

Though the book is in letter form it is a simplified and straightfor-

---

[8] *Henry Crabb Robinson on Books and Their Writers*, ed. Edith J. Morley (London, 1938), iii. 843.

ward historical narrative, with no interplay between narrator and correspondent. The first letter asserts the need to feminize historiography by making it less 'tedious', voluminous, and time-consuming, giving female readers better access to 'this necessary, rather than attractive, study' by appealing to what are supposed to be feminine habits, interests, and tastes. The work is to be apolitical, or free 'from those prejudices of party which pervade and disfigure many histories of our country'—a familiar claim—and 'the facts will be impartially collected from the best historians'. It is to be optimistic and more social than political in giving 'some idea of the manners of the successive ages, by which may be traced the progress to that refined state of society which those who live at the present period may thus contemplate with increased satisfaction' (i. 1).

Hays's portion of the work, from the accession of Charles II to the resumption of war after the Peace of Amiens, is somewhat livelier than Smith's, more open in opinion, and more emphatic about the relation of progress to peace—a timely topic just after the resumption of global warfare in 1803. Hays, like Smith, deplores the machinations of courts and the corruption they spread through society, but Hays also condemns the violence of the common people. In dealing with the French Revolution, for example, she criticizes both the intrigues of the court and the excesses of the Jacobins and the Revolutionary mobs. She is, however, sympathetic to the middle-class Irish rebels, or United Irishmen, and notes that their rebellion of 1798 revived loyalty to the government and a sense of patriotic nationalism in the face of the threat from France. Hays's account of manners and culture also differs from Smith's, as Phillips complained. Whereas Smith focused on social culture and class distinction, and even describes men's and women's fashions in different eras, Hays ignores these 'feminine' topics to concentrate at the end of volume three on the progress of arts, manufactures, and science (letters 174–7). She does so on the grounds that intellectual, economic, and social progress are inseparable from peace and social harmony, and thus inseparable from the feminization of society and culture. For example in discussing the reign of Queen Anne she implies both a historical parallel between the Augustan age and the Revolutionary aftermath of the 1800s and a necessary relationship between revolutionary energy and post-revolutionary civil society. Revolutionary times, such as the English Civil War and the 1790s, produce controversy and conflict, here given an overtone of masculine sexual aggression as a 'spirit of enquiry' that is 'aroused' and taken to unnatural excess in 'domestic warfare', but then subsumed in a civil society dominated by feminine values as a 'germ' 'maturing in the womb of time' and nurtured by a female monarch (iii. 227). This plot of historical progress is figured as a natural process gendered female, thereby advancing a vision of post-Revolutionary mediation, reconciliation, and harmony found in Williams, Hays, Hamilton, and many women writers.

Hays's work on *The History of England* showed her the potential of this kind of hack-work for feminist social criticism and she immediately produced a more thorough feminization of history in *Historical Dialogues for Young Persons* (1806–8). It claims the same aim as *The History of England*—to overcome 'the disinclination' of young women 'for the study of history', a conventionally masculine discourse which had long been recommended in female conduct-books as an antidote to novel reading but which, Hays felt, ignored women's experience and interests, excluded women from its purview, denatured them if they assimilated it, and condemned them to cultural marginality if they did not. Yet Hays believes that study of history can help women acquire the intellectual discipline that Revolutionary feminists thought necessary to rescue women from their historic assimilation to court culture and inscribe them in the professional middle-class cultural revolution. To achieve this end, however, historiography must begin with women as they are by 'nature' and in the present state of society. It must be feminized:

History, excepting to the statesman and political economist, can be interesting and amusing only in proportion as it is biographical, or as it treats of individual character. Disquisitions and statements of finance, political revolutions and changes, general descriptions of wars, of alliances, and of treaties, afford but little delight to the imagination, which dwells only with pleasure on single portraits, on minuter and characteristic delineations, on pictures of the passions and manners, of the habits, incidents, and affections of individual life. We must feel an interest and a personal sympathy in the books we read, to give them their effect on the heart and mind.

Like *Female Biography*, *Historical Dialogues* aims to repair women's alienation from both history and historiography.

Accordingly, it employs narratives, scenes, and events 'from popular historical productions' in order 'to lead the mind to reflect on the facts presented', asserts 'general moral principles' 'unconnected with system or sect', and avoids both sensational novelizing of history likely to appeal to the sensibility rather than the reason and merely utilitarian synopsis of received knowledge. For the work is designed 'for youth, from the age of twelve years and upwards', when the reasoning must be trained to counterbalance the feelings, though it may provide 'recreation, or exercise, for the elder pupils in schools' where, Hays hopes, it 'may prove an acceptable present'—part of the system of books as 'rewards of merit'. In short, *Historical Dialogues* is designed to contribute to the formation of autonomous subjectivity in women— the core of the Revolutionary feminist programme—by appropriating a discourse conventionally gendered masculine and used to subordinate women within culture. *Historical Dialogues* feminizes history in several ways. It uses the domestic dialogue long associated with writing for women, as Mrs Neville recounts for her nieces Mary and Emma and nephews William and Henry a succession of 'true stories'. These are designed to appeal to their curiosity, which she calls 'the most powerful spring of the mind, the source of its activity, and the foundation of all its improvements'—a view held by Enlightenment materialist philoso- phers and the Godwin circle. In fact, most of the work's historical narrative is continuous, with the dialogue taking place by way of preamble or moralizing conclusion. The text as a whole is a desultory selection of representative events and personages rather than an exhaus- tive or monumental narrative, and 'philosophical' reflections by Mrs Neville demonstrate for her pupils a critical approach to history as subject-matter and historiography as a learned discourse, within a framework of instruction in a domestic setting founded on familial rela- tions.

Taken together, the narratives set forth a social critique related to pre-Revolutionary Sentimental feminism but adapted to the Revolu- tionary aftermath. Pre-Revolutionary themes include the horrors of war and imperial conquest, sympathy for oppressed colonial peoples, condemnation of luxury and courtly decadence, criticism of the patron- age system and insistence on merit in private and public life, and rejection of religious 'fanaticism'. Certain themes echo interests of Enlightenment 'philosophical' historians and eighteenth-century classi- cal republicans and commonwealthmen: Greek and Roman republican virtues contrasted with the sexual and political intrigue of the tyrants' and emperors' courts, the brutality and oppression of feudalism and the extravagance and folly of chivalry, the futility of aristocratic 'heroism' and monarchic martial 'glory', the subversive nature of conspiratorial and fanatical religious organizations such as the Jesuits, the cruelty and greed of European imperialism as seen in the Spanish conquest of America, the patriotism and selflessness of rulers such as Cyrus and Henry IV, and—echoing *Female Biography*—the incompatibility of women and domestic virtues with the masculine public and political sphere under court government. These themes acquired new edge in the Revolution debate and new relevance in post-Revolutionary criticism of aristocratic and royal decadence, Britain's inability to defeat a resurgent Revolutionary France led by Napoleon, and the government's obstruction of political reforms many thought necessary to resolve this national and international crisis.

Mrs Neville's feminized Enlightenment historiography includes other themes of particular relevance in the Revolutionary aftermath, including an account of the Revolution (following Helen Maria Williams) in terms of a feminized Girondin phase and an excessively masculine Jacobin phase, the dangers of 'mob' politics, the proper conduct of public controversies (such as the Revolution debate, but recalling Hays's first book), and the practicability of reform under particular historical circumstances. Conscious that such topics were considered 'unfeminine' in the 1790s and even more so in the Revolutionary aftermath, Hays brings the matter into the open. When young Emma comments that she thought 'women were forbidden to intermeddle in politics; and that questions of government, of constitutions, and of laws, were wholly out of their sphere', Mrs Neville replies:

A female political partizan, or zealot of a faction, must be always ungraceful and uncharacteristic, and can in rare circumstances only be tolerated. But the subjects of government and laws, as connected with the morality and happiness of the human species, and with the characters and history of mankind, cannot fail of being interesting to every benevolent and enlightened mind. There is nothing masculine and unbecoming in knowledge: from the perfection of human reason perhaps true gentleness is only to be expected: presumption, pedantry, and violence, are engendered by ignorance, by narrow views and partial information . . . (ii. 130–1)

The gendering of discourse is thus associated with the conditions that produced Revolutionary violence, while the ungendering of discourse is associated with the feminized culture ('true gentleness') being advanced as a resolution of social and political conflict ('faction').

Historical Dialogues closes with Mrs Neville's promise to deal in a similar fashion with the history of Britain, virtually excluded from the present work, though covered in Hays and Smith's *History of England*.

Historical Dialogues is also as good as anything of the kind and better than most, but Hays did not publish again for several years; she seems to have lived in various lodgings on a small legacy and hovered on the fringes of literary circles. By 1813 she hoped to live with the Southeys, with a lady in Northamptonshire, or 'in some picturesque country', though Crabb Robinson feared 'an over-strained sensibility joined to precise manners will make her offensive and ridiculous to the many'.[9] But in the mid-1810s she resumed publication with two works following the example of Maria Edgeworth's didactic fiction and designed to reinforce social discipline of two groups seen as potential sources of disaffection—the lower ranks and women.

The first of these works was *The Brothers; or, Consequences: A Story of What Happens Every Day; Addressed to that Most Useful Part of the Community, the Labouring Poor* (1815), published by the London firm of W. Button and Son, who sold religious tracts of various kinds, but printed by Whittingham and Rowland, the former of whom was known for publishing elegant inexpensive editions of English 'classics'. A postscript by Hays states that the story is designed 'to exemplify and illustrate the leading principles' of a Bristol philanthropic organization, 'The Prudent Man's Friend Society', designed to encourage the investment mentality among the poor by affording them a bank for small savings and loans, 'guaranteed by men of known property and respectability'. Such a project accorded with post-Revolutionary middle-class schemes of ideological and social control, but Hays gives it a feminist turn by pointing out that the Society was led and planned by a woman, 'with a spirit of enlightened and sound philosophy, a perspicuity and a comprehensiveness, that would reflect credit upon our best writers on political economy'. She then assimilates the project to post-Revolutionary social reconciliation by quoting the project's claim that 'statesman and political economists' will soon see 'that the stability of government, and the strength and happiness of an empire, depend not upon a numerous, degraded and half-starved population; but on one in which, from the prevalence of a spirit of virtuous independence, the necessaries if not the comforts of life are enjoyed by *all*; and where, from early formed habits of industry and prudence, the firmest foundation is laid for the superstructure of a highly moral and religious national character'. One reviewer did think *The Brothers* was timely: 'The present *rush* of employment in some of our manufactories, will

---

[9] *Crabb Robinson*, ed. Morley, i. 235, 131.

lead many of the unthinking to false dependences, and bad, or extravagant habits: a work calculated to restrain this presumption, would be
essentially useful.'[10]

The Brothers resembles the pseudo-popular literature developed in
the 1790s by Hannah More and continued after 1800 by Maria Edgeworth's *Popular Tales* (1803), Elizabeth Hamilton's *The Cottagers of
Glenburnie* (1808), Revd Legh Richmond's *Annals of the Poor* (1809–
14), Barbara Hofland and Mary Sherwood's many tales, and the
publications of the Religious Tract Society, the Sunday-School Society,
and numerous other middle-class organizations aiming to exercise
social control over the lower orders through the power of print. This
was a genre which women writers could dominate because of their
supposed expertise in narrative, fiction, and domestic realism, and their
supposed ability to extend their domestic virtues into projects of social
amelioration. Nevertheless, Hays gives a libertarian and original turn
to the form. *The Brothers* is cast not as prose narrative but as nine scenes
of dialogue with descriptions of the settings, giving the didacticism
freshness and vigour while remaining true to the long-established use
of dialogue to teach those supposed to be intellectually and culturally
unsophisticated, such as children, women, the lower classes, and 'primitive' peoples. Like other texts with similar aims, it uses conventions of
the Sentimental tale of lower-class life, including simple language,
linear plot, one-dimensional protagonists, moralizing authoritative
characters, a *deus ex machina* in the form of upper-class patrons for the
worthy poor, pathetic scenes of reconciliation, and poetic justice.

As the title suggests, the book uses the familiar didactic device of
contrasting characters—the working-class brothers William and Robert
Jennings, the former thoroughly imbued with the middle-class investment economy, as shown by his willingness to use the savings bank set
up by the philanthropic local squire, and the latter corrupted by the
plebeian lottery mentality. The plot follows the familiar didactic
pattern of contrasting destinies, domestic conflict, paternalistic intervention, and reconciliation. In spite of the lectures and illustrative anecdotes
of their mother, Mrs Jennings, Robert is encouraged in improvidence
by his fiancée, the coquette Fanny, whereas William and his fiancée,
Susan, postpone their marriage so that she can care for her sickly
stepfather. Afraid of losing Fanny to the attractions of a soldier from
the nearby garrison, Robert marries her before they have saved

---

[10] *Literary Panorama*, NS 3 (Mar. 1816), 949.

enough money to start life together on a firm footing; as expected, their housekeeping is slovenly and their marriage soon falls apart when Robert takes to drink and Fanny resorts to the dances at the Shamrock. The local philanthropist, Lady Goodville, refuses to let William and Susan sacrifice their own savings and happiness to help Robert and Fanny. She makes William her steward and gets Robert and Fanny work in her brother's factory. William's success inspires the drunkard Ralph to reform and he rejoins the savings club. After a few years Robert leaves the country, a broken man, but William and Susan have a neat farmhouse with children of their own and care for Robert's abandoned daughter. One day a crippled soldier falls at their door; it is of course Robert, who has returned repentant to tell his tale and spend a last Christmas with his family before he dies.

The work was Hays's first since *Cursory Remarks* to reach a second edition, being reprinted in Dublin in 1820, though Hays's name was left off the title page, apparently not considered useful for selling such a book. In 1817 she produced a follow-up entitled *Family Annals; or, The Sisters*, directed at middle-class women and published by the energetic firm of Simpkin & Marshall. Like *The Brothers*, *Family Annals* contrasts two characters and their destinies in order to recommend self-discipline as the best defence against poverty and social ruin. The Preface praises Maria Edgeworth for having effected 'a revolution in works of imagination' by her 'delineations of real characters and manners, pictures of the age and times in which we live, (to which future historians and philosophers will be glad to refer) good sense, sound principle and unaffected feeling', thereby supplanting 'the wonders of ancient romance' and 'the intricate incidents[,] inflated descriptions, and still more inflated sentiments, of the modern novel'. This ideological and cultural work will, the Preface claims, have major social and cultural effects by blending 'amusement and instruction' to make certain views 'more widely and generally diffused'. Hays claims that she has resumed her pen in order to participate in the post-Revolutionary social conciliation led by women writers such as Edgeworth, but her continuing commitment to Revolutionary feminism is suggested by the book's dedication to Eliza Fenwick, former member of the Godwin circle.

Family Annals is characteristically post-Revolutionary in subsuming the pre-Revolutionary critique of decadent court culture in stronger insistence on the investment mentality and domestic ideology. Two daughters of a minor landed gentleman take different courses in life because of their different educations. The elder, Ellen, has been educated in self-restraint and the investment mentality whereas her sister Charlotte, raised by her indulgent aunt Mrs Percy, lives for the moment. While Charlotte's pursuit of fashion and social emulation repeatedly lead her into debt, Ellen conserves her money and is thus able to devote it to books and beneficence. As Mr Seymour tells his daughters, 'The true art of economy, like the true spirit of generosity, has its origin in *self-denial;* without it no fortune will prove sufficient, nor will there be any merit in bestowing' (p. 6). Yet Charlotte marries an elderly businessman, Mr Wycherly, so that she may continue her career of luxury, whereas Ellen makes a love match with the virtuous (and therefore impecunious) barrister Mr Neville. Improvidence enforces calculated self-interest, but self-discipline enables expression of authentic selfhood as romantic love. Meanwhile, young Seymour, who will inherit the family estate, has imbibed a spirit of romantic 'chivalry' and not only shares Charlotte's extravagance but feels compelled by 'honour' to marry Clara, a foolish coquette who has fallen in love with him.

The opening chapters set up this pattern of contrasts, and the rest of the story, largely told through the conventionally feminine medium of letters between Charlotte and Ellen, shows the differing destinies of the two sisters and their brother in conjugal life. Young Seymour and his foolish wife soon run through the family estate. Charlotte's fashionable pursuits weaken her husband's business. Ellen and her husband at first seem destined to misfortune when his illness forces him to retire from his profession. But the family retires to the country and an entirely domestic existence that is divinely validated. Their life of cultivated, intellectual, and socially ameliorative domesticity was already becoming a figure for the *embourgeoisement* of rural England, or resiting professional middle-class culture from town to country, thereby culturally and ideologically dispossessing the historic agrarian classes, the gentry and rural labourers. Much space is devoted to describing the Nevilles' domestic life and their participation in 'modernizing' the rural lower classes after the example of Elizabeth Hamilton's *Cottagers of Glenburnie*.

Charlotte indicates Ellen's significance as a figure for post-Revolutionary feminism by calling her both 'romantic' and a 'philosopher' for preferring such a life to Charlotte's own worldly and courtly existence. The sisters also exchange letters reminiscent of Hays's in *Essays and Letters* and the *Monthly Magazine*; they recapitulate the Enlightenment debate on luxury as a cause of progress or decadence in society and culture. Meanwhile, disappointed in business and his marriage, Charlotte's husband takes to drink and dies before her remorse can make a difference. She tries living with the Nevilles, is at first delighted with their romantic domesticity, eventually becomes bored, and accompanies her brother and his wife to the Continent, where they have been forced to retire in order to retrench their extravagant way of life. But Seymour takes up the aristocratic vice of gambling, his wife is seduced by a foreign gallant and elopes, and Charlotte is forced to become the parasite of a wealthy and domineering dowager and eventually retires to Switzerland where, insensitive to the beauties of nature and the pleasures of rustic simplicity, she dies discontented. The Nevilles live happy and useful lives, and even after her husband's death Ellen gains new energy from supplying the place of father to her children and looks forward to rest and reward with God, the source of all excellence—implicitly, the kind of professional middle-class excellence exemplified by Ellen herself.

Family Annals is minor hack-work and Hays continued to seek professional work, social usefulness, and domestic security. In 1817 Henry Crabb Robinson found her again about to move lodgings and still looking for 'literary employment'. In 1819 he visited her after another move and wrote that 'she wants society': 'But alone she rather *bores*, though she is a sensible as well as very excellent and worthy woman, and her improved health and spirits render her society less burdensome than when she was more sentimental.'[11] Hays was also still well enough informed about the Godwin–Shelley circle to tell Crabb Robinson that Wollstonecraft's daughter Fanny Imlay had committed suicide—an event hushed up by Godwin. Hays seemed to be sinking into obscurity, hardship, and discontent, like other women writers whose great personal and professional opportunity had been in the Revolutionary decade. But an unexpected national political crisis gave her a final opportunity to show the relevance of Revolutionary feminism to the post-Revolutionary era.

The coronation of George IV and the return of his long-estranged consort to claim her royal rights focused popular opposition to the monarch and the entire system of 'Old Corruption'.[12] The king's

---

[11] *Crabb Robinson*, ed. Morley, i. 212, 234.

[12] See Christopher Hibbert, *George IV: Regent and King 1811–1830* (London, 1973), chs. 10–14; Thomas W. Laqueur, 'The Queen Caroline Affair: Politics as Art in the Reign of George IV', *Journal of Modern History*, 54 (Sept. 1982), 417–66.

extravagance, his mistresses, decades of scandal surrounding him and his brothers, his failure to maintain his youthful support for political and institutional reform, recent economic distress, rioting, Luddism, the 'Peterloo Massacre', and demands for Catholic emancipation— these events seemed to culminate in what was seen as a glaring instance of court government's exploitation of women, now a symbol for many vocal but powerless groups in society. The Whig opposition exploited the situation for their own ends and many conservatives feared that the convergence of various popular protest movements in support for the queen would be used by 'Jacobins' to precipitate a revolution. Themes and symbols from the Revolutionary 1790s resurfaced, though transformed by new circumstances, and the 'Queen Caroline Affair' gave impetus to successful reform movements of the 1820s and 1830s.[13]

T. & J. Allman, who published books for the popular market and advertised themselves as 'Booksellers to Her Majesty', commissioned Hays, as a writer familiar with issues of the wronged woman and experienced in writing female biography, to produce a book for the occasion, *Memoirs of Queens Illustrious and Celebrated*, published in the summer of 1821. It was a catchpenny compilation but its frontispiece, showing Queen Caroline's portrait surrounded by those of Marie Antoinette, Anne Boleyn, Elizabeth I, and Mary Queen of Scots, suggests a project similar to *Female Biography*, and the Preface is a forthright statement of Hays's post-Revolutionary feminism and her service to the cause of women, including Queen Caroline:

Having more than once taken up my pen, how humble soever its efforts may have been, in the cause, and for the honour and advantage, of my sex; and having deeply at heart, as connected with the welfare of the human species, and of society at large, the moral rights and intellectual advancement of *woman*, I acceded cheerfully, though declining in physical strength and mental activity, to the request of the publishers of the present volume, that I would select, compress, and compile, from the records of female eminence and worth, a memoir of *Queens* only, illustrious for their great qualities, or celebrated for their endowments and fortunes. The throne itself, with but few exceptions, secures not woman from the peculiar disadvantages that have hitherto attended her sex. (pp. v–vi)

Basing her argument on 'nature, equity, philosophy, and the Christian

---

[13] E. P. Thompson, *The Making of the English Working Class*, rev. edn. (Harmondsworth, 1968), 778–9.

religion', she insists 'that there can be, but *one moral standard of excellence for mankind*, whether male or female'. Court government's 'spirit of tyranny, selfishness, and sensuality' is responsible for 'the heaviest evils that have afflicted, degraded, and corrupted society', and though women's capacity 'for rational and moral advancement are, at this day, no longer a question', the education of women is still 'for adornment rather than for use; for exhibition rather than for moral and mental improvement; for the delights of the harem, rather than to render her the friend, the companion, the assistant, the counsellor of man, the former of his infant habits, the instructor of his early years, the source from which his character takes its bias, his principles their rise' (pp. vi–vii). This is less the rational civic woman of Hays's earlier Revolutionary feminism and more the national nurse, conscience, and cultural repository sketched during another national crisis, in Hannah More's *Strictures on the Modern System of Female Education*.

Considering the occasion for *Memoirs of Queens*, it is not surprising that many themes from *Female Biography* reappear here—the corrupting effect of court culture, the trivialization of women by courtly 'gallantry' and the 'mistress system', the susceptibility of uneducated women to 'romance' and 'superstition', the compatibility and interdependence of intellectual and aesthetic cultivation with domestic virtue, the dependence of women's public civism on such cultivation and virtue, and the incompatibility of such cultivation and virtue with courtly decadence and political conflict. Hays argues that where women are merely pawns in court intrigue, they are victims; where they rule directly, they are as capable as men; but where they are happiest and most useful is in domestic life. The domestic ideal of woman applies especially, because of their role as examples, to queens. Because of this focus, *Memoirs of Queens* also differs from *Female Biography*. It relies on virtually the same repertory of sources as its predecessor and it too lacks proportion, the last half of the alphabetical series being crammed into the last fifth of the book. But it is more reflective and philosophical, more consistent in providing rationalist sociological explanations for what its readers would see as the often extravagant and bizarre conduct of women placed so high above others and above readers of Hays's book. *Female Biography*, like many of the sources it drew on, contains an apology for female victims of court culture led into error, vice, and crime and exploited by a system they were not intellectually trained to analyse and therefore not morally armed to overcome; in *Memoirs of Queens* that apology focuses on Queen Caroline, whose errors and wrongs, as the book's frontispiece suggests, have been shared by others in her situation, and several of the other lives echo the themes set forth in hers, thus forming a history of the wrongs of women in the highest ranks of society.

For example, in imperial Rome a bad marriage and a corrupt court also led Agrippina the younger into moral decline; in Byzantium the virtuous empress Eudocia, too, had a mind 'probably too elevated to be a match for the veterans of political intrigue', and during the Renaissance Mary Queen of Scots was also the victim of feminine sensibility placed in hostile circumstances:

Who is there, that considers the unparalleled and trying circumstances in which she was placed, and who has ever looked into human nature and his own heart, that will dare to be severe? Mary possessed fine talents, but with that flexibility of mind and softness of temper that are inseparable from great sensibility. This might render her weak and infirm of purpose, might expose her to fall an easy victim into the snares of the artful and interested; but it seems to preclude the idea of the more atrocious crimes alleged against her. (pp. 421–2)

These were the same terms used in 1820 and 1821 to exculpate Queen Caroline, and Hays gives similar treatment to controversial queens of modern times. During the 1790s Hays held Marie Antoinette and her court responsible for the outbreak of the Revolution and its later excesses, but now Hays portrays the French queen too as a victim of court culture, her own sensibility, and the political volatility of the common people. When the Revolution broke out, Marie Antoinette 'experienced the vanity and uncertainty of popular favour', for 'the liveliness of the French character, prone to extremes, led them from the excess of attachment towards their monarchs to an equal extravagance of hatred and reprobation' (389–90). As Hays's readers would know, Queen Caroline was similarly showered with popular support, praise, and even gifts during the Parliamentary debate on the government's Bill of Pains and Penalties against her, and the abandonment of the Bill produced national rejoicing. But this soon cooled, and when she tried to force her way into her husband's coronation in July 1821 she was hissed and laughed at. Hays's book was published late in July, before the queen's unexpected death in August revived her political popularity.

In her biography of Marie Antoinette and numerous other lives Hays not only invokes themes of the 1790s, as demonstrators in the streets were doing, but reworks a long line of comment on women and politics, comment that became particularly acrimonious during the 1790s and such episodes as the 'Queen Caroline Affair'. The Revolution debate gave a new turn to historic anti-feminist critiques of the political, moral, and sexual excesses at courts dominated by women such as Cleopatra, Messalina, Catherine II of Russia, and Marie Antoinette, while Burke stirred a controversy over political activity of women, especially from unenfranchised classes. During the mid- and late 1790s courtly licence and Revolutionary excess in France were linked in accounts of manners and morals under the Directory; in Britain Revolutionary feminism was associated with social and political insubordination as well as sexual immorality, and some readers would remember that Hays herself had been implicated in this association. The anti-feminism of the Jacobin government and Napoleon's regime had echoes in Britain. There was an element of anti-feminism in opposition to Queen Caroline for two decades before her 'trial' in 1820, and supporters of the king and the government used it in 1820 and 1821 to discredit Caroline and her supporters—especially women—by associating political liberalism with sexual licence and social disorder.[14]

Hays begins her life of Queen Caroline by acknowledging the danger and difficulty in taking up matter liable 'to call forth, to aggravate, and to irritate every passion and every prejudice of the public mind' (pp. 93–4). Therefore she adopts the rhetorical posture of the 'impartial' and 'dispassionate' historian rather than the advocate, and professes to give 'a mere sketch of prominent and undisputed facts, with deductions immediately arising out of those facts'. In fact, Hays adapts the Revolutionary feminist critique of court culture to place Caroline in a historic line of female victims of court government. The pattern of Caroline's life as Hays presents it resembles that of the lives of queens in similar situations, also described in *Memoirs*, and is shaped in such a way as to elicit sympathy for the subject by showing her 'natural' character denatured and corrupted by her circumstances. Before marriage Caroline 'was of a gay and lively temper' and 'sought the love and confidence rather than the homage and respect of her inferiors'. After marriage the Prince of Wales's disappointment over Parliament's expected repayment of his debts—the reason he had married—led to coolness toward his wife that was manipulated by

[14] Laqueur, 'The Queen Caroline Affair', 446.

court intriguers for their own ends. Thus the court system is to blame, rather than Caroline, or even the Prince. The interrelated domestic and political situation of Caroline is the focus of Hays's life of her, as of the other lives in *Memoirs of Queens*, and Hays passes lightly over the separation of the Prince and Caroline, the 'Delicate Investigation' of 1807 into her alleged adultery, restriction of her access to her daughter, Princess Charlotte, her departure from England in 1814 in return for an annual pension of £35,000, and the secret investigation of her conduct while abroad.

Like others at the time, then, Hays portrays the queen's character and situation—however the queen herself may be judged—as products of the court system of government and sees popular support for the queen as an aspect of widespread desire for a revolutionary transformation of that system. To support this view she recalls the place of woman in the Revolution debate inaugurated by Burke in 1790:

Burke, had he now lived, would have retracted his assertion, that the age of chivalry had passed away; it revived, in all its impassioned fervour, amidst the soberest and gravest people in the civilized world. Every manly mind shrank from the idea of driving, by protracted and endless persecutions, a desolate unprotected female from her family, her rank, from society and from the world. *Woman* considered it as a common cause against the despotism and tyranny of man. Morals are of no sex, duties are reciprocal between being and being, or they are abrogated by nature and reason. Brute force may subjugate, but in knowledge only is real strength, and to truth and justice is the last and only legitimate appeal. With the feudal institutions fell the childish privileges and degrading homage paid to the sex; and to *equity* not gallantry do they now prefer their claim. Oppression and proscription, it is true, still linger, but old things appear to be passing away; and, in another century, probably, should the progress of knowledge bear any proportion to its accelerated march during the latter half of the past [century], all things will become new. We live in eventful times, and at a critical era of the world. Happy those who understand the signs of the times; who seek not to oppose to a flood feeble mounds and inadequate barriers; but who suffer its waters gently to flow and expand through prepared appropriate reservoirs and channels, carrying fertility as they glide. (pp. 127–8)

Many others in 1820 and 1821 used Burke's sentimental invocation of 'antient chivalry' in the cause of Marie Antoinette to characterize their support for Britain's 'injured Queen', just as many liberals, Whigs, and reformers saw support for the queen as a portent of sweeping changes in the state. But Hays feminizes these commonplaces, portraying the

revolution to come as extraordinary yet natural ('a flood'), and feminine ('gently to flow . . . carrying fertility').

Hays also portrays Caroline as the last in a historical line of corrupted,
degraded, and wronged queens stretching back to antiquity; thus Hays
implies that her own perspective and authority are supra-historical and
that she is 'above' the plane of experience on which queens have
existed, continue to exist, and will exist until the imminent revolution
transforms the conditions that produce the kind of women represented
in *Memoirs of Queens*. The supra-historical perspective of the book's
narrator is both illustrated and explained by her ability to generalize
from the lives of these historical individuals, past and present. This
ability arises from the similarity and difference between Hays and her
subject, and is demonstrated in such passages as Hays's comment on
Caroline's victimization by court politics:

The intrigues and manoeuvres of a court are perhaps little understood, or
imagined, by those without its vortex. Temptations and excitements surround
situations of eminence, to the influence of which those in humbler stations are
seldom or never exposed. (p. 102)

Her authority for such remarks must be 'philosophical' rather than
empirical, the product of critical reflection rather than experience, for
she herself could not have direct knowledge of Caroline's social milieu.
Hays implies that she is able to reflect in this way because she is not
subject to Caroline's experience, but since the oppression of women by
court culture is disseminated through all classes, Hays has similar
experience to ground both her understanding of Caroline's situation
and her sympathy for it. Class experience may divide Caroline and her
biographer, but gender experience unites them. Thus class and gender
together enable Hays to construct herself in her text as both a 'philosopher' and a woman, enough like the queen to understand and sympathize with her situation but different enough to escape the limits of
that situation and become a 'female philosopher', thus implicitly superior to the queen. Hays establishes this superiority in order to propose
herself, or the 'female philosopher' constructed in her text, as the
model of the revolution, or radical restructuring of the social hierarchy,
that *Memoirs of Queens* shows is necessary and predicts is imminent.

Memoirs of Queens demonstrates continuity between the Revolution
debate—including Revolutionary feminism—and the Revolutionary
aftermath, now represented as the beginning of a revolutionary future.
Thus *Memoirs of Queens* also demonstrates the continuing relevance of

Revolutionary feminism. But 'old things' did not pass away as quickly as Hays and others would have liked. Though Hays lived to see the popular agitation over Queen Caroline pass into the debate on Catholic Emancipation, the Reform Bill of 1832, reform of the poor law, reform of the criminal law, and many other changes that seemed imminent in the early 1790s, she published no more. On 21 February 1843 Henry Crabb Robinson recorded his last news of her:

Last night I received an account of the death of my old friend Mary Hays (turned eighty), one of the oldest of my friends—a very worthy woman. In her day she had a sort of popularity, that is with those who could tolerate a warm friend of Mrs. Wollstonecraft. She was very liberal in her opinions and had stuck fast in them.[15]

[15] *Crabb Robinson*, ed. Morley, ii. 629.

8

Elizabeth Hamilton: Domestic Woman and National Reconstruction

HELEN MARIA WILLIAMS and Mary Hays found their Sentimental and Revolutionary feminism increasingly under attack in the later 1790s and the Revolutionary aftermath, and had to turn to other ways of sustaining their social critiques. By contrast, Elizabeth Hamilton seemed well positioned to become a major post-Revolutionary critic of feminism. In fact, she moved closer to Revolutionary feminism after 1800, resisting the increasing remasculinization of culture and restriction of women to narrowly defined domesticity. Like a number of other women writers, she did so by following the lead of Hannah More's *Strictures on the Modern System of Female Education*, reconstructing domestic woman of the earlier conduct-book tradition for the post-Revolutionary crisis of 'national' unity and imperial defence. At the same time, she continued her work of feminizing 'masculine' discourses, aiming to intellectualize women's culture by popularizing, novelizing, and thereby disseminating philosophy, theology, and history, and doing so in a way that offered herself as model for the new intellectual-domestic woman.

Her first move in this programme was *Letters on Education* (1801), a feminization of Enlightenment epistemology and moral philosophy in the acceptably 'feminine' guise of educational writing. This was less like More's *Strictures* than Catharine Macaulay Graham's *Letters on Education* (1790), a Bluestocking feminist synthesis and popularization of a wide range of learned discourses and philosophical, cultural, and social issues. Hamilton's synthesis takes in a range of such discourses that would have been congenial to Williams, Hays, and even Wollstonecraft. It includes Enlightenment epistemology (Dugald Stewart, Thomas Reid), liberal theology (Joseph Priestley, Bishop Taylor), 'philosophical history' (Edward Gibbon), cultural anthropology and cultural criticism (Kames), and education and socialization (Maria and Richard Lovell Edgeworth's *Practical Education*). But like her argumentative and didactic novels of the Revolutionary decade, her non-fiction work is composed so as to exemplify the kind of cultural revolutionary for which the work argues—a woman intellectual able to contribute to national peace and progress without abandoning acceptably feminine discourses of the domestic, the educational, the local, and the practical. In the context of post-Revolutionary anti-feminism, remasculinization of literary discourse, and hostility to 'blue-stockings', the textual construction of such an 'author' constitutes an act of cultural resistance and political polemic.

In fact *Letters on Education* constructs its 'author' as something like the 'female philosopher' in the texts of Mary Hays, one of Hamilton's main satiric butts during the Revolution debate. On one hand the text is epistolary, pretends to be no more than a simplified rendering of eighteenth-century liberal theology and associationist psychology, deals dialogically with objections raised by the correspondent, and uses illustrative anecdotes—compositional elements often used by women writers dealing with subjects some might have found unfeminine. Yet the book is organized like a philosophical treatise, starts from first principles and elaborates consequences, proceeds in a formal argumentative way, deploys the language of eighteenth-century epistemology, and is less informal and uses fewer anecdotes and common-life observations than most books by women on such a subject. Hamilton also distinguishes her position on the education of women from that of the Revolutionary feminists without distancing herself from it, advancing the same Pricean theology of spiritual equality that grounded Wollstonecraft's *Vindication*, declaring that the aim of education is to cultivate 'the powers of *human beings*, so as to bring them to the greatest perfection of which they are capable', thus making 'no distinction of sex' in matters of intellect and dismissing 'natural' female inferiority as a 'hereditary prejudice'—a phrase by now associated with Revolutionary sympathizers (pp. 36–7). But she also blames Revolutionary feminists for 'this *portentous crisis*', arguing that 'the human character' is elevated 'into dignity and importance' and 'Divine favour' by 'an equality of moral worth' rather than 'an equality of employments and avocations, founded upon the erroneous idea of a perfect similarity of powers' and 'admission into the theatre of public life' that is pervasively contaminated by courtly values of 'honour', 'glory', and 'ambition' (pp. 243–4). Finally, Hamilton assimilates this revised Revolutionary feminism to the post-Revolutionary concern for social reconciliation, toleration, and sense of common 'national' identity and purpose. In short, the argument and form of *Letters on Education* are designed to manifest a way of being a woman intellectual and social critic without going as 'far' as the Revolutionary feminists and without relapsing into counter-feminism.

But there was a fine line between the wish to popularize 'philosophy' for women readers and the need to construct an authoritative 'female philosopher' in the text. Concerned that the book was too abstract and philosophical, Hamilton quickly rewrote it to 'render the subject perfectly clear and intelligible to readers of every description' ('Advertisement'), and republished it as *Letters on the Elementary Principles of Education*, 'second edition' (1801). Reviewers were also ambivalent, welcoming *Letters on Education* for its moral and political principles but deploring its 'unfeminine' philosophical character. Paradoxically, the *Monthly Review* was glad to see Hamilton write a 'more serious and important' work than a novel and one that 'would produce a most desirable revolution in the state of the world' by causing 'a wonderful change in the knowledge, opinions, and habits of mankind'. The reviewer also expected that 'readers will be rather surprized, perhaps, on seeing a lady undertake to tread' in the path of Locke and Watts, but reassured them that 'here is no female champion arisen, who seeks to contest the prize with those veteran heroes', for Hamilton takes 'a more humble station' than the philosopher, aiming only 'to furnish parents, nurses, and superintendants of young children, with the proper theory of the infant mind, and with the most effectual method of fostering the tender bud of intellect'. The *Critical Review* thought the book showed 'great judgement, an intimate knowledge of the human heart, and delicacy of sentiment', though ignorance of real children. The reviewer agreed that 'No man of sense will hold a well-educated woman in contempt', and insisted that women may 'possess . . . an elegance, and often an elevation of sentiment, which renders them capable, in many instances, of instructing and directing their husbands', yet 'they do not naturally possess that strength of judgement, that force of mind, competent to adapt them to the more important, the more abstracted, intellectual functions'. The *British Critic* contrasted More and Hamilton, the former 'an humble Christian, of more than ordinary reading and observation', and the latter 'a metaphysician of the school of Hartley' that was associated with Revolutionary 'metaphysicians', and pursuing interests 'ill becoming the elegance of the female mind'.[1]

---

[1] *Monthly Review*, NS 38 (Aug. 1802), 408; 39 (Sept. 1802), 49; *Critical Review*, NS 34 (Feb. 1802), 181, 187; see also 36 (Nov. 1802), 291–8; *British Critic*, 19 (Mar. 1802), 232–3.

This reception and Hamilton's own doubts about her method in *Letters on Education* may have affected a different work she was engaged on, feminizing theology in an analysis of Paul's epistle to the Romans. Hamilton was drawn to this text because it dealt with a problem that was central to her own religious belief—whether salvation was predestined or the result of free will. This was also the basis of difference between the Presbyterianism in which Hamilton was raised and the Episcopalianism to which she adhered as an adult. In the 1790s many had seen a parallel between this religious issue and the difference between English Jacobin 'necessitarianism' and anti-Jacobin emphasis on individual responsibility. Thus the heart of the epistle to the Romans has several resonances for Hamilton and the immediate Revolutionary aftermath. It also had relevance to her as a woman, for the epistle was notoriously difficult of theological interpretation, controversial, and the subject of learned dispute—on all counts supposedly beyond the education and capacity of women. Women could practise devotional writing because, unlike theology, it was by convention personal and emotional and did not require any great learning or powers of reasoning. In a fragmentary preface addressed to her sister, Hamilton acknowledges this gendering of religious discourse but brushes it aside. Male theologians consider the Epistle to the Romans as the 'most abstruse and difficult' of Paul's writings, yet she confidently embarks on interpreting it, sarcastically attributing her boldness to 'some deficiency of capacity' or 'a deficiency in that stock of learning which is necessary in order to enter into the associations of the learned'. She declares her intention to pay 'little attention' to the learned theologians because 'the Scriptures themselves' supply 'the solution of every difficulty', and rather than proceed as a man would, by 'abstract reasoning' and analysis of separate parts, she prefers 'a system of our own'—a feminizing, integrative method, reconciling difficulties 'not to any particular and favourite theory, but to the general tenor and spirit of the author'.[2] This attitude is characteristic of the disregard of merely professional theology found in Scottish philosophers Hamilton was reading, especially Thomas Reid and Dugald Stewart, and of the post-Revolutionary reaction against narrowly professional and dehumanizing 'philosophy' supposed to have inspired French Revolutionaries and

---

[2] Elizabeth Benger, *Memoirs of the Late Mrs. Elizabeth Hamilton*, 2nd edn., 2 vols. (London, 1819), ii. 240–1.

'English Jacobins' such as those Hamilton satirized in *Memoirs of Modern Philosophers*. The same attitude was expressed in the 1790s by writers such as Helen Maria Williams, but in the post-Revolutionary remasculinization of culture it was adopted by many men, but especially Coleridge, in what would later be called Romanticism. Hamilton's essay in theology expresses her awareness of the contradictions in being a woman writer in other ways. Her theologizing clearly arises from daily experience, the conventionally ascribed site of women's knowledge, and is first personal and private, like much women's writing. Secondly, her experiment in personal and domestic yet rational and reflective theology may have been, like her satire on Revolutionary feminists, a reaction to the scandalous activity of another woman, Joanna Southcott, an uneducated servant who proclaimed prophecies and led a millenarian movement made up largely of lower-class women in the late 1790s and 1800s. Hamilton herself did not complete or publish her experiment in theology—perhaps another indication that she thought the price of transgressing gendered boundaries of discourse too high at this time—though she continued such writing in journal form, published in part after her death.

She was also preoccupied with feminizing yet another 'masculine' discourse—historiography—while illustrating her argument for a feminized state and civil society founded in individual subjectivity and domesticity and validated by Christian faith. *Memoirs of the Life of Agrippina, the Wife of Germanicus* (1804) is another experimental work, a quasi-novel or text in which non-fiction material predominates over fiction. Like *Letters of a Hindoo Rajah* and *Memoirs of Modern Philosophers* it presents a critique of the present by defamiliarizing it, through historical analogy rather than the alien perspective or burlesque distortion.[3] This again was a technique associated with men's writing, especially eighteenth-century 'classical republicans' and 'commonwealthmen', and the French *philosophe* Barthélemy used it in *Voyage du jeune Anacharsis* (1788), a critique of the *ancien régime*. But women became interested in the form, with such works as the Bluestocking Cornelia Knight's *Marcus Flaminius; or, A View of the Military, Political, and Social Life of the Romans* (1793), because the historical quasi-novel enabled them to practise various discourses conventionally reserved for men, including historiography, archeology, and classical studies, literary

[3] On the quasi-novel see Gary Kelly, *English Fiction of the Romantic Period 1789–1830* (London, 1989), 252–60.

and art criticism, and political and cultural critique, under the guise of the acceptably feminine form of prose fiction.

Hamilton's Preface declares the aim of communicating her intellectual and moral philosophy to a wider readership by means of 'a more agreeble medium' than the 'didactic form' of *Letters on Education*. She rejects fiction as such because it enables an author 'to promote the reception of a favourite theory' but 'can never be considered as a confirmation of its truth'. Biography, however, both engages the reader's sympathetic interest and makes a deeper moral impression because it is known to be true (vol. i, pp. xiii–xiv). Hamilton's biographical method is based on the Enlightenment epistemology, set forth in *Letters on Education*, that also underpinned English Jacobin 'necessitarianism': 'to trace the progress of an extraordinary mind from the first dawn of genius to maturity; to mark the circumstances from which it received its peculiar bent; to develope the sources whence the understanding derived its stores; and thus . . . to pourtray the characteristic features of the soul'. But an element of fiction is required because history is 'imperfect': public acts may be recorded but the exercise of subjective virtues is 'not of a nature to be disclosed' and the exercise of domestic virtues' is or ought to be 'for ever veiled from vulgar eyes' (pp. xvii–xviii). Yet these virtues are more important and instructive than the actions of 'conquerors and disturbers of the earth', on which biography and historiography have hitherto focused (p. xxvi)—a reference to the French Revolution and Napoleon. By contrast, Hamilton intends to favour 'Minerva' over 'Mars' and to avoid modern controversies by choosing a subject both domestic and classical. This 'may have the appearance of presumption', but a woman may popularize learned discourse, especially for the improvement of her own sex, and will know how to describe with 'probability' those 'domestic avocations, society, &c.' which 'it suited not the dignity of history to record' (pp. xxviii, xxxii), but which are the foundation of the national character and destiny.

Hamilton first feminizes classical studies by popularizing them in a 'Genealogical Sketch' of her main characters and 'Preliminary Observations on the History and Character of the Ancient Romans', similar to the 'Preliminary Dissertation' in *Letters of a Hindoo Rajah*. This framing device gives an Enlightenment sociology of the rise, decline, and fall of republican Rome, a favourite theme of eighteenth-century classical republicans and commonwealthmen.[4] Like these men, Hamilton at-

---

[4] See John A. W. Gunn, *Beyond Liberty and Property: The Process of Self-Recognition in*

tributes the greatness of Rome to its citizens' love of liberty; because their 'idea of liberty' was connected with the common good, ambition 'swelled the tide of national prosperity' rather than 'the selfish gratification of individual interest'. Hamilton feminizes this argument, however, by insisting that this 'patriotic zeal' in turn depended for its strength and dissemination on 'the influence of female manners':

Taught to place her glory in the faithful discharge of the domestic and maternal duties, a Roman matron imperceptibly acquired an elevation of sentiment, a dignity of manners, which rendered her equally the object of esteem and of respect. Her country was no less dear to her than to her husband; but the same spirit of patriotism which impelled him to exert his valour in the field, or his wisdom in the senate, animated her mind in the instruction of her children, and the regulation of her family. (i. 18–19)

She further feminizes the argument by insisting that the only thing lacking to soften and perfect this 'patriotic' character was the Christian religion.

The fall of Rome, like its rise, depended on the same factors. Lacking the check of Christianity, the Romans' love of freedom and country degenerated into love of 'power' over others, including conquered nations, slaves, and even members of the same family. Foreign conquests expanded slavery, introduced luxury and decadence from the Orient, encouraged social emulation, and resulted in the decline of the female character: 'The Roman females soon caught the contagion of licentiousness', chastity was no longer 'the matron's glory, or the maiden's pride', and 'the care and instruction of her children' and 'management of domestic affairs, no longer conferred dignity' (i. 46–7). This plot of Roman history has two obvious modern parallels—Revolutionary history from the early 1790s, through the republican turmoils and expansionism of 1792–4, the decadence of the Directory, and the rise of a new 'Emperor'; and Britain's decline from virtuous liberty established by the Glorious Revolution, through the increasing luxury and orientalization of the eighteenth century, the civil strife of the 1790s, and post-Revolutionary social decadence and political corruption.

The story of Agrippina and Germanicus illustrates this historical process outlined in Hamilton's 'Preliminary Observations'. Much of volume one is spent describing their ideal companionate and egalitarian

Eighteenth-Century Political Thought (Kingston, Ontario, 1983), ch. 1, 'Parliament and the Caesars: Legal Tyranny in the Political Rhetoric of Eighteenth-Century England'.

marriage and contrasting it with others of the time, especially within the imperial family. When Germanicus is stationed in Germany, the couple find the domestic virtues and respect for women equally prevalent among this 'primitive' people, but in Rome Germanicus and Agrippina stand out from the vice and intrigue of the imperial court and become objects of envy and resentment. Even their virtues are limited without Christian faith, however, and when Germanicus falls victim to court intrigues Agrippina indulges in grief and a desire for revenge. Although the populace loved Germanicus they too lack the basis for principled and effective political action and are easily corrupted by flattery and bribes, for ancient philosophy—a parallel to Revolutionary and English Jacobin 'philosophy'—remained the diversion of an elite few. Even Agrippina's children, Agrippina and Caligula, were corrupted in such a divided, selfish, and individualistic society and became two of the most notorious characters of antiquity. Agrippina herself is banished, abandoned by the intimidated 'giddy multitude', and in frustration tries to starve herself to death.

This is the low point of Agrippina's story, but the narrator reminds the reader that meanwhile another event was occurring to transcend and transform this history of degeneration:

While Tiberius, the creature of a moment, whose lengthened reign is but a speck in the annals of time, was exercising his power in spreading terror and desolation, the messenger of the MOST HIGH announced to the righteous the tidings of everlasting joy! In the resurrection of CHRIST, such full assurances were given of a future state, as should thenceforth render the transitory ills of life only dust in the balance! (iii. 282–3)

The narrator's exclamations signal her participation in this triumph over history as irredeemably temporal, relative, and conflicted, a condition caused by class difference: 'In the separation made by rank and circumstances, the tie of a common nature, that tie which ought to bind man to man, was in the pagan world completely lost.' Worse still, Roman society lacked the religion necessary to overcome these differences:

The rich and the poor, the noble and the lowly, knew not what it was to meet on equal terms in the house of GOD, to join in the same acts of humility and contrition, to rejoice in the same hopes of mercy, and to send their prayers and praises in unison to one common Parent, one universal LORD, one great Creator! They considered not each other as joint heirs of immortality, beings equally frail by nature, and who might be equally enriched by grace! (iii. 327–8)

Here Christian virtues are equated with those conventionally ascribed to women, and society is envisaged as a family, though a patriarchal one. The narrator's concern is obviously less with pagan Rome than with un-Christian, socially divided Britain and un-Christian, warlike, and imperialist France. Agrippina's fate shows that despite her feminine virtues she lacked true religion as ideological defence against the passions and ambition of her time, thus 'cherished the seeds of misery and corruption' even in her own family, and thereby unintentionally contributed to the decline and fall of her country.

The narrator concludes with a moral for the present: 'Let those who have an opportunity of forming [their idea of virtue] upon a purer model, learn to prize the inestimable privilege they enjoy, in having clearer views of moral excellence, and brighter prospects of future reward, than ever opened on the unfortunate Agrippina!' For in *Memoirs of Agrippina* Hamilton attempts to go beyond the Revolution debate in three ways. In giving her version of the transition from republican to imperial Roman society she invokes a central theme of the eighteenth-century classical republicanism that was a common source of Revolutionary politics in France and English Jacobinism in Britain, but she adapts that theme for her counter-revolutionary politics by insisting that Christian faith is necessary to complete classical republican private and social virtue. At the same time, by relativizing private virtue, political principles, and history in the light of eternity she appropriates the historicism of the eighteenth-century classical republicans and the social critiques of the Enlightenment. Secondly, by feminizing history and social analysis, and by asserting that the motive force of both is the private and domestic affections extended into the public and national arena, she gives her own interpretation to the post-Revolutionary idealization and heroization of domestic woman as source of the 'national' identity, culture, and destiny. Finally, in her experimental quasi-novel Hamilton attempts to go beyond the Revolutionary decade's conflicts of form, genre, and discourse by feminizing historiography.

This experiment did not succeed, at least in the view of reviewers, who were polite but did not believe that a woman could purposely transgress boundaries of discourse; experiment, especially when by a woman, was again read as bad writing. The *Annual Review* doubted 'the expediency of composing historic novels' and complained of 'an inconvenient confusion of fact and fiction'. The *Monthly Review* faulted Hamilton's scholarship, thought the mixture of ancient history with

Christian reflections showed ignorance of literary decorum, and considered the book 'too didactic and too moral ever to become a favourite at the circulating libraries' as Hamilton seemed to hope. The *Critical Review* thought that 'there is nothing essential in the work to distinguish it from a novel' but that women readers would not get past the third page. In contrast, the *British Critic* thought that Hamilton's 'talents' had never been so 'conspicuous', that she would fix 'the reader's attention' completely 'through the whole three volumes', and that the 'Preliminary Observations' contained 'judicious reflections' offering 'lessons of practical wisdom' for 'Britons of every rank and every age'. Nevertheless, this reviewer, too, thought the fiction vitiated the biography and that the Roman world was too different for any moral to be inferred from it for the present.[5]

Nevertheless, Hamilton's earlier counter-revolutionary contributions were recognized with a royal pension in 1804; the penetration of her counter-revolutionary feminism into the dominant class was recognized in a request from a Scottish nobleman to supervise his daughters' education. She was reluctant, having told a friend in 1803, 'in our sex, the cultivation of the intellectual faculties is so much considered as a secondary object, that to undertake the education of a female is in some respects to be put on a footing with fiddlers and dancing-masters; in short, to be deprived of the respectability of independence.'[6] She accepted the position on condition of having a 'separate establishment' to maintain her status as a genteel professional, but after six months she found her 'personal independence' was compromised and declined to continue.[7] The experience did produce another book, *Letters, Addressed to the Daughter of a Nobleman, on the Formation of Religious and Moral Principle* (1806), aiming to exemplify in practice the theory of *Letters on Education* and to feminize both 'philosophy' and theology. It is, accordingly, in epistolary and dialogical form, based on a professionalized relation of domestic affection, and addressed to 'Lady Elizabeth' (Bingham, daughter of Lord Lucan), a former pupil, in order to render the author-teacher's mentorial presence permanent, in print. It incorporates personal observations and short illustrative narratives, and has a more belletristic range of reference and quotation than Hamilton's earlier *Letters on Education*. It stakes out a middle ground between books such

[5] *Annual Review*, 3 (1804), 542; *Monthly Review*, NS 50 (July 1806), 274–8; *Critical Review*, 3rd ser., 7 (Feb. 1806), 190, 189; *British Critic*, 26 (July 1805), 26–33.
[6] Benger, *Memoirs of Hamilton*, ii. 53.
[7] Ibid. i. 177–8.

as Hays's *Letters and Essays* and More's *Strictures on the Modern System of Female Education*, both of which Hamilton knew, being less miscellaneous, materialist, and feminist than the former and more 'philosophical' and less Evangelical than the latter, aiming to reconcile Revolutionary feminism and counter-revolutionary feminism by emphasizing the common objective of both—to confer autonomous subjectivity and thus a degree of social independence on women by training them in the same self-discipline and critical thinking necessary to professional men.

Thus the Preface rejects the rote learning usually imposed on women in favour of training in critical thought, while insisting that only relations of domestic affection buttressed by orthodox religion, not mere professional method, can sustain such training. The first volume outlines the religious and philosophical rationale for 'constant and habitual exercise' of both critical thought and moral sensibility, validated by religious principle, extended to every activity, relationship, and moment of life, thereby relativizing merely social categories of personal worth and internalizing the professional middle-class discourse of subjective merit and capitalist investment mentality, validated by the light of eternity and, in an aptly financial yet biblical metaphor, called 'accountableness' (i. 30, 31). Such internalization of the moral economy of professionalized 'virtue' is necessary because merely social 'securities' are ever-changing due to 'fashion', social conflict, and the fluctuations of 'power' in society. This is especially the case with the upper class, who are always being flattered and manipulated by courtly intriguers, 'for who but the self-interested and depraved will practise the arts necessary to obtain an ascendancy over the mind either of an equal or superior?' (i. 129). The second volume describes the religious basis of this programme, subsuming features of rational Dissent in the Anglican doctrine of good works as well as true faith, and confronting Eve's place, as representative woman, in the Christian scheme of time and eternity. This was a major theme in Revolutionary feminist critique of patriarchal religion, and Hamilton tries to reconcile anti-feminist and feminist interpretations by reading Eve's punishment as an allegorical act of divine mercy, offering women 'a peculiar hope' for redemption through means appropriate to their condition of maternity and domesticity (ii. 28–30), but insisting that this option cannot be exercised without intellectual training and the freedom to acquire moral discipline (ii. 131–2).

But she condemns social protest, whether based on gender or class, as a sign of sinful pride. Though sympathetic to the dependent and impoverished condition of most women, she represents 'the distinctions of society' as 'not only essential in a political, but necessary in a moral, point of view, as means of exercising and proving our virtue', and anticipates 'the hour' when 'the transient distinctions' that separate 'the owner of the rich domain' and 'the rustic hind who labours it' will 'be annihilated', along with 'all the unhallowed passions which these distinctions might have inflamed' (ii. 169–72). The same cold comfort had been offered to the oppressed by Burke and More in the 1790s and was being offered again in the Revolutionary aftermath by the likes of the Religious Tract Society. Paradoxically, Hamilton argues that the trials of social difference benefit the middle class most because their 'selfishness, as well as pride, meets with so many checks, and is so universally opposed and reprobated, that even by the common inter-courses of life it must be in some measure subdued, or at least restrained', resulting in 'benevolent feelings' toward others, expressed in acts of charity (ii. 253). Implicitly, therefore, it is women and the middle classes, differently but equally oppressed, who are best placed to ameliorate social conflict and misery, thereby leading social and national reconciliation on earth while acquiring the spiritual merit necessary to salvation hereafter.

Though a second edition of *Letters* was soon called for, reviewers were becoming impatient with Hamilton's feminization of 'masculine' discourses. The *Monthly Review* writes condescendingly that she 'occasionally wanders a little out of her depth' and 'has not sufficiently studied the subjects of Christian theology, to justify her public discussion of them'. The *Critical Review* objects to some of her theological arguments and questions her intellectual competence by accusing her of 'grammatical inaccuracies', 'uncouth expressions', and 'unmanageable or broken metaphors'. The *British Critic* distinguishes her previous work from that of most women writers in displaying 'powers of thinking, and of thinking justly', and acknowledges the 'many profound as well as useful reflections, expressed in elegant language' in her present work. But the reviewer also deplores the 'petulant self-sufficiency' of her preface as 'unbecoming the female character', worries about her venturing into 'the thorny labyrinth of controversy' where 'a lady' would not commonly 'choose to take her literary walk', and devotes almost two pages to Hamilton's grammatical and stylistic errors.[8]

---

[8] *Monthly Review*, NS 54 (Sept. 1807), 17–20; *Critical Review*, 3rd ser., 9 (Nov. 1806), 303; *British Critic*, 29 (Apr. 1807), 347–57.

Letters to the Daughter of a Nobleman attempts to feminize both philosophy and theology while subsuming Revolutionary feminism in her counter-revolutionary project of religious, social, and political reconciliation in the aftermath of the Revolution debate. Hamilton carried out a similar project in her personal and public life to challenge the post-Revolutionary remasculinization of literary culture. Though 'most Scotchwomen read, and were not inferior to their southern neighbours in general information and good taste, very few had ventured to incur the dangerous distinction of authorship' and there was a widespread prejudice against 'bluestockings', which Hamilton 'set at defiance' by avoiding any appearance 'that she valued her literary reputation on any other ground but as a means of usefulness', by 'her cheerfulness, good sense, and good humour', and by managing a number of charitable institutions, especially the Edinburgh House of Industry.[9]

This was 'instituted for the purpose of affording assistance to aged females of respectable character, when thrown out of employment, and of training the young to habits of industry and virtue'. Located near the Magdalene Asylum established in 1797 to receive prostitutes from prison, the House of Industry was probably meant to complement the Asylum by rescuing women who were on the verge of prostitution.[10] It had three branches. The spinning room provided work-for-welfare for older women on the verge of indigence or prostitution—growing concerns to middle-class reformers and ratepayers. The lace factory employed girls and young women for ten hours every day, giving six hours 'to lace-working, three to needlework, and one to reading and spelling'. All meals were provided, payment was by piecework with deductions for materials and overheads, a shilling and sixpence a week went to each girl's parents, any surplus was put aside to buy clothes, and the girls later went into the School for Servants, where lack of funds meant that there was only one meal of bread and broth a day. Those employed from the School were investigated annually and rewards given to those with good behaviour. The managers of the House also aimed to reform the inmates' parents by drawing them into the economy and the religious services of the institution. Despite this comprehensive plan for a self-supporting programme of

[9] Benger, *Memoirs of Hamilton*, i. 193–4; the description of the Edinburgh House of Industry is a separately paginated four-page notice bound at the end of Hamilton's *Exercises in Religious Knowledge*, originally written for the inmates.

[10] Linda Mahood, *The Magdalenes: Prostitution in the Nineteenth Century* (London, 1990), 75.

social reform and education for subordination, the House of Industry remained dependent on local middle-class subscribers who worried that educating the poor would give them ambitions above their station, or that the workhouse would compete with other businesses. Consequently, the managers assured subscribers that 'it is not so much their object to make accomplished readers and needleworkers, as to make active, diligent, and sober-minded servants, well instructed in their duty to God and man, and who have acquired habits which may accord with and support their principles'.

At about this time Hamilton began a fictional work to disseminate the same diminutive form of professional middle-class ideology and culture. Sometime in 1805 or 1806 she began 'a little tale for the lower orders' as the first in a series of tracts designed to resemble Hannah More's Cheap Repository of the 1790s, but probably inspired by Maria Edgeworth's *Popular Tales* (1804), published a year after Hamilton and Edgeworth had met in Edinburgh, and short stories by women writers such as Harriet and Sophia Lee and Amelia Opie, adapted from the Sentimental tale of the late eighteenth century in reaction against 'novels of manners', 'Gothic romances', and 'political romances' of the 1790s.[11] Despite their modest appearance, these tales represent the *embourgeoisement* of domestic and rural life as the basis for a national moral and cultural reconstruction in the Revolutionary aftermath. Hamilton's *The Cottagers of Glenburnie: A Tale for the Farmer's Ingle-nook* was published in 1808 and it too addresses major post-Revolutionary developments, including increasing class alienation, uncertainty over Britain's governability, the deepening international crisis, and especially concern for the condition of the lower classes, seen in such works as Thomas Malthus's *Essay on Population* (1798, revised 1803) and Patrick Colquhoun's *Treatise on Indigence* (1806), and numerous local and national projects to 'improve' the lower classes through education in basic literacy, distribution of Bibles and religious tracts, the 'suppression of vice', and institutions of charitable relief and social reclamation. Philanthropic aims justified efforts at ideological subjection and social control by replacing the lower-class lottery mentality with a middle-class investment mentality. Like the Edinburgh House of Industry, *The Cottagers of Glenburnie* was intended to contribute to this

---

[11] Marilyn Butler, *Maria Edgeworth: A Literary Biography* (Oxford, 1972), 198–9; Kelly, *English Fiction of the Romantic Period*, 71–4.

effort, but like Cheap Repository its form, format, and price indicate that it was to be bought by the middle classes and distributed to the 'lower ranks'.

Its political purpose is indicated by the dedication to Hector Macneill, whose *Skaith of Scotland* assimilated the popular dialect verse tradition of Robert Burns but eliminated Burns's 'licentiousness' and 'immorality', and especially his pro-Revolutionary sentiments, in order to 'reform' the lower classes while creating a 'national' Scottish identity within that of Britain—in fact a projection of middle-class culture. Hamilton claims that her 'dull prose' is beneath the dignity of poetry such as Macneill's, yet it too may interest 'the well-wishers to the improvement of their country'. First, however, she criticizes nationalism that is mere nostalgia or produces 'a blind and indiscriminating partiality for national modes, manners, and customs; and a zeal that kindles into rage at whoever dares to suppose that our country has not in every instance reached perfection' (pp. viii–ix)—both confrontational anti-Jacobin jingoism and reform-minded regional patriotism that had threatened Britain's stability in recent years. She also follows Maria Edgeworth in promoting the modernization of her part of Britain in order to eliminate social, cultural, and economic disparities that threatened the unity of state and empire. Such work of conciliation would be considered as acceptably feminine involvement in public and political affairs, yet Hamilton declares that it may accomplish more than the 'politician' or economist can:

The great mass of the people are, in their estimation, as so many teeth in the wheels of a piece of machinery, of no farther value than as they serve to facilitate its movements. No wonder if, in their eyes, a regard to the moral capacities and feelings of such implements should appear visionary and romantic. Not less so, perhaps, than to the war-contriving sage, at the time he coolly calculates how many of his countrymen may, without national inconvenience, be spared for slaughter!

Happily, there are others, to whom the prosperity of their country is no less dear, though its interests are viewed by them through a very different medium. National happiness they consider as the aggregate of the sum of individual happiness, and individual virtue.... They forget not that the pleasures of the heart, and of the understanding, as well as those of the senses, were intended by Providence to be in some degree enjoyed by all; and therefore, that in the pleasures of the heart and the understanding, all are entitled to participate. (pp. ix–xi)

Discourses conventionally gendered masculine and feminine are contrasted and the latter declared to have their special, and even superior province in subjectivity, domesticity, and individual experience that are the basis of the national interest and character. Hamilton's specific targets here are political economy ..nd utilitarianism, newly prominent factions in the professional middle-class cultural revolution, associated with both Revolutionary 'philosophy' and the Revolution's latest embodiment, the 'war-contriving sage' Bonaparte.

Thematically and formally *The Cottagers of Glenburnie* is designed to promote Hamilton's own post-Revolutionary social vision. It takes up central themes of the professional middle-class cultural critique, as redefined during the Revolutionary aftermath. It shows how decadent court culture has permeated all levels of society, from the landed gentry to rural and factory labourers, from the towns to remote villages, bringing individuals and families to the brink of ruin and opening the populace to 'Jacobinism', and requiring national reform necessarily beginning at the local level in the individual family. It takes up pre-Revolutionary projects such as Sarah Trimmer's *The Œconomy of Charity*, urging middle-class women to take their domestic expertise into local social work and policing, reinforced during the Revolution debate by Hannah More, Jane West, and others, illustrated with numerous examples in Trimmer's second edition of 1801, and now extended by Hamilton to national social reconciliation, renewal of the paternalistic social structure, and resistance to evils of urbanization and industrialization. *The Cottagers of Glenburnie* is constructed to appeal to a readership unconcerned with high art and probably suspicious of 'mere' novels. It uses familiar didactic devices such as the 'Socratic' dialogue, one-dimensional or 'humour' characters, a progressive main plot, parallel sub-plots showing characters with similar or diverging destinies, closure according to narrative justice or appropriate rewards and punishments, a protagonist of almost godlike power to transform the world around her, and a hierarchical linguistic universe centred by standard written English—rapidly becoming the cultural property and dialect of the professional middle class. At this period these devices are also characteristic of didactic writing for children and for the 'lower orders', who were seen by their 'betters' as childish or childlike.

The most prominent formal devices are characterization of the protagonist, use of language, progressive plot, and characterization of the narrator-author, and they are chosen, shaped, and interrelated so as to address such a readership and represent clearly Hamilton's social vision. The protagonist Mrs Mason (aptly named social rebuilder) is a local reformer and reconciler and therefore appropriately a woman; she is also a professional, though within acceptably feminine callings such as housekeeper, governess, and companion, and when she performs her reforming ministry in Glenburnie she has retired from employment and acts as a social volunteer. As a pragmatist she is guided by the Church of England Arminianism Hamilton adopted in the early 1790s and affirmed in her educational writings after 1800, asserting that true faith, good works, and the exercise of free will are necessary to salvation. Mrs Mason's successful reform of all ranks suggests that all have similar problems and common or parallel interests and that this process need not be sought through political revolution. At the same time, Mrs Mason's failures and the intervention of social forces and accidents of mortality beyond her control indicate the importance of free will in individual and social destiny, while relying on divine benevolence and justice in the long term. This is a post-Revolutionary vision of social reform without social conflict, in the 'national' interest.

Hamilton uses two forms of language in *The Cottagers of Glenburnie*—English and Scots. Scots is used in accord with the new, non-burlesque treatment of lower-class life and the representation of 'national' character. Hamilton had used Scots in her youthful writing and expressed her patriotic feelings toward it in a letter of 1801 to Hector Macneill, claiming that its 'simplicity' is 'infinitely better adapted' to descriptions of nature 'than the cold refinement of modern language', and hoping that the work of Macneill and Burns will soon make 'the study of *gude braid Scotch*' a part of upper- and middle-class education.[12] Like many professional intellectuals at the time she was concerned at the loss of a separate 'national' identity and power through loss of the distinctive 'national' language. But the standard written language of Scotland, as of the rest of Britain, was English. To represent Scottish 'national' identity within Britain and commanded by the professional middle class, Hamilton uses a written form of spoken Scots, but distributed almost entirely to lower- or lower middle-class characters and subordinated within the text to the standard English of the omniscient third-person narrator, a figure for the author who, implicitly, alone commands both 'national' dialects.

This linguistic structure connects with characterization of protagonist and narrator by implying a hierarchy in which narrator and reader are

---

[12] Benger, *Memoirs of Hamilton*, ii. 12–13.

on the same narrative plane, 'above' the dialect speakers. Mrs Mason 'speaks' the same dialect of standard written English as the narrator, clearly indicating her place in the novel's hierarchy of truth and value. The narrator is further characterized for the reader by energetic and mildly ironic tone of description and sharp evaluative commentary on the characters and incidents. Mrs Mason is implicated in these devices, too, especially when the narrator uses free indirect discourse to report Mrs Mason's thoughts and feelings, establishing another basis of identity between her and the narrator. The plot of re-education is managed by these two characters, within the novel by Mrs Mason and for the novel by the 'author', an implied character constructed as the narrator.

Like many 'tales', *Glenburnie* opens *in medias res*. Mrs Mason, returning to Scotland from England, stops with her friends the Stewarts on her way to retirement after a lifetime of service to the upper-class Longlands family. Mr Stewart is a virtuous professional man, formerly the Longlands' steward (hence his name). But his two daughters, Bell and Mary, have contrasting characters (as their names indicate), the former spoiled by friendship with the courtly Mrs Flinders and the latter educated to be like her father. In the first third of the novel Mrs Mason tells Mary, her ideological and cultural daughter, the story of her life from humble beginnings to servant and then governess to the children of Lord and Lady Longlands. Through self-culture and self-discipline she became a professionalized domestic woman and as such saved the Longlands family and their estate from ruin by reforming their insubordinate servants, their courtly domestic intrigues, their aristocratic extravagance, and their false social relations. But the Longlands estate was inherited by a son spoiled by his courtly mother, Lord Longlands' first wife; the family disperses and Mrs Mason is forced into retirement. This part of the story can be read as an allegory of Britain's history in the eighteenth century, from courtly decadence, through reform and progress culminating in the reign of George III, to imminent return of court government led by the decadent Prince of Wales and his social and political followers. Mrs Mason's actions in the rest of the novel show the way forward to social reform without political revolution, through the feminization of private and community life.

Mrs Mason retires to the remote village Glenburnie to live on the proceeds of stocks acquired during her lifetime of professional domestic service—apt symbol of her commitment to the investment mentality. Her friends are surprised, since Glenburnie is notorious locally for its disorderly and vulgar inhabitants and consequent dilapidation, dirt, and poverty. Scotland and the Celtic fringe had a similar reputation with the English, as did Britain's overseas empire. Mrs Mason finds Glenburnie to be as she was told; she also finds that the cottagers of Glenburnie are unwilling to take responsibility for their situation. Most blame it on some secular or religious version of the lottery mentality—custom, luck, fate, predestination. Others blame it on their 'betters', and take up Jacobin doctrines of 'liberty and equality'. Mrs Mason rejects custom, Presbyterian predestination, and Jacobin sedition; as the basis of her reform programme she enunciates an Anglican theology of true faith, good works, and free will. When Mr MacClarty stoutly maintains that ' "We maun trust a' to the grace of God' ", Mrs Mason replies:

'God forbid that we should put trust in ought beside . . . but if we hope for a miraculous interposition of divine grace . . . without taking the means that God has appointed, our hope does not spring from faith, but from presumption. It is just as if you were neither to plough, nor sow your fields, and yet expect that Providence would bless you with an abundant crop.' (p. 186)

Later Mrs Mason confronts the secular version of the MacClartys' Calvinist theology of predestination when she tells them that taking 'trouble', or in local dialect 'being fashed', becomes habitual and saves labour. Her hostess responds, ' "Ilka place has just its ain gait, . . . and ye needna think that ever we'll learn your's. And indeed to be plain wi' you, cusin, I think you have our mony fykes' " (p. 205). The phrases 'Ilka place has just its ain gait' and 'I canna be fashed wi' it' recur throughout the novel, becoming figures for a popular culture relying on custom and a lottery mentality and corresponding to the popular Presbyterianism of the Scottish lower classes. Indeed, the novel made these phrases into popular expressions with the reading public. But as Mrs Mason observes, 'this *fear of being fashed* is the great bar to all improvement' (p. 206). She proclaims an ideology of 'improvement', demonstrates the method required to achieve it, and organizes an investment economy to sustain it. Ideology, practice, and institution are validated by her Arminian theology, seconded by the authoritative figure of the good pastor, Mr Gourlay, who assists Mrs Mason's work.

Mrs Mason exemplifies this theology by intervening in history as the transmission over generations of false consciousness including custom, the lottery mentality, predestinarian apathy, and courtly intrigue and emulation, which either sustain court government by disarming resistance or encourage 'Jacobinism' by leaving no alternative but violent resistance. Mrs Mason emphasizes the importance of free will guided by 'reason', or the analytical, critical, reconstructive mentality characteristic of the virtuous professional. She demonstrates her programme for local and thus national reconstruction by relationships with two contrasting families, the MacClartys and Morrisons, and through them with all the 'cottagers of Glenburnie'—implicitly all residents of Britain and its empire.

The feckless, vulgar, unteachable MacClartys are Mrs Mason's relations and first hosts in Glenburnie. The dirt and disorder of their household are detailed by the narrator with a comic energy characteristic of eighteenth-century novelists such as Hamilton's fellow Scot, Smollett. Such 'domestic realism' was becoming a leading feature of post-Revolutionary fiction, serving a renewed taste for fiction of common life in reaction to novels of manners in high life and 'Gothic romances' of the exotic, and to what was seen as the merely theoretical character of 'political romances' of the 1790s. Thus such 'realism' has a polemical and political edge, partly through being figural as well as representational, for the dirt and disorder of the MacClartys' house are both the result of and correlative to the moral and social disorder in the family divided within by conflicts of gender and generation and without by competition with neighbours. These divisions make the MacClartys resistant to Mrs Mason's reform programme and it is only when Mr MacClarty dies and Mrs MacClarty is 'incapacitated' by illness that Mrs Mason is able to reform the household economy, beginning, significantly, with the younger females:

The girls, though at first refractory, and often inclined to rebel, were gradually brought to order; and finding they had no one to make excuses for their disobedience, quietly performed their allotted tasks. They began to taste the pleasure of praise, and encouraged by approbation, endeavoured to deserve it; so that though their tempers had been too far spoiled to be brought at once into subjection, Mrs Mason hoped that, by steadiness, she should succeed in reforming them. (pp. 258–9)

But Robert MacClarty, 'who had ever shewn a sulky antipathy to Mrs Mason', inherits the farm and the girls 'relaxed into indolence, and became as pert and obstreperous as ever'. In language reminiscent of the Revolution debate, the narrator observes, 'Mrs Mason saw that the reign of anarchy was fast approaching' (p. 278).

Reluctantly she finally leaves the MacClartys to lodge with William and Peggy Morrison:

They were poor; and therefore the small sum she could afford to pay, might to them be particularly useful. They were humble, and therefore would not refuse to be instructed in matters which they had never before had any opportunity to learn. She might then do good to them and to their children; and where she could do most good, there did Mrs Mason think it would be most for her happiness to go. (pp. 281–2)

The Morrisons are poor because William became infected with social emulation and ambition. He confesses to Mrs Mason:

'had I been contented to go on with my business, as my father did before me, on a scale within my means, my profits, though small, would have been certain. But I wished to raise my wife and bairns above their station; and God, who saw the pride of my heart, has punished me.' (p. 286)

Pride gives a theological cast to William's ideological error, but it is used throughout the novel to describe what readers would recognize as social emulation leading to a fall.

The significance of this error is developed further when Mrs Mason is called away to Gowan-brae, the home of the Stewarts, whose daughter Bell, misled into social ambition by her courtly friend Mrs Flinders, has married the extravagant and ostentatious 'Captain' Mollins. But Mrs Mason recognizes Mollins as a tradesman's son whose '"ambition to be genteel led him into the society of the showy and dissipated'" where he was soon ruined, and he married Bell Stewart thinking she was an heiress. Nevertheless he loves her and has a kind heart, and Mrs Mason mediates a family reconciliation. Mr Stewart is delighted to learn that his son-in-law is middle class after all, and promises to help him in business. Stewart blames the Flinders, who are vulgar upstarts themselves, and tells his daughter Bell:

'I do not despise the Flinders's on account of their want of birth, but on account of their paltry attempts at concealing the meanness of their origin by parade and ostentation. It is them, and such as them, who, by giving a false bent to ambition, have undermined our national virtues, and destroyed our national character; and they have done this, by leading such as you to connect all notions of happiness, with the gratification of vanity, and to undervalue the respect that attends on integrity and wisdom.' (pp. 342–3)

As elsewhere in this and Hamilton's earlier novels, it is the women who are first seduced by courtly 'parade and ostentation' and spread the evil to their menfolk and thence through all classes in society.

Having established social harmony on the foundation of middle-class values at Gowan-brae, Mrs Mason returns to her work reforming Glenburnie. She improves the Morrisons' domestic economy and, following Mr Gourlay's suggestion, puts William Morrison in place of the old schoolmaster, a pedant and thus a bad teacher. Such criticism of the 'mere' learning practised by men is found elsewhere in Hamilton's work and is common in women writers conscious of their socially acceptable yet subordinate role as popularizers of learning for practical, everyday use. Gourlay and Mrs Mason direct Morrison's efforts and reorganize the school according to the Lancasterian monitorial system, emphasizing order, discipline, and subordination as the necessary context for constructing the pupils' subjective selves for 'obedience and self-government'. These are in turn necessary for the pupils to become efficient workers later in life (pp. 285–6). The connection between education and the rural socio-economic order is reflected in the school's organization:

Each of the three classes were . . . divided into three distinct orders; viz. landlord, tenants, and under-tenants. The landlord prescribed the lesson which was to be received as rent from his tenants: Each of the tenants had one or two under-tenants, who were in like manner bound to pay him a certain portion of reading, or spelling lesson; and when the class was called up, the landlord was responsible to the master, as superior lord, not only for his own diligence, but for the diligence of his vassals. The landlord who appeared to have neglected his duty, or who permitted the least noise or disturbance in his class, was degraded to the rank of an under-tenant. (pp. 387–8)

This system applies only to the boys.

The girls are educated to be domestic producers and Mrs Mason teaches them herself, since their character will determine that of Glenburnie. In principle and method the system she adopts resembles that advanced by Wollstonecraft in *A Vindication of the Rights of Woman*, designed to imbue women with the same powers of critical thought and consequent self-discipline essential to the education and careers of professional men. Mrs Mason has concluded that the relative intellectual inferiority of girls to boys of the same age in Glenburnie is due to the fact 'that their education had been more neglected', not so much in schooling as its application in everyday life. Boys were called upon to use observation and analytic reasoning learned in school in their occupations out of it but the girls were not; accordingly, Mrs Mason endeavours 'to rouse the sleeping faculties' by engaging the girls in critical appraisal of each others' work, which is predominantly domestic in nature, in effect professionalizing the 'household work' to which most 'girls in their station' are destined by subjecting it to the same intellectual 'operations' and 'exercise' required by boys in their work. The result is the girls' 'improvement in personal neatness and good-breeding' (pp. 391–2).

This 'revolution in female manners', in Wollstonecraft's phrase, spreads from the school to the village and beyond. It also coincides with a domestic revolution on the Longlands estate. The sudden death of the wastrel Lord Longlands leaves the estate to his younger brother, aptly named Mr Meriton, the man of merit whom Mrs Mason had saved from a fire in his infancy and whom she had taught when he was a boy. As a result of this change, Mrs Mason 'received a great addition to her consequence in the eyes of her neighbours', and the new Lord Longlands' approval of the revolution in Glenburnie validates her 'wisdom'. Patronage may be useful after all, and the revolution in Glenburnie spreads. The school is soon 'increased by scholars from all parts of the country':

To have been educated at the school of Glenburnie was considered as an ample recommendation to a servant, and implied a security for truth, diligence, and honesty. And fortunate was the lad pronounced, whose bride could boast of the tokens of Mrs Mason's favour and approbation; for never did these fail to be followed by a conduct, that ensured happiness, and prosperity. (pp. 399–400)

The schoolmaster, Morrison, soon pays his creditors, 'and from that moment he seemed to enjoy the blessings of life with double relish', and Mrs Mason allows his daughters 'to succeed her in the charge of the school'.

By contrast, the MacClarty family disintegrates. Robert is tricked into marrying a smuggler's daughter and quarrels with his mother. She enters factory work with her daughters in a nearby town, where Meg MacClarty is seduced and abandoned. Having been 'exposed to disgrace' in her local community, she is forced to seek 'service' in Edinburgh 'and was never heard of more'—implying that she became a prostitute. Throughout the novel, as in Henry Sydney's account of Scotland in *Memoirs of Modern Philosophers*, towns and factories are seen as places of moral, social, and political corruption, in part reflecting the experience of the 1790s, when manufacturing towns such as Glasgow were hotbeds of plebeian 'Jacobinism', attributed to the relative independence afforded working men and women by factory wages. As the women of Glenburnie put it, ' "Glasgow, by a' accounts, is an unco place for wuckedness: but than wha can wonder, whar there's sae mony factories'" (p. 219). Meg MacClarty disappears into Edinburgh, the more fashionable city, but her fate still represents the interconnection of moral and political transgression; the fact that once there she 'was never heard of more' suggests a loss of social identity resulting from such transgression. In the second edition Hamilton added a letter from a traveller who found Jean MacClarty and her husband running a roadside inn of predictable squalor, again described with Smollettian comic vigour. Domestic disorder reproduces itself and disappears or escapes into the public sphere.

Mrs Mason herself 'at length acceded to the wishes of her friends, and took possession of the pretty cottage, which had been built for her by Lord Longlands, in the midst of the pleasure grounds at Hill Castle', where 'she tranquilly spent the last days of a useful life; looking to the past with gratitude, and to the future with the full assurance of the hope which is mingled with peace and joy' (p. 402). Having instilled Hill Castle, Gowan-brae, and Glenburnie with her feminized version of professional ideology and culture, Mrs Mason receives her earthly reward and merely awaits its final validation after death. The relationship between Hill Castle, Gowan-brae, and Glen-burnie remains unchanged, like the patriarchal and paternalist structure of rural society, but revolutionized from within by a woman symboli-cally stationed in a paradise on earth, between past and future, earth and heaven—like Hamilton herself, the mediator between them. As promised in the novel's Dedication, Hamilton has shown how a woman may revolutionize the revolution while remaining within 'her' sphere, and thus accomplish what men, in their public and political sphere, apparently could not.

Its publisher had been reluctant to take *Glenburnie*, but it became one of the books of the season—at first with middle-class readers rather than 'the lower orders'. The *Scots Magazine* reported in September 1808 that it had 'excited an extraordinary sensation' in Edinburgh.[13] According to Hamilton's biographer 'the demand for the work . . . induced the publishers to print a cheap edition, which circulated to the Highlands, where even the genius of the mountains'—supposedly resistant to innovation—'confessed the influence of good sense, and the

---

[13] *Scots Magazine*, 70 (Sept. 1808), 678–9.

importance of domestic economy.' It was read with such 'avidity' in Stirlingshire that one of Hamilton's poorer friends was able to make some money 'by lending her single copy for a penny each reader'. Another friend later claimed:

Perhaps few books have been more extensively useful. The peculiar humour of this work, by irritating our national pride, has produced a wonderful spirit of improvement. The cheap edition is to be found in every village-library; and Mrs. M[a]cClarty's example has *provoked* many a Scottish housewife into cleanliness and good order.[14]

The novel was widely read in England, too: ' "I canna be fash'd" became a popular phrase; and the name of Mrs. M[a]cClarty resounded in the polished circles of fashion, of elegance, and beauty.'[15] It was one of Maria Edgeworth's favourite novels.[16]

Many reviewers and readers, English and Scottish alike, placed its 'realism' in the vanguard of a literary revolution. The English *Lady's Monthly Museum* found Hamilton's 'picture of the national character-istic of the Scottish peasantry' to be 'both accurate and amusing'. The *Scots Magazine* thought the picture would not apply to 'the opulent farmers of Lothian and Berwickshire', but certainly 'to the little farmers in remote districts, and to most of the peasantry'. Anna Lætitia Barbauld, the leading woman intellectual of English Dissent, praised Hamilton's realism for both rhetorical effectiveness and femi-nine delicacy: 'perhaps few writers, without "overstepping the modesty of nature," can produce scenes equally comic, or, without departing from the airiness of narration, administer counsel equally weighty.' The *Edinburgh Review* declared that *Glenburnie* contained 'as admirable a picture of the Scot[t]ish peasantry' as Edgeworth's *Castle Rackrent* and *Popular Tales* did of the Irish, 'and rivals them, not only in the general truth of the delineations, and in the cheerfulness and practical good sense of the lessons which they convey, but in the nice discrimina-tion of national character, and the skill with which a dramatic represen-tation of humble life is saved from caricature and absurdity'. The *Edinburgh* recognized that 'humble life', for centuries considered mate-rial mainly for comic or burlesque literature, was now being given serious and not necessarily sentimental treatment. The *Critical Review* found this treatment feminine in character, the story 'blended . . . with

[14] Quoted in Benger, *Memoirs of Hamilton*, i. 196–7.
[15] Ibid. i. 184.
[16] Butler, *Maria Edgeworth*, 199.

much sweetness, good sense, and sound morality', and the characters 'drawn to the life, with much force of outline' but also 'with a delicate discrimination in the colouring'. A decade later, after male novelists and poets had endowed such realism with 'literary' status, Elizabeth Benger insisted that Hamilton gave it characteristics one might expect from a woman writer: 'Glenburnie affords a striking example that deep and intense interest may be excited by a narrative composed of the most simple and even homely materials, but which exhibits the real workings of the human heart.'[17]

Reviewers saw Hamilton's handling of dialect as central to the novel's cultural politics, for good or ill. The *Scots Magazine* thought Hamilton had performed a national service by exhibiting 'perhaps the purest colloquial Scots that ever appeared in print', free from admixture of English, thus enabling 'the language and manners of our country, with all their imperfections', to be 'handed down to posterity in full purity'. The Englishwoman Anna Lætitia Barbauld found the dialect an obstacle, though intelligible enough 'to gratify every reader of taste, and every lover of humour'. The *Edinburgh Review* found it 'a specimen of the purest and most characteristic Scotch which we have lately met with in writing' but thought it could be 'intelligible' to only a 'small number of readers' and admitted 'a sort of malicious pleasure' in thinking that English readers would not understand it unless they 'take the trouble thoroughly to familiarize themselves with our ancient and venerable dialect'.[18] This attitude would have confirmed Hamilton's fear that such representations of 'national' culture would increase differences within Britain. The *Scots Magazine* thought the novel's portayal of the Scots would, unintentionally perhaps, reinforce such divisive 'national' stereotypes and prejudices, and portrayed the relation between England and Scotland as a war in which the 'fortress' had been betrayed to the 'enemy' by a 'strong a part of the garrison'—its innermost, domestic quarter.

The century-long debate in Scotland over the benefits of union with England was redirected in the Revolutionary aftermath by continuing political instability and the problem of harnessing the new nationalism,

---

[17] *Lady's Monthly Museum*, NS 5 (Sept. 1808), 138; *Scots Magazine*, 70 (Sept. 1808), 679; *Monthly Review*, NS 60 (Oct. 1809), 217; *Edinburgh Review*, 12 (July 1808), 401–2; *Critical Review*, 3rd ser., 15 (Dec. 1808), 421; Benger, *Memoirs of Hamilton*, i. 185–6.

[18] *Scots Magazine*, 70 (Sept. 1808), 678–9; *Monthly Review*, NS 60 (Oct. 1809), 217; *Edinburgh Review*, 12 (July 1808), 402–3.

supposedly inspired by Revolutionary ideas, to the kind of cultural, social, political, and economic modernization that would strengthen Britain's resistance to French imperialism. The Scottish professional middle class led this drive to eradicate negative, pre-modern aspects of the Scottish 'national character', attributed to 'prejudice' and stubborn attachment to 'custom' and 'tradition'. It was generally felt that Hamilton's novel would reinforce this effort. The *Edinburgh Review* thought such a 'reformation' unlikely to be effected by *Glenburnie* alone:

But a strong current of improvement runs at present through all Scotland, and a much smaller impulse than would once have been necessary, will now throw the peasantry within the sphere of its action. Besides, *our* cottagers [unlike those elsewhere in Britain] are reading and reasoning animals; and are more likely perhaps to be moved from their old habits by hints and suggestions which they themselves may glean up from a book, than by the more officious and insulting interference of a living reformer.

The *Satirist* expected 'extensive benefit to all classes of society' because 'In its affecting pages the rich may read a clear statement of the best mode to ensure popularity, the moderate in fortune and desire may trace the best source of domestic comfort, the poor may perceive the best way to independence, and even the indigent may learn how to grow content'.[19] But the *Edinburgh Review* also thought the book's form and price would limit its usefulness 'to our peasants at home' unless Hamilton would 'strike out all the scenes in upper life' and 'print the remainder upon coarse paper, at such a price as may enable the volume to find its way into the cottage library'.[20] Such claims for the social effect of books like *The Cottagers of Glenburnie* may seem exaggerated, but they were reprinted in editions of varying cheapness well into the period that saw the 'rise of respectable society' in all classes. This fact suggests that if such books did not directly inspire social and cultural change, they at least reinforced decisions to change that individuals, families, and classes were taking for other reasons.[21]

Hamilton pressed on with ideological and cultural reformation of all classes. *Exercises in Religious Knowledge; for the Instruction of Young*

[19] *Edinburgh Review*, 12 (July 1808), 410; *The Satirist*, 3 (Dec. 1808), 542–3.
[20] *Edinburgh Review*, 12 (July 1808), 402.
[21] Thomas W. Laqueur, *Religion and Respectability: Sunday Schools and Working Class Culture 1780–1850* (New Haven, Conn., 1976); F. Michael L. Thompson, *The Rise of Respectable Society: A Social History of Victorian Britain 1830–1900* (London, 1988).

Persons (1809) is a catechism 'originally composed for the use of young persons brought up in a charitable institution'—her Edinburgh House of Industry[22]—but now offered 'to the consideration of those of higher rank'. The implication is provocative, calling for a democracy of subjectivity: 'Whatever be the station, it must be of importance to impress the heart and understanding at an early period, with a sense of individual interest in the scripture doctrines of salvation; as until they are thus brought home to the conscience, there is little room to expect that they will have any powerful influence on the conduct' (p. vi). Such restructuring of the subjective self is again to be achieved by avoidance of rote learning in favour of understanding, for mere memorization is not incorporated in the self, leaves subjective space free for undesirable kinds of self-construction, and so enables the pupil to elude the policing of the self by the instructor. In *Exercises* the 'Teacher' delivers a discourse followed by question and answer with the pupil—an asymmetrical dialogue in which one side is always right and has all the answers, a dramatization of knowledge as power. Yet *Exercises* also covertly challenges that power-knowledge as gendered discourse: in overall form it is an analytical outline of the Bible, enabling Hamilton to present her own interpretation of the Word and thus to practise theology, a discourse conventionally gendered masculine, under the guise of the acceptably feminine discourse of religious education.

Hamilton's confidence in carrying on this kind of work and recommending it to other women seems to have derived from her own self-construction as woman *and* intellectual. Throughout her life she was aware that intellectual pursuits were widely considered unfeminine, and like such friends as Joanna Baillie and Maria Edgeworth, she successfully maintained a literary career without sacrificing the appearance of domesticity. Hector Macneill mingled 'feminine' and 'masculine' traits in his description of Hamilton when he recalled never having known a woman 'with a finer mind, a warmer heart, a clearer head, or a sounder understanding', but he was particularly impressed with her powers of critical thought: 'Such was the clearness of her conceptions, and such the quickness of her discrimination, that she seldom or never hesitated a moment to give her opinion decidedly on any subject introduced,—and what is equally remarkable, seldom or never were her opinions erroneous.'[23] These powers of 'mind' were

[22] Benger, *Memoirs of Hamilton*, i. 183 n.   [23] Ibid. 238–9.

the basis of professional middle-class work and culture; they were claimed for women by Revolutionary feminists of the 1790s in order to end gender inequality vitiating the professional middle-class cultural revolution; and in the Revolutionary aftermath they were prescribed for women by writers from More to Hamilton in order to sustain the cultural revolution without threatening social stability or national unity. Like many women, however, Hamilton found that the stress of sustaining a contradictory identity caused periodic psychosomatic illness and doubts about her intellectual and artistic ability, such as her delay in completing *Letters of a Hindoo Rajah*, her failure to complete her analysis of Paul's Epistle to the Romans, and her inability, due to 'doubt and diffidence', to complete a novel she sketched in 1813.[24] This experience stimulated a philosophical interest in the nature of subjectivity, and the 'chosen companions of her private hours' were Dugald Stewart's *Philosophy of the Human Mind* (1792) and *Outlines of Moral Philosophy* (1793), Archibald Alison's *Essay on Taste* (1790), and William Paley's *Moral and Political Philosophy* (1785) and *Natural Theology* (1802).[25] Like Wollstonecraft, Hays, Edgeworth, and other women intellectuals of her time, she sought to validate her sense of self through Enlightenment epistemology and moral philosophy, together with a strongly personal religious outlook.

To this end she kept a private journal consisting 'of a series of papers, composed with a view to assist the writer in the exercise of self-examination, which she considered as the basis of moral and religious improvement'. Significantly, she kept this journal from 1788, just after her brother's arrival from India, to just before her death, and in it she developed a 'mental philosophy' similar to the materialism she had satirized during the Revolutionary decade, based on the belief that circumstances form character and that the authentic self is private and domestic, in contrast to the social self. 'Women have more frequent opportunities' for observing this self than men do, she argues in her journal, 'but women seldom generalise: their attention is solely occupied with little particulars, from which they draw no general inferences', though women who 'are more capable' have the 'power' to gain considerable 'insight into the mind and disposition' by domestic observation alone.[26] The restriction of women to the domestic sphere deprives them of training in the professional's ability to generalize, but it is precisely this restricted experience that gives women their peculiar

---

[24] Ibid. 216.   [25] Ibid. 221.   [26] Ibid. 270–1.

'power'—a superior understanding of the authentic being of others. A similar point was made by women writers from Wollstonecraft, Hays, and Williams to Edgeworth and Austen. Hamilton felt she possessed this power herself, and believed she could 'trace the mental peculiarities of individuals to circumstances over which they had no control', such as education and social and economic conditions, for 'whatever state of mind these circumstances tend to produce, will, by the frequent recurrence of them, become habitual; and when thus habitual, all new ideas will be rejected that do not accord or correspond with it'.[27] This confers on women skilled in subjective analysis, such as herself, a unique and valuable insight into the public, political sphere in an age of transgressive individualism.

This argument informed all Hamilton's work but she advances it with new clarity and emphasis in *A Series of Popular Essays, Illustrative of Principles Essentially Connected with the Improvement of the Understanding, the Imagination, and the Heart* (1813). As the title suggests, by popularizing 'mental philosophy' it again treats a conventionally masculine discourse in an acceptably 'feminine way'. This aim is implied in the dedication to Archibald Alison, the Scottish philosopher, addressed here as minister of an Episcopal Chapel in Edinburgh rather than as a philosopher, for Hamilton again feminizes Scottish Enlightenment epistemology by fusing it with Anglican (in Scotland, Episcopalian) ethical theology. She again disclaims any intention to transgress discursive boundaries, ironically assuring her readers that though she discusses 'the science of mind' she does not mean 'to be dull, deep, and metaphysical', for 'as it is not in my power to be very deep, I have taken care to be as little dull as possible'. Her 'conclusions' and illustrations have been drawn from 'the objects of our familiar observation'—the conventionally acknowledged scope of women's knowledge—justifying the term 'popular' in the title (vol. ii, p. xvi). She claims to be content with the established female role of popularizing 'the observations or discoveries of superior minds'—implicitly men—though she also claims only partial dependence on them, 'not having been as yet convinced, that there is any subject within the range of human intellect, on which the capacity of any intelligent Being of either sex, may not be profitably, or, at least, innocently employed' (p. xxxi). In fact, her aims were shared by a number of women writers in the Revolutionary aftermath. First she aims to recuperate 'philosophy'

---

[27] Benger, *Memoirs of Hamilton*, i. 231.

from the odium it acquired during the Revolution debate: 'if it can be proved that a knowledge of the various powers and faculties of the human mind may be rendered essentially instrumental in confirming our religious faith, and in improving our moral qualities, no science can be put in competition with it, either as interesting or useful'. Secondly, this science is necessary both to understand the 'selfish principle' behind post-Revolutionary increase in commercialism and luxury and to engage the opposing, divinely implanted 'benevolent affections', or conventionally feminine values of social sympathy and philanthropy. Finally, this 'science' is required for extending 'the benefits of education to the lower orders of society' (p. xlii), thus ensuring social stability and national harmony. To make her arguments more accessible she planned illustrations from 'history, sacred and profane', but abandoned them because the book would have become even more expensive than its £1.4s.—hardly a 'popular' price.

In fact the book is a philosophical rationale in laywoman's language for Hamilton's post-Revolutionary programme of social transformation. The first of the five essays, on 'the utility of the study of the mind' and its relation to educational reform, is a theoretical justification for the rest; the second essay deals with Hamilton's favourite idea that 'attention' is the key to intellectual development and thus the focus for education; and the third essay relates this argument to the development of 'imagination' and 'taste'. But the centre of Hamilton's politics is in the last two essays, 'on the propensity to magnify the idea of self' and development of the providentially implanted 'benevolent affections', arguing that the critical thought essential to professional work is the basis of liberty and political stability for a society divided by class, gender, and 'party'. Thus the core of the book is a social psychology of power, a theory of the politics of ideology and culture. Hamilton argues that the basis of the 'selfish principle' is the 'love of power', diffused through society by emulation as the less powerful magnify themselves by identifying with the more powerful. This argument was long established in critiques of court government, but the recent history of France and Britain raised the question of how this principle operates in democracies or republics. Hamilton argues that each faction tries to attain complete and permanent power over the others, becoming a despotism. But 'this lamentable conclusion of the history of a free people' may be prevented by 'the intellectual energy that inevitably results from a free exercise of the intellectual powers' (ii. 19)—another way of describing the professional middle-class discourse of critical thought. Hamilton then postulates a historical dialectic between the 'love of power' and 'intellectual energy', concluding that 'the propensity to magnify the idea of self, appears indeed to have been the prime agent in the revolutions of empires'.

For magnifying the self through power requires controlling the thoughts of the ruled and produces the desire of the ruled to identify with the ruler. Paradoxically, this leads in turn to the decline of 'intellectual powers' of the ruled, the basis of that national glory ('wealth, grandeur, and power, produced by the industry, wisdom, taste, and valour of the people') by which the ruler's self is magnified (ii. 27). Similarly, the upper classes magnify their own 'glory' by adopting 'the tastes and opinions which prevail in the court' and, consequently lacking 'any exercise to the noblest faculties of the mind', 'degenerate into a race of puny triflers' (ii. 30). Here 'noblest' subverts social rank with intellectual merit in an obvious reference to both the *ancien régime* in France and the Regency in Britain. Hamilton concludes that the form of government best suited to the national interest is a constitutional monarchy with 'the powers and prerogatives of royalty so accurately defined, as necessarily to lay a restraint on that selfish principle' which leads to national decline, and giving 'the benevolent principle' 'perpetual exercise' in the monarch's 'breast'; this advantage was 'conferred on the kings of Great Britain by the Revolution' of 1688 (ii. 33).

Hamilton goes on to consider gender difference as a form of 'magnifying the self' through 'party' and 'an instance sufficiently extensive, as it comprehends the whole of the human race', for 'every individual of each sex' is, 'in his or her mind, identified with the whole of the sex to which he or she individually belongs'. This implicitly explains Revolutionary feminism. Women of 'strong feelings and generous hearts' become 'champions' of their own sex and 'anxious, not only to defend the character, but to extend the privileges of the sex with which the idea of self is particularly connected', they consider 'every circumstance which marks their situation in society' as a 'grievance', blaming the other sex for their own ills 'when blame probably attaches in equal portions to both' (ii. 81). Hamilton gives her own historical sociology of women's oppression, from subjection of women by mere physical force in the 'savage state' to intellectual subjection in court societies, arising from the desire of men to magnify themselves. Gender oppression is similar to political despotism and requires the same remedy—free exercise of professionalized critical thought.

Clearly, *Popular Essays* is, despite its modest title and ostensible subject, a very ambitious book—nothing less than a political theory of ideology, culture, and politics designed to account for the past quarter-century of revolutionary upheaval—including Revolutionary feminism—and recommend a way to sustain necessary and desirable social transformation without resort to such upheaval. But reviewers were as condescending to Hamilton's feminization of political philosophy as they had been to her feminizations of epistemology, theology, and historiography. The *Monthly Review* calls her 'not unknown as a novelist' though 'still more distinguished as a preceptress', but accuses her of listening 'too much to the metaphysicians', wrongly attributing intellect to education rather than heredity, and writing a book that is 'prosing because it studiously shuns the picturesque or brilliant colouring of poetic eloquence', supposedly more appropriate for a woman writer. The *Critical Review* gave unusually prominent, lengthy, and detailed consideration for such a work, especially by a woman, and compared 'three distinguished ladies' of England, Scotland, and Ireland, known for their devotion to the 'improvement' of 'their fellow creatures': 'Mrs. More is grave, sensible, and discriminative; Miss Edgeworth fertile of invention, witty, and humourous; and Mrs. Hamilton calm, observant, and metaphysical.' Yet 'nothing is more fatiguing than too much good sense', and the reviewer finds Hamilton's book well-intentioned and an honour to her sex, but 'more allusive and illustrative, than original or profound', self-contradictory, often unclear, and restating the obvious.[28]

Popular Essays was followed by a far less ambitious work, though one that sketched out the practical basis for her feminized social revolution. *Hints Addressed to the Patrons and Directors of Schools* (1815) is a handbook for application of Hamilton's ideas on education, dedicated to the Edinburgh Education Society, addressed to the educational movement for social control of the lower ranks, and ostensibly based on Pestalozzi's educational theories, but in fact aimed at the growing number of middle-class women who were engaging openly in political activity through various philanthropic movements. Hamilton assumes that 'the wisdom and eligibility of teaching the children of the poor to read and write' are widely accepted and the only question is the appropriate means. She holds out the example of Scotland, where

---

[28] *Monthly Review*, NS 74 (Aug. 1814), 402–6; *Critical Review*, 4th ser., 5 (Mar. 1814), 225–41.

lower-class literacy was well established, with 'moral effects' 'exhibited in the conduct of our countrymen in every quarter of the globe' (p. 3)—reference to the Scots' contribution to the just-concluded wars with Revolutionary and Napoleonic France. During the 1790s there were claims that the literacy of Scottish artisans had opened them to Paine and 'Jacobinism', but Hamilton blames urbanization and industrialization (p. 6) and aims 'to effect such a radical improvement in the intellect, temper, and dispositions of the hundreds of children who may be assembled under the same roof, as will, when converted into habits, render them good and useful members of society, promote their interests in this world, and lead to the attainment of everlasting happiness in the world to come' (p. 76). She condemns 'those who take no farther interest in the education of the lower orders than as it affords additional security to property' (p. 144 n). In laying out her own method she plays the mediator between contending supporters of the Bell and Lancaster monitorial systems and insists that careful management and domestic reinforcement of the programme are more important than theoretical niceties. She again opposes mere rote learning for 'exercise' in 'principles' until they become 'habits', and seeks confirmation in Pestalozzi's method (also promoted by the Edgeworths) for adapting instruction to the growth of the child's mind, abolishing artificial inducements of reward and punishment, and establishing a relation of 'domestic affection' between pupil and teacher.

Hamilton assigns women a special place in this feminized, domesticated educational system but insists that they must first be professionalized by intellectual training and religious belief, or ideological discipline, if they are 'to enlarge their sphere of usefulness, and to extend, beyond the narrow precincts of the domestic roof, the beneficial influence of maternal solicitude and maternal tenderness'. For, Hamilton claims, women have 'instituted and endowed' more than three-quarters of the small charity schools in Britain and Ireland and almost all those established for girls (pp. 42–3). Yet such projects are bedevilled by gender and class difference because women volunteers too often defer to the men who are usually appointed heads of these institutions. 'Is it in these enlightened times to be supposed,' she demands, 'that women of good sense and good education are so incompetent to judge or to act, that the choice and application of proper means for the education of their own sex cannot properly be committed to them?' (pp. 74–5). Men also interfere in the administration of schools to distribute '*patronage*,—the root of many evils', in the appointment of teachers and other employees (p. 177). The result is that such institutions fail, as evidenced by the claim that 'a vast proportion' of the women who fall into prostitution 'have been brought up in charitable institutions, endowed and supported for the very purpose of preserving them in virtue' (p. 156). Hamilton ignores the possibility that prostitution may be a form of social rebellion by women subjected to incarceration and social control by their 'betters'. She argues that these institutions fail because they provide neither the 'exercise' of mind necessary for moral independence and the religious principles to bolster it, nor the practical skills needed to obtain 'honest' employment. Even needlework, a staple of training in such schools, including Hamilton's Edinburgh House of Industry, is taught as a mere mechanical skill rather than as a branch of 'that cultivation of the moral and intellectual faculties, which is essential to the performance of every duty' (p. 127). On the same principle she offers 'Examples of Questions Calculated to Develop the Faculties of the Infant Mind', the kind of catechism promoted by Evangelicals and others to ensure that the right 'principles' have been internalized in the pupil's subjective being, thus protecting him or her against both upper-class courtly values and the plebeian lottery mentality and subjecting him or her to a diminutive version of professional middle-class culture.

This was Hamilton's last work published in her lifetime. Its views were by now shared by many throughout Britain, in movements ranging from Evangelicalism and Utilitarianism to Romanticism. But as the great cycle of revolutions and wars begun in 1789 was drawing to an end, Hamilton, like many others, turned for understanding of it to the Bible and especially the Book of Revelation.[29] Hamilton was probably aware that the plebeian woman prophet Joanna Southcott (who died in 1814) was particularly associated with this text, having claimed to be the woman clothed with the sun in Revelation. As with her earlier, unfinished reflections on Paul's Epistle to the Romans, however, Hamilton was more concerned with defying the conventional restriction of biblical interpretation to professional men. She again insists that such interpreters have only further mystified a divine message designed for common understandings (ii. 245–6), and she feminizes theology in several ways. Rather than compose a systematic treatise based on extensive scholarship for professional peers, she writes daily reflections

---

[29] 'Remarks on the Revelation', in Benger, *Memoirs of Hamilton*, ii. 245–371.

on chapters and verses of Revelation as they occur to her amidst the realities of local daily domestic life, addressed to her sister. Unlike many who read Revelation as a prophecy of particular recent public events, she insists that it contains only a general message warning believers against moral and spiritual enemies in private life (ii. 362), and she particularly rejects reading it in terms of an increasingly nationalistic or sectarian triumphalism that saw the defeat of France as a sign of divine favour to Britain, its people, its government, and its religion (ii. 338–9). Hamilton insists that Revelation recommends tolerance and forbearance and announces salvation for all peoples, of any nation or religion, including those in the empire (ii. 292–3).

She does, however, condemn what she sees as the perversion of reason by sceptical philosophy, meaning the Enlightenment materialism that was blamed for the French Revolution and which she had attacked in her novels of the 1790s (ii. 331). For she reads Revelation as a condemnation of 'idolatry', by which she means the worship of things made by man; these could include the French Revolution, with its claims to remake humanity without divine assistance, but they could also include the British constitution or established Church (ii. 311–12). In fact, concerned more with Britain's internal condition than its international situation, Hamilton reads Revelation as a warning against 'bigotry', or any creed, sect, or party claiming a monopoly of truth—a reference to competition between various factions of cultural revolutionaries, including Evangelicals, Utilitarians, industrial capitalists, political economists, Orientalists, Romantics, and new Dissent—as well as the power of the state and state religions to exclude certain groups. For 'It has been the aim of this deformed and degenerate spirit, in every age, to arrogate to itself the sole disposal of temporal honours, and temporal enjoyments' (ii. 307–9)—an allusion to parliamentary rejection of Catholic emancipation and denial of full citizenship to various groups on grounds of religion. Hamilton emphasizes prophecy as well as admonition in Revelation—the prophecy of a great teacher coming to spread truth and destroy the heresies that afflict the present age. Then good works as well as true faith will be judged, and division and discord will cease. Underlying this reading is a cyclical view of history, from an original harmony of the human and divine, through the Fall and millenniums of discord, conflict, and death, to redemption and reharmonizing of mankind and the divine. Such a reading particularly suited those, including women writers such as Hamilton, Hays, and Williams but also others such as Edgeworth, Austen, Morgan, and

Hemans, who undertook the task of national reconciliation and mediation after the shock of Revolutionary rupture. Furthermore, in its main arguments Hamilton's reading of Revelation anticipates that of modern feminist theology, just as her approach to theology and religion in general anticipates in certain respects that of modern feminism, rejecting an avenging God for one of compassion, insisting on the authenticity of women's religious experience, and claiming that experience as a valid basis for understanding of deity, Scripture, and ecclesiastical doctrine.[30]

Hamilton's reading of Revelation advances what many in her own time would have seen as a woman's theological discourse, and she had some intentions of publishing it as a 'tract'. But her health was failing, and an inflammation of the eyes drove her to Harrogate spa for relief, where she died on 23 July 1816. Some of her work continued to be reprinted. Part of *Hints Addressed to the Patrons and Directors of Schools*, entitled *Examples of Questions Calculated to Exercise the Infant Mind*, was published in London in 1815 and republished in Dublin in 1841 as a 'valuable work', though 'comparatively but little known' ('Preface'). *Letters on the Elementary Principles of Education* went through five editions by 1818 and was reprinted in 1837 in an elegant small edition by Charles Tilt's 'Miniature Classical Library'. But her best-known work was *The Cottagers of Glenburnie*, which reached a seventh edition in 1822 and survived well into the nineteenth century. Though originally a pseudo-popular fiction designed, like Hannah More's Cheap Repository tracts, to supplant the chapbooks of the common people, it did become a popular classic, judging by an Irish edition of the 1830s in a series that included old chapbook favourites such as *Joe Miller's Jests*, *Robin Hood's Garland*, and *Valentine and Orson* as well as chapbook versions of more recently popularized fashionable novels such as *The Children of the Abbey*, *Paul and Virginia*, and *Elizabeth; or, The Exiles of Siberia*, and lives of Irish patriots.[31] *Glenburnie* was also reprinted by William and Robert Chambers, great purveyors of 'useful' books to

---

[30] Elizabeth Schüssler Fiorenza, *The Book of Revelation: Justice and Judgment* (Philadelphia, 1985); for a survey of the work of Fiorenza, Mary Daly, Rosemary Ruether, and others see Marie Tulip, 'Religion', in *Feminist Knowledge: Critique and Construct*, ed. Sneja Gunew (London, 1990), 229–68; see also Letty M. Russell (ed.), *Feminist Interpretation of the Bible* (Philadelphia, 1985), and Adela Yarbro Collins (ed.), *Feminist Perspectives on Biblical Scholarship* (Chico, Calif., 1985).

[31] According to the title-page, the edition was published by C. M. Warren of Dublin, but a yellow paper cover of the kind commonly put on chapbooks bears the imprint of J. Smyth, Belfast.

the people, who hoped that their cheap edition of 1859 would be 'peculiarly suited by its price for popular use', and thereby become 'the means of conveying into still more minute channels the excellent moral and economical lessons of the Authoress'.[32]

Nevertheless, the post-Revolutionary remasculinization of literature, culture, and civil society was already marginalizing the contribution of Hamilton and others to this phase of the professional middle-class cultural revolution. By the time Elizabeth Benger's biography of Hamilton appeared in 1818 she was referred to condescendingly as 'this most conscientious, most principled, most industriously useful, and most zealously religious author', and as 'an excellent woman' and 'useful writer' whose *Memoirs of Modern Philosophers* successfully exposed 'the morbid sensibility and pseudo-philanthropy of the French Revolutionary school', though 'its immediate day is perhaps gone by', and whose *Cottagers of Glenburnie* 'is considered a grand national work' in Scotland.[33] Maria Edgeworth, the leading post-Revolutionary woman popularizer of conventionally masculine discourses from science to political economy, praised Hamilton's novels of the Revolution debate but claimed that *The Cottagers of Glenburnie* was much read in Ireland and had done much good there because of its 'humour', implying an opposition between the confrontational discourse of satire and the conciliatory discourse of 'humour'. Edgeworth thought Hamilton's major contribution to literature and society was of 'a more solid and durable nature', in 'works on education' that freed 'philosophy', or critical thought, from its associations with the Revolution and Revolutionary feminism and made it accessible, attractive, and usable for women, without encouraging dangerous gender conflict. More important, Edgeworth claimed that Hamilton exemplified throughout life 'that uniform propriety of conduct' and 'all those virtues which ought to characterize her sex, which form the charm and happiness of domestic life, and which in her united gracefully with that superiority of talent and knowledge that commanded the admiration of the public'.[34] Edgeworth justly inscribes Hamilton in her own post-Revolutionary conjunction of 'domestic woman' with popularizing and femi-

---

[32] *The Cottagers of Glenburnie: A Tale* (London and Edinburgh: William and Robert Chambers, 1859), p. viii.

[33] *Monthly Review*, NS 88 (Feb. 1819), 221–2; *British Critic*, NS 10 (July 1818), 96.

[34] *Monthly Magazine*, 42 (Sept. 1816), 133–6. Edgeworth's account is printed, with some variations, in Benger, *Memoirs of Hamilton*, i. 224–7, though there the source is said to be an Irish newspaper.

nizing discourses conventionally gendered masculine. Hamilton's intervention in the Revolution debate was by now overshadowed, as she wished, by her 'practical' and 'useful' contributions to post-Revolutionary conciliation in the 'national' interest.

Hamilton's writing in the Revolutionary aftermath, like that of Williams and Hays, seems more disparate, less politically focused, less confrontational, and less polemical than during the 1790s. In part this appearance is due to continuing realities and changed circumstances. In the Revolutionary aftermath women such as Williams, Hamilton, and Hays still had to respect commercial considerations in order to support themselves and their relations by writing, negotiate past commercial and literary gatekeepers or even (in Williams's case) police censors in order to get published, observe changing social conventions in order to avoid moral or critical condemnation, and compromise literary convention and innovation in order to challenge an oppressive discursive order and generic and stylistic practices without confusing or alienating their readers. It is true, too, that in contrast to the expanding opportunities of pre-Revolutionary Sensibility and the heroic struggles of the Revolutionary decade, the horizons of possibility for women writers such as Williams, Hays, and Hamilton seemed relentlessly narrowed by post-Revolutionary counter-feminism and remasculinization of culture. As Joan Kelly points out, 'if we apply Fourier's famous dictum—that the emancipation of women is an index of the general emancipation of an age—our notions of so-called progressive developments, such as classical Athenian civilization, the Renaissance, and the French Revolution, undergo a startling re-evaluation.'[35] The relation of women, writing, and revolution from the 1790s to the 1820s may seem not a history of triumph but at best a history of resistance within the professional middle-class cultural revolution while serving that revolution in ways permitted to women, even as it increasingly discouraged, marginalized, and silently appropriated their work.

Yet during the Revolution debate women writers such as Williams, Hays, and Hamilton insistently feminized politics, ideas of civil society, and discourses previously gendered masculine, especially 'philosophy' as social critique, themes that were already becoming central in representations of the Revolution and in Romantic culture, in part at least

---

[35] Joan Kelly, 'The Social Relation of the Sexes: Methodological Implications of Women's History', *Signs*, 1 (Summer 1976), repr. *Women, History and Theory* (Chicago, 1984), 2–3.

because of these women's work. They and others met the challenges of the Revolutionary aftermath with, if anything, even more determination and inventiveness than in the era of Revolutionary possibility and struggle. If political polemic came to be seen as still more 'unfeminine' after 1800 than before, writers such as Hays, Hamilton, and even Williams turned their social critique into cultural themes and genres only apparently apolitical, and in some ways more effectively political because more acceptably 'feminine', less dismissible, and more accessible than their work of the 1790s. The relationship between these writers and their younger contemporaries and immediate successors is difficult to determine, and may well have been mediated partly by men writers who appropriated their work. But there is some evidence that elements of Revolutionary feminism were continued in radical political circles such as the Owenite socialists, and that elements of post-Revolutionary or counter-revolutionary feminism, often further reshaped into femininism, were continued into the work of women writers as diverse as Felicia Hemans, Letitia Landon, Anna Wheeler, Sarah Ellis, Harriet Martineau, Maria Jane and Geraldine Jewsbury, Agnes and Elizabeth Strickland, Anne Katharine Elwood, Barbara Bodichon and the Langham Place feminists, Anna Brownell Jameson, and George Eliot.[36] But even if these connections remain obscure, the work of writers such as Williams, Hays, and Hamilton, their complex, subtle, and shifting negotiations with contradictions of class, gender, and writing in an age of revolutionary crisis, challenge not only the literary, cultural, and social history of their time, but the history and definition of women's writing and feminism themselves.

[36] See Barbara Taylor, *Eve and the New Jerusalem: Socialism and Feminism in the Nineteenth Century* (London, 1983); Philippa Levine, *Victorian Feminism: 1850–1900* (London, 1987); Norma Clarke, *Ambitious Heights: Writing, Friendship, Love—The Jewsbury Sisters, Felicia Hemans, and Jane Welsh Carlyle* (London, 1990).

Bibliography

I. MANUSCRIPTS

Dr Williams's Library, London

Samuel Kenrick and James Wodrow Correspondence
Mary Hays Correspondence

Bodleian Library

William Godwin Correspondence

Pforzheimer Collection, New York Public Library

Mary Hays Correspondence

2. WORKS BY HAMILTON, HAYS, AND WILLIAMS

[HAMILTON, ELIZABETH,] Letter by 'Almeria', *The Lounger*, 46 (24 Dec. 1785), 181–4; repr. in Elizabeth Benger, *Memoirs of the Late Mrs. Elizabeth Hamilton, with a Selection from Her Correspondence, and Other Unpublished Writings*, 2nd edn., 2 vols. (London, 1819), i: 297–311.
—— Translation of the Letters of a Hindoo Rajah; Written Previous to, and During the Period of His Residence in England; To Which is Prefixed a Preliminary Dissertation on the History, Religion, and Manners of the Hindoos, 2 vols. (London: G. G. & J. Robinson, 1796).
[——] *Memoirs of Modern Philosophers*, 3 vols. (Bath: R. Cruttwell, for G. G. & J. Robinson, London, 1800).
—— *Letters on Education* (Bath: R. Cruttwell, for G. G. & J. Robinson, London, 1801).
—— *Letters on the Elementary Principles of Education*, '2nd edn.', 2 vols. (Bath: R. Cruttwell, for G. & J. Robinson, London, 1801).
—— *Memoirs of the Life of Agrippina, the Wife of Germanicus*, 3 vols. (Bath: R. Cruttwell, for G. & J. Robinson, London, 1804).
—— *Letters, Addressed to the Daughter of a Nobleman, on the Formation of Religious and Moral Principle*, 2 vols. (London: T. Cadell & W. Davies, 1806).
—— *The Cottagers of Glenburnie: A Tale for the Farmer's Ingle-nook* (Edinburgh: Manners & Miller, and S. Cheyne; London: T. Cadell & W. Davies, and William Miller, 1808).

HAMILTON, ELIZABETH, *Exercises in Religious Knowledge; for the Instruction of Young Persons* (Edinburgh: Manners & Miller; London: T. Cadell & W. Davies, 1809).

—— *A Series of Popular Essays, Illustrative of Principles Essentially Connected with the Improvement of the Understanding, the Imagination, and the Heart*, 2 vols. (Edinburgh: Manners & Miller; London: Longman, Hurst, Rees, Orme, & Brown; and T. Cadell & W. Davies, 1813).

—— *Hints Addressed to the Patrons and Directors of Schools; Principally Intended to Shew, That the Benefits Derived from the New Modes of Teaching May Be Increased by a Partial Adoption of the Plan of Pestalozzi; To Which Are Subjoined Examples of Questions Calculated to Excite, and Exercise the Infant Mind* (London: Longman, Hurst, Rees, Orme, & Brown, 1815).

—— *Examples of Questions Calculated to Excite and Exercise the Infant Mind* (London: Longman, Hurst, Rees, Orme, & Brown, 1815).

HAYS, MARY, 'A Sonnet: Ah let not Hope', *Universal Magazine*, 77 (Dec. 1785), 329; repr. in Mary Hays [and Elizabeth Hays], *Letters and Essays, Moral, and Miscellaneous* (London: T. Knott, 1793), 257.

—— 'Ode to her Bullfinch', *Universal Magazine*, 77 (Dec. 1785), 329; rev. in Mary Hays [and Elizabeth Hays], *Letters and Essays, Moral, and Miscellaneous* (London: T. Knott, 1793), 258–60.

—— 'The Hermit; An Oriental Tale', *Universal Magazine*, 78 (Apr. 1786), 204–8; (May 1786), 234–8; rev. in Mary Hays [and Elizabeth Hays], *Letters and Essays, Moral, and Miscellaneous* (London: T. Knott, 1793), 219–53.

[——] *Cursory Remarks on an Enquiry into the Expediency and Propriety of Public or Social Worship: Inscribed to Gilbert Wakefield*, by 'Eusebia', 2nd edn., with a postscript (London: T. Knott, 1793).

—— [and Elizabeth Hays,] *Letters and Essays, Moral, and Miscellaneous* (London: T. Knott, 1793).

—— *Memoirs of Emma Courtney*, 2 vols. (London: G. G. & J. Robinson, 1796).

—— Letter on Freedom of Enquiry, *Monthly Magazine*, 1 (June 1796), 385–7, signed 'M. H.'.

—— Letter on Sexual Superiority, *Monthly Magazine*, 2 (July 1796), 469–70, signed 'A Woman'.

—— Letter on Sexual Superiority, *Monthly Magazine*, 3 (Mar. 1797), 193–5, signed 'M. H.'.

—— Letter on Whether or Not Mental Talents Produce Happiness, *Monthly Magazine*, 3 (May 1797), 358–60, signed 'M. H.'.

—— Letter on Novel Writing, *Monthly Magazine*, 4 (Sept. 1797), 180–1, signed 'M. H.'.

[——] Obituary of Mary Wollstonecraft, *Monthly Magazine*, 4 (Sept. 1797), 232–3.

[——] *Appeal to the Men of Great Britain in Behalf of Women* (London: J. Johnson & J. Bell, 1798).

—— *The Victim of Prejudice*, 2 vols. (London: J. Johnson, 1799).

—— 'Mary Wollstonecraft', in *The Annual Necrology, for 1797–8; Including, Also, Various Articles of Neglected Biography* (London: R. Phillips, 1800).

—— *Female Biography; or, Memoirs of Illustrious and Celebrated Women, of All Ages and Countries*, 6 vols. (London: Richard Phillips, 1803).

—— *Harry Clinton: A Tale for Youth* (London: J. Johnson, 1804).

—— *Historical Dialogues for Young Persons*, 3 vols. (London: J. Johnson, J. Mawman, 1806–8).

—— *The Brothers; or, Consequences: A Story of What Happens Every Day; Addressed to that Most Useful Part of the Community, the Labouring Poor* (London: W. Button & Son, 1815).

—— *Family Annals; or, The Sisters* (London: Simpkin & Marshall, 1817).

—— *Memoirs of Queens Illustrious and Celebrated* (London: T. & J. Allman, 1821).

—— *The Love-Letters of Mary Hays (1779–1780)*, ed. A. F. Wedd (London, 1925).

[—— and] CHARLOTTE SMITH, *The History of England, from the Earliest Records to the Peace of Amiens; in a Series of Letters to a Young Lady at School*, 3 vols. (London: R. Phillips, 1806).

[WILLIAMS, HELEN MARIA,] *Edwin and Eltruda: A Legendary Tale* (London: T. Cadell, 1782).

[——] *An Ode on the Peace* (London: T. Cadell, 1783).

—— *Peru: A Poem; In Six Cantos* (London: T. Cadell, 1784).

—— *Poems*, 2 vols. (London: T. Cadell, 1786).

—— *A Poem on the Bill Lately Passed for Regulating the Slave Trade* (London: T. Cadell, 1788).

—— *Julia: A Novel; Interspersed with Some Poetical Pieces*, 2 vols. (London: T. Cadell, 1790).

—— *Letters Written in France, in the Summer of 1790, to a Friend in England; Containing, Various Anecdotes Relative to the French Revolution; and Memoirs of Mons. and Madame du F——* (London: T. Cadell, 1790).

—— *A Farewell, for Two Years, to England: A Poem* (London: T. Cadell, 1791).

—— *Letters from France: Containing Many New Anecdotes Relative to the French Revolution, and the Present State of French Manners*, 2nd edn., 'vol. 2' (London: G. G. & J. Robinson, 1792).

[——] *Letters from France: Containing a Great Variety of Interesting and Original Information Concerning the Most Important Events that Have Lately Occurred in that Country, and Particularly Respecting the Campaign of 1792*, 'vols. 3 and 4', 2 vols. (London: G. G. & J. Robinson, 1793).

—— *Letters Containing a Sketch of the Politics of France from the Thirty-first of May 1793, till the Twenty-eighth of July 1794, and of the Scenes which Have Passed in the Prisons of Paris*, 2 vols. (London: G. G. & J. Robinson, 1795).

—— *Letters Containing a Sketch of the Scenes which Passed in Various Departments of France During the Tyranny of Robespierre*, 'vol. 3' (London: G. G. & J. Robinson, 1795).

WILLIAMS, HELEN MARIA (trans.), Jacques-Henri Bernardin de Saint-Pierre, *Paul and Virginia* (London: G. G. & J. Robinson, 1795).

—— *Letters Containing a Sketch of the Politics of France, from the Twenty-eighth of July 1794, to the Establishment of the Constitution in 1795, and of the Scenes which Have Passed in the Prisons of Paris,* 'vol. 4' (London: G. G. & J. Robinson, 1796).

—— *A Tour in Switzerland; or, A View of the Present State of the Government and Manners of those Cantons: with Comparative Sketches of the Present State of Paris,* 2 vols. (London: G. G. & J. Robinson, 1798).

—— *Sketches of the State of Manners and Opinions in the French Republic, Towards the Close of the Eighteenth Century, in a Series of Letters,* 2 vols. (London: G. G. & J. Robinson, 1801).

—— (trans. and ed.), *The Political and Confidential Correspondence of Lewis the Sixteenth; with Observations on Each Letter,* 3 vols. (London: G. & J. Robinson, 1803).

—— (trans.), Friedrich Wilhelm Alexander von Humboldt, *Personal Narrative of Travels to the Equinoctial Regions of the New Continent, During the Years 1799–1804,* 5 vols. in 6 (London: Longman, Hurst, Rees, Orme, & Brown [vols. 1–5]; J. Murray [vols. 1–3]; H. Colburn [vols. 1–3], 1814–21).

—— (trans.), Friedrich Wilhelm Alexander von Humboldt, *Researches, Concerning the Institutions & Monuments of the Ancient Inhabitants of America, with Descriptions & Views of Some of the Most Striking Scenes in the Cordilleras!,* 2 vols. (London: Longman, Hurst, Rees, Orme, & Brown; J. Murray; H. Colburn, 1814).

—— *A Narrative of the Events which Have Taken Place in France, from the Landing of Napoleon Bonaparte, on the 1st of March, 1815, till the Restoration of Louis XVIII; With an Account of the Present State of Society and Public Opinion* (London: John Murray, 1815).

—— *On the Late Persecution of the Protestants in the South of France* (London: T. & G. Underwood, 1816).

—— (trans.), Xavier de Maistre, *The Leper of the City of Aoste: A Narrative* (London: George Cowie & Co., 1817).

—— *Letters on the Events which Have Passed in France since the Restoration in 1815* (London: Baldwin, Cradock, & Joy, 1819).

—— *Poems on Various Subjects; With Introductory Remarks on the Present State of Science and Literature in France* (London: G. & W. B. Whittaker, 1823).

—— *Souvenirs de la Révolution française,* trans. Charles Coquerel (Paris: Dondey-Dupré, père et fils, 1827).

[—— *et al.,*] *Copies of Original Letters Recently Written By Persons in Paris to Dr. Priestley in America, Taken on Board of a Neutral Vessel* (London, 1798).

3. OTHER BOOKS AND ARTICLES

ANDERSON, BENEDICT, *Imagined Communities: Reflections on the Origin and Spread of Nationalism*, rev. edn. (London, 1991).

ANSTEY, ROGER, *The Atlantic Slave Trade and British Abolition 1760–1810* (London, 1975).

ARIÈS, PHILIPPE, *The Hour of Our Death*, trans. Helen Weaver (Harmondsworth, 1983).

ARMSTRONG, NANCY, and LEONARD TENNENHOUSE (eds.), *The Ideology of Conduct: Essays on Literature and the History of Sexuality* (New York, 1987).

ASHCROFT, BILL, GARETH GRIFFITHS, and HELEN TIFFIN, *The Empire Writes Back: Theory and Practice in Post-Colonial Literatures* (London, 1989).

[BARBAULD, ANNA LÆTITIA,] *Devotional Pieces, Compiled from the Psalms and the Book of Job; To Which Are Prefixed, Thoughts on the Devotional Taste, on Sects, and on Establishments* (London, 1775).

—— 'The Origin and Progress of Novel-Writing', *The British Novelists*, vol. i (London, 1810).

BARR, PAT, *The Memsahibs: The Women of Victorian India* (London, 1976).

BENGER, ELIZABETH, *Memoirs of the Late Mrs. Elizabeth Hamilton, with a Selection from Her Correspondence, and Other Unpublished Writings*, 2nd edn., 2 vols. (London, 1819).

BEN-ISRAEL, HEDVA, *English Historians on the French Revolution* (Cambridge, 1968).

BIRE, EDMOND, *La Légende des Girondins* (Paris, 1881).

BOULTON, JAMES T., *The Language of Politics in the Age of Wilkes and Burke* (London, 1963).

BRISSENDEN, R. F., *Virtue in Distress: Studies in the Novel of Sentiment from Richardson to Sade* (London, 1974).

BURKE, EDMUND, *Reflections on the Revolution in France*, ed. Conor Cruise O'Brien (Harmondsworth, 1968).

BURMAN, SANDRA (ed.), *Fit Work for Women* (London, 1979).

BUSHAWAY, BOB, *By Rite: Custom, Ceremony and Community in England 1700–1880* (London, 1982).

BUTLER, MARILYN, *Maria Edgeworth: A Literary Biography* (Oxford, 1972).

—— *Jane Austen and the War of Ideas* (Oxford, 1975).

—— (ed.), *Burke, Paine, Godwin, and the Revolution Controversy* (Cambridge, 1984).

CAGE, R. A., *The Scottish Poor Law 1745–1845* (Edinburgh, 1981).

CAMPBELL, COLIN, *The Romantic Ethic and the Spirit of Modern Consumerism* (Oxford, 1987).

CANNON, GARLAND, *Oriental Jones: A Biography of Sir William Jones (1746–1794)* (Bombay, 1964).

CASEY, JAMES, *The History of the Family* (Oxford, 1989).

CHAMBERLAIN, LORI, 'Gender and the Metaphorics of Translation', *Signs*, 13 (Spring 1988), 454–72.

CLARK, J. C. D., *English Society 1688–1832: Ideology, Social Structure and Political Practice During the Ancien Regime* (Cambridge, 1985).

CLARKE, JOHN, *The Price of Progress: Cobbett's England 1780–1835* (London, 1977).

CLARKE, NORMA, *Ambitious Heights: Writing, Friendship, Love—The Jewsbury Sisters, Felicia Hemans, and Jane Welsh Carlyle* (London, 1990).

CLAYDEN, P. W., *The Early Life of Samuel Rogers* (London, 1887).

COLLIER, JANE FISHBURNE, 'Women in Politics', in Michelle Zimbalist Rosaldo and Louise Lamphere (eds.), *Women, Culture, and Society* (Stanford, Calif., 1974), 89–112.

COLLINS, ADELA YARBRO (ed.), *Feminist Perspectives on Biblical Scholarship* (Chico, Calif., 1985).

COLQUHOUN, PATRICK, *Treatise on the Police of the Metropolis* (London, 1796).

CONE, CARL B., *The English Jacobins: Reformers in Late 18th Century England* (New York, 1968).

CORRIGAN, PHILIP, and DEREK SAYER, *The Great Arch: English State Formation as Cultural Revolution* (Oxford, 1985).

COTT, NANCY F., *The Bonds of Womanhood: 'Woman's Sphere' in New England 1780–1835* (New Haven, Conn., 1977).

CREASEY, JOHN, 'The Birmingham Riots of 1791: A Contemporary Account', *Transactions of the Unitarian Historical Society*, 13 (1963–6), 111–17.

CRONE, PATRICIA, *Pre-Industrial Societies* (Oxford, 1989).

DALLAS, RICHARD CHARLES, *A Refutation of the Libel on the Memory of the Late King of France, Published by Helen Maria Williams* (London, 1804).

DANSETTE, ADRIEN, *Religious History of Modern France*, trans. John Dingle, 2 vols. (Freiburg, 1961).

DAVIS, NATALIE ZEMON, 'Women on Top: Symbolic Sexual Inversion and Political Disorder in Early Modern Europe', in Barbara A. Babcock (ed.), *The Reversible World: Symbolic Inversion in Art and Society* (Ithaca, NY, 1978).

DEAN, MITCHELL, *The Constitution of Poverty: Toward a Genealogy of Liberal Governance* (London, 1991).

DICKINSON, HARRY T., *Liberty and Property: Political Ideology in Eighteenth-Century Britain* (1977; London, 1979).

—— 'Popular Loyalism in Britain in the 1790s', in Eckhart Hellmuth (ed.), *The Transformation of Political Culture: England and Germany in the Late Eighteenth Century* (London, 1990), 503–33.

DINWIDDY, JOHN, 'England', in Otto Dann and John Dinwiddy (eds.), *Nationalism in the Age of the French Revolution* (London, 1988), 53–70.

DONOVAN, JOHN, Introduction, Jacques-Henri Bernardin de Saint-Pierre, *Paul and Virginia*, trans. John Donovan (London, 1982).

DOYLE, WILLIAM, *The Oxford History of the French Revolution* (Oxford, 1989).

DUGAW, DIANNE, *Warrior Women and Popular Balladry 1650–1850* (Cambridge, 1989).

DWYER, JOHN, *Virtuous Discourse: Sensibility and Community in Late Eighteenth-Century Scotland* (Edinburgh, 1987).

EASTWOOD, DAVID, 'Patriotism and the English State in the 1790s', in Mark Philp (ed.), *The French Revolution and British Popular Politics* (Cambridge, 1991), 146–68.

EHRARD, JEAN, and PAUL VIALLANEIX (eds.), *Les Fêtes de la Révolution: Colloque de Clermont-Ferrand* (Paris, 1977).

ELIAS, NORBERT, *The Court Society*, trans. Edmund Jephcott (Oxford, 1983).

EMSLEY, CLIVE, *British Society and the French Wars 1793–1815* (London, 1979).

FELSKI, RITA, *Beyond Feminist Aesthetics: Feminist Literature and Social Change* (Cambridge, Mass., 1989).

FENTRESS, JAMES, and CHRIS WICKHAM, *Social Memory* (Oxford, 1992).

FINKE, LAURIE A., *Feminist Theory, Women's Writing* (Ithaca, NY, 1992).

FIORENZA, ELIZABETH SCHÜSSLER, *The Book of Revelation: Justice and Judgment* (Philadelphia, 1985).

FITZPATRICK, MARTIN, 'Heretical Religion and Radical Politics in Late Eighteenth-Century England', in Eckhart Hellmuth (ed.), *The Transformation of Political Culture: England and Germany in the Late Eighteenth Century* (London, 1990), 339–72.

FORDYCE, JAMES, *Sermons to Young Women*, 3rd edn., corr., 2 vols. (London, 1766).

FOUCAULT, MICHEL, 'The Political Technology of Individuals', in Luther H. Martin *et al.* (eds.), *Technologies of the Self: A Seminar with Michel Foucault* (Amherst, Mass., 1988), 145–62.

FRASER, DEREK, 'The Poor Law as Political Institution', in Derek Fraser (ed.), *The New Poor Law in the Nineteenth Century* (London, 1976), 111–27.

GAGNIER, REGENIA, *Subjectivities: A History of Self-Representation in Britain, 1832–1920* (New York, 1991).

GALLAGHER, CATHERINE, and THOMAS LAQUEUR (eds.), *The Making of the Modern Body: Sexuality and Society in the Nineteenth Century* (Berkeley, Calif., 1987).

GELLNER, ERNEST, *Reason and Culture: The Historic Role of Rationality and Rationalism* (Oxford, 1992).

GIROUARD, MARK, *The Return to Camelot: Chivalry and the English Gentleman* (New Haven, Conn., 1981).

GOODMAN, DENA, 'Enlightenment Salons: The Convergence of Female and Philosophic Ambitions', *Eighteenth-Century Studies*, 22 (Spring 1989), 329–50.

GOODWIN, ALBERT, *The Friends of Liberty: The English Democratic Movement in the Age of the French Revolution* (London, 1979).

GUILLOIS, ANTOINE, *Le Salon de Madame Helvétius* (Paris, 1894).

GUNN, JOHN A. W., *Beyond Liberty and Property: The Process of Self-Recognition in Eighteenth-Century Political Thought* (Kingston, Ontario, 1983).

GUTMAN, HUCK, 'Rousseau's *Confessions*: A Technology of the Self', in Luther

H. Martin *et al.* (eds.), *Technologies of the Self: A Seminar with Michel Foucault* (Amherst, Mass., 1988), 99–120.

HAMILTON, CHARLES (trans. and ed.), *An Historical Relation of the Origin, Progress, and Final Dissolution of the Rohilla Afghans in the Northern Provinces of Hindostan; Compiled from a Persian Manuscript and Other Original Papers* (London, 1787).

—— (trans. and ed.), *The Hedaya, or Guide: A Commentary on the Mussulman Laws*, 4 vols. (London, 1791).

HARGREAVES-MAWDSLEY, W. N., *The English Della Cruscans and Their Time, 1783–1828* (The Hague, 1967).

[HAWKINS, LÆTITIA MATILDA,] *Letters on the Female Mind, Its Powers and Pursuits; Addressed to Miss H. M. Williams, with Particular Reference to her Letters from France*, 2 vols. (London, 1793).

HELLMUTH, ECKHART (ed.), *The Transformation of Political Culture: England and Germany in the Late Eighteenth Century* (London, 1990).

HEMLOW, JOYCE, 'Fanny Burney and the Courtesy Books', *Publications of the Modern Language Association of America*, 65 (1950), 732–61.

HENRIQUES, URSULA, *Religious Toleration in England 1787–1833* (London, 1961).

HIBBERT, CHRISTOPHER, *George IV: Regent and King 1811–1830* (London, 1973).

HOBSBAWM, ERIC J., *Nations and Nationalism since 1780: Programme, Myth, Reality* (Cambridge, 1990).

HOLMES, GEOFFREY, *Augustan England: Professions, State and Society, 1680–1730* (London, 1982).

HONE, J. ANN, *For the Cause of Truth: Radicalism in London 1796–1821* (Oxford, 1982).

HUGHES, GRAHAM W., *With Freedom Fired: The Story of Robert Robinson, Cambridge Nonconformist* (London, 1955).

INNES, JOANNA, 'Politics and Morals: The Reformation of Manners Movement in Later Eighteenth-Century England', in E. Hellmuth (ed.), *The Transformation of Political Culture: England and Germany in the Late Eighteenth Century* (London, 1990), 57–118.

JANES, R. M., 'On the Reception of Mary Wollstonecraft's *A Vindication of the Rights of Woman*', *Journal of the History of Ideas*, 39 (1978), 293–302; repr. in Mary Wollstonecraft, *A Vindication of the Rights of Woman*, ed. Carol H. Poston, 2nd edn. (New York, 1988).

KAMENKA, EUGENE, *Bureaucracy* (Oxford, 1989).

KEENER, FREDERICK M., and SUSAN E. LORSCH (eds.), *Eighteenth-Century Women and the Arts* (New York, 1988).

KELLY, GARY, *English Fiction of the Romantic Period 1789–1830* (London, 1989).

—— 'Revolutionary and Romantic Feminism: Women, Writing and Cultural Revolution', in Keith Hanley and Raman Selden (eds.), *Revolution and English Romanticism: Politics and Rhetoric* (Hemel Hempstead, 1990), 107–30.

—— 'Unbecoming a Heroine: Novel Reading, Romanticism, and Barrett's *The Heroine*', *Nineteenth-Century Literature*, 45 (Sept. 1990), 220–41.

—— Revolutionary Feminism: The Mind and Career of Mary Wollstonecraft (London, 1992).

KELLY, JOAN, 'The Social Relation of the Sexes: Methodological Implications of Women's History', Signs, 1 (Summer 1976), repr. in Joan Kelly, Women, History and Theory (Chicago, 1984), 1–18.

KENNEDY, EMMET, A Philosophe in the Age of Revolution: Destutt de Tracy and the Origins of 'Ideology' (Philadelphia, 1978).

KIMMEL, MICHAEL S., Revolution: A Sociological Interpretation (Cambridge, 1990).

KNIBIEHLER, YVONNE, 'Femme', in Dictionnaire Napoléon, ed. Jean Tulard (Paris, 1987).

KNOX, VICESIMUS, Essays Moral and Literary, 2 vols. (London, 1778–9).

KOSELLECK, REINHART, Critique and Crisis: Enlightenment and the Pathogenesis of Modern Society (1959), trans. (Oxford, 1988).

KOWALESKI-WALLACE, ELIZABETH, Their Father's Daughters: Hannah More, Maria Edgeworth, and Patriarchal Complicity (New York, 1991).

KRAMNICK, ISAAC, Republicanism and Bourgeois Radicalism: Political Ideology in Late Eighteenth-Century England and America (Ithaca, NY, 1990).

LAMB, CHARLES, and MARY LAMB, The Letters of Charles and Mary Anne Lamb, ed. Edwin W. Marrs, Jr., vol. i (Ithaca, NY, 1975).

LANDES, JOAN B., Women and the Public Sphere in the Age of the French Revolution (Ithaca, NY, 1988).

LANDRY, DONNA, The Muses of Resistance: Labouring-Class Women's Poetry in Britain, 1739–1796 (Cambridge, 1990).

LAQUEUR, THOMAS W., Religion and Respectability: Sunday Schools and Working Class Culture 1780–1850 (New Haven, Conn., 1976).

—— 'The Queen Caroline Affair: Politics as Art in the Reign of George IV', Journal of Modern History, 54 (Sept. 1982), 417–66.

—— 'Orgasm, Generation, and the Politics of Reproductive Biology', in Catherine Gallagher and Thomas Laqueur (eds.), The Making of the Modern Body: Sexuality and Society in the Nineteenth Century (Berkeley, Calif., 1987), 1–41.

—— Making Sex: Body and Gender from the Greeks to Freud (Cambridge, Mass., 1990).

LAWLESS, VALENTINE BROWNE, 2nd Baron Cloncurry, Personal Recollections of the Life and Times, with Extracts from the Correspondence (Dublin, 1849).

LEITH, DICK, A Social History of English (London, 1983).

LERNER, GERDA, The Creation of Patriarchy (New York, 1986).

LEVINE, PHILIPPA, Victorian Feminism: 1850–1900 (London, 1987).

LLOYD, GENEVIEVE, The Man of Reason: 'Male' and 'Female' in Western Philosophy (London, 1984).

LOVELL, TERRY, Consuming Fiction (London, 1987).

LURIA, GINA, 'Mary Hays: A Critical Biography', Ph.D. thesis (New York University, 1972).

LURIA, GINA, A Note on the Authorship', in Mary Hays, *Appeal to the Men of Great Britain in Behalf of Women*, repr. (New York, 1974).

LYOTARD, JEAN-FRANÇOIS, *The Postmodern Condition: A Report on Knowledge*, trans. Geoff Bennington and Brian Massumi (Minneapolis, 1984).

MACCOBY, S., *English Radicalism 1786–1832: From Paine to Cobbett* (London, 1955).

'MacSarcasm, Rev. Sir Archibald, Bart.' (possibly Abraham Elton), *The Life of Hannah More, with a Critical Review of Her Writings* (London, 1802).

MAHOOD, LINDA, *The Magdalenes: Prostitution in the Nineteenth Century* (London, 1990).

MALCOLMSON, ROBERT W., *Popular Recreations in English Society 1700–1850* (Cambridge, 1973).

MARTIN, LUTHER H., *et al.* (eds.), *Technologies of the Self: A Seminar with Michel Foucault* (Amherst, Mass., 1988).

[MATHIAS, THOMAS J.,] *The Pursuits of Literature: A Satirical Poem; in Four Dialogues*, 7th edn., rev. (London, 1798).

MAY, GITA, *Madame Roland and the Age of Revolution* (New York, 1970).

MAYO, ROBERT D., *The English Novel in the Magazines 1740–1815* (Evanston, Ill., 1962).

MCHUGH, PAUL, *Prostitution and Victorian Social Reform* (New York, 1980).

MCKENDRICK, NEIL, JOHN BREWER, and J. H. PLUMB, *The Birth of a Consumer Society: The Commercialization of Eighteenth-Century England* (London, 1982).

MESSER-DAVIDOW, ELLEN, ' "For Softness She": Gender Ideology and Aesthetics in Eighteenth-Century England', in Frederick M. Keener and Susan E. Lorsch (eds.), *Eighteenth-Century Women and the Arts* (New York, 1988), 45–55.

MILROY, JAMES, and LESLEY MILROY, *Authority in Language: Investigating Language Prescription and Standardisation* (London, 1985).

MINGAY, GORDON E., *The Gentry: The Rise and Fall of a Ruling Class* (London, 1976).

MORAVIA, SERGIO, *Il tramonto dell'illuminismo: Filosofia e politica nella società francese (1770–1810)* (Bari, 1968).

MORE, HANNAH, *Essays on Various Subjects, Principally Designed for Young Ladies* (London, 1777).

——— *Strictures on the Modern System of Female Education, with a View of the Principles and Conduct Prevalent among Women of Rank and Fortune*, 2 vols. (London, 1799).

MUKHERJEE, S. N., *Sir William Jones: A Study in Eighteenth-Century British Attitudes to India*, rev. edn. (London, 1987).

MULLAN, JOHN, *Sentiment and Sociability: The Language of Feeling in the Eighteenth Century* (Oxford, 1988).

MYERS, MITZI, 'Reform or Ruin: "A Revolution in Female Manners" ', in Harry C. Payne (ed.), *Studies in Eighteenth-Century Culture*, 11 (Madison, Wis., 1982), 199–216.

MYERS, SYLVIA HARCSTARK, *The Bluestocking Circle: Women, Friendship, and the Life of the Mind in Eighteenth-Century England* (Oxford, 1990).

NEWMAN, GERALD, *The Rise of English Nationalism: A Cultural History 1740–1830* (London, 1987).

OGILVIE, MARILYN BAILEY, *Women in Science: Antiquity through the Nineteenth Century; A Biographical Dictionary and Annotated Bibliography* (Cambridge, Mass., 1986).

OKIN, SUSAN MOLLER, *Women in Western Political Thought* (Princeton, NJ, 1979).

—— 'Patriarchy and Married Women's Property in England: Questions on Some Current Views', *Eighteenth-Century Studies*, 17 (Winter 1983/4), 121–38.

ORTNER, SHERRY B., 'Is Female to Male as Nature is to Culture?', in Michelle Zimbalist Rosaldo and Louise Lamphere (eds.), *Woman, Culture, and Society* (Stanford, Calif., 1974), 67–87.

OUTRAM, DORINDA, *The Body and the French Revolution: Sex, Class and Political Culture* (New Haven, Conn., 1989).

OWEN, DAVID EDWARD, *English Philanthropy 1660–1960* (Cambridge, Mass., 1964).

OZOUF, MONA, *La Fête révolutionnaire 1789–1799* (Paris, 1976).

PARKER, HAROLD T., *The Cult of Antiquity and the French Revolutionaries: A Study in the Development of the Revolutionary Spirit* (Chicago, 1937).

PAULSON, RONALD, *Representations of Revolution (1789–1820)* (New Haven, Conn., 1983).

PEDERSEN, SUSAN, 'Hannah More Meets Simple Simon: Tracts, Chapbooks, and Popular Culture in Late Eighteenth-Century England', *Journal of British Studies*, 25 (Jan. 1986), 84–113.

PHILIPS, CYRIL H., *The East India Company 1784–1834*, corr. edn. (Manchester, 1961).

PHILP, MARK (ed.), *The French Revolution and British Popular Politics* (Cambridge, 1991).

PILBEAM, PAMELA M., *The Middle Classes in Europe 1789–1914: France, Germany, Italy and Russia* (Basingstoke, 1990).

PIOZZI, HESTER LYNCH THRALE, *The Intimate Letters of Hester Piozzi and Penelope Pennington 1788–1821*, ed. Oswald G. Knapp (London, 1914).

—— *Thraliana: The Diary of Hester Lynch Thrale (Later Mrs. Piozzi) 1776–1809*, ed. Katherine C. Balderstone, 2nd edn., 2 vols. (Oxford, 1951).

POLLIN, BURTON R., 'Mary Hays on Women's Rights in the Monthly Magazine', *Études anglaises*, 24 (1971), 271–82.

[POLWHELE, RICHARD,] *The Unsex'd Females: A Poem; Addressed to the Author of The Pursuits of Literature* (London, 1798).

POOVEY, MARY, *The Proper Lady and the Woman Writer: Ideology as Style in the Works of Mary Wollstonecraft, Mary Shelley, and Jane Austen* (Chicago, 1984).

POYNTER, J. R., *Society and Pauperism: English Ideas on Poor Relief, 1795–1834* (London, 1969).

PRICE, RICHARD, *A Discourse on the Love of Our Country, Delivered on Nov. 4, 1789, at the Meeting-House in the Old Jewry, to the Society for Commemorating the Revolution in Great Britain*, 2nd edn. (London, 1789).

PROCHASKA, FRANK K., 'Women in English Philanthropy, 1790–1830', *International Review of Social History*, 19 (1974), 426–45.

—— *Women and Philanthropy in Nineteenth-Century England* (Oxford, 1980).

REDFORD, BRUCE, *The Converse of the Pen: Acts of Intimacy in the Eighteenth-Century Familiar Letter* (Chicago, 1986).

RENDALL, JANE, *The Origins of Modern Feminism: Women in Britain, France and the United States 1780–1860* (Basingstoke, 1985).

ROBBINS, CAROLINE, *The Eighteenth Century Commonwealthman: Studies in the Transmission, Development and Circumstance of English Liberal Thought from the Restoration of Charles II until the War with the Thirteen Colonies*, repr. (New York, 1968).

ROBERTS, JOHN M., *The Mythology of the Secret Societies*, repr. (London, 1974).

ROBERTS, WILLIAM, *Memoirs of the Life and Correspondence of Mrs. Hannah More*, 3rd rev. edn., 2 vols. (London, 1835).

ROBINSON, HENRY CRABB, *Henry Crabb Robinson on Books and Their Writers*, ed. Edith J. Morley, 3 vols. (London, 1938).

RODGERS, BETSY, *Cloak of Charity: Studies in Eighteenth-Century Philanthropy* (London, 1949).

ROE, NICHOLAS, *Wordsworth and Coleridge: The Radical Years* (Oxford, 1988).

ROSA, ANNETTE, *Citoyennes: Les Femmes et la Révolution française* (Paris, 1988).

ROSALDO, MICHELLE ZIMBALIST, and LOUISE LAMPHERE (eds.), *Woman, Culture, and Society* (Stanford, Calif., 1974).

RUSSELL, LETTY M. (ed.), *Feminist Interpretation of the Bible* (Philadelphia, 1985).

SALVAGGIO, RUTH, *Enlightened Absence: Neoclassical Configurations of the Feminine* (Urbana, Ill., 1988).

SCHIEBINGER, LONDA, 'Skeletons in the Closet: The First Illustrations of the Female Skeleton in Eighteenth-Century Anatomy', in Catherine Gallagher and Thomas Laqueur (eds.), *The Making of the Modern Body: Sexuality and Society in the Nineteenth Century* (Berkeley, Calif., 1987), 42–82.

SOLOWAY, R. A., *Prelates and People: Ecclesiastical Social Thought in England 1783–1852* (London, 1969).

SPACKS, PATRICIA MEYER, *Gossip* (Chicago, 1986).

SPEAR, PERCIVAL, *The Nabobs: A Study of the Social Life of the English in Eighteenth Century India*, rev. edn. (London, 1963).

SPENCER, JANE, *The Rise of the Woman Novelist: From Aphra Behn to Jane Austen* (Oxford, 1986).

SPENDER, DALE, *Mothers of the Novel: 100 Good Women Writers before Jane Austen* (London, 1986).

STANTON, JUDITH PHILLIPS, 'Statistical Profile of Women Writing in English from 1660 to 1800', in Frederick M. Keener and Susan E. Lorsch (eds.), *Eighteenth-Century Women and the Arts* (New York, 1988), 247–54.

STAVES, SUSAN, *Married Women's Separate Property in England, 1660–1833* (Cambridge, Mass., 1990).

ST CLAIR, WILLIAM, *The Godwins and the Shelleys: The Biography of a Family* (London, 1989).

SUMMERS, ANNE, 'A Home from Home—Women's Philanthropic Work in the Nineteenth Century', in Sandra Burman (ed.), *Fit Work for Women* (London, 1979), 33–63.

TAYLOR, BARBARA, *Eve and the New Jerusalem: Socialism and Feminism in the Nineteenth Century* (London, 1983).

THIÉBAULT, BARON DIEUDONNÉ, *Mémoires du Baron Thiébault*, 5 vols. (Paris, 1893–7).

THOMPSON, EDWARD P., *The Making of the English Working Class*, rev. edn. (Harmondsworth, 1968).

THOMPSON, F. MICHAEL L., *The Rise of Respectable Society: A Social History of Victorian Britain 1830–1900* (London, 1988).

TICKNOR, GEORGE, *Life, Letters, and Journal of George Ticknor*, 2 vols. (London, 1876).

TODD, JANET, *The Sign of Angellica: Women, Writing, and Fiction 1660–1800* (London, 1989).

TOMALIN, CLAIRE, *The Life and Death of Mary Wollstonecraft* (London, 1974).

TOMPKINS, JOYCE M. S., *The Popular Novel in England 1770–1800* (1932; Lincoln, Nebr., 1961).

TOMPSON, RICHARD, *The Charity Commission and the Age of Reform* (London, 1979).

TRIMMER, SARAH, *The Œconomy of Charity; or, An Address to Ladies Concerning Sunday-Schools; The Establishment of Schools of Industry under Female Inspection; and the Distribution of Voluntary Benefactions; To which Is Added an Appendix, Containing an Account of the Sunday-Schools in Old Brentford* (London, 1787); rev. edn., *The Oeconomy of Charity; or, An Address to Ladies; Adapted to the Present State of Charitable Institutions in England: With a Particular View to the Cultivation of Religious Principles, among the Lower Orders of People*, 2 vols. (London, 1801).

TULIP, MARIE, 'Religion', in Sneja Gunew (ed.), *Feminist Knowledge: Critique and Construct* (London, 1990), 229–68.

UNGER, RHODA K., 'Psychological, Feminist, and Personal Epistemology: Transcending Contradiction', in Mary McCanney Gergen (ed.), *Feminist Thought and the Structure of Knowledge* (New York, 1988).

WAKEFIELD, GILBERT, *An Enquiry into the Expediency and Propriety of Public or Social Worship*, new edn. (London, 1792).

WALKOWITZ, JUDITH, *Prostitution and Victorian Society: Women, Class, and the State* (Cambridge, 1980).

WALPOLE, HORACE, *Horace Walpole's Correspondence with Mary and Agnes Berry and Barbara Cecilia Seton*, ed. W. S. Lewis and A. Dayle Wallace, vol. i (London, 1944).

WOLLSTONECRAFT, MARY, *Collected Letters of Mary Wollstonecraft*, ed. Ralph M. Wardle (Ithaca, NY, 1979).

WOODWARD, LIONEL D., *Une anglaise amie de la Révolution française: Hélène-Maria Williams et ses amis*, repr. (Geneva, 1977).

Index